Foreign Direct Investment in Post Conflict Countries

Opportunities and Challenges

Published by
Adonis & Abbey Publishers Ltd
P. O. Box 43418
London
SE11 4XZ
http://www.adonis-abbey.com
Email: editor@adonis-abbey.com

First Edition, October 2010

Copyright 2010 © Virtus C. Igbokwe, Nicholas Turner and Obijiofor Aginam

British Library Cataloguing-in-Publication Data
A catalogue record for this book is available from the British Library

ISBN: 9781906704667 (HB)/9781906704674(PB)

Layout Artist/Technical Editor, Jan B. Mwesigwa

Printed and bound in Great Britain

Foreign Direct Investment in Post Conflict Countries

Opportunities and Challenges

Edited by

Virtus C. Igbokwe,
Nicholas Turner and
Obijiofor Aginam

Adonis & Abbey
Publishers Ltd

Contents

Contributors

Obijiofor Aginam: Academic Officer, United Nations University Institute for Sustainability and Peace, Tokyo, Japan & Adjunct Research Professor of Law, Carleton University, Ottawa, Canada.

Henri Bezuidenhout: School of Economics, North-West University, Potchefstroom, South Africa.

Estelle Bierman: Postgraduate, School of Economics, North-West University, Potchefstroom, South Africa; Credit Analyst, ABSA Retail Banking, Johannesburg, South Africa

Tai-Heng Cheng: Associate Professor of Law & Associate Director, Center for International Law, New York Law School.

Luis Jorge Garay: Associate Research Fellow, United Nations University Institute on Comparative Regional Integration Studies, Bruges, Belgium.

Virtus C. Igbokwe: Barrister and Solicitor (Of the Bar of Ontario), Toronto, Canada.

Philippe De Lombaerde: Associate Director, United Nations University Institute on Comparative Regional Integration Studies, Bruges, Belgium.

Patricia J. McCall: Regional Director, Middle East & North Africa, Duke University, United Arab Emirates.

Ibironke T. Odumosu: Assistant Professor, College of Law, University of Saaskatchewan, Canada.

Nicholas Turner: Academic Programme Associate, United Nations University Institute for Sustainability and Peace, Tokyo, Japan.

Kojo Yelpaala: Professor of Law, University of the Pacific, McGeorge School of Law, Sacramento, USA.

Chapter 1

Introduction:
Foreign Direct Investment in Post-Conflict Countries

Virtus C. Igbokwe and Obijiofor Aginam

...The foreign investor expects the host State to act in a consistent manner, free from ambiguity and totally transparently in its relations with the foreign investor, so that it may know beforehand any and all rules and regulations that will govern its investments, as well as the goals of the relevant policies and administrative practices or directives, to be able to plan its investments and comply with such regulations...The foreign investor also expects the host State to act consistently, i.e. without arbitrarily revoking any preexisting decisions or permits issued by the state that were relied upon by the investor to assume its commitments as well as to plan and launch its commercial and business activities.[1]

The twentieth century witnessed a number of violent conflicts around the world – from Africa to Europe, Asia and Latin America. Particularly with respect to sub-Sahara Africa, the roots of these conflicts have been traced to social and economic factors such as poverty and unequal distribution of natural resource wealth.

Post-conflict countries face economic ruin, internal governance difficulties and uncertainties. In the aftermath of these conflicts, much of the responsibility for initial post-conflict reconstruction has been shouldered by the World Bank and its affiliate institutions, the United Nations, donor agencies and international NGOs. Indeed, international aid agencies have acted as first responders in the post-conflict conflict reconstruction process, providing immediate relief, restoration of law and order, establishment of interim governance institutions, resettlement of refugees and internally displaced persons, demobilization and reintegration of ex-combatants, and reconstruction of security institutions.[2] Notwithstanding the laudable effort of international donor agencies, it is clear that foreign aid alone cannot provide sustainable economic development, political stability and consolidation of peace in post-conflict countries. Taking into consideration the broader context of conflict, the task of policy makers in the post-conflict reconstruction process is to create an integrated and comprehensive approach to post-conflict reconstruction with a view to sustainable economic development, political stability and consolidation of peace. The core of such an approach is post-conflict reconstruction that is driven by foreign direct investment (FDI) rather than dependent on foreign aid. A well articulated and efficiently executed foreign investment strategy will bring much needed private capital, generate employment and transfer new skills and technology. More importantly, employment opportunities generated through FDI will help to assimilate former combatants (and others who depended on the war economy) into legitimate economic activities and thus strengthen state effectiveness by reducing the chances of renewed conflict.

As previously noted, post-conflict countries face economic and institutional devastation – damaged infrastructure such as schools, factories, communication networks, roads, railways, and water systems. War also results in diminished human resources, a very weak legal structure, and very weak, non-existent or dysfunctional governmental institutions (including judicial and administrative institutions). Thus there are many investment opportunities and potential for high returns in post-conflict countries. Even for those without abundant natural resources, such as Rwanda, investment in infrastructure (roads, bridges, telecommunications, and power stations) is of critical importance for peace consolidation and economic development. However, a post-conflict country is generally an unpredictable environment for foreign investment. Foreign investors in post-conflict countries face unique economic and political risks. In a post-conflict environment, there may be inadequate or non-existent legal and regulatory rules relating to foreign investment. Governments may breach contractual obligations with foreign investors, frequently interfere with property rights of investors, and may even nationalize or expropriate the investments. There is also the overriding fear that the investment climate may quickly deteriorate in the event of resumption of conflict, leading to loss of all the investments. Against this background, the task of policy makers in post-conflict countries is to improve the investment climate, which will not only attract new investments but also encourage the return of foreign investors that fled during the conflict.

This leads us to the main focus of this volume: laws and policies for FDI in post-conflict countries. For post-conflict countries seeking foreign investment for sustainable economic development, political stability and consolidation of peace, legal and regulatory reform is imperative. Despite the abundant investment opportunities, the economic and political risks of foreign investment in a post-conflict country may far outweigh its benefits. Among others, prospective investors are concerned with the protection of property rights, the risk of nationalization or expropriation by the host state, and the host state's commitment to its contractual and other obligations.[3] In developing countries in general and post-conflict states in particular, some of the overarching questions include: are there sufficient measures for the protection of the investor's legitimate expectations? Are there assurances that the host state will honor its contractual and other obligations particularly after the investment has been made? What are the fiscal and other incentives available to the foreign investor? At what forum are disputes between the host state and the foreign investor to be resolved? Particularly for capital intensive projects that may take some time to realize, the decision of a prospective investor may well depend on how adequately these questions are addressed in the host state's legal and regulatory framework for foreign investment.

Against this background, the contributors to this volume critically examine various issues relating to foreign investment in post-conflict states. The essays in this volume cover the perspectives of both the foreign investor and the host state, bearing in mind that the ultimate goal is a mutually beneficial relationship between the host post-conflict state and the foreign investor. For a post-conflict state's policy makers, the task is to design a foreign investment strategy that brings real and meaningful economic development and aids the state in achieving political stability. Attracting foreign investment for the attainment of these objectives can only be possible if the investor's legitimate expectations are adequately protected by the host state's legal and regulatory framework for foreign investment. FDI in post-conflict states is discussed from different methodological perspectives – comparative law and comparative politics – and some contributors draw on case studies from different post-conflict states.

The impact of FDI on the economic transformation of developing countries has been a subject of intense debate and contradictory studies. Kojo Yelpaala's chapter questions the effectiveness of conventional FDI as the central focus in the reconstruction and economic development of post-conflict states. He vigorously argues for a paradigm shift – a shift of focus from conventional FDI to non-conventional FDI for the reconstruction and development of post-conflict states. He refers to numerous studies which show that left to its own devices, FDI is unlikely to generate growth, lead to meaningful technology transfer or create internal links necessary for the economic development of developing countries. Against this background, he strongly argues that the transformation of post-conflict states requires "an industrial strategic policy architecture" that targets specific sectors and projects and emphasizes domestic *value added* – technology and knowledge transfer and meaningful linkages with the local economies.

One type of non-conventional FDI that can play a meaningful role in the transformation of post-conflict states, Yelpaala suggests, is the project finance model that incorporates irreversible high value build operate and transfer (BOT) or similar operations with the potential for the greatest development impact. The BOT will be supported by a Post Conflict Guarantee Fund and operated by sponsors for a limited time period. The projects will be turned over to local owners after they have paid for themselves. Rather than general FDI incentives which may further deplete the revenues of post-conflict states, the necessary FDI incentives can be constructed and directed at ensuring the realization of the developmental objectives of the host post-conflict state. Undoubtedly, BOT projects are capital intensive projects that could only be realized over a long period of time, with political and related risks. In this regard, Yelpaala notes the complexity of economic development agreements and suggests BOT legislation for post-conflict states that adopt the BOT system. The BOT legislation would provide a clear and stable regulatory framework, guarantee the legitimate expectations of the investor(s), and the settlement of disputes by conciliation, mediation or international arbitration procedures.

Given the peculiarities of a post-conflict environment, legal and regulatory reforms relating to FDI may be slow for reasons that may include the lack of resources and expertise for such reforms. Such reforms may also rank lower in priority than security and other immediate needs of the state. In his chapter entitled "Law on Loan: Legal Reconstruction After Armed Conflict," Tai-Heng Cheng suggests two main ways that a post-conflict state may *borrow* laws to fill the legal vacuum and thus be able to attract foreign investment: forum selection clauses in investment contracts and the international legal framework for FDI. With respect to the forum selection clause, the investment contract may stipulate the laws of the investor's state and its court as the governing law and the forum for adjudicating disputes respectively. The host state could further demonstrate its commitment to investment protection and promotion by express waiver of its sovereign immunity from lawsuits. This mechanism, the author argues, "replaces the nascent laws of the post-conflict state with the developed commercial laws of the state of the investor". In addition to forum selection clauses in investment contracts, the post-conflict state should accede to various international legal instruments for FDI, specifically the United Nations Convention on the Recognition and Enforcement of Foreign Arbitral Awards (the New York Convention), the ICSID Convention and BITs. The author argues that these steps can be taken without undermining the state's regulatory powers and suggests the following five strategies that policy makers in post-conflict states could take to mitigate the possible risks of "borrowing" laws: circumscription, clarification, communication, control, and compensation.

In his chapter, Virtus Igbokwe evaluates the guarantee of access to international arbitration, particularly ICSID arbitration, in the domestic Investment Codes of the Democratic Republic of Congo (DRC), Sierra Leone and Liberia, all of which have ratified the ICSID Convention. Despite this, investors in these countries may not have access to ICSID arbitration or any other neutral arbitral forum because these countries have signed few BITs. For instance, since Sierra Leone has signed only one BIT with the United Kingdom, foreign investors in Sierra Leone who are not nationals of the UK would not benefit from the guarantees and protections provided in the treaty. For a prospective investor whose home state does not have a BIT with the host post-conflict state, the guarantee of access to a neutral arbitral forum in the domestic investment code of the host post-conflict state is a critical consideration in the decision to make an investment, particularly given the volatility and unpredictability of the investment climate of post-conflict states.[4]

In addressing this important concern of foreign investors, the governments of the DRC, Sierra Leone and Liberia follow different approaches. Under Liberia's Incentive Code, the investor's right to international arbitration is implicit – an incentive to be negotiated between the investor and the host state. In contrast, the domestic investment codes of the DRC and Sierra Leone guarantee investors' *unconditional* right to a neutral arbitral forum for resolving investment disputes with the host state. Investors in both the DRC and Sierra Leone have a unilateral, standing offer by the host state to submit disputes to international arbitration under the auspices of ICSID or the ICSID Additional Facility or pursuant to UNCITRAL Arbitration Rules. This offer can be accepted by the investor either at the time of making the investment or after a dispute has arisen.[5] Igbokwe argues that the guarantee of investors' right to international arbitration under the DRC and Sierra Leonean codes is not sacrosanct because the unilateral offer could be withdrawn by the state before it is accepted, i.e. by the state's exercise of its sovereign right to amend or repeal the law. For post-conflict states seeking to attract foreign investment, he suggests a stability provision in the investment codes that preserves the investors' right to international arbitration even in the event of adverse legislative changes.[6] He submits that this is important because the investment climate of a state, particularly a post-conflict state, must be understood as referring not only to the present but also to the investor's "legitimate expectations" in the future, i.e. the basic and legitimate expectations that were taken into consideration by the investor before making the investment.

Pre-conflict Rwanda was largely dependent on foreign aid, and relatively little effort was made to attract foreign investment. However, post-conflict Rwanda has made considerable efforts towards attracting foreign investment for economic development and political stability. Ibironke Odumosu critically examines the legal and regulatory reforms for the promotion and protection of foreign investment in post-conflict Rwanda. Rwanda's economic blueprint, she points out, is contained in a Vision

Statement called "Vision 2020", published in 2000 by the country's Ministry of Finance and Economic Planning. The Vision Statement identifies private sector led development as pivotal to Rwanda's post-conflict reconstruction – a private sector led development that is anchored on the twin pillars of liberalization and privatization. The government has pursued a liberalization of its foreign investment policy in the belief that promoting macroeconomic stability and wealth creation from the private sector will reduce dependence on foreign aid. The liberalization of Rwanda's foreign investment regime is evident in its domestic investment laws, international and regional treaty commitments. The primary domestic law is the Law Relating to Investment and Export Promotion and Facilitation ("Investment Code"), which does not preclude investment in any sectors of the economy. The Investment Code establishes the Rwandan Investment and Export Promotion Agency (RIEPA), a government agency that promotes and facilitates the entry and establishment of foreign investment in Rwanda. While the Investment Code does not mandate performance requirements or technology transfer, it strongly suggests and encourages foreign investors to use available local materials and to transfer technology and expertise. Subsidiary domestic laws relating to foreign investment include Law No. 2 on Privatization and Public Investment which was enacted on March 11, 1996, Organic Law Determining the Modalities of Protection, Conservation and Promotion of Environment in Rwanda ("Environmental Law"), and the Law Establishing the Labor Code ("Labor Code").

At the international level, Rwanda has concluded five Bilateral Investment Treaties (BITs), including one with the United States in 2008. Besides the few BITs, Rwanda has ratified the Conventions for the promotion and protection of foreign investments such the ICSID Convention and the Convention establishing the Multilateral Investment Guarantee Agency (MIGA). At the regional level, Rwanda has ratified various regional instruments for the promotion and protection of foreign investment, including the Treaty Establishing the East African Community ("EAC Treaty") and the Treaty Establishing the Common Market for Eastern and Southern Africa ("COMESA Treaty"). Among other things, the COMESA Treaty binds member states to establish a liberal and transparent investment climate, protection of property rights (including intellectual property rights and concessions), fair and equitable treatment in accordance with the customary international law standard, national treatment, guarantee of capital repatriation, most favored nation treatment, guarantee against expropriation or nationalization, and investor-state dispute settlement pursuant to the UNCITRAL Arbitration Rules, the ICSID Convention and ICSID Additional Facility Rules. It is evident that Rwanda has made admirable progress since the end of one of the most violent conflicts in human history and has created a friendly climate for foreign investment through its laws and policies. However, this author cautions against a rush to label Rwanda a success story before it is determined in the future that FDI has made significant impact in the country's post-conflict economy.

Patricia J. McCall, in "Transitional Commercial Law and Foreign Direct Investment in Afghanistan: A Case Study," maps out the progress of legal reforms relating to FDI, the gaps that still remain and how these gaps can be temporarily closed. Post-conflict Afghanistan faces unique challenges because of extended periods of economic and political instability, lawlessness and general insecurity. At the end of the campaign to remove the Taliban regime in 2001-2, the judicial system was virtually non-existent and many municipal and provincial authorities relied on Islamic law, traditional/tribal codes of justice and other informal justice processes. Before the conflict, there was generally no legal regime relating to private sector participation in the economy. Policy makers, experts and international organizations faced the daunting task of reconstructing and modernizing the country's legal system as there were no laws on private investment, contract, property, customs, trade and financial sector law, bankruptcy, corporate and partnership laws. However, evidence of progress with respect to legal and regulatory reforms includes a new banking law, Income Tax Law, Insurance Law, Customs, and Minerals Law.[7] A new Private Investment Law was enacted in 2004 with the stated purpose of "maximizing private investment, both domestic and foreign, in the economy..."[8] The law established the Afghanistan Investment Support Agency (AISA) as a "one-stop shop" responsible for registration, licensing and promotion of new investments in Afghanistan. Despite the progress that has been made, post-conflict Afghanistan still faces significant challenges. Through her case studies of the investment climate of post-conflict Afghanistan, Ms McCall documents the slow pace of legal reforms, lack of infrastructure development, corruption and general insecurity and a general lack of legal certainty and predictability in the investment climate of post-conflict Afghanistan. Instances of this include reversal of policies and lack of clarity on the part of regulators and the unreliability of policies relating to taxes and customs. With respect to infrastructure, there is a general lack of electricity with the result that many companies rely on private generators to carry out their business.

Estelle Bierman and Henri Bezuidenhout empirically examine the role of "FDI in the Economic Transformation of the Post-Civil War Economies of Angola and Mozambique." After the end of the Angolan civil war in 2002 and the Mozambican war in 1992, both countries made significant progress in improving their foreign direct investment laws and policies. Besides reforms of domestic laws relating to foreign investment, Angola has signed five BITs while Mozambique has signed twenty-one BITs. Both have also ratified other international and regional instruments for the promotion and protection of foreign investments. While these countries are becoming increasing less restrictive to foreign investment, barriers that still exist include political instability, administrative burdens, bureaucracy, corruption and shortage of skilled labor. In evaluating their current investment climate, the authors used three general indicators: (i) social political indicators, (ii) good governance indicators, and (iii) economic indicators. These indicators are then compared with those two countries' Southern African neighbors South Africa and Botswana, as well as with China and Brazil. Data analysis shows that Angola and Mozambique have less attractive investment climates than those Southern African neighbors, and far worse investment climates than Brazil and China. Angola has a less stable political environment but a more stable economic environment, while Mozambique has the more stable political environment. Angola's more stable economic environment may be attributed to the country's abundant natural resources, particularly oil and diamonds. From their study, however, the authors argue that a country with a more stable political environment (like Mozambique) will attract more sustainable FDI over the long term than a country with a less stable political environment (like Angola). Notwithstanding the disparity in FDI flows to the two countries, empirical evidence presented by the authors shows that FDI has a positive impact on economic growth, directly through an increase in capital stock and the subsequent capital flows, and indirectly through spill-over effect. The authors suggest that African countries in particular and post-conflict states in general can maximize the benefits of FDI through targeted public and private initiatives that link industry, education, human capital and institutional capacity.

Philippe De Lombaerde and Luis Jorge Garay examine the FDI policies of Colombia amid a continuing conflict. Until the late 1980s, Colombia's FDI policy mirrored the Andean foreign investment regime established by the Cartagena Agreement of 1971. This regime was very restrictive, with FDI in certain sectors of the economy prohibited, including infrastructure, communications, electricity, public services, waste collection and the financial sector. The hostility to foreign investment in the Andean region began to wane in the late 1980s. By 1991, the Andean countries had liberalized FDI, eliminating the discrimination between foreign and domestic investors. Moreover, individual countries were free to design their own foreign investment policies. Colombia has since pursued a policy of foreign investment liberalization through its domestic investment laws, BITs and other international instruments for the promotion and protection of foreign investment, such as ICSID. As a result of this policy shift, Colombia has attracted more investment, though the continuing conflict has affected the flow of foreign investment. Surveys among private businesses in Colombia indicate that indirect costs of the continuing conflict could be significantly higher than the macroeconomic estimates. Also, results of the authors' study show minimal spillover effects of foreign investment in Colombia, perhaps due to the continuing conflict.

In the concluding chapter, Nicholas Turner and Obijiofor Aginam highlight some of the various approaches employed by the post-conflict states examined in this volume, drawing out common factors of success and failure in their practices seeking to attract and regulate beneficial FDI.

FDI laws and policies of post-conflict states have not received much attention in post-conflict discourse. This volume represents a significant step towards extending the discourse. However, it remains to be seen whether and to what extent FDI can impact the economic recovery of post-conflict states as well as contribute to peace consolidation and political stability. Time and data will provide the evidence.

Notes

[1]   ICSID Arbitral Tribunal in *Técnicas Medioambientales Tecmed, S.A. v. United Mexican States (Tecmed)* (ICSID Additional Facility, Award of May 29, 2003), para. 154. Available at: <http://ita.law.uvic.ca/documents/Tecnicas_001.pdf>

[2]   In 1997 for instance, the World Bank established the Post-Conflict Fund (PCF) to support countries in transition from conflict to sustainable political stability and economic growth.

[3]   Paul E. Comeaux and N. Stephen Kinsella, *Protecting Foreign Investment under International Law: Legal Aspects of Political Risk* (1997).

[4]   See generally, M. Sornarajah, *The Settlement of Foreign Investment Disputes* (2000).

[5]   *Southern Pacific Properties (ME) Ltd & SPP Ltd v. The Arab Republic of Egypt*, 3 ICSID REPORTS, 131 (Decision on Jurisdiction, 14 April, 1988); *Zhinvali Development Limited v. Republic of Georgia*, 10 ICSID REPORTS, 3 (Award of 24 January 2003)

[6]   *Rumeli Telekom A.S. & Another v. Republic of Kazakhstan* (ICSID Award, July 29, 2008). Available at: <http://ita.law.uvic.ca/documents/Telsimaward.pdf>.

[7]   The text of the various laws are available at: <http://www.aisa.org.af/invest mentlaws.html>

8   See Article 2, *Law on Private Investment in Afghanistan* (2004, amended December 2005).

Chapter 2

Rethinking the Foreign Direct Investment Process and Incentives in Post-Conflict Transition Countries[*]

Kojo Yelpaala[**]

Introduction

Burdened by the remnants of conflict, continuing threats of security lapses, significant market failures and weak institutions, post-conflict transition countries can hardly be described as normal economies. The task of transforming them into vibrant, productive and self-sustaining economies is no simple assignment. Constructing the blueprint for reconstruction and economic development requires creativity of the first order. Conventional theories or pure neo-liberal market driven policy levers preached by the Washington Consensus group are not likely to be productive. The design of the investment regime for development should therefore focus on non-conventional policy constructs. Contrary to the received theories, the record of conventional foreign direct investment (FDI) as an engine of growth and development in developing countries has been disappointing. It is doubtful whether such FDI can play the necessary transformative role in countries facing more extraordinary economic and political conditions than other developing countries. What post-conflict transition countries need for their transformation is an industrial strategic policy architecture that emphasizes domestic value added, high value investment demand targeting specific sectors and projects. Non-conventional FDI policies should then play a complementary role to the domestic investment demand for economic development. One type of non-conventional FDI that can play a meaningful role in post-conflict transition countries is the project finance model that incorporates irreversible high value build operate and transfer (BOT) or similar operations with the potential for the greatest development impact. The BOT will be supported by a Post Conflict Guarantee Fund and operated by sponsors for a limited time period. Any necessary FDI incentives can then be constructed and directed at actual impediments to achieving the specific developmental objectives of each country.

Prominent among the many challenges facing post-conflict transition countries is how to design and implement the strategic architecture for transforming their economies into vibrant and self-sustaining economies.

Shattered by conflict and deprived of skilled labor and capital from brain drain and capital flight, post-conflict economies are seldom normal economies. Laboring under the weight of severe security problems and significant market failures, they tend to be underperforming economies characterized by rent seeking, with bureaucratic and elite groups capturing power. In this context, we must start by realizing that post-conflict transition countries are in the second-best world. They suffer from many constraints and distortions, particularly those relating to investments. In many of these countries there may be weak financial institutions, poor access to capital or low investment demand, due to unattractive private conditions for ownership or low social returns on investment.[1] Investments may also be held back by wrong perceptions of market size that can support economies of scale. If weak institutions hamper entrepreneurial investments in developing countries, and are the root causes of underdevelopment, the conditions of weak institutions in transition countries will be magnified at least threefold. Consequently, transforming these economies is no ordinary task. As the UNDP stated, "extraordinary creativity in policy design" and implementation is necessary.[2] Conventional policy levers are most likely ill suited to the task. It is in this light we approach the issue of the role of foreign direct investment (FDI) in transformation of post conflict transition countries.

It must be stressed that post-conflict transition countries are varied. At one end of the spectrum are failed states such as Liberia, Sierra Leone, Somalia, Democratic Republic of Congo and Bosnia-Herzegovina that are recovering from collapse and are on the path to some level of security, stability, and legitimacy. At the other end of the spectrum are countries that emerged from conflict with their political and other institutions relatively intact. This category of states includes Guatemala, Sri Lanka and the former Yugoslav Republic. There is yet a third category of post-conflict transition countries, such as Rwanda, that have managed to reconstruct the essential institutions for transformation and have embarked on what appears to be an irreversible path towards development. The last category of such countries did not experience an outbreak of violence that completely destroyed the state, but nevertheless continue to experience sufficient levels of periodic violence to put them in the same category as the others. It is this assemblage of states for which the question is posed as to the role of FDI in their economic development and the extent to which incentives for FDI might be relevant.

FDI is only a sub-category of the investment regime required to transform these countries. Experience has shown that FDI flows to the least developed countries are insignificant by comparison with other regions of the world.[3] Moreover, as appropriately pointed out by a World Bank study and the experience of recent development success stories, development requires two types of complementary investment: public and private.[4] So the critical question is, what are the investment needs of post conflict transition countries if their economies are to be transformed into vibrant systems within the larger global economy? The issue is framed more broadly to draw attention to certain misconceptions about FDI and development.

What is important about FDI is its perceived beneficial impact on development. It is often assumed that FDI will spur growth and induce the transfer of technology and much needed know-how to the host country. This perception gained greater credibility with the outstanding economic performance of the Asian Newly Industrializing Countries (NICs) such as Taiwan, South Korea, Singapore, Hong Kong and Malaysia.[5] The emergence of China and India as major economies on the rise has further given greater prominence to the beneficial impact of FDI on development.[6] However, the complexity of the underlying reasons for the Asian NICs' success does not permit any isolated categorical statement about the impact of FDI on their development. Recent studies point to a host of complex mixtures of macroeconomic and government market interventions as significant contributing factors.[7]

Notwithstanding the multiplicity of contributing factors, the general perceptions about assumed beneficial effects of FDI mask the complexity of FDI and its role in economic development. Since the decades of the 1970s and 1980s, various studies have questioned the claims of FDI's positive impact on development.[8] The studies showed that the impact of FDI on development is not always unambiguously positive. In other words, any benefits that accrue from FDI may depend critically on the absorptive capacity of the host country, the nature of the internal linkages created with the local economy, the quality (*high value*) of the investment and, to a large extent, the role of the host government in channeling or guiding the process toward specific developmental goals.[9] Other studies challenged the efficacy of tax and other fiscal incentives for attracting FDI. Indeed, one of these studies questioned the theoretical foundations of tax incentive policies and concluded that not only were tax and other fiscal incentives ineffective instruments for attracting FDI, but they also provided a form of perverse reverse subsidy from impoverished and weak recipient states to affluent capital exporting countries.[10] This irony of the poor subsidizing the wealthy through their incentives for FDI should not be lost on policy makers confronted with the difficult task of designing programs for transforming weak and impoverished post conflict states laboring under severe resource constraints.

Over two decades later, the United Nations Conference on Trade and Development (UNCTAD), in a most revealing study on FDI in Sub Saharan Africa (SSA), not only questioned the perceived beneficial impact of FDI in the region but also expressed serious skepticism about the utility of conventional thinking on the subject in that region.[11] We have had occasion to comment briefly that although the recommendations of the study were in the right direction, they were not bold enough.[12] However, because many of the post-conflict transition countries are within Sub-Saharan Africa, and the call by UNCTAD for rethinking FDI has wider implications beyond SSA, it will be useful to examine some of its core arguments. The following observations deserve particular attention.

First, the UNCTAD study found that the SSA region is lagging behind others in terms of the size, performance and beneficial impact of FDI.[13] Second, contrary to familiar arguments, the unattractiveness of SSA and the poor developmental impact of FDI in the region cannot easily be attributed solely to the failure of market-oriented governance reforms.[14] Third, FDI carries with it costs and benefits which must be critically assessed by policy makers if host countries are to capture some of the hoped-for positive contributions to their economic development objectives.[15] Fourth, since the colonial era, Africa has been the victim of FDI-led enclave economies, described elsewhere as *scoop and ship* operations, particularly in the mining sector.[16] Extractive institutions which were established during the colonial era have continued to burden African economies as constraints to development.[17]It is therefore hardly surprising that the UNCTAD study correctly observed that any lack of sensitivity to this enclave phenomenon in FDI policy design will entrench a relationship that has been least beneficial to the continent.

Fifth, the UNCTAD study also pointed out a major fallacy in current thinking that greater openness and downsizing of the state will attract FDI. Not only has this proved to be empirically false, it also has the effect of distracting policy makers from focusing on the fundamental determinants, drivers or theories of FDI and growth.[18] Sixth, following the steps of earlier studies critical of incentives as instruments for FDI, the study concluded that tax and other fiscal incentives might produce the perverse effect of subsidizing the rich capital exporting countries, even as the benefits to poor host countries are highly questionable.[19] Finally, the study stressed that an FDI policy cannot be justified merely because it provides the highest returns to FDI. Rather, FDI can only be justified if it is *high value* and contributes significantly to technological spill-over effects or jobs. Otherwise, FDI might keep the host country in a low-level development trap.[20]

One of the inescapable lessons from the numerous studies of FDI's impact on development is that left to its own devices, FDI is unlikely to generate growth, lead to meaningful technology transfer or create the internal links necessary for the development of certain regions of the world. In view of this, it is highly questionable whether the policy framework for transforming post-conflict transition countries can have reliance on FDI as its central focus. Indeed, as will be shown below, a brief review of the characteristic attributes and distinctive behavior of foreign investors suggests that such reliance would likely be unproductive. This Chapter therefore advocates for the use of the Build Operate and Transfer (BOT) model within the context of industrial project finance for developing local enterprises and an entrepreneurial class in post conflict transition countries.

Patterns of FDI in Post-Conflict Transition Countries

Most post-conflict transition countries are burdened by significant market failures, relatively small market size, severe economic constraints and failed or weak institutions necessary for a well functioning economy. Many of them fall into the category of countries described as least developed; they are located in SSA, some of them are landlocked countries and a few of them suffer from the natural resource curse.[21] Although there are no available statistics dedicated to this group of countries, one can get a sense of their FDI attractiveness from an examination of the categories they fall into.

A study by UNCTAD of FDI in LDCs provides a general picture of FDI flows to LDCs and flows to specific countries, some of which are in post-conflict transition.[22] It is observed that in the decades of the 1990s, LDCs appeared to be more attractive to foreign direct investors than in previous decades. For instance, the annual growth rate of FDI to these countries was about 20% and they seemed to be keeping pace with the annual growth rate of FDI to developing countries, which stood at about 22%.[23] While this annual growth rate of FDI might be indicative of the future attractiveness of these countries to FDI, what is of interest to policy makers in developing countries and post-conflict transition countries is not so much the size of FDI flows but their impact on and contribution to the developmental objectives of the host country. This requires a closer examination of the data.

It would appear that the general positive trend of FDI flows to LDCs masks certain specific troublesome indicators. For instance, FDI flows to LDCs constituted only a very small fraction of total FDI flows to the world and to other developing countries. From 1986 to 1990, FDI flows to LDCs were only 0.4% and 2.2% of total world and developing countries FDI flows respectively.[24] By 1999, the share of LDCs in world FDI dropped to 0.3%, but its share of total flows to developing countries increased slightly to 2.4%.[25] Consistent with the location patterns of FDI, it is hardly surprising that the general picture is that LDCs do not appear to be very attractive to FDI. To the extent that many of the post-conflict transition countries fall into this category, one must ask what amount of energy should be devoted to attracting FDI unless it is deliberately targeted at some specific industrial policy objectives.

FDI flows to post-conflict transition countries face additional difficulties which are characteristic of those countries specifically, and of developing countries in general. First, some countries, such as Angola and the Democratic Republic of the Congo (DRC), are endowed with significant mineral resources, particularly in petroleum and minerals. Others, such as Liberia and Sierra Leone, are also known for their diamond deposits. All of these countries stand to attract FDI investments in those sectors. Unfortunately it is also precisely because of these resources and the conflicts that there may be capital flight or FDI may be of the wrong origin or the wrong type. In countries such as Sierra Leone, divestments exceeded new investment flows in the 1990s.[26] The DRC experienced significant fluctuations between negative and positive inflows during this period. It is reported that the current government of the DRC is even engaged in various forms of infrastructure for natural resources barter investment schemes with foreign governments and their investors, reminiscent of the classic *scoop and ship* investments.[27] In other countries, FDI may come at significant cost to the host country. Resources may be in the hands of incompetent bureaucrats or captured by elite interest groups working in cahoots with foreign investors for siphoning away valuable natural resources in *scoop and ship* investment operations, with little beneficial impact on the development of the host country. Second, their natural resource endowments may also put them in the paradoxical position of suffering from underdevelopment precisely because of their riches, a phenomenon generally referred to as the Dutch Disease,[28] discussed in greater detail later. This is a problem said to be a perverse characteristic of mineral rich countries where abundant natural resource endowments may be a curse, not a blessing.[29]

There is, however, another category of countries, such as Angola and Liberia, which seems to have attracted FDI even in their condition as post-conflict transition countries. A closer look at that picture reveals FDI behavior very much consistent with the patterns observed above. With significant petroleum reserves, Angola has always been attractive to FDI, despite its post-conflict status, particularly in an era of high global energy demand and short supply.[30] Liberia has also experienced relatively high spikes in its FDI inflows during the period, mostly due to Japanese investments aimed at exploiting the tax haven status of Liberia.[31] By any definition of the term, Liberia has been for decades a tax haven attractive to *flag of convenience* investment. Liberia does not levy any taxes on the foreign source income of Liberia corporations. Finally, landlocked and small post-conflict transition countries such as Rwanda face certain constraints in attracting conventional

FDI. Not only are their markets too small, they also face legal questions regarding transit rights if they ship their products to foreign markets.

There are certainly differences in the conditions of post-conflict transition countries. However, what emerges from the general and specific analysis of FDI inflows is a picture that screams at policy makers to pay attention if they want to assign a role to FDI in the positive development and economic transformation of these countries. It is obvious that unless great creativity is invoked, an industrial policy design that focuses on FDI in its conventional form is likely to be ineffective and disappointing in results and impact. Transforming post-conflict transition countries should be, in the words of Easterly, "homegrown," based primarily on a domestic industrial policy crafted by "searchers" within the swamps of local conditions.[32] In this context, searchers are those policy makers looking for the type of *high value* FDI that can make positive contributions to the transformation of the swamp.

Although it seems counterintuitive to call on countries that have been devastated by conflict to take their own fate into their own hands, the transformation of post-conflict transition countries cannot be achieved by outside "planners" relying primarily on conventional FDI.[33] The necessary transformation can best be achieved by the hands of locals with the savvy and adaptability to take only those FDI resources that will assist them in the task at hand. If the resources of developing countries have been used, exploited and adapted to keep the industrial engines of many countries of the world running for centuries, has the time not come for developing countries to take a page from self-reliant industrial strategies of successful countries, many of which they have supported to their own detriment with their raw materials? This is the crucial question to be faced by policy makers. Though conditions in these countries may be bad, optimism must guide policy design and implementation.

The argument made so far is not that FDI cannot contribute to the economic development of a host country. Rather, it is that FDI in one country may contribute to the development of other countries, while at times imposing a cost on the host country. Further, it is also argued that in order for FDI to transform developing countries, particularly post-conflict transition countries, some positive and proactive measures must be taken to ensure that FDI fits into some domestic investment demand systems, in such a way that FDI creates the necessary spill-over effects and internal linkages with the local economy.

FDI by any MNE does not necessarily constitute a simple isolated investment in the host country. Rather, each FDI operation forms part of a system, a network of interdependent and interconnected operations pursuing a general MNE corporate strategic vision. The system provides the parent with great flexibility since it essentially operates an internal market of its own which excludes outsiders and the open market from its intra-firm transactions. Through this internal market, it can shuttle its resources within the system to achieve various objectives which would have been difficult, if not impossible, if it had to rely on third parties in an open market setting. This does not mean that the FDI operations constitute a complete closed system. Internalization theory states that where the market will work well the MNE will rely on outsourcing, delocalization and other forms of external open market transactions.[34] What is important to note is that these transactions that rely on other efficient producers, wholesalers or channels of distribution are not FDI based.

Post-Conflict Transition Countries and the MNE System

In the context of post-conflict transition countries, three countries, Angola, the DRC and Liberia, best exemplify the nature of the FDI flows to such countries and the role of those countries in the functioning of the MNE network of subsidiaries. As an oil producing country, Angola is by far the most attractive to FDI in this sample of countries and shares that level of attractiveness with other oil producing countries on the Continent.[35] In spite of its attractiveness to natural resource seeking investments, Angola also suffers from the same swings in investment flows. In 2003 FDI in Angola reached its peak in the era, $3,500 million, but this was followed by declines culminating in significant negative inflows three years later. Lower levels of volatility were experienced by Liberia and the DRC. What is perhaps significant about the DRC is that the country is reported to be endowed with significant quantities of all minerals known to man, and yet the FDI flows to that country are hardly reflective of its potential.[36] On the other hand, FDI flows to Sierra Leone shows an insignificant but crawling upward trend. In short, whatever the reasons for this volatility in FDI might be, it does not bode well for a country trying to rely on FDI as an instrument for development.

All of the countries examined here have been part of the network of countries brought into the MNE system as suppliers of raw materials, and in Liberia's case also as a tax haven. Even during its internal conflict, Angola remained attractive to foreign investors, primarily in the petroleum sector. In its post-conflict transition phase, Angola has remained one of the leading overall recipients of FDI in Africa, but still primarily in the petroleum sector.[37] Endowed with significant amounts of extractive natural resources, the DRC has been attractive to natural resource seeking FDI.[38] However, with weak institutions, persistent post-conflict security challenges and poor governance, and without an industrial strategic policy architecture of the type advocated for in this study, the DRC seems to have had flirtations with perhaps the wrong types of foreign investors in its extractive industries. As raw material suppliers, neither country benefits from value added activities, technology transfer and linkages with their local economies. The case of the DRC deserves particular attention. In a normal context, raw material supplier countries in the MNE system do not stand to benefit significantly when they are purely in that role. In the case of the DRC, the continuing tensions and administrative difficulties the country faces raise serious questions about what benefits it can even reap from its position as supplier of raw materials.[39] The internal governance difficulties and uncertainties faced by post-conflict transition countries, such as Angola and the DRC, do not make them attractive to irreversible site-specific conventional FDI.

Unlike Angola and the DRC, Liberia plays a dual role in the MNE system. It has been both a supplier of raw materials and a tax haven for MNEs. Starting with the notorious Firestone rubber plantation in the 20th century, Liberia became a major supplier of iron ore to American and Swedish industries in the 1960s.[40] These MNEs established just enough railroad transportation links between the mining sites and the port to facilitate the export of the ore for processing elsewhere. Hardly any internal linkages were made with the local economy, nor did the operations foster the developmental goals of the country. Despite the efforts of policy makers, subsequent timber concessions granted in the 1970s suffered a similar fate.[41] Thus, Liberia was and remains largely unattractive to irreversible *high value* site specific or cheek-by-jowl investments. As a prototypical small country, the small local market size cannot support the economies of scale essential for market seeking FDI.

One of the enduring characteristics of Liberia's international economic policies has been openness. Throughout its history, in crisis and challenging economic times, Liberia remained wedded and unwavering in its commitment to an open economy.[42] An important aspect of this open policy is a liberal tax jurisdiction which is based on the territoriality or source principle. That is, Liberia does not levy any taxes on income earned by Liberian nationals or corporations outside its territorial borders. Thus, Liberian subsidiaries of foreign MNEs are only subject to taxation for income earned within Liberia. In addition to the policy of an open economy, Liberia is also a "flag of convenience" state which allows the registration of foreign owned ships in Liberia. The combined effect of these policies is that Liberia is attractive to FDI motivated by the benefits conferred by a tax haven. This has wide ranging implications for the country if FDI is to play a meaningful role in its economic development. To the extent that income earned outside Liberia is not subject to Liberian taxes, there is hardly an incentive for foreign investors to engage in activities, transformative or otherwise, within the country that would subject them to taxation. In a perverse way, the tax haven status of the country discourages the type of high value investments that would be beneficial to its economic development because, as much as possible, income generating activities will be engaged out of jurisdiction. There is an obvious incentive for FDI in the extractive industries to be primarily *scoop and ship* operations.[43] Local processing which generates higher value would also subject a higher amount of operational revenues to local taxes. It is therefore hardly surprising that since the 1990s Liberia has attracted relatively large amounts of "flag of convenience" FDI, primarily from Japan.[44]

Flag of convenience FDI is essentially a tax haven book-keeping device that does not involve any actual capital inflow. The value of the ships registered under this process constitutes the FDI. Such book-keeping driven investments, while very valuable to the MNE, are *slippery and easily switch-able* between jurisdictions in the book-keeping process. Moreover, since the ships are likely to be used in international trade between countries and points outside Liberia, the income generated in that process will escape Liberia taxation.[45] Thus, Liberia may be used as an instrument for sheltering income of other countries from taxation without the positive capital accumulation effects. The flexibility inherent in the MNE system makes this not only possible but also easy.

Of course, the political economy of Liberia is a very complex one which cannot be addressed here.[46] However, if the goal of the liberal tax jurisdiction regime and the "flag of convenience" policy is to encourage FDI for the economic development of the country, that goal may be elusive. Viewed as a regime, these policies would encourage the least amount of operational activities in the country, particularly in the extractive industries where the country has natural endowments and comparative advantage. That is, FDI operations would involve mostly the extraction and export of raw materials, which would deny the country beneficial value-added activities, technology transfer and essential links with the local economy. They would also discourage irreversible investments and encourage transitory FDI with little or no actual capital inflows. In particular, "flag of convenience" investments in a tax haven such as Liberia are likely to contribute less to economic development. By their very nature nothing may be done or is required to be done in the host country. In a vertically or horizontally integrated MNE system, significant amounts of income may be earned by Liberian registered ships without contributing any value to the local economy except the registration fee. In all of these cases the contribution by FDI to the development of Liberia would be minimal unless some proactive development driven policies are put in place.

Given the functional dynamics of the MNE system, no country can count on conventional FDI making the type of contribution it needs for its growth and economic development *without some guidance*. In other words, the search for the contributions of the MNE system to local economies must be a double-sided search that raises a series of questions. What motivates MNEs in the choice of their host countries? Put differently, what is the role of any specific FDI from the point of view of the investor? Why are some countries suppliers of raw materials and others manufacturers of products? What contributions to the system are expected from each of the countries and their subsidiaries in the system? What local conditions in each host country might contribute to the position of that country in the MNE system? In view of the fact that the distribution of the benefits of the MNE system among the participating countries might be uneven or even inequitable, which type of FDI operations could *positively* alter the distribution of those benefits? Which types of FDI are likely to expose the host country to negative externalities in the form of social and environmental costs, or expose the vulnerability dependence associated with the volatility of the global economy? Indeed, the risks of detrimental impact associated with certain investments might be too high for policy makers to ignore.

In the specific case of post-conflict transition countries, this understanding is even much more crucial since they are likely to face several additional problems and constraints. The sample of countries examined here, Angola, the DRC and Liberia, all fit well into the model of the MNE system discussed above. All three countries have been long-time suppliers of raw materials. This would seem to suggest that MNEs in those countries made decisions which minimized certain uncertainties or avoided the vulnerabilities associated with irreversible high value asset specific investments in local processing or manufacturing. Yet, the raw materials demands of MNEs are such that they made investments even in the midst of political turmoil and severe insecurity. So, even during its internal conflict, Angola continued to attract FDI, primarily in the petroleum sector. Notwithstanding the volatility of its political conditions, Angola remained one of the leading recipients of FDI in Africa. Also, in spite of governance difficulties, the DRC also attracts investments in the extractive industry. As discussed above, within the context of the post-conflict chaos and governance difficulties that seem to exist within the DRC, it is doubtful how much benefit the country could receive in its position as raw material supplier.

Transformative Industrial Strategic Policy Architecture

This chapter proposes a transformative strategic industrial policy architecture in which non-conventional FDI plays a complementary role as an engine of development within a carefully crafted domestic investment demand. This entails a direct reversal of roles in the creation of MNE FDI systems in which the host country exercises greater control over the type, timing and duration of FDI. Through screening, targeting and sequencing, industrial projects and technologies with the greatest potential for generating sustained growth and development should be funded through a Project Finance and Build Operate and Transfer format. As will be explained below, project sponsors, as foreign investors, should play an important but transitory role in responding to the developmental objectives of the host country for profit. In that context, we shall argue that conventional neo-liberal, anti-state market based prescriptions that dominated the decades of the 1980s and 1990s are perhaps misguided and ill suited to the needs of post-conflict transition countries in search of instruments for development. This is particularly the case when uncompromising market based principles are preached and imposed on countries where market failure of the first order dominates their economies.

Contextualising the Strategic Policy Architecture of the Post-Conflict State

The picture painted earlier of the post-conflict transition state within the system of traditional FDI raises serious questions about whether FDI can play a meaningful transformative role in their economic development. First, from the point of view of the strategic mindset of MNEs, post-conflict transition countries play only a limited role in the achievement of their corporate objectives. Any developmental impact of MNE activities in the host country is a by-product or consequence and not *necessarily* a directed corporate objective. Second, certain prevailing conditions in post-conflict transition countries make them attractive only to certain types of conventional FDI with limited transformative possibilities. We have already addressed these above. However, for emphasis and to clarify the approach advocated below, a summary of the conditions of post-conflict transition countries is necessary.

According to various classifications of countries by the United Nations, its organs and other international institutions, post-conflict transition countries are some of the poorest countries in the world. Some of them fall into the category of countries classified as least developed countries, fragile economies or landlocked. Some belong to more than one of these categories. Several of them are found in Sub-Saharan Africa, a region notorious for consistently lagging behind other developing countries in its basic economic indicators such as GDP growth, per capita income and general economic performance. Standing alone, most post-conflict transition countries constitute small markets either because of their population or because of low per capita income. Such is the case of Liberia and Sierra Leone. Others, such as the DRC, with larger population and greater market potential, lack basic infrastructure, transportation, and telecommunications that can support a successful marketing strategy. In response to the limitations of small markets and the demands of economies of scale for production that can support market seeking manufacturing FDI, cross-cutting and overlapping regional trade organizations and free trade agreements have mushroomed in Africa. For instance, COMESA, of which Rwanda is a member, has 19 member countries that stretch from South Africa to Egypt. As they cover larger geographic areas with huge populations and diverse economies, one would have thought that the market size problems faced by manufacturing FDI would have been removed by the formation of these regional trade organizations. Unfortunately, the intended regional markets are also hampered by similar inadequate infrastructural linkages and other barriers to effective marketing. Thus, the effective markets for FDI continue to be national markets.

With these conditions and constraints, post-conflict transition countries appear to be unattractive to high value FDI with the transformative capacity they need. From our earlier discussion of the enduring characteristics of FDI, the poorest of poor countries are hardly ever attractive to MNEs in search of markets and profits unless those countries are endowed with abundant natural resources. Besides, in view of lingering security questions and the vulnerabilities associated with specific asset investment inherent in long-term irreversible and high value FDI, conventional FDI has tended to be primarily in the extractive or natural resource industries. Designed to minimize investor exposure to vulnerabilities, and purely for the export of raw materials, these types of operations cannot transform the host country. Instead, they tend to expose the host country to the vagaries and volatilities of the world commodity markets.

It is clear from this summary and the arguments advanced so far that left alone, FDI cannot deliver the goods on growth and economic development in post transition countries. Indeed, it seems that such an expectation of MNEs would be a mismatch of expectations and responsibilities. The primary objective of MNEs is not economic development, although they stand to benefit from it and can contribute to it. On the other hand, economic development is one of the primary responsibilities of the state. And it is incumbent on the state to take all necessary measures to achieve its developmental objectives. For developing countries in general, the evidence so far seems to suggest that economic development cannot easily be achieved without some deliberate and active state intervention. The state cannot relinquish that responsibility to the so-called pure market forces guided, as it were, by the invisible hand. *Just as a farmer tills the land, plants and nurtures his crops for a great harvest, so must the state take measures for the development of its economy.* This is the context in which one must see the role of post-conflict transition countries in the design of an industrial strategic policy architecture for development.

Modeling Industrial Strategic Policy Architecture: Lessons from Success Stories

The argument advanced is not that market principles are not relevant in fundamental industrial policy design. Rather, it is that post-conflict transition countries in search of techniques to jump start their economies should benefit from the lessons of recent success stories of other countries. In particular, they should look to the newly industrializing economies (NIEs) of South East Asia for clues and ideas that could inform their choice of policies and techniques for laying the framework for development. The lessons from this region are particularly instructive given that the countries do not constitute a homogenous group. In an informative and careful study of a sample of 119 countries, John Page offered some reasons for the miraculous success of these countries.[47] At the outset, he pointed out that the East Asian miracles are hardly homogenous or monolithic in culture, economic conditions, resources, population or historical experience.[48] In spite of such diversity, they all shared certain common characteristics in their success. They all enjoyed simultaneously sustained growth and equitable distribution of income. That is, they debunked the view once held that there is an inverse relationship between growth and equity. Instead they demonstrated that high levels of growth can be positively correlated to high income equality.[49] For as these economies enjoyed unprecedented growth rates the gap between the rich and poor simultaneously narrowed significantly. The policy architecture that produced such miraculous results is worth the attention of other developing countries, particularly countries in search of a framework for development after conflict and major economic disruptions. The critical question is, what policies produced these impressive results?

The answer to this question is particularly important to countries that have suffered severe and untold devastation, but coming out of that face the opportunity for a fresh bold start. However, according to Page, there are two schools of thought on the reasons for the East Asian miracle. One school, the *fundamentalists,* hold that these countries relying on market principles got the basics right. They focused on policies that increased physical and human capital per worker and efficient allocation of resources. In essence, they concentrated on getting the "price right."[50] The *mystics,* on the other hand, argued that markets have consistently failed to guide investments into industries with the greatest potential for growth. It was activist governments in the region that intervened directly in getting the "price wrong" by channeling investments and technologies into predetermined industries and projects with the greatest potential for growth which normal market forces would have rejected.[51] It would, however, appear that the explanation of the success of NIEs is too complex to be cast in an either-or choice between the *fundamentalist* and *mystics* arguments.

The overall evidence from Page and numerous other studies suggests that a combination of policies played a significant role in the productivity growth and development of these countries.[52] It appeared that all countries, at different phases and at different rates, combined market oriented capital accumulation and allocation policies with state interventionist policies that promoted specific industries and technologies believed to have high value transformative effects. More specifically, common to all countries were the combinations of the following policies: (1) market oriented capital accumulation and allocation, (2) state interventionist policies that promoted specific industries and technologies, (3) unusual macroeconomic stability spurred by sound policies and management, (4) improved integrity of the banking systems with carefully designed and monitored directed credit that increased profitability for the banks, (5) educational policies that focused on primary and secondary education which generated a rapid increase in the pool of skilled labor and (6) agricultural policies which did not over-tax rural communities.[53]

With due regard to the other complementary policies, it would appear that rapid human capital growth was perhaps the most important element in the success of the industrial policies pursued. The industrial targeting policies and the manufactured export orientation based on new technologies all required a skilled labor force. High productivity growth, high quality output and efficiency driven low cost production, which in turn were also essential for global competitiveness of their exports, could not have been achieved without a growing pool of skilled labor. Perhaps one of the most important reasons for the high simultaneous growth rates and the rapid narrowing income gap was the emphasis on increased supply of skilled labor achieved through primary and secondary education.[54] Without such resources, the achievement of the industrial transformation as designed would have been difficult, if not impossible. But as skilled labor productivity increased, so were labor's rewards in wages and other compensation, which then narrowed the income inequality gap.

The Role of the Developmental State

One of the important lessons to be discerned from the success stories of the East Asian Miracles is the role of the *"developmental state"* in economic development.[55] The "developmental state" is one which does not approach the development task as a dichotomized tension between the state and markets, seen by neo-liberal economists and the so-called Washington Consensus as virtually incompatible. Nor does it see any bipolarity between market-driven, export-led growth and an inward looking or import substitution development agenda. The development task of these countries does not easily fit into such simple dichotomies or bipolarities. There is not a simple choice between free and unfettered markets and "statist" restrictive and protectionist policies, or between a domineering or dominant state control over entrepreneurial decisions and free market structures. Rather, the need is for marshalling various forces of the political and bureaucratic elites, entrepreneurs and industry leaders, various economic rent seekers and other stakeholders into a symbiotic organism with a single national mission for industrial development.

The pessimists and skeptics might view the success of these East Asian Miracles as too much of a cultural phenomenon unique to that region and therefore of little value to post-conflict transition countries. If so, one might ask why neo-liberal free market driven policies have transcendent cultural and universal characteristics. Moreover, as pointed out by Page, the East Asian Miracles are hardly culturally homogenous, yet they employed similar industrial policies with similar remarkable results.[56] Certainly, culture plays some role in how a sound industrial policy might be adapted in any country, be it Liberia, Bosnia or Angola. However, the soundness of an industrial policy emphasizing high value manufacturing investment is not culturally driven. Besides, why should any person put a ceiling on what other peoples or cultures can do in any country by denying them access to successful and workable models? Some might even call the approach used by the successful countries as "state capitalism" in a pejorative use of the term, suggesting that there is only one road to development and it is the unfettered free market system. Diversity of development theories and instruments cannot be a detriment but rather a major asset, unless we underrate the adaptive capacity of humanity.

The experience of the Asian Miracles suggests that what post-transition countries need is an industrial policy design that is outside conventional norms but well suited to their developmental needs. The push for non-conventional policy design is nothing extraordinary. It conforms with the earlier call for creativity of the first order if post-conflict transition countries are to be transformed amidst the significant and extraordinary circumstances they face. It is also consistent with a growing unease with the once dominant neo-liberal policy prescription of the 1980s and 1990s. A paradigm shift seems to be in the offing among development economists about the role of the state in development. And institutions such as the World Bank and many development economists seem to recognize the limitations of the neo-liberal economic policy prescription for developing countries.[57] The neo-liberal anti-state, market-oriented approach to development policy has not borne fruit in many poor countries, and not from lack of effort.[58] As Easterly might describe it, the diagnosis and medicine of the "Planners" have not worked.[59] The task of poor developing countries and particularly those emerging from years of conflict cannot be left *solely* to market forces. The task requires the hand of an activist "developmental state" that must harness and weld together a multiplicity of forces into a symbiotic organism with a single national economic development mission.[60]

The Developmental Post-Conflict State

It is apparent from our discussion so far that the needs of post-conflict transition countries for transforming their economies into sustainable growth and development point to the choice of adopting the role of the "developmental state."[61] First, those countries are afflicted with several severe market failures and constraints on their economies that cannot easily be resolved by reliance on pure neo-liberal, anti-state market driven policies. They need a pragmatic, developmental, "activist" or "interventionist" state with the right industrial policy framework.[62] Second, it is also clear that conventional FDI and its system of interconnected operations as currently configured is unlikely to be a meaningful instrument for economic development in these countries. Most of them are suppliers of raw materials within the MNE system, which does not create any beneficial links with the local economy. Notwithstanding these facts, MNEs have the capital, technology, know-how and other resources essential for economic development. These resources can be harnessed and channeled to that end by the state. Third, the evidence from countries that have made a meaningful and sustained transition toward industrialization suggests models and pathways to development that can inform the choices to be made by post-conflict transition countries. The success stories have demonstrated that the "developmental state" can, through ingenuity, craft a complex and deliberate commingled policy design that relies substantially on domestic investment demand and local physical and human capital accumulation for the manufacture of products aimed at external markets.

The task of the "developmental state" is to focus on the answer to the critical question, what is the meaning and purpose of development? According to Amartya Sen, winner of the Nobel Prize in Economics in 1998, ancient religious and philosophical texts have struggled with the purpose of wealth.[63] According to him, Aristotle saw wealth merely as an instrument for something else.[64] Similarly, the industrial policy architecture of the "developmental state" might be aimed at a chain of purposes: the empowerment of the economy which in turn empowers people towards self-fulfillment and liberty. Thus, industrial policy is ultimately not about growth indices as such but about economic, social and cultural enrichment of individual citizens for the expression of their liberty. Indeed, for all its brilliance, Hernando De Soto's celebrated book *The Mystery of Capital* about unlocking the vast amounts of the invisible capital of the poor has, at its core, the purpose of enlightening the poor to help them transform their vast unstructured wealth toward self realization.[65]

In view of the foregoing, the goal of this section is to develop, or at least to suggest, an industrial strategic architecture for a developmental state that benefits from the positive elements of successful countries, while taking into account the conditions of the post conflict transition countries. Such a strategic architecture will draw on the positive contributions of foreign investors outside the framework of conventional FDI. It will seek the contributions of capital, technology, know-how and other resources generally generated and bundled in FDI, while avoiding the attributes of permanent ownership and control of conventional FDI as well as its cost. As a general policy, the industrial strategic architecture contemplated will insist on investment activities that create meaningful links with the local economies. This will require, as its primary focus, the elimination of the export of raw materials without some local processing. Put more directly, as a general policy, *post-conflict transition countries with abundant natural resources must resolve never to export those resources in their raw form.* Such a policy will be perhaps the single most important policy decision made. It will establish a major paradigm shift, the acquisition of a mindset that demonstrates the belief and willingness of the country to alter its position permanently in the global commodities regime. It will at once constitute an immediate break with the past and compel the adoption of several necessary and complementary policies essential to local value added and economic development in general. The feasibility, sequencing and intensity of the required productive activities will be a matter of policy, based on the nature of the resources in each country.

The strategic policy architecture must take into account the mineral and natural resources of the country. However, the industrial policy prescription for transforming post-conflict transition countries must go beyond the processing of raw materials and reducing the vulnerabilities associated with them. The strategic architecture must include policies for industrial upgrading involving other sectors and industries, with a view to value-added investment activities. According to John Dunning, a country should improve upon any processes it does well, in addition to venturing into other sectors that hold promise for industrial upgrading.[66] In particular, consideration might be given to investments in what has been described as flexible factories for the manufacture of standardized products or manufacture-to-order operations for spare parts, clothing and similar operations in services.[67] The current wave of outsourcing globally captures this phenomenon. Independent factories not committed to the continuous process of the manufacture and sale of specific products have great flexibility and a great opportunity for sharing fixed costs with customers.[68]

However, a manufactured-export led industrial strategy necessarily demands the achievement of a second goal in the design of industrial policy: the recognition of the important and inevitable link between trade and investment policies to export-led growth and development.[69] The evidence from the Asian Tigers demonstrates clearly that a successful export-oriented industrial policy had to address three crucial elements: (1) the demand side of the equation: which products to manufacture and for which markets; (2) the essential elements of global competitiveness for those products (high quality, low cost and low price); and (3) the issue of market access. Policy makers understood that globally competitive products needed a free trade regime that assured market access to target markets.[70] The achievement of these goals was a collective effort of government officials in the relevant ministries and trade negotiators and entrepreneurs, particularly industry leaders. For instance, working within the framework of the gaps and ambiguities in GATT and employing tactical "bilateral/unilateral" voluntary export restraints, Japan was able to gain and retain access to some high per capita income markets such as the US for its high demand export products in the 1970s and 1980s.[71]

The third goal of the industrial strategic architecture for the developmental state is *self-reliance*. Ultimately, the transformation of the economies of post-conflict transition countries must be in the hands of locals who are most familiar with their needs and the complexities of welding together competing forces into a coherent whole for the national good. Foreign planners, advisors and other well wishers can assist but cannot do it for them. From Japan to South Korea and more recently from India to China, the evidence is mounting that the development task is "homegrown."[72] It requires the building of foundational institutions and adopting fundamentally sound macroeconomic policies. The concept of self-reliance might seem counterintuitive in the case of countries that are just emerging from severe conflict, but the experience of Vietnam and Rwanda might contradict that. With the right framework and mindset much is achievable, even in post-conflict states.

Fourth, and more specifically, it is clear from our discussion of the success stories that the economic fate of post-conflict transition countries cannot be left *totally* in the hands of the free-market forces under the type of neoliberal policies that dominated the decades of the 1980s and 1990s. Nor can the transformation of these countries be purely the function of the interventionist and activist state. In the post-conflict transition state, either of these approaches in isolation will be an unmitigated disaster. The severe market failure and the potentially excessive political power that normally befall post-conflict countries do not bode well for an either-or policy framework. What is required is the "developmental state" that designs an industrial policy drawing from a combination of sources. Under its guiding hand, private investments play the primary role in investment activities targeted toward certain industries and manufactured exports with the greatest potential for development, while the government simultaneously engages in infrastructural development and various forms of regulation of industry suited to the task at hand.

Finally, it is clear from our discussion so far that the "developmental state" does not believe in unfettered or unregulated access to its productive resources with the greatest potential for generating growth and development. That path was avoided by the East Asian Miracles towards FDI. Through different policies and regulations, South Korea and Taiwan channeled FDI towards industries where their contribution would advance some national objectives. In certain industries foreign investors were permitted only as equal or minority joint venture partners with local enterprises.[73] In the case of Japan, there appeared to be a preference for the acquisition of foreign technology instead of FDI. The most recent example of the "developmental state" at work is China.[74] The foreign investment laws of China do not encourage unfettered or unregulated FDI in all industries.[75] The foreign investment laws distinguish between the more desirable high technology investments and others for differential treatment.[76]

It is apparent from this discussion that the policy response to FDI was not hostility but one geared towards harnessing its positive effects and contribution to the local economies. Where FDI could make a difference it was not left to its own devices to make the needed contribution. Rather, foreign investors were prodded, guided or channeled toward certain industries or projects. If this was the context within which FDI operated beneficially under much more favorable circumstances, the question presented here is whether FDI could produce similar beneficial consequences under less hospitable circumstances and without guidance in post-conflict transition countries.

The Role of Project Finance in Industrial Policy Implementation

The argument advanced so far is that if the goal of any strategic industrial policy architecture in a post-conflict transition country is the transformation of its economy, conventional FDI is an unlikely candidate for that task. Burdened by severe economic constraints and endemic uncertainties compounded by ever looming risks, post-conflict transition countries are hardly attractive to the type of high value FDI that could transform a country. The foreign investment opportunities that tend to attract MNEs to those countries are mostly in enclave and natural resource activities with minimal developmental impact. Enclave investments in abundant natural resource countries might even infect them with the so-called "Dutch Disease."[77] Yet in the midst of this disappointing picture the opportunities for high value transformative foreign investment abound, if only a different type of investor and investment opportunities is sought after. The investment instruments that hold great promise for transforming these countries is project finance or a variation of it generally referred to as "build operate and transfer" (BOT). The self-reliant industrial policy framework advocated in this study could benefit from project finance projects that result in an eventual transfer of the projects to local interests. Although BOTs are generally analyzed under the framework of project finance for the purposes of emphasis and clarity in policy implementation we shall examine them separately below.

Project finance is a tried and true old-fashioned medieval merchant banking investment practice that seems to have escaped the attention of foreign investment theorists. As an investment instrument, project finance is a non-recourse or limited recourse financing scheme used by private investors to fund specific projects or ventures solely on the basis of the ability of the projects to pay for themselves from their cash flow.[78] The sponsor of the project does not guarantee repayment of the principal and interest should the project fail to produce sufficient proceeds to service the debt. In that sense, the financing is a non-recourse funding in which the lenders, creditors and equity investors do not look to the general assets of the sponsor for repayment of the loan. In the case of limited recourse financing the lenders look to the sponsors' assets for a repayment of a portion of the debt.

Project finance is employed by developed and developing countries in a variety of projects ranging from infrastructure, power generation, oil and gas and mineral explorations and exploitation, orbiting communication satellites to manufacturing and research and development.[79] The modern proliferation of project finance seems to be a phenomenon concentrated most in developed countries, Asia and Latin America.[80] Naturally, the return of project finance has also produced a growing body of literature addressing its various complexities as an investment instrument, which cannot be explored here.[81]

Impact of Project Finance on Industrial Policy Objectives

From its inception to its current modern configurations, project finance has continued to offer several benefits to foreign investors and host governments that permanent capital in the form FDI does not easily provide. The benefits and advantages examined below should also engage the attention of policy makers in post-conflict transition countries.

From the point of view of the equity investors, project finance provides sponsors with financial independence on a project-by-project basis and insulates their general assets from the financial obligations associated with the loan for the project. This is often referred to as "off-balance-sheet" debt since the project finance debt does not show up in the consolidated financial statements of the sponsor.[82] This permits the sponsor to maintain a certain debt/equity ratio and not to dilute its existing equity.[83] Even when the project finance is on a limited recourse basis the commitments of the sponsor are still substantially less than full recourse obligations. For host governments risky and complex ventures with developmental potential can be funded and implemented.

The cost of the typical complex project finance transaction runs from tens of millions to billions of dollars. For example, while the cost of the Nghe An Tate & Lyle Sugar Mill in Vietnam was $90 million the cost of the Australian-Japan Cable project stood at $520 million, and that of the Chad-Cameroon Pipe Line was $4 billion.[84] The financial demands of these projects exposed lenders to such high risks that no single lender was willing to undertake them alone. The funding of projects is therefore generally undertaken by a multiplicity of parties – banks, equity investors and multilateral institutions – to spread the risks associated with each project.[85] Risk distribution works to the benefit of host developing countries since it allows more deserving projects to be funded at a lower cost to the participants and governments.[86] Besides, the parties can participate in multiple projects without risking huge amounts of capital in any of them. Conventional FDI, even within its risk sharing joint venture format, is unlikely to commit such huge amounts of permanent equity to these ventures in risky countries.

Moreover, the demands of project finance are fairly rigorous. As an IFC report aptly stated, there is no free lunch in project finance.[87] Since each project must stand on its own and pay for itself, the selection process is guided by careful capital budgeting techniques. Qualifying projects must then meet basic corporate capital budgeting requirements in terms of their cash flow and the ability to pay for themselves. Although objections might be raised about the government picking winners one ought to keep in mind that this process compels the host government to pick wisely and therefore brings some discipline in any policy of industrial targeting used by the government.

For countries with abundant natural resources, manufacturing based project finance confronts directly the enclave characteristics of conventional FDI, lamented by the World Bank and other international institutions.[88] If, as we have argued, no resources may be exported without local processing, project finance provides several advantages in that regard. Establishing a local processing plant would bring about the infusion of capital, technology and know-how, the very assets and contributions generally sought after in conventional FDI. With project finance, the host country receives those resources and benefits in the industries and projects that matter to its industrial development goals, the achievement of which is not guaranteed by conventional FDI. Moreover, local processing not only provides value-added contribution to local resources but also creates linkages with the local economy generally considered as essential for development. Besides, conventional FDI in natural resources may create a perverse effect on supplier countries. It may expose them to vulnerability dependence created by the volatility of global commodity markets on which they have to rely.

The growth rates and economic fortunes of mono-crop economies or those heavily dependent on one or two commodities traded in the world commodities markets are dictated by forces outside their control. Their growth rates rise and fall with the swings in world prices. Such is the current experience of many African countries that seem to be enjoying high GDP growth rates mainly because of current favorable commodity prices.[89] However, with local processing the growth rates of post-conflict transition countries will be stabilized over time. Consider what the economic fate of Angola and the DRC would be if these countries employed the strategy of compelling or at least insisting on local processing of their raw materials. The crude oil of Angola would be refined before export; so would the numerous ores and minerals of the DRC. Producers of coffee beans such as Rwanda would, through project finance, establish flexible coffee roasting facilities with the capacity to roast beans to the specifications of any foreign buyer. Over time countries such as Rwanda, Ethiopia and Kenya could develop their own national brands of roasted coffee for the global market place.

The point that ought to be stressed here is the need to redirect national policy towards new empowering possibilities for developing countries. The limitations on local processing in poor countries may be more an issue of limited imagination and generalizations than one of limited human capacity in specific cases. For instance, in 1998, Mozambique, one of the least developed countries in the world, with the assistance of THE IFC obtained project finance funding of $1.2 billion for a green field investment in an aluminum smelter called MOZAL.[90] This project was the largest private sector project in the country. Kaiser Aluminum has since the 1960s operated an aluminum processing plant in Ghana using imported bauxite and initially imported technical labor.[91] Neither of these two countries could be said to have had the requisite supply labor at the outset. The possibilities and feasibility of local processing were assessed against the backdrop of the global supply of human capital and other resources in the short term and the necessary long-term adjustments.

Labor policies in an industrial policy framework for local processing ought to be addressed separately. Local processing ultimately will require skilled local labor in the form of engineers and technicians if the benefits of know-how transfer are to be realized. In the typical post-conflict transition country such skilled labor may be absent because of inappropriate educational programs or the brain drain. Both of these can be addressed in the short and long term. Initially, the productivity of the local processing plant can be handled by hiring foreign skilled labor. The world offers an almost inexhaustible pool of skilled labor for the needs of any specific project in any country. However, the future needs of the processing plant must be addressed through a deliberate training program whose cost is incorporated in the cost of the project. In other words, built into the project cost must be the training of a pool of local engineers and skilled labor to replace the foreign technical work force in the long run. The sponsor must undertake to implement this program with yearly targets for an agreed number of years. Thus, at the end of that period the technical labor necessary for efficient operations would have been substantially provided.

What is perhaps even more important to the policy requiring local processing is its impact on other government policies if the entire industrial policy can be beneficially implemented. This single policy should trigger complementary policy changes in education, banking, investments, commercial laws, public expenditures on infrastructure, macroeconomic management and others essential to the industrial development goals pursued.[92] Thus, to ensure the continuous flow of technical labor, the general educational policies of the country will have to be adjusted and realigned. As discussed above, the East Asian Miracles focused on primary and secondary education, to great effect not only in increasing labor productivity but also in closing the income inequality gap.[93]

One of the benefits of local processing of raw materials for exports is the irrelevance of the constraints imposed by small, underdeveloped or inaccessible local markets. The target markets for the output are external hard currency global markets which are infinitely larger than the supply capacity of any single small country. The existence of these markets should not be in question since they are the same markets that foreign raw materials processing plants aim to serve. The real issue will be global competitiveness of the output with respect to quality, cost and price. But under project finance the project would most likely not be funded if these requirements were not met. However, a well constructed link between trade, investment and industrial policy should ensure market access.[94] At least, the policy of local processing of raw materials for export compels a comprehensive, coherent and integrated policy framework that ties all the pieces together. *There are neither half measures nor free lunches in the development game.*

Industrial Upgrading of Light Manufacturing Industries and Other Sectors

The emphasis on local processing of raw materials for export should not be read as a limited policy prescription. Rather it is to stress the need for a *paradigm shift* in the policy orientation of developing countries in general and post-conflict transition countries in particular. After all, the possibilities for industrial upgrading even in countries with abundant natural resources extend beyond those resources, and several countries are not endowed with abundant natural resources. The general argument we seek to make is that industrial policy should be aimed at empowering the local productive forces through value-added industrial upgrading investment activities in sectors with the greatest promise for growth and development. Such empowerment may focus on exploiting the comparative advantage of the country together with whatever opportunities the global economic resources may offer.

Project finance can be employed fruitfully in establishing manufacturing facilities for the production of generic or standardized global products such as spare parts, component parts, original equipment manufactured products, or bottles and soda cans that be used by many soft drinks manufacturers. In the high technology sector, data processing and related computer based service centers offer yet other opportunities for servicing multiple clients within the current global outsourcing regime. Factories with multiple output capacities have been aptly described as flexible, independent or batch-process in that the manufacturer does not own the products and is not producing a single line of products tied to a brand name or logo.[95] The use of project finance under these circumstances provides the manufacturer with great flexibility in managing risks and maintaining stable profits. Flexible factories are capable of producing different types of unbranded or branded products for different foreign customers, as in manufacture-to-order facilities that produce different brand name designer clothing or customized goods or components for different customers. The manufacturer is not unlike the typical village blacksmith of yesteryear who made different wares and products on order for different customers.[96]

For post-conflict transition countries, the batch-process manufacturing plant offers several advantages for industrial upgrading. As already pointed out, the manufacture of goods destined for foreign customers and markets minimizes or removes the domestic and regional market constraints faced by these countries. As an independent manufacturer of different products under contract for different customers, the manufacturer retains great flexibility for profitable operations. The cash flow of the manufacturer that is so essential for project finance is not linked to a single product or market but determined by a variety of its manufactured products marketed globally. The manufacturer is to a large extent insulated from the consequences of competition between its customers for global market share. Losses and gains in market share by customers may result in a loss of some customers but they do not necessarily change its production volume and the resulting cash flow.[97]

Project financing of flexible factories or production services opens up other possibilities for a host country in the area of strategic alliances. It is now clear that one of the goals of the strategic alliances of the 1980s was the search by enterprises for opportunities to convert their fixed cost into variable cost by sharing them with as many partners as possible. Flexible manufacturing facilities fit into this mold. Through them many competitors save money by not building their own plants; without investing any money in the manufacturer they share their fixed costs by contractual arrangements. These arrangements permit economies of scale, lower per unit cost and better global price competitiveness.

The impact of project finance on independent value-added manufacturing facilities would produce effects similar to those gained from the processing of local raw materials. The investment would involve the transfer of capital, technology and know-how and create linkages with the local economies. Of course, the efficacy of this policy would depend critically on the availability of skilled labor, the productivity of labor, output quality and cost. The response to these issues has already been discussed above. Similarly, the efficacy of independent export oriented factories would depend on a well coordinated investment and trade policies also discussed above.

In conclusion, the search for transformative policies and investment strategies in post-conflict transition countries must start not only with what the domestic economy offers but, even more so, with what the global economic environment offers in terms of capital, technology, other resources and markets. In the short term the picture may be dim, but policy makers should focus on laying the foundations for sustained future growth and development. With project finance, some of the short-term and long-term constraints can be addressed by utilizing available global resources to empower local industries to be self-reliant in the long term.

Use of Build Operate Transfer Industrial Policy Implementation

One of the key elements of the strategic industrial policy architecture advocated for post-conflict transition countries is the use of self-reliant economic development policies. We have argued that ultimately outsiders, no matter how well intentioned, cannot transform those economies.[98] They do not have much directly at stake, nor are they in the best position to assess the complexities of the local conditions and make the most critical choices necessary. The locals are better suited for that job and can do it effectively if given the proper support. We have argued such support can be given within the framework of project finance funding of private sector projects that hold the greatest promise for growth and development. As part of that empowerment we now argue that the project finance model should be Build Operate Transfer (BOT) in which projects arre transferred to local owners after a specified term.

The term BOT is said to have been the brainchild of Turgut Ozal, Prime Minister of Turkey, who used the term in 1984 during the privatization of Turkish public projects.[99] Soon after its introduction, the concept caught the imagination of governments in Europe, Asia and elsewhere seeking funding for various infrastructural projects at the time of severe fiscal constraints. The BOT approach became an attractive instrument for funding infrastructural projects such as power generation plants, toll roads and tunnels such as Eurotunnel.[100] For policy makers, it made sense to invite foreign capital for the construction and management of basic infrastructural projects and have them transferred to the host government after the projects had paid for themselves. The attractiveness of the eventual transfer of an efficient and effective operating facility to local owners is one of the reasons why the BOT model is advocated here for the private sector in post-conflict transition countries.

Under the BOT approach, one or more private sector sponsors are authorized to create a private project company to build a manufacturing plant or other facility using the project finance system to raise the necessary capital for the project. Under an agreement, the sponsors will build, manage, operate and maintain the facility through the project company as a separate and distinct legal entity for a specified time period, after which the plant is transferred to local owners. The duration of time given to the sponsors to manage and operate the plant will vary with the size of the debt, the risks associated with the venture and its projected cash flow.[101] BOT projects vary in characteristics, sectoral conditions, risks and costs. No two BOT projects are exactly the same. With non-recourse or limited recourse lending based on the notion that each project must pay for itself, the duration of the contract for the transfer to local ownership must reflect the risks and conditions of each project. In other words, the duration must reflect how long it would take for each project to pay for itself and provide the equity investors with a reasonable return. The BOT technique has two short- and long-term policy elements. In the short term it can be used to jumpstart an industry and in the long term to develop successful local entrepreneurial skills.

Just as project finance has ancient roots, the underlying conceptual framework of BOTs is also traceable to 18th century French concessionized scheme used to develop the French water system.[102] Thus, the BOT approach shares the same attributes and characteristics with the typical project finance analyzed above. However, the BOT model shares essential characteristics with production sharing agreements and service contracts that emerged in the 1960s in the oil and gas industry.[103] Under these agreements, foreign enterprises acting as independent contractors provided debt capital to host governments for the exploration and exploitation of oil and gas which was paid for in cash or in kind according to a set of complex contractual provisions. Similarly, as part of the project finance schemes, BOTs constitute a series of complex transactions and contractual relations involving multiple parties, different resources, several phases and risks.

The purpose of this study is not to explore all the complexities of BOT transactions and operations. Rather our goal is to focus on the issues that are relevant to the use of BOTs as instruments of empowering local entrepreneurs for economic development. Attractive as the BOT concept might be for developing local entrepreneurs, it presents certain challenges for policy makers and governments. The BOT structure, parties, contracting framework and risks are so complex that success demands the utmost attention to how all the pieces of the system of contracts fit together. The complexities inherent in the BOT framework are best captured by Diagram 1 below.

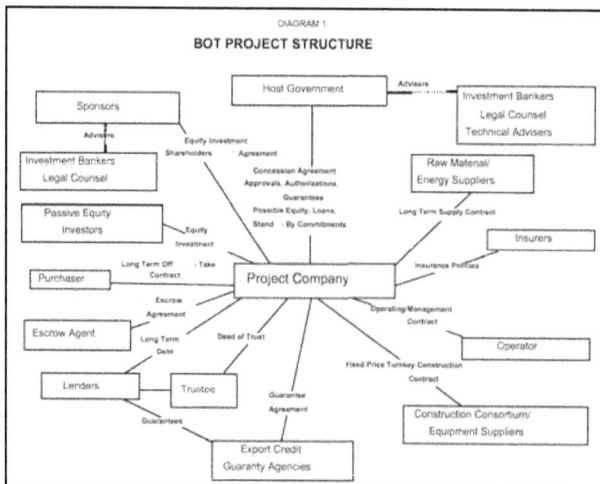

DIAGRAM 1
BOT PROJECT STRUCTURE

Diagram 1 captures the basic structure of project finance and provides a detailed depiction of the parties and the series of contractual relations involved. However, our discussion of Diagram 1 shall focus only on issues that are relevant to the role of BOTs in industrial policy implementation. For the purposes of this study the following subjects will be addressed briefly: (1) the nature of the BOT project, (2) the parties, (3) the central role of the law of contracts, (4) the risks and (5) the role of incentives for achieving the development objectives.

The Nature of the BOT Project

Implicit in the BOT structure captured in Diagram 1 is the relevance of the project itself to the developmental objectives of the host country. As discussed above, not every project is suitable for project finance generally or under the BOT model. To ensure the developmental impact and empowerment of local entrepreneurs, projects should be screened against the industrial strategic policy architecture. In this regard, projects may be identified by the host country before or after feasibility studies to determine their viability. Having selected the industries with the greatest potential for developmentally sound projects, the host country may also invite the private sector to submit BOT project proposals that meet its goals and objectives.

BOT projects selected under this scheme should satisfy three essential criteria. First, they must be financially viable in that they should generate a cash flow sufficient to service the debt. Second, they must advance some economic development goals of the host country. Third, each project must have the capacity for creating a sustainable local entrepreneurial class in the industry involved. The central theme of these arguments and the policy prescriptions suggested is that the impact of BOTs on the local economy cannot be left completely to chance.

The Parties

It is apparent from Diagram 1 that the typical BOT project involves a large number of direct parties and many more associated with different aspects of the project. The large number of parties presents certain strengths and weakness in BOTs. In the first place, given the non-recourse and limited recourse nature of funding involved, BOT projects are likely to receive greater scrutiny by different lenders and equity investors concerned about the risk of loss. In this way, qualified projects would have a greater probability of success. For the host country, the greater the number of participants the greater the likelihood of getting the project funded, since the risks will be shared by many as opposed to a single foreign investor.[104]

Risk sharing also benefits the participants since each of them will absorb only a small share of the financial and other burdens of the project. Lower levels of financial exposure and risks allow lenders, sponsors and others to participate in multiple projects simultaneously. Besides, operating as a collective provides the parties with collective security against potential post-contractual opportunism, threats of expropriation, nationalization or measures having equivalent effects.[105] Measures of that nature that affect the interests of a syndicate of banks, other lenders, suppliers and equity investors in different industries from different countries and international financial institutions would visit significant, if not irreversible, detriment on the international interests of the host country. The cost to the host country would be too high for it to try.

Corruption continues to be a major problem in many countries and post-conflict transition countries might be even more exposed to that phenomenon than others. However, the great number of participants in BOT projects might create a buffer to corruption by compelling greater transparency. The theory of cartels suggests that numbers are antithetical to cartel formation.[106] That is, the greater the number of members the greater the difficulty of forming and maintaining a cartel. The same can said of BOT project participation. Corruption will be difficult to carry out when so many parties have so much at stake in the project. It would be difficult to pay off all or some government officials quietly for individual gains. The legal risks, costs and reputational damage associated with corruption under these circumstances might discourage the practice on the part of those involved.

Notwithstanding these advantages, the multiplicity of parties presents some difficulties in the implementation of BOT projects. One of the key elements of BOT transactions is the identification, assessment and distribution of risks among the parties. The greater the number of parties the greater the difficulty of distributing risks. Sponsors and others involved in these complex transactions might be able to conceal risks which in turn would increase agency or monitoring cost and the incidence of moral hazard.[107] Moreover, the complexities of the transactions and the legal regime essential for their success might over-task the legal capacity of the host country, particularly in the post-conflict context. Thus, an essential element for the success of BOTs in post-conflict transition countries would be legal reform that would facilitate the transactions consistent with their industrial policies.

The BOT Contract

Central to the BOT transaction is the role of the law of contracts as an instrument for welding together different independent groups with different interests into a coherent system of contracts toward the common goal of a successful venture. An industrial strategic policy architecture that assigns a significant role to BOTs in its implementation must develop the appropriate legal environment for the enforcement of contractual obligations. A better understanding of the nature of the BOT contractual relations will be essential if the appropriate response is to be made. Although BOT is mostly an open markets process it shares several characteristics with its counterpart, the firm, even as it seeks to operate outside the firm. In his seminal paper on "The Nature of the Firm" published in 1937, Coase argued that the reason why the firm emerged as an organization for internalizing all those transactions its owners could not rely on the open markets was to minimize transaction costs.[108] Put differently, the firm was a response to market uncertainties and misalignments in open market contractual relations managed by the firm through integration. Having removed the necessity of dealing with independent third parties, internalization and integration permitted the owners to manage the internal relationships by fiat.[109] This situation rarely occurs in post-conflict transition countries. However, modern commentators argue that the firm is a nexus of contracts.[110] In their view, in its attempt to avoid certain costly external markets transactions, the firm created its own internal organization based on a nexus of contracts between the owners, managers, employees, suppliers, customers and others. The internal dynamics of the nexus of contracts of the firm are governed by authority and fiat under a management command system; the firm sought to replace costly open market contracts with its own system of internal contracts.

In many respects the BOT transaction seems to mimic the firm by relying on a nexus of a series of contractual relations aimed at creating a system that allows it to minimize risks, reduce costs and receive the benefits of internalization without the cost of its authority structure or management by fiat. The preference for markets suggests a preference for party autonomy and contract management system based on mutuality of interests. Thus, the BOT approach would flourish within a matured and stable contractual regime. To the extent that the BOT approach is a policy choice, the market preference elements should be reinforced by reforming the legal framework in contracts for better results.

However, just as the firm suffers from agency costs, so does the BOT transaction.[111] In the modern firm with widely diffused ownership, the separation of ownership and control imposes a monitoring cost on owners concerned about managers pursuing interests other than those of the owners.[112] According to Michael Jensen, one can identify three types of agency cost in the context of the firm.[113] In spite of incentives for proper conduct by managers the owners must incur the cost of monitoring aberrant behavior of managers. As agents, managers also incur what is termed a bonding cost in trying to give guarantees of performance. The third agency cost has to do with the residual welfare loss occasioned by agents' decisions that do not maximize the interest of the owners.[114] If these are the agency costs associated with organizations managed by fiat, the potential agency costs are significantly higher in complex systems of multiparty transactions such as BOTs organized purely on the basis of contractual relations. Each party and each transaction within the project brings its own category of risks that must be identified, assigned and monitored. The agency costs associated with these cannot be underestimated.

The relationship between the bankers and the project company is purely one of creditor and debtor, which nevertheless has agency cost implications. Creditors have to incur monitoring costs to ensure that repayment commitments are valid and honored. Guarantees, commitments, and undertakings by the host government to sponsors, lenders and other equity investors face similar agency costs. An appreciation of the nature and sources of these agency costs by policy makers should result in appropriate policy measures and incentives targeted at addressing them and facilitating the functioning and eventual transfer of the project to local interests.

BOT transactions also share many characteristics with other long-term complex contractual relations such as joint ventures, licensing agreements and strategic alliances.[115] All of these transactions are notoriously burdened by incomplete contracts because of bounded rationality and opportunism. While bounded rationality has to do with the computational incapacity of the human brain, opportunism relates to human motivations behind transactions.[116] Parties to a contract may seek to take advantage of others through non-disclosure of relevant facts, half-truths, even outright falsehoods, or by skirting obligations *ex post facto*. The complexity and the multiparty nature of BOT transactions expose them to the same level of obligational and contingent incompleteness as other contracts long term contracts.[117] Perhaps even more important in the BOT context is the risk of post-contractual opportunism. Under the BOT model advocated here, each transaction would involve the making of irreversible specific asset investments in the form of plant, equipment and technology which cannot easily be redeployed. Oliver Williamson has explored the vulnerabilities associated with such investments.[118] Once a refinery or manufacturing facility is built it cannot easily be relocated or converted to other uses, and the salvage value of the assets could hardly satisfy the cost of building them. Other BOT projects such as toll roads or tunnels suffer from similar vulnerabilities.

Given that the financing of BOTs is non-recourse or more likely limited recourse, the lenders, sponsors and all other equity investors are exposed to *ex post* contractual opportunism by the host government. In unstable regimes of post-conflict states such as the DRC, Liberia or Angola, subsequent changes in policy or laws may compromise the cash flow of the project, or the availability of hard currency to service debt or import necessary inputs. Such measures would undermine the financial viability of the project and its ultimate developmental objectives. In response to these risks, the host government may be required to provide contract stabilization measures and other guarantees that changes in policy and law would not alter the commitments, obligations and repayment terms of the BOT project. In appropriate cases sinking funds against revenue shortfalls may be recommended.

This cursory examination of the contracting environment of BOTs suggests that a country that embarks on the BOT approach must address simultaneously all the fundamental policy issues relevant for an effective regime for the enforcement of contracts. An essential element of an effective BOT system is stability in expectations, which can be provided through BOT legislation that provides a clear and stable regulatory framework for BOT transactions.[119] Such legislation would lay out the process, the criteria for participation, the process for project initiation, the bidding procedures and the general rights and obligations of the parties. Equally important for providing stability of expectations is the issue of dispute resolution. The complexity of economic development agreements and their inherent political ramifications make them better suited to alternative dispute resolution than litigation in any courts. It would therefore be necessary for the BOT legislation to provide for the resolution of BOT disputes by conciliation, mediation or arbitration under any of the international arbitration procedures. It must however be stressed that while a country may opt to be a signatory to the various international conventions for the settlement of investment disputes such as ICSID, the need for settling such disputes by arbitration does not necessarily mandate subscribing to such treaties. Mandating arbitration in the BOT legislation should be sufficient as long as the parties are given freedom to make the choice of the arbitration institution or procedure. However, an effective arbitration mandate may require subscription to the New York Convention on the Enforcement of Foreign Arbitral Awards.[120] For post-conflict transition countries this gives additional confidence to lenders and other investors contemplating participation in BOT projects. It would appear that among the post-conflict transition countries Liberia, Bosnia, and Mozambique, but not Angola, the DRC and Rwanda, are signatories to this Convention.[121]

Managing BOT Project Risks

Critical to the success of any BOT project is the identification, evaluation and allocation of the project risks.[122] Each project type carries with it certain characteristic risks that must be addressed. Infrastructural and industrial projects are dissimilar not only in their characteristics but also in their associated risks factors. The allocation of the different categories of BOT risks has been the subject of some intellectual investigation which the interested reader can consult elsewhere.[123] An in-depth analysis of how these risks are identified, assessed and distributed is beyond the scope of this work. Our interest is limited to investigating how BOT risks might be addressed within the context of the framework of industrial policy to facilitate the management of such risks. Recalling that the industrial strategic policy architecture is aimed at local processing of raw materials, value-added industrial upgrading, manufactured exports, technology transfer and creating linkages with the local economy, one may ask, what project risks might undermine these objectives, and how might they be managed for the success of the industrial policy?

As a general matter, BOT risks might be described or identified by the type of project, the phases of the project or the type of risk. To some, each project has pre-implementation, implementation, construction, operating and transfer risks.[124] To others, the risks might be viewed as startup, operating, technology, markets and political risks.[125]

Irrespective of the classification of these risks, the basic principle in risk allocation is that risk should be distributed on the basis of its source and the party that can best manage it.[126] So the question of great relevance is, what risks are attributable to the host government and which risks can it more easily and effectively manage?

Since the focus of this study is primarily on BOT projects for transforming post-conflict transition countries the discussion that follows will address only those risks factors that the host government must manage to ensure success of its BOT policy objectives. In focusing on this limited set of risks factors we are nevertheless aware of the variety of other risk elements in BOTs that have generally been the subject of discussion. The following risks will be examined briefly below: (1) risk of government disinterest, (2) political risks, (3) foreign currency and input risks, (4) infrastructural risks, (5) force majeure risks and (6) transfer risks.

Risk of Government Disinterest. Once an industrial project has gone through its feasibility and approval phase and lending and investment commitments have been secured, the host government may simply move on to the next project. However, construction may be stalled for various reasons including shortages, cost overruns and other events. Or the entire project may collapse at that stage. For lenders, equity investors and others with different types of financial exposures such an event would be financially disastrous. The cash flow from the project is essential for the loan repayment and some reasonable returns on investment are contingent on a completed and operational project. None of this would come to pass if the project fails at its construction phase. It is therefore generally argued that the success of project finance projects depends on some level of host government involvement.

There are different ways in which the host government's interest in the success of the project can be sustained beyond approving it and hoping for its success. This can be achieved by government participation in the project company as an equity investor. The government participates in the project company as an equity joint venture partner with the sponsors directly or as one of the sponsors under the shareholder agreement. With an equity investment in the project the government is unlikely to walk off and remain aloof from the fate and fortunes of the projects. In the alternative or even in combination with its equity participation, the government may offer certain guarantees and commitments to make funds available should some unforeseen events threaten the completion of the construction phase of the project.

One of the constraints post-conflict transition countries face is lack of financial resources and inadequate access to international money markets where they can raise capital for these projects at a reasonable cost. So, one may legitimately ask how the host government can make these financial contributions. The answer may lie in having access to a "Dedicated Project Finance Fund" earmarked for the transformation of post conflict transition countries. Every year the G8 makes promises of increasing foreign development assistance aid to poor countries. Many other developed countries offer various forms of development assistance to developing countries. In his book, *The End of Poverty*, Jeffery Sachs has advanced as passionate a case for development assistance aid as one could possibly make.[127] He argues that foreign aid that raises the per capita stock from $900 to $1,800 over several years will help countries break out of the poverty trap.[128] However, several studies have argued that decades of foreign development aid programs have failed as instruments of economic development.[129] One must then question not the passion or the compassion but the wisdom of a policy prescription that most people believe is faulty and ineffective. Sachs' mission in *The End of Poverty* is to end poverty through mostly donor aid, which is vastly different from empowering private entrepreneurial risk taking in targeted industries with the greatest potential for development impact. The one has minimalist elements and the other is rather boldly self-reliant. Thus, in the case of post-conflict transition countries, a much more fruitful approach might be to redirect some of the development assistance funds to a special fund to support the economic transformation of these countries through project finance and other private enterprise driven programs.

The benefit of such a fund is that it can be designed not to be a handout to governments but rather to aim at projects that have been approved under the rigorous project finance requirements. In this sense the funds would not go to the government but to projects that are capable of achieving the development objectives through private investment activities. So much criticism is often leveled at the corruption that comes with foreign development aid. We wonder whether this direct approach to supporting private risk taking in development driven projects would not reduce corruption but actually lead to successful development driven projects. However, the government may borrow from it for its equity contribution to a project company. The government may also borrow from it for its guarantee for cost overruns or shortfalls in revenue and similar risks. In this sense the funds do not go directly to the government, nor is there a free lunch. The Fund may also be accessed by local sponsors involved in the project to whom the project will ultimately be transferred after it has paid for itself. Thus the Fund, once established, would have the capacity to replenish itself over time from successful projects through the repayment of loans taken from it either by the government or local sponsors. Finally, because each project will be substantially financed by non-recourse or limited recourse debt access to this fund is less likely to be abused, particularly if certain restrictive criteria are imposed to address the potential for abuse.

Political Risks. One of the most significant risks in BOT projects in developing countries is political risk. Political risks cover a wide spectrum of politically motivated events and government policies ranging from labor unrest and government fiscal and economic policies to outright expropriation and nationalization.[130] These events may undermine the construction or operational efficiency of BOT projects. In the context of post-conflict transition countries, the ever present security risks tend to magnify the actual or perceived political risks. In most circumstances, the source of BOT political risks tends to be the host government. In any event, because of the nature of these risks, the host government is generally better positioned to manage them. The focus of any political risks management strategy should be on shifting the cost of these risks to the host government by employing techniques similar to those used in the basic turnkey or production sharing/service contract models.

With the project funded substantially by debt and some equity, the private parties face specific asset investment vulnerabilities should they hold direct or collateralized property rights in the assets of the project company, for any government measures that compromise the cash flow or the viability of the project would cause significant losses to the private parties. Since the goal is to transfer the project to local interests the materialization of political risks could precipitate that transfer in a fire sale to the detriment of lenders and equity investors and other creditor stakeholders. And it would be no consolation to them that such measures may destroy the creditworthiness of the country and its investment climate.

However, a combination of *ex ante* political risk management techniques could be used to shift substantially the specific asset vulnerabilities to the host government. Under the production sharing/service contract model, the government and the future private interest holders have ownership interest in the project, as in the basic turnkey agreement.[131] The sponsors, as service providers, may operate the project under a lease or concession granted by the government for a period sufficient to service the debt and give investors a reasonable return on their capital. Such arrangements may include various forms of subsidiary contracts such as technical assistance agreements to ensure that the technology of the project is upgraded as often as needed. The key point here is that *the government cannot expropriate what it owns.* It may however interfere with the lease or the activities of the project company and additional measures may be required. An agreement to indemnify the lessee and all creditors for the full amount of the outstanding debt and equity, taking into account a reasonable return on equity laced with a cross default clause, could serve as a significant deterrent to breach.[132] To ensure that guarantees of indemnity are not empty promises, the government may be required to carry political risk insurance covering the value of project as security. But the creditors and equity investors may also carry political risk insurance with any of the many political insurance programs such as OPIC and MIGA. Ultimately, the insurers will have the right to recover any pay-out from the host governments, thereby shifting the risk of loss again to the host government. Finally, to encourage lenders and equity investors to participate in the economic development objectives of developing countries, the private parties should be allowed to recover all political risk induced losses from the Dedicated Project Finance Fund, at the cost of the host government. In other words, the Fund would charge the payout amount to the host government as debt to be paid to the Fund.

These political risk shifting techniques may appear harsh, but we should not lose sight of the goals and objectives of the host governments. The basic strategy of relying substantially on non-recourse or limited recourse lenders and some equity investors to create industrial enterprises with developmental impact imposes significant risks on the lenders and investors. It is not asking too much to insist that political risk management techniques be employed to eliminate post-contractual opportunism by the government. Nor should the government expect a handout from the private parties willing to take some risk to advance its development goals.

Foreign Currency and Inputs Risks. One of the most significant risks in project finance transactions of any type is foreign currency risk.[133] In addition to the complexity of the contractual relations among the multiplicity of parties and funding source, there are the currency requirements for debt service. While the project funding and debt service obligations might be in hard currency the revenue generation might be in local currency that must be converted into the appropriate currency to meet those obligations.[134] Moreover, the BOT project may require foreign currency for the importation of equipment, raw materials or other inputs for effective operational success. In this regard, BOT projects face several foreign exchange risks including inflation, the unavailability of foreign currency, restrictions on transfers, exchange controls and currency devaluation risks. The currency risks could extend to the restrictive allocation of hard currency necessary for the importation of materials and inputs for the BOT manufacturing facility. There are various currency risk management techniques advocated in the project finance context, including political risk insurance with OPIC and MIGA or even commercial currency swaps by lenders and other project participants.[135] However, our focus is on those measures that should be undertaken by the host government proactively to mitigate the currency risk to ensure a greater potential for successful projects.

Government measures aimed at mitigating currency risks should be part of the basic BOT policy framework. We have argued above that as part of its industrial strategic policy architecture the government should enact BOT legislation that provides the framework for all BOT transactions. Mitigating or even eliminating currency risks should be one of the goals of BOT legislation. The BOT legislation must guarantee currency convertibility under a single exchange rate if multiple exchange rates exist. In addition, BOT projects should be given equal access to the allocation of foreign currency with other enterprises and institutions. In short, the host government must liberalize its exchange control regime in the project finance and BOT framework even if there are legitimate economic reasons for general exchange controls.

A special exchange control liberalization program within the BOT legislative structure would serve several purposes. It would permit the BOT process to bypass some of the bureaucratic approval bottlenecks in an area critical to BOT funding. It would provide a statutory process that streamlines and eliminates bureaucratic or administrative consensus based decisions or discretion, often the source of corruption.[136] The experience in some Asian countries suggests that the administrators charged with implementing these laws must be given clearly defined responsibilities to prevent bureaucratic graft.[137] It will be difficult if not impossible to get lender participation if there is little confidence that the necessary foreign currency will be available for debt service. Hence the BOT legislation might include the approval of offshore accounts and the use of local foreign currency accounts.[138] Indeed, an offshore account might be a condition for foreign lender participation in BOT projects. Legislation that permits such accounts will impose a legal obligation on the Central Bank to authorize the accounts and the amounts of money that can be held in them. In the case of industrial projects with manufactured export products, purchasers could then make payments directly to these offshore accounts from which various disbursements can be made. The authorization of local foreign currency accounts will also give BOT projects direct access to foreign currency to address their foreign currency needs and bypass the bureaucratic issues associated with exchange controls and Central Bank allocation of foreign currency to BOT projects.

Infrastructural Risks. The central feature of the industrial strategic policy architecture for transforming post-conflict transition countries is an emphasis on industrial upgrading based on local processing of raw materials, local value added and manufactured exports. An essential element of this policy architecture is the existence of basic infrastructure such as power plants, roads and other public facilities that can support manufacturing activities. One of the reasons for the miraculous economic performance of the Asian Tigers is the development of basic infrastructure either through direct public expenditures or through project finance.[139] Unfortunately, one of the major constraints affecting post-conflict transition countries is the absence of such basic infrastructure. Conflict often leaves countries with devastated infrastructure, weak, low grade unreliable power plants, terrible roads and inadequate ports and airport. So any industrial policy aimed at transforming these countries through manufacturing facilities must confront the infrastructural problems at hand.

The host government must then confront the inadequate infrastructural needs within the industrial strategic policy architecture. Not only must the host government implement an industrial upgrading policy, it must simultaneously upgrade its infrastructure as a necessary element of that policy. Infrastructural development can be undertaken through direct government expenditures, but in view of the financial constraints of post-conflict transition countries project finance is the likely candidate for meeting that need. An examination of the power plants project finance practices in Asia suggests various models that can be used by the host country to achieve its objectives.[140] Indeed, one might argue that the prerequisite for the industrial strategic policy architecture of any country is the existence of basic infrastructure. Developing such basic infrastructure would stabilize the infrastructural needs of the country to meet current demand and the building of a series of BOT industrial projects would create additional demand for the power generation projects. The sequence of investment activities in this regard would be critical. With the power plants in operation, the government can guarantee the power supply to the projects through various arrangements and techniques common to power plant and other infrastructural projects.

Transfer Risks. The basic premise of the BOT model is the eventual transfer of projects to local interests. Such a transfer may take place after the project has paid for itself and the equity investors have received a reasonable return on their investment. The transfer may also take place after an agreed upon time has expired. Whatever triggers the eventual transfer, that final phase of BOTs is not free from risks. Assuming that the project achieves its objectives and expected cash flow levels and lenders and equity investors are fully paid as expected, the local joint venture sponsor partners must now take over the operations. However, their initial investment in the project will not be sufficient to cover the current market value of the project. They must come up with additional financing to purchase the entire facility or invite other local investors to participate in the venture. The likelihood that they or the other local investors will have access to capital at a reasonable cost may be low. The host government may then address this capital scarcity by offering loan guarantees to the local investors to seek private funding either domestically or in the international money markets.

If on the other hand the transfer is triggered by the expiry of a fixed contractual term but the lenders and equity investors have not yet been fully paid, a new set of risks faces the private party stakeholders. There will be no guarantee that the facility under new local management will be able to generate the necessary revenue to pay the outstanding debt and equity interest. It may well be argued that such a risk of loss is what the lenders bargained for. However, because BOT contracts are notoriously incomplete, certain adjustments should be made to address the equities in the relationship. A well constructed BOT contract would have made provision for adjustments particularly in the case of a fixed term contract. In view of this, the host government might be required to settle the outstanding obligations and take equity interest in the project, or provide a loan or loan guarantees to the local sponsors and other interested parties to buy out the foreign private interest. As an alternative, the Dedicated Project Finance Fund could provide a standby loan guarantee for the private parties to acquire the project.

Other transfer risks may materialize when a fixed contract term expires. The products of the project may lose their competitiveness in the market place because of declining demand, changing consumer taste or other business conditions. The technology of the project might also be overtaken by new innovations, thereby increasing cost and dampening price competitiveness.[141] These markets and technology risks might materialize even when the feasibility studies were well conducted and proven technology was chosen. Under these circumstances, all the parties and stakeholders face some risks. The lenders and investors may have to absorb some losses; the new local owners will inherit an underperforming enterprise and there will no incentive for them to pay off the outstanding debt. Besides, the policy objectives of the host government may not be achieved.

The response to market and technology risks would require some additional capital outlay by the new local owners. In the case of projects with flexible factories, changes in demand and consumer tastes and preferences may not affect productivity. The projects may lose some manufacture-to-order clients but gain others. However, changes in technology can be addressed by retooling and upgrading through government guaranteed loans. The response to market and technology risks for industrial projects is less straightforward. Changes in consumer tastes may require a total new product design or may lead to collapse of the project. The cost of responding to market and technology changes could be substantial, and again the new local owners would need substantial financial support in the form of government guaranteed or subsidized loans to respond to these changes if the projects can continue to serve the development objectives of the host country.

Shifting the Focus of Incentives in BOT Policies

In his famous book *The Economics of Welfare* published in 1920, Pigou advanced the broad conceptual basis for incentives granted to enterprises to correct for the greater social returns on private investment than the private returns received by the investors.[142] According to Pigou, private investment might result in positive externalities such as economies of scale, increase in new knowledge, and new, herd mentality induced, investment generated by the initial investment. Whatever the private returns on investment might be they will not reflect these positive externalities because the market is incapable of rewarding such contributions. Incentives are therefore necessary to correct for these unrewarded contributions. In more recent times, others have advanced what might be termed a dynamic growth development thesis for incentives.[143] They argue that incentives might be appropriate within the context of growth and development dynamics in developing countries. In their formative stages, industries in developing countries may face higher cost, other challenges and constraints characteristic of countries forging their industrial paths through infant industries. Incentives might play an essential role of supporting these industries at their formative stages.[144] Such was the experience of Japan and many other Asian economies that followed its extraordinary transformation. And the question is whether these two broad conceptual frameworks can support the case for incentives for FDI in post-conflict transition countries, and if so in what form.

A Brief Historical Review of Incentives

Notwithstanding the general conceptual framework advanced by Pigou and the dynamic growth and development theory of incentives, the theory of incentives for FDI is less settled than the practice by host countries.[145] For decades, numerous theoretical and empirical studies have challenged the theoretical basis for incentives, questioned the efficacy of incentives for FDI, and doubted the causal link between incentives and the actual investment behavior of investors.[146] Indeed, in an earlier study, we provided a comprehensive review of contemporary legal, survey and economic studies on the efficacy of tax incentives in the FDI process.[147] The survey studies covered a geographic area stretching from North America to Europe in developed countries and from Latin America to Africa and Asia in developing countries. Similarly, these studies covered a long time frame, running from the 1920s to the 1980s. Consistent in all of these studies were findings that tax incentives had little if any impact on FDI location decision process.[148] More recent survey studies and more rigorous econometric time series analysis of the same question have yielded substantially the same results: tax incentives do not have an impact on the location decisions of FDI.[149] The results of the survey studies are hardly surprising; survey studies always run the risk of manipulation by respondents motivated by objectives other than rational investment decision choices.[150] For instance, in a study of the tax holidays experience of Indonesia Louis T. Wells and Nancy J. Allen reported that although the Japanese firms complained bitterly about the repeal of the tax holidays in Indonesia, Japanese investments continued to grow rapidly.[151] This clearly confirms the argument that tax incentives are often redundant in that the investment would be made without them, like the Japanese investments in Indonesia.[152]

Although the theory and empirical evidence seem to point in one direction host countries competing for scarce FDI resources seem to be looking in the opposite direction. Since the 1990s there has been a remarkable and almost irreversible competition for FDI through generous incentives. According to Andrew Charlton, the competition is so pervasive that countries, states within federal systems and regional trade organizations and even regions within countries find themselves pitched against one another with generous incentives for wooing FDI.[153] An UNCTAD study in 1994 of 103 countries found that only four of them did not offer any incentives for investments.[154] The intense competition for FDI has also led to a global legislative movement toward the liberalization of the foreign investment climate and regulatory regime in many countries. According to the UNCTAD *World Investment Report* of 2000, of about 1,035 changes in the regulatory environment worldwide, about 94% made the legal environment

more favorable.[155] Globally, there is growing convergence and harmoniza-
tion of the regulatory environment toward greater favorable treatment of
investors. It is important to note that most measures undertaken by countries were liberalization measures made from the point of view of the dynamic growth and development thesis. And this is the context in which we
shall approach the case for incentives in post-conflict transition countries.

The history of disappointing performance of incentives in attracting FDI
compels caution in crafting any policy prescriptions for post-conflict transition countries. The case for caution is further bolstered by the fact that
decades of liberalization of investment regimes worldwide have yet to bear
fruit in FDI inflows. The proliferation of bilateral investment treaties in
developing countries as instruments for investment protection and promotion seems to make little difference in attracting FDI to developing countries.[156] However, incentives impose a direct and indirect cost on host
countries without the necessary corresponding benefits. Incentives are not
only a burden on the treasuries of the host countries but also work as reverse subsidies to affluent countries and their investors by poor developing
countries.[157] For this to continue there must be some rational justification. It
therefore seems incumbent on any investment policy design that has as one
of its objectives the attraction of FDI through incentives to investigate why
these incentives have not worked.

The Framework for Incentives in the BOT Model

The policy architecture for transforming post-conflict transition countries
advocated in this study does not rely on conventional FDI as a primary
instrument. Its focus on the combination of substantial debt and some equity
in economic development suggests that conventional incentive policy levers
would be unsuitable for the task at hand. That notwithstanding, any design
of an incentives policy framework must start with the reasons why incentives have failed to be effective and respond to them effectively.

As is apparent from the discussion above, several reasons have been
suggested for the ineffectiveness of incentives. The first line of reasoning
traces the problem to the theoretical basis upon which incentive policies are
designed. Incentives do not address the real determinants of FDI such as
market size, the possession of exploitable intangibles assets, or the imperatives of circumventing costly open market transactions burdened by uncertainties and chronic market failures that require internalization.[158] Distilled
from these theory-based arguments is a simple but powerful suggestion that
incentives and their policy constructs are often misguided, and this is an
observation that policy makers cannot ignore. Incentives are misguided
when they are not aimed at known or proven impediments to, or the real

motivations for, FDI. Rather, most incentives tend to be general in the sense that they are made available to all qualifying investors, who are not always required, if ever, to make some positive contribution to some developmental objectives or address some specific national problem. Even when incentives are targeted at specific industries, investment activities, technological contribution or labor absorption investments, they still retain their basic general characteristics.

Incentives also face other problems. Most incentive regimes disaggregate the responsibilities of granting incentives from those of assessing their costs. Investment promotion agencies, charged with the single task of increasing investment flows, are eager to grant incentives to achieve that goal. However, investment promotion goals may be pursued without regard to the cost of incentives to society and the treasury. Moreover, incentive schemes tend to give discretionary powers to administrators. The consensus seems to be that discretion based incentives tend to fail because they are prone to induce corruption, increased costs and other obstacles that discourage serious investors from pursuing the incentives.[159]

The misguided nature of general incentives should be eliminated within the context of the industrial strategic policy architecture advocated in this study. To the extent that projects are chosen on the basis of their potential contribution to some developmental goals of the host country, there are greater opportunities to make incentives work. As a start, any incentives regime cannot be general but must be specific to types of projects. Because projects differ by type and level of complexity, the incentives can be tailored to the needs of each project type or each specific project. Generality and redundancy in incentives can be eliminated by subjecting incentives to cost-benefit analysis within the capital budgeting process of each project. For instance, incentives may be given for training a specific number and caliber of technical and management personnel per year for the project. Incentives can also be given based on the value of manufactured exports per annum generated by the project. Both of these are performance based and their costs and benefits can be estimated within the capital budgeting process.

The central theme of any incentive regime is to encourage investment that would otherwise not take place. The goal of the incentive regime within the project finance and BOT context should be to channel potential sponsors and other equity investors toward specific projects for the achievement of certain development objectives. Thus, the basis for any specific incentives should be some *quid pro quo* between the incentive recipients and the host government. Each incentive or incentive type can more easily be assessed in terms of cost and benefits if some bargain for exchange formula is used. Achieving such a *quid pro quo* may not be easy but the search for it will compel a higher level of transparency and deliberateness in the granting of incentives.

One of the drawbacks of general incentives is that they tend not to take into account the fact that all development incentives are not perfect substitutes for one another. Different incentives have different levels of value to the investor and different costs to the host government.[160] Low value incentives, in whatever form they come, are unlikely to be effective although they are a charge on the treasury of the host government. However, with the project chosen the specific investors will be known and their incentive preferences or which incentives would work best in the specific context can be identified. A requirement for some *quid pro quo* will compel tighter scrutiny of incentives and increase their likelihood of efficacy.

The BOT model can also address effectively problems associated with highly discretionary incentive regimes. We have already argued that BOT legislation is essential to provide a clear and concrete regulatory framework for project participants. One of the goals of such legislation is to reduce the exercise of discretionary power, which is often the source of corruption. The general framework for incentives should be designed within the BOT legislation with the goal of reducing discretionary incentives. Categories of incentives might be earmarked for different project types as long as their use is contingent on the cost-benefit analysis within the capital budgeting process of each project. The use of incentives and qualifying investors might involve limited discretion, but ultimately the grant of incentives will still be subjected to the rigors of the capital budgeting process.

Conclusion

Several post-conflict transition countries, where people are living on less than $2 a day, are some of the poorest countries in the world. Such abject poverty in a world where affluent nations wallow in transcendent abundance is unacceptable and demands a response as a moral or humanitarian imperative. In 2000, all the members of the United Nations adopted the Millennium Development Declaration and Goals (MDGs) aimed at, among many other objectives, eradicating extreme poverty and hunger. The MDGs stands as a colossal beacon inviting the attention of any person charged with constructing a blueprint for the transformation of post-conflict transition countries. Nevertheless, the achievement of the MDGs had remained largely elusive by 2005.

The MDGs do not, and cannot, claim monopoly over the concerns or the solutions for poverty eradication in the world. Clamoring for equal attention in any poverty eradication policy design and directed objectives are two other very popular instruments: (1) Official Development Aid (ODA) and (2)

FDI. ODA programs are best exemplified by the Africa Commission Report of March 2005 commissioned by Tony Blair's British Government and presented at the G8 Conference in Scotland, calling for ending poverty in Africa as the primary focus of that Conference. Every year, the G8 focuses attention on addressing development needs through ODA. The G8 Conference of 2008 held in Hokkaido in Japan continued to pursue ODA as an instrument for addressing poverty and development. Given the historic central role assigned to ODA in development, logic would dictate that ODA must be in play in any industrial strategic policy architecture with the goal of transforming post-conflict transition countries. After all, most if not all of them are the targets of ODA and poverty alleviation measures. Many have also assigned a significant role to FDI in the achievement of economic development goals.

In this paper, we reject these approaches as the starting point for crafting industrial policies for transforming post-conflict transition countries. In doing so, we do not reject the necessity for poverty alleviation. The real question is, what is the most effective way of putting these countries on the path to sustained economic self-transformation over time so that poverty does not remain a burning and recurrent issue. After decades of ODA programs, the poor countries have remained poor and some have gotten even poorer relative to their own history and in relation to the rest of the world. Although the poverty alleviation policies may often be well intentioned, unimpeachably humanitarian, and passionately argued, at their core they are mostly minimalist both in intent and in potential impact. Poverty alleviation instruments would have greater effect within a larger industrial framework that focuses on empowering the entire economy through projects and industries with the potential for the greatest development impact. Conventional FDI instruments may also be misplaced both in post-conflict transition countries and in other developing countries. An understanding of the systems characteristics, the strategic vision, and the mission of MNEs would suggest that we should not put the developmental burden of countries on MNEs when, as direct instruments, they are not well suited for that task. This also does not mean that FDI cannot play a role. It only means that the role FDI plays must be complementary and should not be left to the investors. It must be guided by the industrial strategic policy architecture of the host country.

In view of the arguments advanced above, we conclude that the industrial strategic policy architecture for transforming post-conflict transition countries must focus on big prizes – that is, investing in and developing industries and projects with the greatest potential impact on economic development that empowers the local economy and entrepreneurs. A policy that keeps its focus on big prizes in the economy is not the same as the current emphasis in certain development circles on a "big push". The basic policy framework for countries with abundant natural and human resources should be to avoid exporting any commodities, products or ideas unprocessed. These countries must seek out investment opportunities with the greatest potential for value-added technology and knowledge transfer and the generation of meaningful linkages with the local economies. Even countries with meager economic resources should reconsider how they fit into the utilization of the vast global resources for their development. The real reasons for poverty might only be the poverty of imagination.

To achieve these goals, we propose the use of the project finance and BOT models. Under these models, industrial projects that can pay for themselves will be funded substantially through non-recourse or limited-recourse debt and some equity. The projects will be turned over to local owners after they have paid for themselves. In this process, the host government provides an effective guiding hand in the selection of industries and projects that serve its development goals. This approach is not free from risks but at least the host governments will take charge of their economic destiny.

Also, under this approach, some of the ODA financial resources that have so far proved to be ineffective can be put to a different use through a dedicated Fund. Such a Fund will finance BOT projects and support private entrepreneurial investment activities. The Fund could produce several benefits: (1) it would provide direct support to carefully selected homegrown economic development projects; (2) it could lend great support to the creation of self-reliant local private industries and an entrepreneurial class which is essential for sustained economic development; and (3) it could break the circle of wasteful and corrupt ODA expenditures with little to show for them.

Finally, no economic development model is without risks. Certainly, there is no silver bullet. However, the need for altering the position of the poorest countries in the global economy demands the use of bold and non-conventional techniques that have worked in other regions of the world. Indeed, although this model is designed for post-conflict transition countries, the basic approach has utility in many developing countries with or without abundant natural and human resources. One only has to look at the examples of the Asian Miracles with diverse cultures and historical experiences to appreciate this point. We maintain that their incredible economic transformation was a function not just of culture but also of sound policy choices.

Notes

* This paper was presented at the conference "Global Development Challenges: Desirable G8 Responses, a G8 Development Country Dialogue for the Hokkaido Summit," July 1, 2008, United Nations University, Tokyo, an International Conference Sponsored by the United Nations University, Centre for International Governance Innovation, and the G8 Research Group. A full version of this chapter is published in Northwestern Journal of International Law & Business, Vol 30, page 23 (2010) © 2008 Kojo Yelpaala,

** I am grateful to the McGeorge School of Law Summer Research Fund for the support of this study. I am also immensely grateful to Dario Mutabdzija for his generous and effective research assistance for this project to Paul Howard for his continuing support of my research efforts. I am also grateful to Melissa Meth, my Research Assistant, for her able and careful work, Jack Schroeder and Dana Botello for footnotes assistance and to the secretarial staff Paul Fuller and Annette Bethea for their prompt, effective support. Special thanks to my colleague John Sims for his support of work. The careful and excellent editorial work of Nicholas Turner of the United Nations University and the editorial staff is greatly appreciated. The author can be reached at kyelpaala@pacific.edu

1 Dani Rodrik and Arvind Subramanian, "Why did Financial Globalization Disappoint?"*IMF Staff Papers*, Vol. 56, at 112 (2009), *available at* http://ksghome.harvard.edu/~drodrik/Why_Did_FG_Disappoint_March_24_2008.pdf.

2 UN Development Programme, *Sustaining Post-conflict Economic Recovery: Lessons and Challenges*, BCPR Occasional Paper 1 (Oct. 2004).

3 UNCTAD, *World Development Report 2007:* "Transnational Corporations, Extractive Industries and Development" at xv-xviii, UNCTAD/WIR/2007 (2007) [hereinafter UNCTAD, *World Development Report 2007*].

4 World Bank, *Global Development Finance: Mobilizing Finance and Managing Vulnerability* (2005), pp.93-98, available at http://siteresources.worldbank.org/INTGDF2005/Resources/gdf05complete.pdf.

5 *See, e.g.,* Il Sakong, *Korea In The World Economy* (Institute for International Economics, 1993)(Hereafter Sakong, *Korea In World Economy*); Sung Yeung Kwack, "The Economic Development of the Republic of Korea, 1965-1981", in Lawrence J. Lau (ed.) *Models Of Development* (San Francisco: ICS Press, 1986), p. 65; Tibor

Scitovsky, "Economic Development in Taiwan and South Korea, 1965-1981", in Lawrence J. Lau (ed.) *Models Of Development* (San Francisco: ICS Press, 1986), p. 135.

6   Justin Yifu Lin, Fang Cai, and Zhou Li, *The China Miracle: Development Strategy And Economic Reform* (The Chinese Univserity Press, 1996)(discussing the strategy employed for China's leap forward in economic reforms and the results of such reform).

7   John Page, "The East Asian Miracle: Four Lessons for Development Policy," NBER Macroeconomics Annual, p. 219 (1994) (hereafter Page, "The East Asian Miracle"); Dani Rodrik, "Getting Interventions Right: How South Korea and Taiwan Grew Rich," Economic Policy, April (1995) (explaining the complexities of the policy mix used by South Korea and Taiwan for achieving development and riches); York W. Bradshaw, Young-Ieong Kim, and Bruce London, "Transnational Economic Linkages, the State and Dependent Development in South Korea, 1966-1988: A Time-Series Analysis," *Social Forces*, Vol. 72, p. 315 (1993)(hereafter Bradshaw, Kim & London, "State and Dependent Development in South Korea")(explaining the direct involvement of the State in development relying heavily on international trade); Alwyn Yound, "The Tyranny of Numbers: Confronting the Statistical Realities of the East Asian Growth Experience," *Quarterly Journal of Economics,*, August (1995)(examining the role of factor accumulation in the extraordinary post war growth of Hong Kong, Singapore, South Korea and Taiwan).

8   Kojo Yelpaala, "Costs and Benefits from Foreign Direct Investment: A Study of Ghana," *New York Law School Journal of International and Comparative Law,* Vol. 2, pp. 72, 91-97 (1980) [hereinafter Yelpaala, "Cost and Benefits of FDI"].

9   John H. Dunning, "Re-Evaluating the Benefits of Foreign Direct Investment," *Transnational Corporations,*Vol. 3, pp. 23, 32-33 (1994).

10   Kojo Yelpaala, "The Efficacy of Tax Incentives Within the Framework of the Neoclassical Theory of Foreign Direct Investment: A Legislative Policy Analysis," *Texas International Law Journal*, Vol. 19, p. 365 (1984) [hereinafter Yelpaala, "Efficacy of Tax Incentives"].

11   UNCTAD, *Economic Development In Africa: Rethinking The Role Of Foreign Direct Investment*, UNCTAD/GDS/AFRICA/2005/1 (2005) [hereinafter UNCTAD, *Rethinking FDI*].

12   Kojo Yelpaala, "In Search of a Model Investment Law for Africa," in Seward M. Cooper et al. eds., *African Development Bank Law for Development Review*, Vol. 1, pp. 2, 74-75 (2006) [hereinafter Yelpaala, "Model Investment Law"].

13   UNCTAD, *Rethinking FDI, supra* note 11,pp. 4-5.

14   Ibid., p.2.

15   Ibid.

16   Yelpaala, "Model Investment Law," *supra* note 12, p. 12. "Scoop and ship" refers to "operations in which the resources of the host country are extracted, loaded onto ships and exported for processing in other countries." Ibid.

17   Daron Acemoglu, Simon Johnson, and James A, Robinson, "The Colonial Origins of Comparative Development: An Empirical Investigation," *American Economic Review*, Vol. 91, pp. 1369, 1376 (2001)(arguing that extractive institutions were necessitated by the inhospitable environment for settlement but the extractive institutions survived independence of the colonies).

18   UNCTAD, *Rethinking FDI, supra* note 11,pp. 35-36.

19   Ibid., pp. 2-3; Yelpaala, "Efficacy of Tax Incentives," *supra* note 10.

20   UNCTAD, *Rethinking FDI, supra* note 11, p. 36.

21   Joseph E. Stiglitz offers some interesting examples of the natural resource curse.; Tsarist Azerbaijan suffered from it at the turn of the twentieth century and even today many resource rich countries have poor people; included in this list are Nigeria, Peru, Venezuela, Mexico, Papua New Guinea and others. In 1975 the number of people in Nigeria living on less $1 a day was about 19 million in 2000 that number reached 84 million. See, Joseph E. Stiglitz, *Making Globalization Work* pp. 133-137 (2006); Jeffrey Sachs and other have also studied this phenomenon in developing countries. See, Jeffrey D. Sachs and Andrew M. Warner, "Natural Resource Intensity and Economic Growth", in: J. Mayer, B. Chambers, and A. Farooq, eds., *Development Policies In Natural Resource Economies,* (Edward Elgar, Cheltenham, UK, 1999), p.13; Jeffrey D. Sachs and Andrew M. Warner, "The big push, natural resource booms and growth", *Journal of Development Economics,*Vol. 59, p. 43 (1999); Jeffrey D. Sachs and Andrew M. Warner, "The curse of natural resources", *European Economic Review*, Vol. 45, p. 827 (2001)

22   UNCTAD, *FDI in Least Developed Countries at a Glance*, UNCTAD/ITE/IIA/3 (2001) [hereinafter UNCTAD, *LDCs*]

23   Ibid., p. 2.

24   Ibid., p. 3.

25   Ibid.

26   Ibid., p. 7.

27   Chinese investments in the DRC are receiving mixed reviews. Although there are elements of creativity there is much fear that they are essentially *scoop and ship* and may ultimately generate more tension with the local communities than would be mutually beneficial. The context and circumstances of the investments are complex and there is not much concrete data for a careful balanced analysis. For the issues raised see, John Farmer and Ann Talbot, "China Steps up Investment in Congo's War in East Continues," World Socialist Web Site, 15 July 2008, http://www.wsws.org/articles/2008/cong-j15.shtml (last visited 9/20/2008) (reporting a $ 9 billion investment deal between China and the DRC in which some of the funds would be used for infrastructure development, mines renovation in return for some minerals); Tim Whewell, "China to Seal $9 billion DR Congo Deal," BBC News, BBC Newsnight, http://newsvote.bbc.co.uk/mpapps/pagetools/print/news.bbc.co.uk/2/hi/progrmmes.newsn (last visited 9/20/2008) (outlining the $9 billion China/DRC deal); for some general information on Chinese investment issues in Africa, see Lydia Polgreen and Howard W. French, "China's Trade in Africa Carries a Price Tag," *New York Times*, August 21, 2007, available at http://www.nytimes.com/2007/08/21/world/africa/21zambia.html1 (last visited 9/20/2008) (discussing Chinese investments in Zambia copper mines and closing of textile factories to export cotton to China); Richard Behar, "Mining Copper in Zambia," Behar, "Mineral Wealth of the Congo," Fastcompany.com, May 9, 2008, http://www.fastcompany.com/magaine/126/congo-a-moment-of -truth.html (last visited 9/21/2008) (suggesting some local resistance to the Chinese investments); Richard Behar, "China Saps Mozambique of Timber Resources," Fastcompany.com, May 9, 2008, http://www.fastcompany.com/magaine/126/congo-a-moment-of -truth.html (last visited 9/21/2008) (suggesting some locals workers are angry over unfair treatment by Chinese investmentors; Perhaps one of the most provocative and disturbing online stories is by Peter Hitchens, "How China Has Created a New Slave Empire in Africa," *Mail Online*, September 28, 2008, http://www.dailymail.co.uk/news/worldnews/

article1063198 (last visited 10/5/2008). One of the difficulties facing scholars is concrete information on Chinese investments in Africa that can inform careful analysis. Without such information these stories will drive the debate and perhaps to everyones' mutual detriment.

28 J. J. M. Kremers, "The Dutch Disease in the Netherlands," in J. Peter Neary and Sweder van Wijnbergen, eds., *Natural Resources and the Macroeconomy,* pp. 96-136 (Cambridge, MA: MIT Press, 1986); United Nations Economic Commission for Africa, *Managing Mineral Wealth: Training Materials on Managing of Mineral Wealth and the Role of Mineral Wealth in Socio-economic Development* (2002) [hereafter ECA, *Managing Mineral Wealth*],p. 22.

29 ECA, *Managing Mineral Wealth, supra* note 28, p.22 (a summary of various studies of the impact of mineral resources concluded that being mineral resource poor may be an advantage for a country because the urban and political elite may engage in rent seeking rather than rent creation).

30 UNCTAD, *LDCs, supra* note 22, pp. 6-7, 10.

31 UNCTAD, *LDCs, supra* note 22, p. 10.

32 William Easterly, *The White Man's Burden* (The Penguin Press: 2006), p. 6 (hereafter, Easterly, *The White Man's Burden*)

33 Ibid., p.17.

34 See, for example, P.J. Buckley, "The Limits of Explanation: Testing the Internalization Theory of the Multinational Enterprise," *Journal of International Business Studies*, Vol. 19, p. 2.

35 UNCTAD, *World Investment Report 2003*, "FDI Policies for Development and International Perspectives," (2003) at 34 (discussing the concentration of FDI in Africa predominantly in oil rich and producing countries such Nigeria, Angola, Chad and Tunisia).

36 See Richard Behar, "Mineral Wealth of the Congo," Fastcompany.Com, May 9, 2008, http://www.fastcompany.com/magaine/126/congo-a-moment-of-truth.ht ml (last visited 9/21/2008) (the DRC has 10% of the planet's known copper, 30% of its cobalt, 80% of its coltan used in everything from playstations to ipods, among many others).

37 UNCTAD, *World Investment Report 2004*, "The Shift Toward Services,"at xvii-xxiv; UNCTAD, *LDCs, supra* note 22; UNCTAD, *Rethinking FDI, supra* note 11 at 4-5.

38 Behar, "Mineral Wealth of the Congo," *supra* note 36. Behar reports that many of the natural resource investors are essentially rogue investors systematically exploiting the country and taking whatever they can with impunity..

39 Ibid. Behar argues that life in the DRC is too precarious and the general environment is too chaotic and dangerous for an orderly exploitation of its vast resources but this might the best reason for the measures advocated in this project.

40 See, Daivd N. Smith and Louis T. Wells, Jr., *Negotiating Third World Mineral Agreements* (Cambridge, MA: Ballinger Pub. Co., 1975) [hereafter, Smith andWells, *Third World Mineral Agreements)*, p. 39. The authors explain in chapter two the structure and substance of mineral agreements in Liberia, arguing that the terms were largely unfavorable; they argue that the financial arrangements of the Liberian-National Iron Ore Company Agreement of 1958 were so disadvantageous that the most charitable interpretation must be that the issue was not clearly understood by Government negotiators. See also Stefan Gullander, "Joint Ventures and Corporate Strategy," *Columbia Journal of World Business*, p. 104 (Spring 1976) [hereafter, Gullander, "Joint Ventures"). Gullander discusses the complex joint venture arrangements involving the exploitation of Liberia's mineral resources). For an extensive discussion of the history and the different phases through which mineral and petroleum and mining agreements moved, see U.N. Center on Transnational Corporations, *Main Features And Trends In Petroleum And Mining Agreements* (1983) [hereafter UNCTC, *Trends In Petroleum And Mining Agreements*].

41 Liberia. E. Timber Corp. v. Liberia, 26 International Legal Materials 647 (1986) (an arbitration between Liberia and Liberian Eastern Timber Corporation (LETCO) over some disagreements between the parties concerning the exploitation of timber under concession agreement).

42 Kojo Yelpaala, *The Efficacy of Fiscal Incentives within the Dynamics of the Multinational Enterprise: The Case of Ghana and Liberia,* (A dissertation submitted in partial fulfillment of the requirements for the degree of Doctor of Juridical Science (S.J.D.) at the University of Wisconsin, Madison (1985)) [hereafter, Yelpaala, *Dissertation]* (an econometric and comparative study of the political economy of a small open economy with a mixed economy and the responses of FDI to various

political and governance variables); Yelpaala, "Model Investment Law," *supra* note 12, p. 25.

43 Gullander, "Joint Ventures," *supra* note 40.

44 UNCTAD, *LDCs, supra* note 22, p. 10.

45 Multinational Gas & Petrochemical Co. v. Multinational Gas & Petrochemical Services Ltd., 3 Western Law Reporter 492 (1983).

46 Yelpaala, *Dissertation, supra* note 42.

47 Page, "The East Asian Miracle," supra note 7, p. 219.

48 Ibid., p.220.

49 Ibid., p. 223.

50 Ibid.

51 Ibid., p. 224.

52 See e.g., Page, *supra* note 7.

53 Ibid.

54 Ibid., p. 234.

55 UNCTAD, *Rethinking FDI, supra* note 11, pp. 59-60 (arguing as follows: The ideology of the developmental State as fundamentally "developmentalist", as its major preoccupation is to ensure sustained economic growth and development on the back of high rates of accumulation, industrialization and structural change. Structurally, such a State has (or develops) the capacity to implement economic policies that effectively delivers development, which in turn gives it legitimacy.); Kojo Yelpaala, "The Impact of Industrial Legislation on the Behavior of Multinational Enterprises and Labor in the Industrializing Countries of East and South East Asia," *Michigan Yearbook of International Legal Studies*, Vol. 6, p. 383 (1984) (explaining the use of coherent industrial legislation across sectors and labor and its impact on foreign investment conduct); Mydal G., *Asian Drama: An Inquiry Into The PovertyOf Nations*, (1968); Castells, M., "The Four

Asian Tigers with a Dragon Head: a Comparative Analysis of the State Economy and Society in the Asian Pacific Rim," in Henderson R. and Applebaum J. eds., *State And Development In The Asia And Pacific Rim*, pp. 33-70 (1992); Mkandawire, T., "Thinking about Developmental State in Africa," *Cambridge Journal of Economics*, Vol. 25, pp. 289-313 (2001)

56   Page, *supra* note 7, p.220.

57   See e.g., Easterly, *supra* note 32 ; Joseph E. Stiglitz, *Globalization And Its Discontents* (W.W. Norton & Company, 2002); Joseph E. Stiglitz, *Making Globalization Work* (W.W. Norton & Company, 2006).

58   The need for and impact of neo-liberal structural adjustments for countries that experienced serious economic malaise have been a subject of much debate in various circles including the Economic for Africa and economists. For a discussion, review and the results of the structural adjustments programs see, Ikubolajeh Bernanrd Logan and Kidane Mengisteab, "IMF-World Bank Adjustment and Structural Transformation in Sub-Saharan Africa," *Economic Geography*, Vol. 69, p. 1 (1993), available at http://www.jstor.org/stable/143877 (last accessed 09/30/2008). After several years the IMF and the World Bank are not exactly celebrating the success of the structural adjustment policies. In its 2005 publication, the World Bank is discussing the issues of global development finance, managing vulnerability and the failures of FDI and the severe challenges to eradicating poverty, see, World Bank, *Global Development Finance, Mobilizing Finance And Managing Vulnerability* (2005)(hereafter, World Bank, *Global Development Finance*); Joseph E. Stiglitz, *Globalization And Its Discontents*, p. 18 (W.W. Norton & Company, 2002)(A Nobel Prize winner in Economics in 2001, Chairman of President Clinton's Council of Economic Advisors and Chief Economist for the World Bank provided a very critical inside view of the World Bank and the IMF and concluded that the structural adjustment program failed to bring sustained economic growth even to those countries that adhered strictly to the program); Easterly, *White Man's Burden*, *supra* note 32, p. 68(pointing out after repeated doses of shock therapy otherwise known structural adjustment loans under austere conditions the economic performance of the recipient countries did not improve).

59   Easterly, *supra* note 32, pp. at 6-7.

60   Several examples exist of how the Asian Miracles combined various policy instruments for success. The lesson from their stories is not that one should copy

them but rather the need for a mélange of various policy instruments from education, demographics to labor. See, Paul Morris, "Asia's Four Little Tigers: A Comparison of the Role of Education in their Development," *Comparative Education*, Vol. 32, p. 95 (1996); Eva Mueller, "The Impact of Demographic Factors on Economic Development in Taiwan,*"* Population and Development Review, Vol. 3, p. 1 (1977); Frederic C. Deyo, "Labor and Development Policy in East Asia,"Annals of the American Academy of Political and Social Science, Vol. 505, p. 152 (1989).

[61] UNCTAD, *Economic Development In Africa: Reclaiming Policy Space*, p. 58, UNCTAD/ALDC/AFRICA/2007/1(2007) [hereinafter UNCTAD, *Reclaiming Policy Space*].

[62] See, Dani Rodrik, "Getting Interventions Right: How South Korea and Taiwan Grew Rich," *Economic Policy* (April 1995) (arguing that the growth in South Korea and Taiwan was a result of subsidized and coordinated investment decisions, government policy engineering to increase private capital); Samuel P. S. Ho, "Economics, Economic Bureaucracy, and Taiwan's Economic Development," *Pacific Affairs*, Vol. 60, p. 226 (1987)(examining the complexities of the institutional, political and administrative interrelationships in development and the successful role of the economic bureaucracy in the development of Taiwan.); Kevin Griceand David Drakakis-Smith, "The Role of the State in Shaping Development: Two Decades of Growth in Singapore," *Transactions of the Institute of British Geographers*, Vol. 10, p. 347 (1985)(discussing how the social and economic development of Singapore has been carefully shaped by the state to ensure national prosperity; nothing seems to have been left to chance); Yung Chul Park, "Development Lessons from Asia: The Role of Government in South Korea and Taiwan," American Economic Review,Vol. 80, p. 118 (1990)(arguing that the governments in both South Korea and Taiwan played an active role in the export-led growth of their economies); Ramesh Thakur and Oddny Wiggen, eds., *South Asia In The World* (United Nations University Press, 2004)(a collection of several conference papers covering a wide range of topics ranging from security to development policy for the region).

[63] Amartya Sen, *Development As Freedom*, p. 13 (Oxford University Press, 1999)(hereinafter, *Development As Freedom*).

[64] Ibid., p. 14.

[65]   Hernando De Soto, *The Mystery Of Capital* (Basic Books, 2000)(hereafter, De Soto, *Mystery Of Capital*)(explaining that capitalism has not worked in poor countries not because of the lack of capital but the invisible and unstructured way in which capital exists that makes it impossible to harness its greatest potential for development).

[66]   John H. Dunning, "Re-Evaluating the Benefits of Foreign Direct Investment,"Transnational Corporations,Vol. 3, pp. 23, 32-33 (1994).

[67]   John W. Kensinger and John D. Martin, "Project Finance: Raising Money the Old-Fashioned Way," Journal of Applied Corporate Finance, Vol. 1.3, p. 69 (1988)(hereafter, Kensinger and Martin, "Raising Money the Old-Fashioned Way"); Thomas L. Friedman, *The World Is Flat* (Farrar, Straus and Giroux, 2005).

[68]   Kojo Yelpaala, "Strategy and Planning in Global Product Distribution–Beyond the Distribution Contract," Law and Policy in International Business, Vol. 25, p. 839, 853-58 (1994)

[69]   See, e.g., Manuel R. Agosin and Francisco J. Prieto, "Trade and Foreing Direct Investment Policies: Pieces of a New Strategic Approach to Development," Transnational Corporations,.Vol. 2, pp. 63, 68 (1993)(advocating linkages between trade and foreign investment policies for effectiveness); Terry Ursacki and Ilan Vertinsky, "Long-Term Changes in Korea's International Trade and Investment," *Pacific Affairs*, Vol. 67, p. 385 (1994); SaKong, *supra* note 5; Sung Yeung Kwack, *supra* note 5; Scitovsky, *supra* note 5.

[70]   See, e.g., Sakong, *supra* note 5; Sung Yeung Kwack, *supra* note 5; Scitovsky, *supra* note 5.

[71]   Andreas Lowenfeld has provided an interesting discussion of the evolution of "voluntary restraints agreements" dating back to the late 1960s when the U. S Congress initiated a series of Bills (at least 22) aimed at imposing quotas and limits on the importation of foreign steel products into the U.S. To forestall such legislation which is often difficult to repeal Mr. Yoshihiro Inayama, the Chairman of the Japan Iron and Steel Exports' Association went to the Washington D.C. for talks with the U.S Department of State proposing import restraints to be imposed by the Japanese exporters. For a full discussion of that history and the legal issues thatfollowed, see, Andreas F. Lowenfeld, *Public Controls On International Trade*, Vol. 6, pp. 195-252 (New York: Matthew Bender, 1983); Comment, "Executive Authority and Antitrust Considerations in Voluntary Limits on Steel

Imports," University of Pennsylvania Law Review, Vol. 118, p. 105(1969); The technique of using voluntary restraints by Japanese industries also came to a head in the Semiconductor industry resulting in the Semiconductor Accord of 1986. See, Dorinda G. Dallmeyer, "The United States-Japan Semiconductor Accord of 1986: The Shortcomings of High-Tech Protectionism," Maryland Journal of International Law and Trade, Vol. 13, p. 179 (1989); Diane P. Wood, "'Unfair' Trade Injury: A competition-Based Approach," Stanford Law Review, Vol. 41, p. 1153 (1989)(arguing that there is no reason for consumers to be deprived low-priced products through the use of trade restraints).

[72]   Easterly, *supra* note 32,p. 6.

[73]   Urban C. Lehner, "Breakup of Dow Chemical's Joint Venture with Koreans Leaves Both Sides Unhappy," *Wall Street Journal,* Jan. 5, 1983.

[74]   UNCTAD, *Reclaiming Policy Space, supra* note 61, p. 58

[75]   Yelpaala, *Model Investment Law, supra* note 12, p. 45; Yabo Lin, "New Forms and Organizational Structures of Foreign Investment in China Under the Company Law of the PRC," Transnational Lawyer, Vol. 7, p.327 (1994).

[76]   Yabo, *supra* note 75,. pp. 333–38, 343.

[77]   J. J. M. Kremers, "The Dutch Disease In The Netherlands," in *Natural Resources and the Macroeconomy,* pp. 96-136 (Blackwell Publishers, 1986)(discussing the term "Dutch Disease" in explaining the internal economic stresses the Dutch economy experienced in the 1960s and 1970s as result of the development of its natural gas reserves); ECA, *Managing Mineral Wealth, supra* note 28 , pp. 22-25, 37 (discussing the Dutch Disease problems within the mineral regimes of Africa).

[78]   Scott L. Hoffman, *The Law And Business Of International Project Finance* (2001)(providing a discussion of a wide range of issues relating to project finance transactions); Benjamin C. Esty, *Modern Project Finance* (2004) (examining the economic analysis and case studies of project finance); Kensinger and Martin, "Raising Money the Old-Fashioned Way," *supra* note 67; Roger S. McCormick, "Legal Issues in Project Finance," Journal of Energy and Natural Resources Law, Vol. 1, p. 21 (1983); Harrold F. Moore and Evelyn D. Giaccio, "International Project Finance," North Carolina Journal of International Law & Commercial Regulation, Vol. 11, p. 597 (1986).

[79]   Ibid., p. 70; IFC, *Project Finance in Developing Countries*, p. 18 (1999)(hereafter IFC, *Project Finance*)(providing a distribution of project finance by category).

[80]   IFC, *Project Finance, supra* note 79; Larry H. P. Lang, *Project Finance In Asia* (1998)(hereafter Lang, *Project Finance In Asia*)(providing a study and analysis of project finance its adaptive configurations in "New Asia").

[81]   For a sample of the growing literature in this field see, Teresa A. John and Kose John, "Optimality of Project Finance: Theory and Empirical Implications in Finance and Accounting," Review of Quantitative Finance and Accounting, Vol. 1, p. 51(1991); S. El-Gazar, S. Lilien and V. Pastena, "The Use of Off-Balance Sheet Financing to Circumvent Financial Covenant Restrictions," Journal of Accounting, Auditing and Finance, Vol. 4, p. 217 (1989); J. C. T. Mao, "Project Finance: Funding the Future," *Financial Executive*, p. 23 (1982); S. Shah and A. Thakor, "Optimal Capital Structure and Project Financing," Journal of Economic Theory, Vol. 42, p. 42 (1987); L. M. Farrell, "Financial Engineering in Project Finance," Project Management Journal, Vol. 33, p.. 27 (2002); John W. Kensinger and John D. Martin, "Project Finance for Research and Development," *Research In Finance*, Vol. 8, p. 119 (1990)(*Project Finance in R&D*).

[82]   Hoffman, *The Law And Business Of International Project Finance, supra* note 78, p. 9.

[83]   Ibid., p. 10.

[84]   Benjamin C. Esty, *Modern Project Finance supra* note 78 (providing a case study of different projects and their related costs); Chad-Cameroon Pipe Line at 71; Australian-Japan Cable Project at 93; Nghe An Tate & Lyle Sugar Company at 190.

[85]   IFC, *Project Finance, supra* note 79, p. 8.

[86]   Ibid.

[87]   Ibid. Stefanie Kleimeier and William L. Megginson, "A Comparison of Project Finance in Asia and the West,"in Lang, *Project Finance In Asia, supra* note 80, p.68.

88   World Bank, *Global Development Finance, supra* note 4, p. 97 (arguing that FDI in natural resources create limited linkage effects, produce the Dutch Disease and make host countries susceptible to the volatility of world commodity prices).

89   International Monetary Fund, *Regional Economic Outlook, Sub-Saharan Africa* (World Economic and Financial Surveys) (2007), p. 4 (arguing that fragile economies such as Sierra Leone, Liberia, and the Democratic Republic of Congo are enjoying higher growth rates because of higher commodity prices).

90   IFC, *Project Finance, supra* note 79, p. 2.

91   David Hart, *The Volta River Project: A Case Study in Politics and Technology*, pp. 59-64 (Edinburgh University Press, 1980).

92   A comprehensive approach to industrial policy complemented by industrial legislation appears to be the approach used by the East Asian Miracles. See, Sakong, *Korea In The World Economy, supra* note 5; Yelpaala, "Model Investment Law," *supra* note 12, pp. 44-46 (discussing the nature of industrial legislation within the framework of industrial policy).

93   Page, "The East Asian Miracle," *supra* note 7, pp. 227-29, 234, 264.

94   Manuel R. Agosin and Francisco J. Prieto, Trade and Foreign Direct Investment Policies: Pieces of a New Strategic Approach to Development? *Transnational Corporations*, Vol 2, p. 63-(1993)

95   Kensinger and Martin, *Raising Money the Old-Fashioned Way, supra* note 67, p. 81

96   Ibid., p. 81.

97   Ibid., p. 74.

98   Easterly, *The White Man's Burden, supra* note 32, pp. 26-33.

99   Mark Augenblick and B.Scott Custer, "The Build, Operate, and Transfer ("BOT") Approach to Infrastructure Projects in Developing Countries," *World Bank Working Papers*, wps no. 498 (1990), p. 2. The BOT concept has several variations to the theme. For instance some may come as "BOOT"(build, own, operate and transfer), "BOO"(build, own and operate), "BRT"(build, rent and transfer), "BOOST"(build, own, operate subsidize and transfer); Paul Handley,

"A Critical View of the Build-Oprate-Transfer Privatisation Process in Asia," Asia Journal of Public Admininistration, Vol. 19, pp. 203, 213 (1997)(hereafter Handley, "Critical View of the Build-Oprate-Transfer") "BTO"(build, transfer and operate).

[100] Handley, "Critical View of the Build-Operate-Transfer,"*supra* note 99; Lang, *Project Finance in Asia, supra* note 80, p.153. Esty, *Modern Project Finance, supra* note 78 (discussing various case studies of infrastructural power plants and other projects including the Eurotunnel).

[101] Handley, "Critical View of the Build-Operate-Transfer," *supra* note 99, pp. 212-213 (explaining the duration of BOT projects: power generation, 10-20 years; toll roads, 20-30 years; and the Eurotunnel, 55 years).

[102] Ibid., p. 212. C. Walker and A. J. Smith eds., *Privatized Infrastructure: The Build Operate Transfer Approach* (Thomas Telford, 1995).

[103] See Smith and Wells, *Third World Mineral Agreements , supra* note 40 (explaining in chapter two the structure and substance of mineral agreements including the production sharing and service contracts); for comprehensive discussion of the history and the different phases through which mineral and petroleum and mining agreements moved, *see* U.N. Center On Transnational Corporations, *Main Features And Trends In Petroleum And Mining Agreements* (1983) [Hereinafter *Trends In Petroleum And Mining Agreements*] (explaining the different techniques including renegotiations used to redistribute gains for trade and maintain stability); for an interesting discussion of the structure and renegotiation of production sharing agreements in Indonesia see, T. N. Machmud, "The Production Sharing Contract in Indonesia," in Thomas W. Walde and George K. Ndi, eds., *International Oil And Gas Investment Moving Eastward*, p. 113 (Kluwer Law International, 1994)(hereafter, Machmud, "Production Sharing Contract in Indonesia")(describing the phases of the Indonesian production sharing agreements and the reasons for renegotiations); new forms of production sharing agreements seem to have adjustments built into them; see generally, Andrei Yakovlev, "Production Sharing Agreements in the Russian Petroleum Sector," *World Competition Law and Economics Review,* Vol. 20, p. 45 (1996) (describing the nature and structure of production sharing under the Russian Production Sharing legislation).

[104] IFC, *Project Finance, supra* note 79, p. 8.

[105] Robert L.K. Tiong, "BOT Projects: Risks and Securities," *Construction Management & Econmics*, Vol. 8, pp. 315, 326 (1990)(hereafter Tiong, "BOT Projects").

[106] See, Katherine Maddox McElroy and John J. Siegfried, "The Economics of Antitrust Enforcement," in Terry Calvani and John Siegfried, *Economic Analysis and Antitrust Law*, 2d. ed., pp. 139-140 (Boston: Little Brown, 1988)(arguing that the fewer the number of firms in an industry, the simpler it would be fir the firms to coordinate their actions and to agree upon common goals). Cartel theory argues that the incentives to cheat on one's cartel partners increase as the number of firms increase and the stability of cartels decrease as a result such is the case of corruption. As the number of partners increase it will be difficult to collude quietly to corrupt government officials.

[107] L.M. Farrell, "Principal-Agency Risk in Project Finance," *International Journal of Project Management*, Vol. 21, pp. 547, 548 (2003)(hereafter Farrell, "Principal-Agency Risk").

[108] Ronald H. Coase, "The Nature of the Firm,"*Economica*, Vol. 4, p. 386 (1937).

[109] Oliver E. Williamson, *The Economic Institutions of Capitalism: Firms, Markets, Relational Contracting*, pp. 78, 85 (The Free Press, 1985); Oliver E. Williamson, *Markets and Hierachies: Analysis and Anitrust Implications*, p. 106 (The Free Press, 1975)(hereafter, Williamson, *Markets and Hierachies*).

[110] Michael C. Jensen, *Foundations of Organizational Strategy*, pp. 135-139 (1998)(hereafter, Jensen, *Foundations of Organizational Strategy*)(arguing that the firm is nexus of contracts written and unwritten among disparate individuals).

[111] Farrell, "Principal-Agency Risk," *supra* note 107.

[112] James S. Ang, Rebel A. Cole, and James Wuh Lin, "Agency Cost and Ownership Structure," *Journal of Finance*, Vol. 55, p. 81 (2000); Farrell, *Principal-Agency Risk, supra* note 107.

[113] Jensen, *Foundations of Organizational Strategy, supra* note 110, pp. 53-55.

[114] Ibid., p. 54.

[115] Kathryn Rudie Harrigan, "Joint Ventures and Global Strategies," *Columbia Journal of World Business*, Spring 1984, p. 7 (offering a dynamic explanation of

corporate joint ventures); Stefan Gullander, "Joint Ventures and Corporate Strategy," Columbia Journal of World Business, Spring 1976, p. 104 (describing joint venture strategies for complex transactions); for strategic alliances a few examples of the vast literature will suffice; Alan S. Gutterman, *The Law Of Domestic And International Strategic Alliances* (1995)(discussing a wide range of complex strategic alliance agreements); Yadong Luo, *Entry and Cooperative Strategies in International Business Expansion* (1999)(providing the theoretical and strategic basis for international cooperative arrangements ranging from joint ventures to strategic alliances); Rosabeth Moss Kanter, "Collaborative Advantage: The Art of Alliances," *Harvard Business Review*, July-August 1994, p. 571(explaining business strategic alliances as living systems, constantly evolving and requiring careful partner management techniques); Ranjay Gulati, "Alliances and Networks," *Strategic Management Journal*, Vol. 19, p. 293 (1998)(discussing alliances as social networks with dynamic structures functioning styles and evolving governance structures).

[116] Williamson, *Economic Institutions, supra* note 109, pp. 45-50; Williamson, *Markets and Hierarchies, supra* note 109, p. 45.

[117] Ian Ayres and Robert Gertner, "Strategic Contractual Inefficiency," *Yale Law Journal*, Vol. 101, p. 729 (1992)(contingently and obligationally incomplete contracts); Richard Craswell, "Contract Law, Default Rules, and the Philosophy of Promising," *Michigan Law Review*, Vol. 88, p. 489 (1989) [hereinafter "Contract Law"]; Ian Ayres and Robert Gertner, "Filling Gaps in Incomplete Contracts: An Economic Theory of Default Rules," *Yale Law Journal*, Vol. 99, p. 87 (1989) [hereinafter *Filling Gaps in Incomplete Contracts*].

[118] Williamson, Economic Institutions, *supra* note 109p. 52 (explaining the nature and vulnerabilities associated with specific asset investments).

[119] See, Philippine Build-Operate-Transfer Law, Republic Act No. 7718, An Act Amending Certain Sections of Republic Act No. 6957, Entitled "An Act Authorizing the Financing, Construction, Operation and Maintenance of Infrastructure Projects by the Private Sector and for other Purposes," Chan Robles and Associates, Virtual Law Library, available at http://www.chanrobles. com/default7.htm (last visited 7/5/2008). For a discussion of this law, see Adora Navarro, *Build-Operate-Transfer Arrangements (BOT): The Experience and Policy Challenges,* (Phil. Inst. for Dev. Studies, Discussion Paper Series No. 2005-01, 2005), available at http://unpan1.un.org/intradoc/groups/public/documents/ EROPA/UNPAN029875.pdf.

120   Convention on the Recognition and Enforcement of Foreign Arbitral Awards, June 10, 1958, T.I.A.S. No. 6997, 330 U.N.T.S. 38 (New York Convention). For a discussion of the Convention, see generally Kojo Yelpaala, "Restraining the Unruly Horse: The Use of Public Policy in Arbitration, Interstate and International Conflict of Laws in California," Transnational Lawyer, Vol.2, pp. 379, 457-462 (1989) [hereinafter, "Restraining the Unruly Horse"]; Paolo Contini, "International Commercial Arbitration: The United Nations Convention on the Recognition and Enforcement of Foreign Arbitral Awards," American Journal of Comparative Law, Vol. 8, p. 283 (1959).

121   UNCITRAL, United Nations Commission on Trade Law, Status, 1958- Convention on the Recognition and Enforcement of Foreign Arbitral Awards, http://www.uncitral.org/en/uncitral_text/arbitration/NYConvention_status.html (Accessed 10/12/2008); Bosnia September 1 1993, Liberia September 16 2005, Mozambique June 11 1998.

122   Tiong, "BOT Projects," *supra* note 105.

123   *See,* notes 130-132 discussing political riks.

124   Tiong, "BOT projects," *supra* note 105.

125   Farrell, "Principal-Agency Risk," *supra* note 107, pp. 549-550.

126   Tiong, *BOT Projects, supra* note 105, pp. 315, 326.

127   Jeffrey D. Sachs, *The End of Poverty* (Penguin Press, 2005)(provides a passionate analysis of root causes of poverty and offers several solutions, sometimes referred as "Big Push" but perhaps better seen as minimalist on how it might be ended).

128   Ibid., p. 250 (assigning a dominant role to donor aid; without donor funding he argues the necessary investment simply cannot be financed and poor people will remain in a poverty trap).

129   Easterly, *White Man's Burden, supra* note 32, pp. 38-40, 50 (arguing that Aid even within the right policy environment does not work; the evidence shows that the poorest countries can grow without Aid); Aart Kraay and Claudio Raddatz, "Poverty Traps, Aid and Growth,"*World Bank Mimeograph* (2005); William Easterly and Ross Levine, "New Data, New Doubts: Comments on Aid. Policies, and

Growth," American Economic Review, Vol. 94, p. 774 (2004)(finding that Aid
does not improve growth in poor countries with sound policies); Raghuram G.
Rajan and Arvind Subramanian, "Aid and Growth: What Does the Cross-
Country Evidence Really Show?" *Review of Economics and Statistics*, Vol. 90, pp.
643-645 (November 2008)(showing that after for possible bias, Aid does not
have an effect, positive or negative growth in developing countries with sound
economic policies).

130   *Tiong, "BOT Projects," supra note 105, p.325; Farrell, Principal-Agency Risk, supra
note 107, p. 550; Hoffman,* The Law And Business Of International Project Finance, supra *note 78,p. 40 (devoting several pages to a discussion of various types of
politically motivated risks that might rise in project finance); Wendy B. Wood, "Risk
Assessment and Options in Project Finance," Project Management Journal, Vol. 23,.pp.
21, 25 (1992)(pointing out the range of political risks including outright hostility to the
project); Dannielle Mazzini, "Stable International Contracts in Emerging Markets: An
Endangered Species?" Boston University International Law Journal, Vol. 15, p. 343
(1997)(discussing the problems encountered by the notorious Enron Corporation in the
State of Maharashtra in India with respect to it power plant and the unilateral termination of the contract by the government); see generally, Frank C Shaw, "Reconciling Two
Legal Cultures in Privatization and Large Scale Capital Projects in Latin America,"*
Law and Policy in International Business, *Vol. 30, p. 147 (1999); S. Baker, D. Pon-
niah andS. Smith, "Techniques for the Analysis of Risks in Major Projects,"* Journal of
the Operational Research Society, *Vol. 40, p. 567 (1998)(providing a general methodology for assessing risks which could then be manged); James E. Smith and John F.
Nau, "Valuing Risky Projects: Option Pricing and Decision Analysis,"* Management
Science, *Vol. 41, p. 795 (1995)(discussing and comparing at the theory level options in
pricing risky projects); Carl R. Beldleman, David Veshosky andDonna Fletcher, "Using
Project Finance to Help Manage Project Risks,"* Project Managemnent Journal, *Vol.
22, p. 33 (1991)(providing a general description of various types of risks that can be
managed through project finance).*

131   For turnkey contracts see, UNCTC, "Features And Issues In Turnkey Contracts
In Developing Countries, A Technical Paper" (1981); for production sharing and
service contracts, see, Ernest E. Smith, "From Concessions to Service Contracts,"
Tulsa Law Journal, Vol. 27, p. 493 (1992) (discussing the evolution of mineral
contracts towards the production sharing and service contracts to give governments greater say and take in the proceeds); Smith and Wells, *Third World
Mineral Agreements, supra* note 40; UNCTC, Trends In Petroleum And Mining
Agreements; Machmud, "Production Sharing Contract in Indonesia," *supra* note
103.

132 Cross default clauses are a staple in syndicated loan agreements because they generally worded broadly enough to work as a deterrent to breach. The typical cross default clause is broadly worded to cover defaults on any indebtedness in the event of which the indebtedness is accelerated or capable of being accelerated. Indebtedness covers all financial obligations to other creditors. See, Philip Wood, *Law And Practice Of International Finance*, p. 256 (1980)(chapter 11 devoted to the loan syndication and its implications); Keith Clark and Andrew Taylor, "Events of Default in Eurocurrency Loan Agreements," International Financial Law Review, Vol. 1, pp. 12, 13 (1982).

133 *Hoffman,* The Law And Business Of International Project Finance, supra *note 78 (discussing a wide range of currency risks associated with project finance).*

134 *Ibid. Tiong, "BOT Projects," supra note 105,p. 323.*

135 *Hoffman,* The Law and Business of International Project Finance, supra *note 78, pp. 44-45.*

136 Lang, *Project Finance in Asia, supra* note 40, pp. 41-43(explaining the absence of legislation in some Asian countries and the politicization of government commitments as a source of corruption and politician jockeying for power as a significant hurdle to project finance.)

137 Ibid., pp.43-46 (explaining that in China the Administrators did treat contracts as binding and although India has a developed legal system the system of corruption was decentralized).

138 Hoffman, *The Law and Business of International Project Finance, supra* note 78; Tiong, "BOT Project", *supra* note 105, p. 323.

139 *Lang,* Project Finance In Asia, supra *note 80(devoting several chapters to power plants and some of the special cases of project finance in Asia); Handley, "Critical View of the Build-Operate-Transfer," supra note 99, pp. 209-211.*

140 Lang, *Project Finance in Asia, supra* note 80, p. 93 (providing an interesting discussion of the background and path to success of Hopewell Holdings in the project finance arena; at hotel project gave rise to the vision of major infrastructural project finance projects).

141 Farrell, *Principal-Agency Risk, supra* note, 107 , p. 550.

142 Alfred C. Piguou, *The Economics Of Welfare* (London: MacMillan and Co., 1920).

143 UNCTAD, *Incentives and Foreign Direct Investment*, U.N. Doc. TD/B/ITNC/Misc. 1 Ge. 95-51297(April 1995), p. 5.

144 Ibid.

145 *Ibid., p. 30.*

146 *See, Yelpaala, "The Efficacy of Tax Incentives,"* supra note 10 *(discussing the weak theoretical basis of tax incentives); G. Reuber,* Private Foreign Investment In Development, *pp. 128-29 (1973); Patrick L. Kelley, "Tax Treaties Between the United States and Developing Countries: The Need for a New U.S. Initiative,"* American Journal of International Law, *Vol. 65, pp. 159, 161 (1971); George E. Lent, "Tax Incentives in Developing Countries," in R. Bird and I. Oldman eds.,* Readings On Taxation In Developing Countries, *pp. 363, 270 (3d ed. 1975); Stanley S. Surrey, "Current Issues in the Taxation of Corporate Foreign Investment,"* Columbia Law Review, *Vol. 56, pp. 815, 843-46 (1956); Surrey & Sunley, "General Report — Part II: Use of Tax Incentives to Achieve Government Goals," Cahiers De Droit Fiscal International, 61A, pp. 28, 30-35 (1976).*

147 *Yelpaala, "The Efficacy of Tax Incentives,"* supra note 146, p. 396.

148 *Ibid., pp. 396-413.*

149 *Louis T. Wells Jr., Nancy J. Allen, Jacques Morisset and Neda Pirnia, "Using Tax Incentives to Compete for Foreign Investment, Are They Worth the Cost?"* Foreign Investment Advisory Service, Occasional Paper, *Vol. 15, pp. 8-15 (2001) (empirical findings that upon removing tax holidays in 1980 FDI in Indonesia increased;p. 77 (arguing that most econometric studies tend to support the results of the survey studies)(hereafter, "Using Tax Incentives to Compete for Foreign Investment").*

150 *Yelpaala, "The Efficacy of Tax Incentives,"* supra note 10, p. 403 *(arguing that surveys allow business executives to reveal their subjective preferences which may have nothing to do with their objective decision processes).*

151 *Louis T. Wells and Nancy J. Allen, "Tax Holidays to Attract Foreign Direct Investment: Lessons from Two Experiments," in "Using Tax Incentives to Compete for Foreign Investment,"* supra note 149, p.14 *(hereafter, "Tax Holidays to Attract Foreign Direct Investment").*

152 *Yelpaala, "The Efficacy of Tax Incentives,"* supra *note 10, p. 392; Wells and Allen, "Using Tax Incentives to Compete for Foreign Investment,"* supra *note 151.*

153 Andrew Charlton, "Incentive Bidding for Mobile Investment: Economic Conse-quences and Potential Responses," *OECD Development Center,* Working Paper No. 203 (Jan. 2003) (offering a review of the nature of the world wide competi-tion for FDI through incentives); For situation in the U.S. see, Steven Kale, "U. S. Industrial Development Incentives and Manufacturing Growth during the 1970s," *Journal of Public, Urban and Regional Policy,* Vol. 15, p. 26 (1984).

154 UNCTAD, *Incentives and FDI, supra* note 143,p. 10.

155 UNCTAD, *World Investment Report 2000,* "Cross-Border Mergers And Acquisi-tions And Development" (2000) [Hereinafter *World Investment Report 2000*] p.1. According to this UNCTAD report, the efforts to attract investment included the conclusion of bilateral investment treaties which increased tremendously be-tween 1980 and 1999. In 1980 there were about 181 bilateral investment treaties concluded. By 1999, the number had increased more than tenfold to 1, 856. Double taxation treaties increase from 719 in 1980 to 1, 982 by the end of 1999.

156 UNCTAD, *World Investment Report 2003, supra* note 35, p. 36. According to this report as of 2003, the conclusion of at least 533 BITs in Africa translated into an average of 10 BITs per country. In addition, African countries had, by the end of 2002, concluded 365 double taxation treaties (DTTs) at the rate of about 7 DTTs per country; Kojo Yelpaala, "Fundamentalism in Public Health and Safety in Bi-lateral Investment Treaties [Part 1]," *Asian Journal of World Health,* Vol. 3, pp. 235, 235-239 (2008)(providing a statistical evidence of the proliferation of bilat-eral investment treaties since the 1950s).

157 Yelpaala, "The Efficacy of Tax Incentives," *supra* note 10pp. 388, 392; Wells and Allen, "Using Tax Incentives to Compete for Foreign Investment," *supra* note 149 p. viii.

158 Yelpaala, "In Search of"; P. Buckley and M. Casson, *The Future of the Multina-tional Enterprise* (London: Macmillan, 1976).

159 Wells and Allen, "Tax Holidays to Attract Foreign Direct Investment," *supra* note 151p. 36 (arguing that highly discretionary approach to incentives may be doomed to failure).

160   David W. Rasmussen, Marc Bendick, Jr. and Larry C. Ledebur, "A Methodology for Selecting Economic Development Incentives," Journal of Public,Urban and Regional Policy, Vol. 15, pp. 18, 24 (1984)(arguing that different incentives have different values to investors and impose different costs on the granting public institution).

Chapter 3

Law on Loan: Legal Reconstruction
after Armed Conflict

Tai-Heng Cheng[1]

This chapter, which is written for policymakers rather than a specialist legal audience, addresses one of many challenges that a government faces after a period of armed conflict: creating a stable legal framework to encourage foreign direct investment (FDI). When a state emerges from armed conflict, it holds out a promise of better and more peaceful times for its people who have survived horrific disruptions. To fulfill this promise, the post-conflict government has to pursue, among several key priorities, economic development.[2] It must usually undertake different tasks to promote development, such as consolidating the authority of a legitimate government, combating crime, generating employment and stimulating local business.[3] One key task is to rapidly create a legal framework to attract FDI. In theory, the government can establish a legal framework by enacting domestic legislation, rebuilding courthouses, training judges and lawyers, and importing computers and law libraries. In practice, this may be all but impossible. A post-conflict government often faces financial and manpower constraints, as well as many other competing priorities for public spending.

The government may instead "borrow law." When borrowing law, a post-conflict government need not confine itself to borrowing the laws of another legal system. It may also borrow its expertise and infrastructure, such as the services of lawyers, judge and arbitrators, as well as physical courthouses and tribunals. It may borrow law through investment contracts and treaties, which can help to rapidly establish a legal framework acceptable to foreign investors, and relieve pressures on the post-conflict state to build its own legal investment framework. This chapter explains how a post-conflict government may solder investment contracts and treaties together to construct a legal framework for investment. It also considers the advantages and risks of such a strategy, and makes recommendations to modify investment agreements to the needs of the post-conflict state.

This chapter accepts as a working assumption that there is a generally positive relationship between FDI and economic development. The United Nations Conference on Trade and Development (UNCTAD) has noted generally "the importance of FDI as a package of internationally mobile assets for growth and development."[4] The World Bank has validated this general statement in granular studies of specific states and regions.[5] Academics have also observed a positive relationship between FDI and growth.[6] There are studies indicating that the precise relationship between FDI and growth depends on various factors,[7] such as the type of FDI, how FDI is deployed in the host state, and other macroeconomic variables.[8] However, a detailed examination of these factors is beyond the scope of this chapter, which concerns establishing a legal infrastructure for FDI.

This chapter also assumes that creating a legal infrastructure through investment treaties is a necessary, but not sufficient condition for attracting FDI.[9] Other political conditions, such as transparency and political stability, may need to be promoted. Economic conditions that enable investors to make a profit must also be present.[10] This set of assumptions is made after accounting for the differing conclusions of academics about the relationship between bilateral investment treaties (BITs) and FDI. Researchers using different models have not uniformly observed a positive relationship. On one hand, Professors Jeswald Salacuse, Nicholas Sullivan, Eric Neumayer and Laura Spess have found a correlation between concluding BITs and increasing FDI.[11] On the other hand, Mary Hallward-Driemeier did not.[12] More recently, however, Professors Susan Rose-Ackerman from Yale Law School and Jennifer Tobin from Oxford have reexamined empirically the relationship between FDI and BITs.[13] They concluded that BITs do generally have a positive impact on FDI flows, but this impact is highly dependent on the political and economic environment surrounding both FDI and BITs. This chapter accordingly examines the creation of a legal framework as one condition for attracting FDI, but does not propose that BITs can absolve post-conflict governments from attending to other political and economic factors necessary to create a favorable investment environment.[14]

With these assumptions, this chapter explains how a post-conflict government might borrow international investment law to attract FDI. Part I argues that post-conflict governments are often not in a position to rapidly establish a domestic legal framework for FDI, and explains how investment agreements may provide an effective alternative. Part II considers the risk that investment agreements may prevent a post-conflict government from discharging core sovereign responsibilities. Part III proposes strategies for post-conflict governments to preserve regulatory space for themselves when entering into the international legal framework for FDI.

Borrowing Law

Every armed conflict has unique geographical, military, historical, and political dimensions. The tribal wars in Rwanda, the sectarian violence in

Iraq, and the "regime change" in Afghanistan were all different in scale, intensity, and persistence. Consequently, the impact of conflict on a state's legal framework can vary considerably from conflict to conflict.

In general, however, severe and lengthy conflicts tend to leave states in a legal vacuum. Judges and lawyers may have fled or been killed. Unpaid law enforcement officials may have joined militias. The new government in a post-conflict state may reject the legitimacy of a prior oppressive government, and treat prior enacted laws as illegitimate and unlawful. Courthouses and other basic infrastructure necessary for a functioning legal system may have been destroyed. There may be no legal scholars for legislators to consult in drafting new legislation. Without these basic elements of a legal system, there simply is no way for a post-conflict state to apply, adjust, and enforce laws.[15]

Foreign investors who might otherwise consider making an investment in a post-conflict state may be deterred by the lack of a legal system. Corporations that do make investments might require a much higher rate of return to account for the increased risks of doing business in a state that may not provide effective legal recourse against unlawful actions by state and non-state actors.

A post-conflict government may lack the resources and expertise to rapidly set up a domestic legal framework to fill this legal vacuum. Training judges, lawyers and police officers, building courthouses, importing and networking basic computer technology, accumulating law libraries, enacting new laws, and explaining laws to local communities all take time and resources. A post-conflict government may face continuing sectarian or tribal violence, malnutrition, unemployment, pressures from foreign powers, as well as a lack of adequate housing, schooling and heath care. Faced with such a daunting list of priorities, it may not be in a position to take the resource-intensive measures necessary to establish a legal framework for foreign investors.

Even if a post-conflict government is able to re-establish its domestic legal system, this may not provide sufficient reassurance for foreign investors. Investors may reasonably be concerned that the judges and laws of the post-conflict state could be biased against their claims. Investors' lawyers may also be unfamiliar with the laws and legal procedures of the post-conflict state. In order to avoid conceding to the post-conflict state a "home team advantage" in potential legal disputes,[16] they may therefore object to investment agreements that are governed by the laws of the post-conflict state and are subject to adjudication by that state's courts.

Post-conflict governments have two non-mutually exclusive policy options to borrow law that may encourage foreign investments. First, the government or corporations of post-conflict states may enter into contractual arrangements with foreign investors that adopt the laws of a foreign state and provide for adjudication of disputes exclusively in the courts of a foreign state. Second, the post-conflict state may enter the international investment law framework, which provides for arbitration of disputes by neutral arbitrators.

Governing Law and Forum Selection Clauses

Investors may wish to structure investment agreements under the laws of the investor's state and to adjudicate investment disputes in its courts. They may do so by inserting governing law and forum selection provisions in investment contracts with the post-conflict government or local corporations. Although some courts are reluctant to entertain claims arising from contracts concluded, implemented, and allegedly breached overseas,[17] many courts do honor forum selection agreements designating them as the venue for dispute resolution.[18]

As a hypothetical illustration of the use of forum selection and governing law clauses in investment contracts, suppose that Anthony Hope's fictional state, Ruritania,[19] has emerged from a period of violent unrest with a newly-elected democratic government. Its despot king has been deposed, but the legal system that remains is in a shambles. Additionally, all its judges have been killed, its courthouses bombed, most of its lawyers have fled, and whatever that is left of a police force are so poorly paid that they are prone to corruption and cannot be trusted to enforce court decisions. Ruritania's hope for economic recovery lies in its vast supply of coal. A US energy corporation, Oro Corp., is willing to enter into a power plant joint venture with Ruritania's only private power corporation, Alum Inc. The joint venture agreement provides that Oro will construct a power plant in Ruritania and Alum will supply coal from its mines. The revenues from the sale of electricity will be divided nine to one between Oro and Alum for twenty years. The joint venture agreement between Oro and Alum might have governing law and forum selection clauses, which state:

> *Governing Law:*
> This contract shall be governed exclusively by the laws of New York.

> *Forum Selection:*
> Any and all disputes arising from or in connection with this contract shall be exclusively adjudicated in the courts of New York, New York.

This provision will probably bind Oro and Alum contractually to adjudicate disputes in New York using State of New York law. In New York, the legislature has enacted a long-arm statute providing that its courts should exercise jurisdiction over contractual disputes if the contract in question had a provision designating New York as the venue for judicial dispute resolution.[20] According to the legislative history of the long arm statute, the legislature did so to build New York as a commercial center and to benefit from business-generating activities that accompany litigation, such as hotels and other litigation-support services.[21] New York courts have accordingly retained jurisdiction over foreign disputes with foreign litigants on the basis of New York forum selection clauses.[22]

The designation of the courts and laws of the investor's state as the adjudication forum and governing law of the investment agreement with the post-conflict state is one way to borrow law to fill the legal vacuum in that state. This mechanism replaces the nascent laws of the post-conflict state with the developed commercial laws of the state of the investor. It borrows the services of foreign judges to discharge adjudicatory responsibilities that the post-conflict state is unable to meet. It allows the post-conflict state and the investor to turn to a pool of lawyers from the investor's state to advance their respective legal claims. It also transfers to the investor state the requirements of providing secondary services critical to the resolution of legal disputes, including hotels, sophisticated computer systems and networks, high-end copy and translation services.

However, transferring legal disputes to the investor state's courts may not always satisfy foreign investors that their investments will be sufficiently protected. In some investments, the investor may enter into an agreement directly with the post-conflict government that designates the investor's state and laws as the adjudicatory forum and governing law, respectively. That agreement might explicitly provide that the post-conflict government waives any sovereign immunity from lawsuits that it might otherwise be accorded under the laws of the investor's state.[23] In such an investment, the investor may feel adequately protected against subsequent actions of the post-conflict government that might hurt its investments.

However, in other investments, the investor might not have contracted directly with the post-conflict government. Instead, it might have entered into a joint venture with a corporation of a post-conflict state, or a government agency. The investor would be legitimately concerned that the central government of the post-conflict state could subsequently take regulatory actions that hurt the foreign investor, such as suspending exchanges out of the currency of the post-conflict state, or denying licenses to do business. Should such fears come to pass, the investor may have neither recourse against the post-conflict government, which was not party to the investment agreements, nor recourse against the local investment partner, which did not breach its contracts with the foreign investor. Even if the foreign investor's attorneys, through skillful pleading in lawsuits, were able to hoist the investment agreement onto the post-conflict government through legal doctrines such as corporate veil piercing, the costs of such elaborate litigation would create a disincentive to investment in the post-conflict state.

Governing law and forum selection provisions that transfer legal disputes to the investor's state courts present serious problems to the post-conflict state as well. Just as investors may perceive the courts of the post-conflict state to be biased or to lack commercial expertise, the post-conflict government may not believe that it would get a fair hearing in the courts of the investor's states, or even a third party state. Those courts may not understand the particular context of the post-conflict state. They may also be required, as a matter of their law, to consider the public policies of their home state and not those of the post-conflict state.[24] Indeed, some scholars have also noted that foreigners may face significant disadvantages in the US courts.[25] A post-conflict government might thus conclude that there are significant litigation risks in ceding authority to US courts to adjudicate investment disputes.

The International Arbitration and Investment Treaty Regime

If a post-conflict state is unable to fill its legal vacuum on its own, and borrowing the courts of a foreign state through contractual provisions in investment agreements is not a complete solution, the post-conflict government may consider additionally borrowing the international legal framework for FDI.

In truth, the suggestion that there is one framework is slightly misleading. There are several distinct but interlocking frameworks. Some pertain to specific concerns, such as the Energy Charter Treaty, which addresses cooperation in the energy sector.[26] Others pertain to specific geographical regions, such as the North American Free Trade Agreement,[27] whose signatories are the North American states, or the 1987 ASEAN Agreement and its progeny,[28] whose signatories are the South East Asian states.

One framework, however, is global in reach and applies to investments generally, comprising two multilateral arbitration treaties and BITs. To borrow this regime, a post-conflict government may take three steps. First, it should accede to the United Nations Convention on the Recognition and Enforcement of Foreign Arbitral Awards (the New York Convention).[29] Second, it should accede to the International Centre for Settlement of Investment Disputes Convention on the Settlement of Investment Disputes Between States and Nationals of Other States (the ICSID Convention).[30] Both Conventions facilitate investment dispute resolution by mandating the recognition and enforcement of international arbitral awards in the courts of any signatory state. Although their mechanics and scopes of application are different, the two Conventions are complementary. The third step for a post-conflict government is to accede to BITs. Each of these steps will be explained in turn.

The New York Convention. The New York Convention applies to any international arbitral award between a foreign investor and a corporation of the post-conflict state, or indeed, the post-conflict state itself. It does not, however, establish procedures for arbitration, which have to be supplied by a separate contractual arbitration agreement between the investor and its counterpart in the post-conflict state. Such an arbitration agreement, might, for example, provide for arbitration under the auspices of the International Chamber of Commerce (ICC) in Paris.

Once an international arbitration tribunal has issued an award, the winning party may seek enforcement of the award in the courts of any signatory state to the New York Convention. Pursuant to Article 2 of the New York Convention, the post-conflict state, and all other signatories to the convention, are obliged to recognize arbitral awards and enforce them. The only limited exceptions to enforcement, which are contained in Article 5, are for serious procedural defects in the arbitration, or cases where enforcement would "be contrary to the public policy" of the country in which enforcement is sought. The New York Convention itself does not define "public policy,"[31] and some national courts have aggressively declined enforcement by interpreting this exception widely.[32] However, most courts limit the public policy exception to narrow situations where enforcement would violate the forum state's most basic notions of morality and justice.[33] It is safe to say that by signing the New York Convention, any properly-made arbitral award against the post-conflict state after the date of accession to the New York Convention will likely be enforceable against the state.[34]

Returning to the example of Ruritania, once Ruritania has signed the New York Convention, Oro and Alum no longer need to provide for adjudication under New York law in New York courts, since that might put Alum in a disadvantaged situation. Instead, their contact might provide the following governing law and dispute resolution clauses:

Governing Law:
This contract shall be governed exclusively by the laws of England.

Dispute Resolution:
All disputes arising out of or in connection with the present contract shall be finally settled under the Rules of Arbitration of the International Chamber of Commerce by one or more arbitrators appointed in accordance with the said Rules.[35]

If a dispute subsequently arises between Oro and Alum, for example if Oro alleges that Alum failed to make good on their contractual promises to deliver the stipulated amounts of coal or if Alum alleges that Oro failed to produce the amount of electricity it was required to generate, either party may commence an ICC arbitration. Once an arbitral award is rendered, the winning party can enforce the award in the courts of any signatory state in which the losing party has assets, including Ruritania and the United States.[36]

A difficulty may arise, however, if the dispute does not involve a breach by either party, but instead results from the acts of the government of Ruritania. For example, suppose the Ruritanian labor unions launched a successful campaign during an election year protesting the foreign workers that Oro brought in to operate the power plant while Ruritanians remained unemployed. The Ruritanian government, in an effort to placate its electorate, might cancel Oro's license to operate the power plant. In this situation, Alum would have done nothing to breach its contract with Oro. The dispute resolution clause in their contract and the New York Convention would not provide Oro with any investment protection because there is no contractual dispute between Alum and Oro. The party that has injured Oro is the Ruritanian government, but neither the New York Convention nor the contract with Alum provide a legal framework for Oro to seek redress against Ruritania.

The ICSID Convention. The solution to the conundrum of protecting foreign investments from acts of the host state lies partially in the ICSID Convention. This applies only to disputes between a signatory state and a national or corporation of another signatory state.[37] It would therefore apply to a dispute between a foreign investor and the state that hosts the investment, but it would not apply to a dispute between a foreign investor and any corporation of the host state. In the hypothetical discussion of Ruritania, the New York Convention would apply to disputes between Oro and Alum, while the ICSID Convention would apply to disputes between Oro and Ruritania.

The ICSID Convention established ICSID as a Centre for conciliation and arbitration of international investment disputes.[38] Pursuant to Article 25 of the ICSID Convention, the Centre has jurisdiction, that is, authority, over any legal dispute arising out of any investment between a signatory state and the nationals or corporations of another signatory state. The aggrieved party may submit a request for arbitration. A tribunal will then be constituted in accordance with the rules and procedures of the ICSID Convention and its Rules and Regulations. It will adjudicate the dispute by applying the laws agreed by the parties or, in the absence of an agreement, the rules of international law and the laws of the signatory state involved in the dispute.[39]

A dissatisfied litigant may request that an ICSID Annulment Committee review the award. The Committee may set it aside only if the tribunal has manifestly exceeded its powers or committed certain procedural errors.[40] However, these are very narrow grounds to upset the award of a tribunal, and its award is immune from broader appeal.[41] For example, even if the tribunal committed an error of law, its award is nonetheless binding on the parties.[42] Thereafter, the wining party may enforce the award in a court of any signatory state, because Article 54 obliges all signatory states to recognize and enforce ICSID awards.[43]

Bilateral Investment Treaties. The ICSID Convention standing alone is not sufficient to provide legal redress for a foreign investor against a host state. The Convention is only triggered when the investment dispute between a signatory state and an investor of another signatory state is of a legal nature. If there is no legal agreement between a host state and a foreign investor, none of their disputes, no matter how acrimonious, is likely to be a legal dispute. In order for a foreign investor to avail itself of ICSID arbitration, it must have a legal agreement between itself and the host state setting out their mutual obligations. Only then will non-compliance of either party with their undertakings under the agreement be a legal dispute triggering the ICSID Convention.

Broadly speaking, a legal agreement between a host state and a foreign investor may take two forms. First, the agreement may be a specifically negotiated contract between the host state and the investor that contains an ICSID arbitration clause. In our hypothetical discussion of Ruritania, Oro and the government of Ruritania might enter into a concession agreement for the power plant project. This concession agreement might provide that Oro and Alum would incorporate a Ruritanian public utility corporation, OrLum, to sell electricity to the Ruritanian public, and that OrLum would be 90% owned by Oro and 10% owned by Alum. It might provide that Ruritania would grant an exclusive license to OrLum for twenty years to sell electricity in Ruritania. It might also contain an arbitration clause that states:

Dispute Resolution:
> The government of Ruritania and Oro hereby consent to submit to the International Centre for Settlement of Investment Disputes any dispute arising out of or relating to this agreement for settlement by arbitration pursuant to the Convention on the Settlement of Investment Disputes between States and Nationals of Other States.

Should disputes arise between Oro and Ruritania, such a concession agreement would permit either party to obtain an award from an ICSID tribunal resolving the dispute.

Second, the host state and the state of the foreign investor may enter into a BIT that provides legal rights and obligations enforceable under ICSID arbitration. BITs are concluded to promote investment between signatory states. They achieve this objective by prescribing that each state will accord certain protections to the investments of investors from the other state. Additionally, BITs provide that even though the parties to the BITs are states and not their investors, their investors may directly bring arbitration claims against the other state for failures to observe these protections. In this manner, BITs create a legal relationship between a host state and a foreign investor. Should the state fall short of its BIT protections, the investor has a case for a legal dispute before an ICSID arbitration tribunal.

There are now over 2,500 BITs globally. Each BIT is individually negotiated between the two state parties to the BIT. Consequently, there are variations among the BITs in the precise investment protections promised, the scope of investments, and investors protected. However, there is a remarkable uniformity across many of the BITs, partly because some states, such as the United States and Canada, use a model BIT as a baseline document when negotiating BITs with other states.

While an exhaustive survey of all the investment protections found in BITs would be beyond the scope of this chapter, a brief introduction to selected protections provides a flavor of the protections necessary to encourage investors to invest in a host state.[44] Most, if not all BITs, absolutely prohibit a host state from directly expropriating a foreign investment without providing compensation.[45] For example, the Treaty between the United States of America and the Republic of Ecuador concerning the Encouragement and Reciprocal Protection of Investment provides:

> Investments shall not be expropriated or nationalized either directly or indirectly through measures tantamount to expropriation or nationalization ("expropriation") except: for a public purpose; in a nondiscriminatory manner; upon payment of prompt, adequate and effective compensation; and in accordance with due process of law and the general principles of treatment provided for in Article II (3). [. . .]

Direct expropriation refers to the actual dispossession of an investor's property by a state against, for example through nationalization, transfer of title, or outright physical seizure. In *Compañía del Desarrollo de Santa Elena S.A. v. Costa Rica*, Costa Rica issued an expropriation decree for a certain property which CDSE had purchased for the purpose of developing a tourist resort and residential community. The tribunal found that Costa Rica had directly expropriated Santa Elena's investment, and was obligated to pay compensation.[46] According to the tribunal, direct expropriation always triggers an obligation by the state to provide compensation to the investor, even if direct taking for environmental reasons is for a public purpose and legitimate.[47]

Many BITs also prohibit indirect expropriation.[48] In the US-Ecuador BIT cited above, the expropriation provision included indirect expropriation in its instructions that "[i]nvestments shall not be expropriated or nationalized either directly or *indirectly* through measures tantamount to expropriation or nationalization" (emphasis added). Indirect expropriation does not involve the actual taking of property or title; instead, a state may interfere with the use, benefits or value of the investor's property to such an extent that it is tantamount to expropriation.

It is not completely clear, however, whether a state may take regulatory measures that eviscerate an investment and still not be deemed to have expropriated an investment if the measures are for legitimate public purposes, are non-discriminatory, and observe due process. In *Methanex v. United States*, the tribunal rejected Canadian corporation Methanex's indirect expropriation claim under Article 1110 of NAFTA against the United States. The regulation in question was California's ban on a chemical called oxygenate MTBE because it contaminated groundwater. This ban allegedly damaged Methanex's investments in the United States significantly. However, the tribunal explained that this ban did not constitute indirect expropriation because it was made for a public purpose, was non-discriminatory, and was accomplished with due process.[49]

However, the tribunal in *Metalclad v. United Mexican States* appeared to take a different view. In *Metalclad*, Mexico granted a US corporation a landfill concession but subsequently issued an Ecological Decree designating an area encompassing the landfill as a preservation zone for a rare species of cactus. The tribunal found that the decree was tantamount to expropriation and violated Article 1110 of NAFTA. It stated that it "need not decide or consider the motivation or intent of the adoption of the Ecological Decree."[50] This statement seems to suggest that even if the environmental regulation was carried out with a legitimate intent, that intent would not cleanse the regulation of its expropriatory taint.

The tribunal in the August 20, 2007 award of *Compañia de Aguas del Aconquija & Vivendi v. Argentina* seemed to support the *Metalclad* rather than *Methanex* approach to indirect appropriation. The *Vivendi* tribunal suggested, citing only *Santa Elena*, that a state will always have to provide compensation for indirect expropriation even if its actions were for legitimate public purposes. This statement, however, does not necessarily settle the matter. *Santa Elena* concerned direct expropriation, and so the *Vivendi* tribunal's analysis of indirect expropriation was not supported by any directly applicable prior arbitral decision. Moreover, the *Vivendi* tribunal found that the indirect expropriation in *Vivendi* was for illegitimate purposes. Accordingly, to the extent that investment treaty arbitration has a system akin to precedent,[51] one could characterize this *dictum* as *obiter*, i.e., it was not an authoritative pronouncement of the law.

The fair and equitable treatment standard is another investment protection commonly found in BITs.[52] Its precise meaning is however not entirely clear,[53] and will often turn on the actual wording on the BIT provision in question. Nonetheless, three recent arbitral awards suggest that a consensus on the meaning of fair and equitable treatment might be emerging. *Saluka Investments BV v. Czech Republic, Azurix Corp. v. Argentina*, and *LG&E v. Argentina* all concluded that while the standard was highly fact-specific, the host state needed to provide measures that would ensure business and legal stability to attract foreign investments.[54] Additionally, the decisions concluded that a state might be guilty of breaching the standard even if it had acted in good faith.[55]

Admittedly, there are a few outlier awards that seem to indicate a different standard. For example, the tribunal in *Genin v. Estonia* held that the standard only prohibited a "willful neglect of duty, an insufficiency of action falling far below international standards, or even subjective bad faith."[56] However, the *LG&E* and *Saluka* tribunals interpreted *Genin* as holding that bad faith was merely one way in which the standard could be breached, but that bad faith was not a necessary requirement for breach. The *Azurix* tribunal concluded that to the extent that *Genin* imposed a bad faith requirement for breach, this was a minority view, and the tribunal elected to follow the majority view that bad faith was not required. In general, therefore, it could be said that the fair and equitable treatment standard requires a host state to respect the legitimate expectations of the foreign investor regardless of whether the host state acts in good or bad faith.

Returning to our example concerning Ruritania, we may now add a US-Ruritania BIT to the bundle of agreements underlying the power plant project. To recap, Ruritania has acceded to two overarching treaties, the ICSID Convention and the New York Convention. Additionally, there is a joint venture contract between Oro and Alum, a concession agreement between Ruritania and Oro, and a US-Ruritania BIT. Assuming the US-Ruritania BIT to be based on the Model US BIT, it might contain, among several protections, the following provisions:

Article 5: Minimum Standard of Treatment

1. Each Party shall accord to covered investments treatment in accordance with customary international law, including fair and equitable treatment and full protection and security. […]

Article 6: Expropriation and Compensation

1. Neither Party may expropriate or nationalize a covered investment either directly or indirectly through measures equivalent to expropriation or nationalization, except:

(a) for a public purpose;
(b) in a non-discriminatory manner;
(c) on payment of prompt, adequate, and effective compensation; and
(d) in accordance with due process of law and Article 5.

If the Ruritanian government summarily cancelled the concession agreement simply to respond to political pressure in an election year, Oro could commence arbitration against Ruritania under ICSID rules. An ICSID tribunal might find that the summary cancellation of the concession violated the provisions on expropriation and fair and equitable treatment. An award of damages would be enforceable in the courts of any ICSID signatory state, including the courts of Ruritania. If Oro commenced arbitration under a different arbitral system, for example under United Nations Commission on International Trade Law or the ICC, it could still enforce the award under the New York Convention in the courts of any signatory state to the New York Convention. Additionally, should Alum, under pressure from the Ruritanian government, breach its joint venture contract with Oro, Oro could seek arbitration against Alum under that contract and could enforce an arbitral award under the New York Convention.

In this manner, the New York Convention, the ICSID Convention and BITs permit a post-conflict state and foreign investors to resolve disputes by using neutral arbitrators and to enforce the awards in the courts of any signatory state. This international dispute resolution infrastructure avoids the difficulties posed by the legal vacuum in a post-conflict state by borrowing the laws of international arbitration, the legal expertise of arbitrators, the infrastructure of foreign states (since arbitrations can take place anywhere), and the enforcement authority of foreign courts.

Succession to Investment Treaties

A post-conflict government may find that before it came to power, the predecessor state or government had already acceded to the ICSID Convention, the New York Convention and numerous BITs. If this was the case, then a question may arise in the minds of policy-makers and attorneys of the post-conflict state as to whether these treaties continue to bind the post-conflict state. This question of succession to treaties does not yield a simple answer.

Lawyers conventionally distinguish between state and government succession. According to this orthodoxy, government succession occurs when there has only been a radical change in the system of government but not in the metaphysical state itself. The regime change in Iraq would be an example of government succession. State succession occurs when a state has undergone a fundamental change in legal personality or has changed its territory. The dissolution of Yugoslavia into five (now six) states is an example of state succession.

The conventional wisdom is that where government succession occurs the state continues to be bound by its treaties.[57] Certainly, a successor government is free to claim that it is not bound by its predecessor's treaties. However, such a claim would incur tremendous diplomatic costs for the government and no successor government appears to have recently made such a claim. Thus, it remains untested in contemporary practice whether such a claim might succeed.

The situation with state succession is less clear. In every succession, the political pressures are so intense and the facts are so unique that centuries of state practice have not yielded clear customary rules addressing the issue of succession to treaties.[58]

Efforts to regulate this problem with the Vienna Convention on Succession of State in Respect of Treaties of 1978 (the 1978 Convention) have not been very successful. The 1978 Convention has entered into force, but only has nineteen signatories, which does not represent widespread acceptance in the global community of states. Even if a post-conflict state had acceded to the treaty prior to its succession, the treaty would not prescribe an answer to whether it is bound by its predecessor state's investment treaties. For the prescriptions of the 1978 Treaty to govern the state's succession to investment treaties, the successor state must first be bound by the 1978 Treaty. This preliminary question as to whether the successor state is bound by the 1978 Treaty, as a logical matter, cannot be addressed by the 1978 Treaty itself.

As a practical matter, however, in recent decades successor states have tended to accept that BITs to which their predecessor states were parties continue to bind them. After the Czech and Slovak Federal Republic (the CSFR) dissolved into the Czech Republic and Slovakia on December 31, 1992, the Czech Republic confirmed to the Kingdom of the Netherlands that the Netherlands-CSFR BIT remained in force between the Netherlands the Czech Republic.[59] After the Soviet Union dissolved, the Russian Federation issued a note to the diplomatic missions in Moscow stating that it would honor the treaty obligations of the Soviet Union.[60]

Where investment disputes have been submitted to arbitration, successor states do not appear to have challenged claims that BITs signed by their predecessor states continued to bind the successor state.[61] Accordingly, tribunals have assumed or asserted that pre-existing BITs were not terminated upon succession.[62]

This trend to accept the continuity of BITs in spite of succession may indicate that successor states recognize the benefits of BITs, the tremendous costs of disrupting the pre-existing international investment infrastructure, and the risks of undermining investor confidence by abandoning pre-existing BITs. Should a post-conflict government discover that its predecessor government had already entered into BITs, the ICSID Convention, or the New York Convention, the post-conflict government should seriously weigh the costs of rejecting any of these treaties before deciding whether to renounce them.

Risk Assessment

A post-conflict state reaps benefits by borrowing international investment law. Providing a stable legal framework for investment is a key requirement for investment.[63] The international investment legal regime provides such a framework when a post-conflict state is unable to do so in the aftermath of conflict. According to a 2005 World Bank report on Afghanistan, consistency and predictability in government acts are additional factors to attract foreign investment.[64] The international investment legal regime also stabilizes government action by binding the post-conflict government to international investment protection standards.

Just as a borrower who takes a loan benefits from the loan but also incurs costs, there are costs involved when a post-conflict state borrows international investment law. In order to attract foreign investment, the state has to persuade investors that it will not take actions that will damage the investments. Investors require a state to legally promise that within reason, it will protect the regulatory framework within which the investment is situated. They also require a state to subject itself to the scrutiny of independent tribunals, which will have the power and authority to enforce these promises. The international legal framework for investments, comprising the ICSID Convention, New York Convention, BITs and investment contracts, provides investors with these assurances. The cost of this framework to a post-conflict state is its loss of authority to take regulatory actions over some sovereign matters.

A calculation of these costs may not be straightforward. As regards the New York Convention, there is in fact only a limited downside in acceding to it. The post-conflict state's accession to the New York Convention is principally for its benefit rather than for the foreign investor's. Article 14 of the New York Convention provides that only a signatory state to the Convention is entitled to avail itself of it, and only to the extent that it is itself bound by the Convention. Assuming that the investor's state is already a party to the New York Convention – and there are currently 141 signatory states, including most of the developed states – the investor may seek enforcement of an arbitral award against the post-conflict state or corporations of the post-conflict state in any of the signatory states. This course of action is available to the investor regardless of whether the post-conflict state is a party to the New York Convention. Suppose, however, that the post-conflict state or its corporations prevails in an arbitration brought against a foreign investor or in an arbitration brought by a foreign investor, the post-conflict state may not enforce that award in a foreign court under the New York Convention unless the post-conflict state is a party to the New York Convention.

The only situation in which a post-conflict state might give up a relative advantage by acceding to the New York Convention is if the state and its corporations do not have assets in any signatory state. In such a situation, an arbitral award against the state or its corporations cannot be meaningfully enforced overseas as there are no assets that may be seized. The only meaningful enforcement will be in the courts of the post-conflict state, and by signing up to the New York Convention, the state's courts become obliged under international law to recognize and enforce arbitral awards against the state or corporations in the state.

This situational advantage, if it exists, is not likely to last long. For the post-conflict state to build its economy, it will need to open its economy to foreign markets. The practicalities of doing business require the state and its corporations to establish foreign bank accounts to pay for goods and services from overseas. Overseas bank accounts may facilitate payments by foreign entities for the state's exports, be they tribal crafts, agricultural products, or oil. Corporations in the post-conflict state may need to establish foreign subsidiaries. Very soon, the post-conflict state and its corporations will have assets overseas and will no longer be able to shield these assets from attachment in foreign courts. At that time, there would be little incentive to refuse accession to the New York Convention.

As regards BITs and the ICSID Convention, the post-conflict state does not give up all its authority over sovereign matters. In some situations, a state may take many regulatory actions so long as they are carried out with due process, in good faith, and for public purposes. As discussed earlier, in *Methanex*, the United States did not violate its NAFTA investment protection obligations even though California's environmental regulation affected the investments of a foreign corporation, in part because the ban was for a legitimate public purpose and was issued in good faith and with due process.

States have another argument to shield their regulatory acts from an obligation to provide compensation. They may argue that an investment obligation takes on a different hue depending on the context of a state's development. In *Genin*, Estonia revoked a foreign investor's banking license for failures to comply with requests for information. The tribunal found that Estonia had not violated the US-Estonia BIT because, *inter alia*, "the circumstances of political and economic transition prevailing in Estonia at that time justified [Estonia's actions]."[65] Although *Genin* may increasingly be regarded as an outlier award, this statement does appear to suggest that a post-conflict state may be allowed to take some actions that a developed state is not allowed.

A state may also raise the necessity defense for acts that would otherwise violate its BIT obligations. The necessity defense completely absolves a state under customary law for actions that would otherwise have breached an investment treaty obligation. Article 25 of the Articles of State Responsibility provides that a state may assert the necessity defense to an alleged breach of an international obligation if four conditions are met:

(1) The act is the only way to safeguard an essential interest against a grave and imminent peril;
(2) The act does not seriously impair an essential interest of the state towards which the obligation exists;
(3) The obligation does not exclude the possibility of invoking necessity; and
(4) The state has not contributed to the situation of necessity.

Similarly, but perhaps not identically, BITs may contain emergency clauses under which a state may shelter. For example, Article XI of the US-Argentina BIT provides:

"This Treaty shall not preclude the application by either Party of measures necessary for the maintenance of public order, the fulfillment of its obligations with respect to the maintenance or restoration of international peace or security, or the protection of its own essential security interests."

A post-conflict government should, however, critically examine whether an act it is considering taking would successfully avoid the duty to provide compensation to an investor. While it can easily avail itself of the defenses described above, it may be more difficult to divine with certainty whether these defenses will succeed in arbitration.

The argument that investment protection obligations are contextual is a double-edged sword. An investor may attack a post-conflict state's regulatory actions by arguing that certain regulatory actions deemed permissible in a highly regulated developed state may be unavailable to a post-conflict state. In *Methanex*, among several reasons the tribunal gave for its decision to reject Methanex's indirect expropriation claim was Methanex's awareness of and participation in the "notorious" US political process that ultimately resulted in the regulation in question.[66] Might an investor in a future dispute invoke this statement to argue that an unregulated state has less latitude to subsequently protect its environment than a highly-regulated state, because an investor in an unregulated state may legitimately have been blissfully unaware that the state might subsequently become more highly regulated?

The scope of the necessity defense is also not fully demarcated. For example, it is not entirely clear whether the necessity defense or an emergency clause in a BIT will extend to economic measures to avert a financial crisis. On one hand, the *CMS Gas Transmission Co. v. Argentina* and *Enron and Ponderossa Assets v. Argentina* awards, which concerned compensation for Argentina's financial measures pursuant to the US-Argentina BIT, stated that such provisions did not apply in their respective disputes,[67] although the *CMS* tribunal did suggest that in other situations economic necessity might well provide a defense.[68] On the other hand, the *LG&E* award, concerning virtually identical measures by Argentina, responding to the same crisis and implicating the same BIT, stated that economic necessity did excuse Argentina from liability.[69]

Another issue is whether or not an emergency clause is self-judging. If it is self-judging, then a state may decide for itself whether its actions were justified. A tribunal may consequently be limited to an inquiry into whether the state made its determination in good faith. If it is not self-judging, a tribunal may substantively examine whether a state's actions were in fact the only means available to avert a national disaster. This is a question of treaty interpretation on which eminent minds might reasonably differ. In the *Enron* dispute, Dean Anne-Marie Slaughter argued in her expert opinion that the emergency clause in the US-Argentina BIT was self-judging,[70] whereas Professor Jose Alvarez took the opposite view.[71]

The risks that a state assumes by taking actions that injure foreign investments are magnified because international investment treaty arbitration does not, at least formally, have a system of precedent binding tribunals to awards of prior tribunals that decided a relevant issue of law.[72] Tribunals do tend to canvass prior awards for persuasive statements that will help them interpret the particular BIT at issue, and many tribunals cite prior awards to support their decisions.[73] However, arbitrators have been known to reach opposite findings in similar disputes. Judge Francisco Rezek sat on the *LG&E* and *CMS* tribunals which reached opposite results, and Professor Albert van den Berg sat on the *LG&E* and *Enron* tribunals, which also reached opposite results. *Lauder v. Czech Republic* absolved the Czech Republic of a duty under the US-Czech Republic BIT to provide compensation to a foreign investor for taking regulatory actions that damaged his telecommunications investment, while *CME v. Czech Republic* awarded damages against the Czech Republic in the very same dispute under a different BIT that had similarly worded provisions.[74] In each of the awards, the tendency for tribunals to survey prior awards was scant consolation to the host state.

Policy Recommendations

Given the risks and benefits of borrowing the international legal framework for FDI, post-conflict states should engage in a careful analysis of not just whether to borrow this framework, but how to borrow and what parts to borrow. Policy-makers can modulate their risks through five strategies: circumscription, clarification, communication, control, and compensation.

Circumscription

A post-conflict government may circumscribe investment protections when negotiating investment agreements. It should tailor the level of protections it promises to the types of investment it hopes to attract and its particular stage of development during the lifetime of the investment agreements. A post-conflict government in an undeveloped state with residual opposition from tribal warlords struggling to rebuild its agrarian economy is unlikely to be overly concerned with carbon emissions from fossil fuels, but might well be concerned about maintaining public security. In such a situation, it may be less important for that government to retain in its BITs its rights to environmental regulation, but critically important to explicitly retain the right to take security measures that might hurt a foreign investment, such as curfews that effectively shut down the investor's factories until peace is restored.

If the post-conflict government is trying to rebuild an economy that is almost completely destroyed, its immediate priority might be to secure micro-financing to support farms and tribal crafts, rather than large scale infrastructure projects such as power plants or super highways. Smaller investment projects cost less and may require lower returns over a shorter period of time to be profitable for the foreign investor. Accordingly, such an investor may be willing to accept weaker protections, or BIT or investment agreements with sunset provisions that terminate the agreements after a number of years.

By comparison, larger projects that involve high capital outlays, such as the construction of large tourist resorts or oil refineries, will require stable returns over a longer period of time. If it is such projects that the post-conflict state hopes to attract, then it may need to voluntarily cede its regulatory authority for more years or decades under its BITs and investment agreements.

Clarification

After a post-conflict state has determined what investment protections to circumscribe according to its economic objectives, it should clarify in investment agreements the limits of its investment protection obligations. The international legal framework for FDI is essentially contractual. As a party to BITs and investment contracts with investors, a state is free to negotiate terms that preserve its authority over sovereign matters and, if necessary, promise an investor greater concessions to account for any corresponding increases in risks that the investor has to consequently bear. For example, the United States Model BIT clarifies in an Annex that under that a BIT, non-discriminatory measures generally do not constitute expropriation if they are taken to protect public welfare objectives, including "public health, safety, and the environment."[75] A post-conflict government should similarly clarify its rights in the BITs it negotiates.

Communication

A corollary to clarification of obligations within investment agreements is communication outside of those agreements. A post-conflict government should communicate to investors, before investment agreements are finalized, the level and types of regulation that it anticipates having to take during the time period of the investment project. It may do so in official statements by government officials in public, or in letters to investors. In this fashion, an investor will be able to properly account for political and regulatory risks when making a business decision whether to invest. If it does invest with knowledge of potential regulatory actions in the future, it will be more difficult for it to complain that the post-conflict government failed to protect its legitimate expectations and should provide compensation when those regulatory acts are eventually taken.

Control

Importantly, before a post-conflict government makes investment protection commitments, it must judge with a suitably jaundiced eye whether it is able to control both government and non-government actors to ensure that they do not unlawfully harm foreign investments. A post-conflict government must exert sufficient control on its instrumentalities and sub-divisions, such as municipal bureaucrats and regulatory agencies. If government officials are open to corruption, or reject the central authority of the government, there is a risk that they may cancel concessions or take other measures that harm foreign investments and place the post-conflict government in breach of its investment protection promises.

A post-conflict government must also train a functioning security force to control religious extremists and separatists in rural areas.[76] Failure to control such non-government actors risks exposing foreign investments to physical damage by militias and incurring liabilities for the government under investment agreements.

Compensation

If, in spite of circumscription, clarification, communication and control, a post-conflict government subsequently discovers that it must take certain actions to neutralize unanticipated threats to the state, it always has the right to expropriate and provide compensation to the investor for its losses.[77] Thus, if a post-conflict state calculates that its priority is to take actions to protect an essential state interest even if those actions will damage a foreign investment, it may repurchase its right to do so by paying compensation to the investor.[78] If borrowing the international legal framework for FDI is like taking a loan, then restrictions on certain state actions are merely covenants from which a state may be released by paying the investor the value of its investments.

The payment of compensation to the investor does not have to occur contemporaneously with the host state's act for an essential public purpose. A state may act first and wait for the investor to complain of its injury before entering into negotiations about compensation. Those negotiations may last for months, or years, and if arbitration occurs, the delay in compensation may stretch into yet more years. Should a settlement be eventually reached or an award be rendered, the state may have to pay interest to soothe the investor for the delay in receiving compensation. However, when a post-conflict government is contemplating an injurious state act, it may consider its current financial state and its projected economic development and conclude that it is rational to delay compensation – even with interest accruing to the investor – until a later time when it anticipates fuller coffers.

Borrowing the international legal framework for FDI is not the panacea for the economic problems that a post-conflict government may face. However, if its domestic legal system is damaged to such an extent that it is not operational, borrowing law may be the best alternative to provide investors with a stable legal foundation on which to build their investment projects. While the international legal framework requires a post-conflict government to voluntarily relinquish some sovereign authority, the essentially contractual nature of this framework provides a post-conflict government with the latitude to decide when to give up its authority, what it will give up, and when to seize it back. These business decisions should be calculated to court foreign investors that the post-conflict state desires.

Notes

1   This chapter was discussed at the Sarah Lawrence College International Law Seminar, at which the title was suggested. Stuart Barden, Brian Kocharsarli, Anthony Kohtio, Robert Trisotto, and Brian Rypkema provided research assistance.

2   *See* United Nations Conference on Trade and Development [hereinafter UNCTAD], *International Investment Agreements: Flexibility for Development*, UNCTAD/ITE/IIT/18 at 11 (2000) [hereinafter *International Investment Agreements*]. ("Development is a fundamental objective of developing countries and has generally been accepted as a goal of the international community as a whole.").

3   UNCTAD, Sept. 24–25, 2007, *Best Practices for Creating an Environment Conducive to Development, Growth and Investment*, ¶ 40, TD/B/COM.2/EM.22/2 (Aug. 8, 2007); Rob Mills & Qimiao Fan, Investment Climate Capacity Enhancement Program, The World Bank Institute, *Policy Research Working Paper: The Investment Climate in Post-Conflict Siutations* at 1, WPS4055 (Nov. 2006).

4   UNCTAD, *Foreign Direct Investment and Development*, UNCTAD/ITE/IIT/10 (vol.1) at 46 (1999).

5 *See, e.g.*, Benard Hoekman & Simeon Djankov, The World Bank, *Policy Research Working Paper: Intra-Industry Trade, Foreign Direct Investment and the Reorientation of Eastern European Exports*, WPS1652 at 23 (Sept. 1996) (noting "conventional wisdom" that export growth in the automobile sector in the Visegrad countries was associated with FDI); Bernard Hoekman & Simeon Djankov, The World Bank, *Policy Research Working Paper: Foreign Investment and Productivity Growth in Czech Enterprises, Summary Findings*, WPS2115 at 20 (May 1999) (noting that firm level data for the Czech Republic suggested that FDI has a positive impact on the firm's growth).

6 *See, e.g.*, Joshua Robbins, *The Emergence of Positive Obligations in Bilateral Investment Treaties*, 13 University of Miami International & Comparative Law Review. 403, 408 (2006) (explaining how FDI contributes to growth).

7 *See, e.g., Policy Research Working Paper: Intra-Industry Trade, Foreign Direct Investment and the Reorientation of Eastern European Exports*, supra note 5, at 23 (noting that for some Eastern European states, "the importance of FDI more generally has not been determined).

8 *See, e.g., Policy Research Working Paper: Foreign Investment and Productivity Growth in Czech Enterprises*, supra note 5, at 2 ("What matters for economic growth are the spillovers [of FDI] to other firms within and across industries").

9 *See generally International Investment Agreements* at 11-15 (describing "policy and normative framework" necessary to attract FDI, but also emphasizing that "economic factors are the principal determinants of FDI flows").

10 Jennifer Tobin & Susan Rose-Ackerman, *When BITs Have Some Bite: The Political-Economic Environment for Bilateral Investment Treaties* at 31 (Nov. 14, 2006) (on file with Yale Law School) ("A stronger political environment and a better local economic environment are complements to BITs.").

11 J. Salacuse & N. Sullivan, "Do BITs Really Work? An Evaluation of Bilateral Investment Treaties and Their Grand Bargain", 46 *Harvard International Law Journal 67* (2005); E. Neumayer & L. Spess, *Do bilateral investment treaties increase foreign direct investment to developing countries?*, Working paper, London School of Economics. London (2004).

12 M. Hallward-Driemeier, *Do Bilateral Investment Treaties Attract FDI? Only a bit...and they could bite*, World Bank Policy Research Working Paper No. 3121 (June 2003).

13 *See* Jennifer Tobin & Susan Rose-Ackerman (note 10).

14 *Cf., id.* at 31 ("Poor countries cannot bootstrap an aggressive program of signing BITs into a major increase in FDI. They cannot avoid the hard work of improving their own domestic environment as it affects the political risks of investment.").

15 *See, e.g., Investment Horizons: Afghanistan* 26 (The Multilateral Investment Guarantee Agency of the World Bank Group, Working Paper No. 34444, 2005) ("Most investors suggest that enforcing contracts is virtually impossible in Afghanistan, and the judicial system is regarded as inadequate and vulnerable to corruption.").

16 *See* Tai-Heng Cheng, *Power, Authority and International Investment Law,* 20 American University International Law Review 465, 500 (2005); Salacuse & Sullivan, supra note 11 at 75 (discussing the interests of foreign investors in host states).

17 *See, e.g., Borden, Inc. v. Meiji Milk Products Co.,* 919 F.2d 822 (2d. Cir. 1991).

18 *See, e.g., Banco do Commercio e Industria de Sao Paolo S.A. v. Esusa Engenharia e Construcoes, S.A.,* 173 A.D.2d 340 (N.Y. App. Div. 1991); *Crédit Français International, S. A. v. Sociedad Financiera de Comercio, C. A.,* 128 Misc. 2d 564 (N.Y. Sup. Ct. 1985).

19 *See* Anthony Hope, The Prisoner of Zenda (1894); Anthony Hope, The Heart of Princess Osra (1896); Anthony Hope, Rupert of Hentzau (1898).

20 N.Y. Gen. Oblig. L. § 5-1402.

21 Memorandum of Legislative Representative of City of New York, 1984 McKinney's Session Laws of New York; *see also* Credit Francais Int'l, S. A., 128 Misc. 2d at 570 ("New York, as the center of international trade and finance, has expressly recognized, as a service to the business community, that its courts will be hospitable to the resolution of all substantial contractual disputes in which

the parties have agreed beforehand that our neutrality and expertise should govern their relationships.").

22   *Id.*

23   *See* 28 U.S.C. § 1605(a) (providing that sovereign immunity can be waived); *see, e.g., Commercial Corp. Sovrybflot v Corporacion de Fomento de La Produccion*, 980 F. Supp. 710 (S.D.N.Y. 1997) (holding that a foreign state shall not be immune from the jurisdiction of the courts if the foreign state has waived its immunity either explicitly or by implication); *Texas Trading & Milling Corp. v. Federal Republic of Nigeria*, 647 F.2d 300 (2d Cir. 1981) (holding that a foreign state shall not be immune from the jurisdiction of the courts if the foreign state's action is based upon a commercial activity within the scope of 28 U.S.C. § 1605(a)).

24   *See Mitsubishi Motors Corp. v. Soler Chrysler-Plymouth, Inc.*, 473 U.S. 614, 659 (1985) (holding that if an arbitration award is contrary to the public policy of a country called upon to enforce it the Convention on the Recognition and Enforcement of Foreign Arbitral Awards does not require it be enforced).

25   *See* William W. Park, *International Forum Selection 8-9*, 13 (1995) (discussing common concern about the home-court advantage in litigation); *see also* 3 Jonathan Elliot, *The Debates in the Several State Conventions on the Adoption of the Federal Constitution* 583 (Philadelphia, Lippincott 2d ed. 1876) (citing James Madison stating, "We well know, sir, that foreigners cannot get justice done them in these [state] courts"). *But see* Kevin M. Clermont & Theodore Eisenberg, *Xenophilia in American Courts*, 109 Harvard Law Review 1120 (1996) (finding no evidence to support the proposition that there is a bias against foreigners in American courts).

26   Energy Charter Treaty, Dec. 17, 1994, 34 I.L.M. 360 (1995); *see* Energy Charter Secretariat, *Energy Charter Treaty and Related Documents*, 3 (2004) ("The Energy Charter Treaty is a unique instrument for the promotion of international cooperation in the energy sector.").

27   North American Free Trade Agreement, U.S.-Can.-Mex., Dec. 17, 1992, 32 I.L.M. 289 (1993).

28   ASEAN Agreement for the Promotion and Protection of Investments, Dec. 15, 1987, 27 I.L.M. 612 (1988); *see also* Protocol to Amend the Agreement for the Promotion and Protection of Investments, Jakarta, Sept. 12, 1996; Framework

Agreement on the ASEAN Investment Area, Makati, The Philippines, Oct. 7, 1998.

29   U.N. Convention on the Recognition and Enforcement of Foreign Arbitral Awards, 330 U.N.T.S. 1 [hereinafter New York Convention].

30   Convention on the Settlement of Investment Disputes between States and Nationals of Other States, Mar. 18, 1965, 575 U.N.T.S. 159 [hereinafter ICSID Convention].

31   *See* New York Convention, art. V(2)(b), 330 U.N.T.S. 38; *Parsons & Whittemore Overseas Co., Inc. v. Societe Generale De L'Industrie Du Papier*, 508 F.2d 969, 973 (2d. 1974) ("The legislative history of the provision offers no certain guidelines to its construction. Its precursors in the Geneva Convention and the 1958 Convention's ad hoc committee draft extended the public policy exception to, respectively, awards contrary to 'principles of the law' and awards violative of 'fundamental principles of the law.'").

32   *See, e.g., Termorio S.A. E.S.P. v. Electranta S.P.*, 487 F.3d 928 (D.D.C. 2007) (refusing to enforce an arbitration award that was set aside by the highest administrative court in Columbia because it violated public policy); *Fotochrome, Inc. v. Copal Co., Ltd.*, 517 F.2d 512, 516 (2d. Cir. 1975); *M & C Corp. v. Erwin Behr GmbH & Co., KG*, 87 F.3d 844, 851, n. 2 (6th Cir. 1996); *Termorio S.A. E.S.P. v. Electranta S.P.*, 487 F.3d 928, 937-939 (D.D.C. 2007); *see also Stawski Distributing Co., Inc. v. Zywiec Breweries PLC*, 2004 WL 2222277, slip op. at 2 (N.D. Ill. 2004) (examining the scope of Article V(2)(b) of the New York Convention).

33   *Parsons & Whittemore Overseas Co., Inc. v. Societe Generale De L'Industrie Du Papier*, 508 F.2d 969, 974 (2d. Cir. 1974) ("Enforcement of foreign arbitral awards may be denied on this basis only where enforcement would violate the forum state's most basic notions of morality and justice.").

34   *See Karaha Bodas Co., L.L.C. v. Perusahaan Pertambangan Minyak Dan Gas Bumi Negara*, 364 F.3d 274 (5th Cir. 2004) (enforcing a Swiss arbitration award against an Indonesian government owned company).

35   *See* International Chamber of Commerce, the standard ICC arbitration clause, *available at* http://www.iccwbo.org/court/english/arbitration/model_clause.asp (last visited Oct. 30, 2007).

36   *Karaha Bodas Co., L.L.C. v. Perusahaan Pertambangan Minyak Dan Gas Bumi Negara*, 364 F.3d 274 (5th Cir. 2004) (enforcing an arbitration and arbitral awards in the United States).

37   *See* ICSID, ICSID Convention, Regulations and Rules, ICSID Doc. ICSID/15 (April 2006).

38   ICSID, ICSID Convention, Regulations and Rules art. 1, ICSID Doc. ICSID/15 (April 2006).

39   *See* ICSID, ICSID Convention, Regulations and Rules art. 42, ICSID Doc. ICSID/15 (April 2006); International Bank for Reconstruction & Development, Report of the Executive Directors on the Convention on the Settlement of In-vestment Disputes Between States and Nationals of Other States at 40 (2006).

40   *See* ICSID Convention art. 52 (1) (stating limited grounds for annulment); *see also Mitchell (Patrick) v. Democratic Republic of the Congo*, ICSID (W. Bank) Case No. ARB/99/7 (2004) (annulling award); *Compania de Aguas del Aconquija S.A. and Vivendi Universal v. Argentine Republic*, ICSID (W. Bank) Case No. ARB/97/3, PP 95-98 (2002) (partially annulling award); *Kloeckner GmbH. v. United Republic of Cameroon*, ICSID (W. Bank) Case No. ARB/81/2, (1986) (annulling award); *Amco Asia Corp. v. Republic of Indonesia*, ICSID (W. Bank) Case No. ARB/81/1, (1986) (annulling award).

41   *See BRIDAS S.A.I.P.C. et al. v. Turkmenistan*, 447 F.3d 441 (5th Cir. 2006) (denying annulment); *Feldman v. Mexico*, ICSID (W. Bank) Case No. ARB/99/1 (2005) (denying annulment); *CDC Group Plc. v. Republic of the Seychelles*, ICSID (W. Bank) Case No. ARB/02/14 (2003) (denying annulment); *CME Czech Republic B.V. v. Czech Republic*, UNCITRAL (2003) (denying annulment); *Wena Hotels Ltd. v. Arab Republic of Egypt*, ICSID (W. Bank) Case No. ARB/98/4 (2002) (denying an-nulment).

42   *See CMS Gas Transmission Company v. Argentine Republic*, Annulment Committee Decision, ICSID (W.Bank) Case No. ARB/01/8 (2007).

43   ICSID, ICSID Convention, Regulations and Rules art. 54, ICSID Doc. ICSID/15 (April 2006).

44   For more detailed discussions of BIT investment protections, see UNCTAD Series on International Investment Policies for Development, Tokyo, Japan, Sept.

1-2, 2005. *International Investment Arrangements: Trends and Emerging Issues*, UNCTAT/ITE/IIT/2005/11 (2006); UNCTAD, *International Investment Agreements: Key Issues*, Vols. I-III; *See also* Andrew T. Guzman, "Why LDCs Sign Treaties That Hurt Them: Explaining the Popularity of Bilateral Investment Treaties", 38 *Virginia Journal of International Law* 639 (1998); Patrick Juillard, "Direct Investment: MAI: A European View, 31 *Cornell International Law Journal* 477 (1998); Kenneth J. Vandevelde, "Investment Liberalization and Economic Development: The Role of Bilateral Investment Treaties", 36 *Columbia Journal of Transnational Law* 501 (1998); Kenneth J. Vandevelde, "The Economics of Bilateral Investment Treaties", 41 *Harvard International Law Journal* 469 (2000).

[45] *See, e.g.,* Agreement Between the Government of the Czech and Slovak Federal Republic and the Government of the People's Republic of China for the Promotion and Reciprocal Protection of Investments, Czech-China, art. 4, Dec. 1991; Treaty between the United States of America and the Republic of Ecuador concerning the Encouragement and Reciprocal Protection of Investment, Unites States-Ecuador, art. 3, Aug. 27, 1993; Agreement between the Government of Australia and the Government of the Republic of India on the Promotion and Protection of Investments, Australia-India, art. 7, Feb. 26,1999.

[46] *Compañía del Desarrollo de Santa Elena, S.A. v. Republic of Costa Rica, Award*, ICSID Case No. ARB/96/1 (Feb. 17, 2000) ¶ 111.

[47] *Id.* at ¶ 68; *see also, Compania de Aguas del Aconquija & Vivendi v. Argentina,* Award, ICSID Case No. ARB/97/3 (Aug. 20, 2007) ¶ 7.5.21 ("As the tribunal in *Santa Elena* correctly pointed out, the purpose for which the property was taken 'does not alter the legal character of the taking for which adequate compensation must be paid.'").

[48] *See, e.g.,* Treaty between the United States of America and the Republic of Ecuador concerning the Encouragement and Reciprocal Protection of Investment, U.S.-Ecuador, Art. 3 § 1, Aug. 27; Treaty between the United States and the Argentine Republic on the Reciprocal Encouragement of Protection of Investment, U.S.-Arg., Art. 3 § 1 Nov. 14, 1991.

[49] *Methanex v. United States of America*, Award, U.N. Commission on International Trade Law ("UNCITRAL") (Aug. 3, 2005), Part IV, Ch.D, at 5.

[50] *Metalclad Corp. v. United Mexican States*, Award, ICSID Case No. ARB (AF)/97/1 (Aug. 30, 2000), ¶ 111; *set aside in part on other grounds*, 2001 B.C.S.C. 664.

51   *See generally*, Tai-Heng Cheng, "Precedent and Control in Investment Treaty Arbitration", 30 Fordham International Law Journal 1014 (2007) (discussing whether there is a system of precedent in investment treaty arbitration).

52   *See, e.g.*, Convention Establishing the Multilateral Investment Guarantee Agency, art. 12(d)(iv), Oct. 11, 1985, 24 I.L.M. 1605; NAFTA, art. 1105; *see also* International Investment Agreements at 54 (citing BITs that impose a fair and equitable treatment standard on host states).

53   *See* UNCTAD, Bilateral Investment Treaties in the Mid-1990s, at 30, U.N. Doc. UNCTAD/ITE/IIT/7.

54   *Saluka Investments BV v. Czech Republic*, Partial Award, Permanent Court of Arbitration, ¶ 61-66 (March 17, 2006); Azurix Corp. v. Argentina, Award, ICSID Case No. ARB/01/12, ¶ 129-136 (July 14, 2006); *LG&E v. Argentina*, ICSID Case No. ARB/02/1, ¶ 29-42 (Oct. 3, 2006).

55   *Id.*

56   *Alex Genin, Eastern Credit Ltd., Inc. & A.S. Baltoil v. The Republic of Estonia*, Award, ICSID Case No. ARB/99/2 (June 25, 2001).

57   *See generally* Tai-Heng Cheng, *State Succession and Commercial Obligations* [State Succession] (2006); Tai-Heng Cheng, *Renegotiating the Doctrine of Odious Debt*, 71 *Duke Law & Contemp. Probs.* (forthcoming 2007).

58   *See* Tai-Heng Cheng, *State Succession and Commercial Obligations* 4 (2006); Oscar Schachter, "State Succession: The Once and Future Law", 33 *Virginia Journal of International Law* 253, 259 (1993) (stating, in the context of succession, that "particularities call for avoiding rigidities and for taking into account of context in specific cases").

59   *Saluka Investments BV v. Czech Republic*, Partial Award, Permanent Court of Arbitration, ¶ 31 (March 17, 2006).

60   *Sedelmayer v. Russian Federation*, slip op. at 17, (July 7, 1998), available at: http://www.iisd.org/pdf/ 2004/investment_sedelmayer_v_ru.pdf.

61   *Saluka Investments BV v. Czech Republic*, ¶ 31 (noting Czech Republic's acceptance of preexisting BIT); *Sedelmayer v. Russian Federation*, at 17 (noting claimants as-

sertion that BIT at issue bound Russia because Russia had sent a diplomatic note to foreign embassies in Moscow accepting all treaties of the Soviet Union).

[62] *Saluka Investments BV v. Czech Republic,* ¶ 31 (stating that tribunal accepted that BIT remained in force because neither party denied its continuity in spite of succession); *Sedelmayer v. Russian Federation,* 63 (not discussing issues of succession and assuming BIT remained in force); *CME Czech Republic B.V. v. Czech Republic,* UNCITRAL Arbitration, ¶ 3 (asserting, without providing reasons, that BIT remained in force in spite of succession) (Mar. 14, 2003); *Lauder v. Czech Republic,* UNCITRAL Arbitration, (assuming, without stating or discussing, that BIT remained in force in spite of succession) (Sept. 3, 2001).

[63] *See, e.g.,* World Bank, *The Investment Climate in Afghanistan: Exploiting Opportunities in an Uncertain Environment,* at 24 (December 2005).

[64] *Id.* at 26.

[65] *Genin v. Republic of Estonia,* Award, ICSID Case No. ARB/99/2, ¶ 370 (June 25, 2001).

[66] *Methanex v. United States of America,* U.N. Commission on International Trade Law ("UNCITRAL") Arbitration, pt. IV, ch. D, p. 5, ¶¶ 9-10 (Aug. 3, 2005), available at: http://www.state.gov/documents/organization/51052.pdf.

[67] *CMS Gas Transmission Co. v. Argentina,* ICSID Case No. ARB/01/08, ¶¶ 354–55 (May 12, 2005); *Enron and Ponderossa Assets v. Argentina,* ICSID Case No. ARB/01/3, ¶339 (May 22, 2007).

[68] *CMS v. Argentina,* ICSID Case No. ARB/01/08, ¶ 354 (May 12, 2005).

[69] *LG&E v. Argentina,* ICSID Case No. ARB/02/1, ¶ 266 (Oct. 3, 2006).

[70] *Enron v. Argentina,* ICSID Case No. ARB/01/3, ¶ 324 (May 22, 2007).

[71] *Id.* at ¶ 328.

[72] Statute of International Court of Justice, June 26, 1945, art. 59, 59 Stat. 1031.

73 Tai-Heng Cheng, "Chinese Law in the Global Context: Precedent and Control in Investment Treaty Arbitration", 30 *Fordham International Law Journal* 1014, 1030–31 (2007).

74 *Lauder v. Czech Republic*, UNCITRAL Arbitration, ¶ 308–09 (Sept. 3, 2001), available at: http://www.investmentclaims.com/decisions/Lauder-Czech-Final Award-3Sept2001.pdf; *CME Czech Republic B.V. v. Czech Republic*, UNCITRAL Arbitration, ¶ 650 (Mar. 14, 2003), available at: http://www.investmentclaims.com/decisions/CME-Czech-FinalAward-14Mar2003.pdf.

75 U.S. Model Bilateral Investment Treaty, Annex B, ¶ 4(b), *available at* http://www.state.gov/documents/organization/38710.pdf.

76 *See Asian Agricultural Products Ltd. V. Sri Lanka*, ICSID Case No. ARB/87/3, ¶ 72 (June 27, 1990) (finding Sri Lanka responsible to investor for takings by militias).

77 *See, e.g.*, Agreement Between the Government of the Czech and Slovak Federal Republic and the Government of the People's Republic of China for the Promotion and Reciprocal Protection of Investments, Czech-China, art. 4, Dec. 1991; Agreement between the Government of Australia and the Government of the Republic of India on the Promotion and Protection of Investments, Australia-India, art. 7, Feb. 26, 1999; Agreement between the Government of the Arab Republic of Egypt and the Government of Kazakhstan on the Promotion and Protection of Investment, art. 4, Feb. 14, 1993.

78 *See* Tai-Heng Cheng, "Power, Authority and International Investment Law", 20 *American University International Law Review* 465 (2005) (discussing how states may regain sovereign authority by paying compensation to investors for sovereign acts that breach BITs).

Chapter 4

ICSID Jurisdiction and the Legal Security of Foreign Investment in Post-Conflict Countries

Virtus C. Igbokwe

Introduction

This Chapter critically evaluates the dispute settlement provisions in the Investment Codes[1] of the Democratic Republic of Congo (DRC), Sierra Leone and Liberia.

Recent years have seen the end of conflicts in those three countries. Backed by the World Bank and its affiliates such as the Multilateral Investment Guarantee Agency,[2] and international Non-Governmental Organizations (NGOs), these states have embarked on post-conflict reconstruction and nation-building. In this regard, they have intensified efforts to shift from aid-dependent to investment-driven post-conflict reconstruction.

The benefits of foreign direct investment (FDI) cannot be overemphasized. FDI brings much needed private capital, modern technology, new skills, and stimulation of local spin-off industries. Indeed, the job opportunities flowing from FDI in post-conflict states will be of vital importance in achieving long-term economic and political stability.

For a prospective foreign investor, there are many investment opportunities in post-conflict states – rebuilding of basic infrastructure such as telecommunication networks, roads, railways, water systems and rehabilitation of the natural resources sector of the host state's economy. However, the various investment opportunities are coupled with substantial risks, political and economic.[3] For instance, there is always the possibility of a relapse into conflict, as ethnic and tribal loyalties may trump the desire for economic recovery and consolidation of the peace process.[4] Judicial and other governmental institutions are weak, dysfunctional and sometimes very corrupt. The host state may re-evaluate its earlier commitments to the foreign investor and may demand more revenue or greater participation in the enterprise. There is also ideological uncertainty inherent in a regime change as the new regime may be ideologically hostile to investment liberalization and thus seek to renegotiate or even nationalize the investment.[5] The opportunities and risks of foreign investment in a post-conflict state are articulated in Liberia's *Investment Guide* as follows:

> ...While the guide describes the advantages of Liberia — its development-oriented governance and its extensive and varied natural resources, from gold and diamonds and iron ore, through timber and rubber, to a coast abounding in marine life — it does not seek to hide the challenges investor face in a post-conflict environment...[6]

In order to attract foreign investment, post-conflict states have taken some necessary legal and regulatory steps toward improving their investment climate by enacting new Investment Codes or revising the existing ones. These Investment Codes provide a wide range of fiscal incentives and other guarantees to foreign investors. Since the DRC, Liberia and Sierra Leone have concluded very few Bilateral Investment Treaties (BITs), a foreign investor may have to rely on the protections provided in the investment laws of the host state, particularly the right to a neutral forum for dispute settlement.[7] Given the likelihood that the foreign investor may not have access to a neutral arbitral forum through a BIT, this chapter focuses on the provisions for international arbitration in the domestic Investment Codes of post-conflict states – the DRC, Liberia and Sierra Leone. These provisions are examined through the prism of arbitration under the auspices of the International Centre for the Settlement of Investment Disputes (ICSID or the Centre), established by the Convention on the Settlement of Investment Disputes Between States and Nationals of Other States (the ICSID Convention or the Convention)[8] and the way certain ICSID jurisdictional requirements are reflected in these Investment Codes.[9] The study is comparative. The provisions on dispute settlement, with particular reference to ICSID, in the Investment Codes of post-conflict states are compared and contrasted with similar provisions in the Investment Codes of other African states and the transition economies of Eastern Europe.

For the purposes of this Chapter, the author fundamentally assumes that all but two requirements of ICSID jurisdiction have been met – whether the host state consented to ICSID arbitration in its investment legislation as required by Article 25 (1) of the Convention and whether the host state agreed in its investment legislation to treat a locally established juridical person as a "national of another Contracting State" because of "foreign control" pursuant to the second clause of Article 25(2)(b) of the Convention.[10] These two requirements are more controversial in the context of domestic investment laws.

Part II of the paper provides an overview of the investment promotion strategies of some African states, particularly post-conflict states, and the various incentives and guarantees under the Investment Codes of these states, including the guarantee, or lack of guarantee, of international arbitration through ICSID or an alternative arbitral forum.

Part III of the paper discusses some key jurisdictional requirements of ICSID arbitration. This part examines two key jurisdictional requirements – "consent" to ICSID arbitration and the exception to the nationality of a juridical person under the second clause of Article 25(2)(b) of the ICSID Convention, and how these key requirements are reflected in the Investment ·Codes of post-conflict states. Comparisons and contrasts are made with similar provisions in the Investment Codes of some African countries, with a view to highlighting their strengths and weaknesses in providing legal security to foreign investors as compared with access to a neutral arbitral forum for adjudicating investment disputes with the host state.

Part IV is summary and conclusion. For greater legal certainty and pre-dictability, it is submitted that the Investment Codes of post-conflict states should contain a stability clause that preserves the guarantee of international arbitration in case of future adverse legislative changes.

The Past and Present Attitude of Developing Countries to Foreign Investment Protection

In the period between the late 1950s and the late 1970s, African countries were in general very hostile to foreign investment[11] and foreign investment arbitration.[12] They relied on sovereignty-centered arguments as legal justification for the restrictive foreign investment policies and hostility toward foreign investment arbitration.[13] They found particularly objectionable the jurisdictional and choice of law clauses in foreign investment contracts and the international law standard of state responsibility. In their view, the domestic law of the host state was the proper law applicable to the substance of foreign investment disputes and remedies for breach of foreign investment contracts, including the amount of compensation for nationalization and expropriation, should be limited to those provided under domestic law.[14]

In 1974, developing countries successfully pushed for three UN General Assembly Resolutions calling for a New International Economic Order (NIEO).[15] The NIEO declaration marked the watershed of the legal position-taking and ideological division between developed and developing countries' scholars and policy-makers on foreign investment protection, particularly the substantive law applicable to foreign investment disputes. In particular, developed, capital-exporting countries rejected Article 2(2)(c) of the Charter of Economic Rights and Duties of States (CERDS) to the extent that it sought to eliminate the role of international law in the settlement of foreign investment disputes.[16] This provision not only recognized the right of states to nationalize, expropriate or transfer ownership of foreign property, it also provided for the settlement of foreign investment disputes in accordance with the domestic laws of the nationalizing states and by its tribunals, "unless it is freely and mutually agreed by all States concerned that other peaceful means be sought on the basis of the sovereign equality of States and in accordance with the principles of free choice of means."[17]

By the early 1980s, developing countries were becoming increasingly aware that statist economic policies had failed and that a new approach to economic development was needed.[18] They began to reassess their attitude to foreign investment.[19] During this period, the Calvo Doctrine, hitherto the dominant theory of foreign investment protection in Latin America, was also in steady decline.[20] Thus, developing countries began to embrace economic liberalization. Openness to foreign investment is evident in the continuing privatization programs[21] and increasing number of Bilateral Investment Treaties (BITs) between developing and developed countries and developing countries *inter se*.[22] The BITs provide wide-ranging substantive protections for foreign investors and their investments in the territory of the other, including protection against direct and indirect expropriation. More important, the BITs provide advance consent to international arbitration for the settlement of investor-state disputes. Besides concluding significant numbers of BITs, developing countries, particularly African countries, have sought to create conducive investment climates by revising their legal and regulatory framework or enacting new laws relating to foreign investment. Today, African States, including post-conflict States, compete vigorously for foreign investment – a policy shift that is reflected in two major ways.

First, the policy change is reflected in institutional arrangements for dealing with foreign investors. In the competition for foreign investments, the establishment of an investment promotion agency is a common practice among African states.[23] These are statutory agencies with the sole responsibility of promoting the state's foreign investment potential and providing information to prospective investors. They perform screening functions – screening applications for investment permits or licenses to ensure that desired investments are admitted and vice versa. They also perform supervisory functions when investments are made to ensure legal and regulatory compliance. The establishment of these agencies is predicated on the assumption that a "one-stop shop" will reduce bureaucratic delays in screening foreign investment applications and fast track the entry of desired investments.[24] In furtherance of this objective, most domestic Investment Codes provide for a maximum period for the approval or rejection of investment application(s) as well as the legal or regulatory implications of an application exceeding the prescribed time limit.[25]

Second, the Investment Codes provide a wide range of fiscal incentives and guarantees to foreign investors.[26] These incentives and guarantees, the eligibility requirements and their duration may be outlined in a separate

Code.[27] In general, there is a great deal of similarity in the incentives and guarantees granted to foreign investors in the Investment Codes of African states. For instance, virtually all the investment codes provide tax and other fiscal incentives to foreign investors. The eligibility for and duration of fiscal incentives may be determined by the importance of the investment to the economic development of the host state. The host state usually designates certain sectors of its economy as the priority sectors and foreign investments in these sectors are granted incentives in consideration of the huge capital resources, risks involved and the contribution to the state's economic development.[28]

Besides fiscal incentives, other provisions that are relatively similar include guarantees against expropriation and nationalization without compensation[29] and guarantees of dispute settlement by a neutral arbitral tribunal.[30] These were hitherto the most controversial issues in the economic relationship between developed and developing countries.[31] Many African states asserted the sovereign right to expropriate or nationalize foreign investments and the exclusive jurisdiction of their national courts or tribunals to determine the amount of compensation for the nationalized or expropriated assets.[32] Thus, the guarantee against expropriation and the offer to submit disputes to international arbitration rather than the state's courts is a rejection of the sovereign-rights ideology relating to the protection of foreign investments – a change in attitude rightly described by Professor Weil as "the no longer stormy relationship of a ménage à trois".[33] These guarantees are intended to reassure a potential foreign investor that the state is a friendly destination for foreign investment.

Despite the progressive developments in foreign investment protection among African states, significant political and economic risks remain, particularly in post-conflict states with poor legal culture and infrastructure. Against this backdrop, the guarantee of a neutral forum for adjudicating investment disputes in the state's Investment Code assumes profound importance in assessing the investment climate. But the state's consent to submit disputes to an arbitral tribunal may not be very clear or may be subject to the fulfillment of certain conditions. It is therefore imperative for a prospective investor to examine the state's legal and regulatory regime, particularly the provisions of the law on the settlement of dispute.

ICSID Jurisdiction and the Legal Security of Foreign Investment in Post-Conflict States

An Overview of the ICSID Convention

The ICSID Convention, which created the ICSID Centre, is a landmark contribution of the World Bank to the settlement of investment disputes between host states and foreign investors.[34] The Convention seeks to stimulate the flow of foreign investment between countries by creating a neutral institution for investor-state dispute settlement.[35] It has been stated that the ICSID Convention seeks to "depoliticize" foreign investment disputes – to remove foreign investment disputes from the realm of diplomacy and crystallize them in the realm of law.[36] Thus, the Convention prohibits Contracting States from giving diplomatic protection to their nationals in respect of cases which the parties have agreed to submit to the Centre.[37]

The Convention strikes a careful balance between the sovereign rights of the state and the interests of the foreign investor.[38] It gives the parties wide latitude to agree on various aspects of their relationship.[39] A state's ratification of the Convention alone does not impose an obligation on that state to submit to the jurisdiction of the Centre; rather, the parties have to agree in writing to submit their dispute to the jurisdiction of the Centre.[40] When both parties agree to submit their dispute to the Centre, the consent cannot be withdrawn unilaterally by either party,[41] nor will the failure of a party to appear or to present his case frustrate the proceedings.[42] Under Article 26 of the Convention, the choice of ICSID arbitration bars recourse to any other forum unless otherwise stated by the parties, although a Contracting State party may require the exhaustion of local administrative and judicial remedies as a condition of its consent to arbitration pursuant to the Convention.[43] At the time of ratifying the Convention or at any time thereafter, a Contracting State may notify the Centre of the class or classes of disputes it would or would not submit to the jurisdiction of the Centre.[44]

Thus, ICSID arbitration is a self-contained, autonomous system, isolated from the interference of national courts of Contracting States.[45] The resulting award is binding and cannot be reviewed by the national courts of Contracting States.[46] Under Article 54(1) of the Convention, a Contracting State is obliged to "recognize an award rendered pursuant to this Convention as binding and enforce the pecuniary obligations imposed by that award within its territories as if it were a final judgment of a court in that State..."[47] However, the Convention provides very narrow grounds for a review and possible annulment of the award or parts thereof by an *ad hoc* Committee constituted pursuant to the Convention.[48]

Briefly, ICSID is an independent, non-state entity whose jurisdictional parameters and other functions are delineated by an international treaty i.e. the ICSID Convention.[49]

Jurisdiction of the Centre

Article 25(1) of the Convention lays down the essential requirements for ICSID jurisdiction:

> The jurisdiction of the Centre shall extend to any legal dispute arising directly out of an investment, between a Contracting State (or any constituent subdivision or agency designated to the Centre by the State) and a national of another Contracting State, which the parties to the dispute consent in writing to submit to the Centre. When the parties have given their consent, no party may withdraw its consent unilaterally.

The above provision delineates the outer limits of the jurisdiction of the Centre, i.e. the limits within which the provisions of the Convention will apply to arbitration under the auspices of the Centre. Thus, the jurisdiction of the Centre, and consequently of the arbitral tribunal constituted thereunder, is subject to fulfilment of four requirements: there must be a legal dispute; the dispute must have arisen directly out of an investment; the parties to the dispute must be a Contracting State (or its constituent subdivision or agency designated to the Centre) and a national of another Contracting State; the parties must have consented in writing to submit the dispute to the Centre.

Consent to International Arbitration in the Investment Codes of Post-Conflict African States: A Comparative Analysis.

Consent is an indispensable requirement for the jurisdiction of the Centre – often referred to as "the cornerstone of the jurisdiction of the Centre."[50] A state's ratification of the Convention alone does not constitute consent to submit to the jurisdiction of the Centre. Under Article 25(1) of the Convention, the Contracting State party and the foreign investor must have agreed in writing to submit their dispute to the Centre. Indeed, arbitral proceedings cannot take place under the auspices of the Centre in the absence of the parties' written consent and neither party can withdraw the consent unilaterally. The Convention does not specify the time at which consent should be given, nor does it require that the consent of both parties should be embodied in the same instrument. The Report of the Executive Directors suggests that:

...a Host State might in its investment promotion legislation offer to submit disputes arising out of certain classes of investments to the jurisdiction of the Centre, and the investor might give his consent by accepting the offer in writing.[51]

This suggestion has been affirmed in ICSID jurisprudence:

...Starting with Article 25 of the ICSID Convention..., it can now be considered as established and not requiring further reasoning that such consent can be also be effected unilaterally by a Contracting State in its national investment laws, the consent becoming effective at the latest if and when the foreign investor files its claim with ICSID making use of the respective national law...[52]

The unilateral offer to submit disputes to a neutral arbitral forum has become a common legislative practice of African states and the transition economies of Europe that seek to attract foreign investment.[53] In general, the various Investment Codes (Investment Promotion Legislation) provide for the amicable or negotiated settlement of disputes and recourse to arbitration if the parties fail to resolve their dispute amicably.[54] Nevertheless, the arbitration provisions of these Codes in the context of Article 25(1) of the ICSID Convention are considerably diverse and open to different interpretations. A prospective investor should be advised to carefully review the consent provisions of the Investment Code of the state in which he intends to make an investment. For present analytical purposes, these consent provisions can be *loosely* categorized as "unconditional" and "conditional" consent clauses. The former refers in general to a host state's unconditional offer to submit disputes to arbitration or a list of dispute settlement options the aggrieved party may choose from. This offer, if accepted by the investor, will be capable of immediately vesting jurisdiction in ICSID. Unlike the former, the latter category is subject to the performance of certain acts or the fulfillment of certain condition(s) and thus is incapable of immediately vesting jurisdiction in ICSID. There can be requirements for separate implementing arbitration agreement between the host state and the foreign investor, for the exhaustion of local administrative or judicial remedies as a condition precedent for recourse to arbitration, or for arbitration procedure(s) only to be utilized for disputes arising from certain class of investments such as "status investments", "licensed business enterprise" or "approved investments".[55] It is pertinent to point out that this is by no means a watertight compartmentalization since a particular Investment Code may combine elements of both categories.

Unconditional consent provisions. Article 38 of the 2002 Investment Code of the DRC is a perfect example of an unconditional consent to arbitration in a state's investment legislation. The Article itself embodies the state's unequivocal consent to ICSID arbitration or, alternatively, to the ICSID Additional Facility (if the investor is not a national of another Contracting State) or the International Chamber of Commerce (ICC) arbitration.[56] The consent portion of the Article states:

> The *consent* of the parties to the competence of [ICSID] or of the supplementary mechanism, depending on the case, required by the governing instruments, *is hereby granted by this article as far as the DRC is concerned* and as far as the investor is concerned, his consent is granted by his application…to be
>
> admitted into the system of this law or subsequently by a separate act.[57] (Emphasis added)

By virtue of this provision, the host state (the DRC), in exercise of its sovereign rights, unequivocally consents to ICSID arbitration or any of the alternative arbitration procedures stipulated therein. Under this law, the investor can give his consent either in his investment application or "subsequently by a separate act".[58] Although the investor has some flexibility with respect to the timing of his consent, a prospective investor may be well-advised to include such consent in his investment application – before the investment is actually made. If the acceptance of the offer to arbitrate is not accepted prior to making an investment, case law supports the proposition that the investor can signify his acceptance of the offer to submit disputes to ICSID arbitration by filing a notice of arbitration after a dispute had arisen.

In the *Tradex* case,[59] an ICSID arbitral tribunal considered Albania's unilateral consent to ICSID arbitration under Article 8(2) of its foreign investment law,[60] which is very similar to the consent provisions of Article 38 of the DRC Code. Albania's consent to ICSID arbitration under Article 8(2) of its investment law states, "…the Republic of Albania hereby consents to the submission thereof to the International Centre for Settlement of Investment Disputes between States and Nationals of Other States…"[61] Albania did not contest its consent to ICSID jurisdiction under Article 8(2) of its 1993 law, rather its argument was that the law came into force after the investment was made and that acceptance of the offer to submit disputes to ICSID arbitration could only apply to disputes that arose after the entry into force of the 1993 law.[62] After evaluating the facts and the evidence, the tribunal held that the 1993 law was applicable to the dispute before it.[63]

Besides the example in the Investment Code of the DRC, a host state's Investment Code may simply provide dispute settlement options from which the aggrieved party may choose. This method is exemplified by

Section 16(2) of Sierra Leone's Investment Promotion Act of 2004. Subsection 2 of Section 16 provides:

> Where any dispute between an investor and the Government in respect of a business enterprise is not settled amicably, it may be submitted at the option of the aggrieved party to arbitration as follows:
>
> (a) In accordance with the rules of procedures for arbitration of the United National (sic) Commission on International Trade Laws (UNCITRAL).
> (b) In case of a foreign investor within the framework of any bilateral or multilateral agreement on investment protection to which the Government and the country of which the investor is a national are parties; or
> (c) In accordance with any other national or international machinery for the settlement of investment disputes as the parties may agree.

It is worth noting that UNCITRAL arbitration is the investor's only option under paragraph (a). Paragraphs (b) and (c) are the investor's only gateways to ICSID arbitration – either by virtue of a BIT between Sierra Leone and the state of which the investor is a national or under an agreement between the parties. Under this scenario, only nationals of the United Kingdom can have recourse to ICSID arbitration under paragraph (b), because it is the only country with which Sierra Leone has concluded a BIT.[64] Section 16(2) of the Sierra Leone Act is similar in all material respects to Section 29(2) of the Ghana Investment Act and Section 26(2) of the Nigerian Investment Promotion Commission Act. Under Section 29(2) of the Ghana Investment Act, the foreign investor can choose from (a) UNCITRAL arbitration procedure; (b) the arbitration procedure(s) in a BIT or multilateral agreement on investment to which Ghana and the country of which the investor is a national are parties; or (c) any other national or international machinery for the settlement of investment disputes *agreed to by the parties*.[65] Section 16(2)(c) of the Sierra Leonean Act, which is the same as Section 29(2)(c) of the Ghanaian Act and Section 26(2)(c) of the Nigerian Act, are however affected by a subsequent subsection in both the Ghanaian and Nigerian Acts which provides for a default option if the parties cannot reach an agreement. Under Section 29(3) of the Ghanaian Act, "the choice of the investor shall prevail" if the parties cannot reach an agreement, while under Section 26(3) of the Nigerian law, "ICSID Rules shall apply."[66] Given that Sierra Leone is a Contracting State of the ICSID Convention, the implied restrictions to ICSID arbitration under Section 16(2) (b) & (c) of its investment promotion legislation are counterproductive, particularly for a post-conflict state seeking to attract foreign investment. These provisions are further undermined by Section 16(3) of the Sierra Leone Act which states that a dispute between an investor and a governmental body that is not resolved amicably and "where no recourse is available through arbitration or previously established contracts or other legal instruments …shall be referred to the relevant legal authority with Sierra Leone for settlement…"

An investor's discretion to choose from different dispute settlement options provided in the host state's investment promotion legislation is supported in ICSID jurisprudence. In *SPP v. Arab Republic of Egypt*,[67] an ICSID Tribunal considered the consent provisions under Article 8 of Egypt's Law No. 43 of 1974.[68] Article 8 provided in relevant part:

> Investment disputes in respect of the implementation of the provisions of this Law shall be settled in a manner to be agreed upon with the investor, or within the framework of the agreements in force between the Arab Republic of Egypt and the investor's home country, or within the framework of the Convention for the Settlement of Investment Disputes between the State and the nationals of other countries to which Egypt has adhered by virtue of Law No. 90 of 1971, where such Convention applies.

Egypt did not challenge the possibility that a state might unilaterally give advance consent in writing to the Centre's jurisdiction through its investment legislation. However, Egypt argued that Article 8 is only a list of possible alternatives to be negotiated by the investor and the Egyptian Government. According to Egypt, "a separate *ad hoc* expression of consent is required to establish the jurisdiction of the Centre."[69] The Tribunal found that Article 8 of Law No. 43 established a mandatory and hierarchic sequence of dispute settlement procedures, and constituted an express consent in writing to ICISD jurisdiction within the meaning of Article 25(1) of the Convention in the absence of an applicable BIT or agreement by the parties on the arbitration procedure.[70] Likewise in *Zhinvali Development Limited v. Republic of Georgia*,[71] the investor (Claimant) initiated ICSID arbitration pursuant to the consent provisions of Article 16(2) of the 1996 Georgia Investment Law which provided in relevant part: "…disputes between a foreign investor and a government body, if the order of resolution is not agreed between them, shall be settled at the Court of Georgia or at the International Centre for the Resolution (sic) of Investment Disputes…"[72] Georgia's argument that Article 16(2) is not a standing offer to submit disputes to ICSID was rejected by the Tribunal; rather the Tribunal agreed with the Claimant's position that the choice between recourse to Georgian courts or to ICSID is solely for the Claimant to make.[73] The Tribunal held that

Section 16(2) of the 1996 Georgia Investment Law "constitute a "consent in writing" by the Respondent to the jurisdiction of ICSID, which offer the Claimant later accepted in writing when it filed its Request for Arbitration".[74]

Investors in both the DRC and Sierra Leone therefore have a unilateral, standing offer by the state to submit disputes to international arbitration. However, under the Investment Code of Sierra Leone, the offer is impliedly limited to UNCITRAL arbitration. The alternatives, such as ICSID arbitration, could only arise if there is a BIT between the host state and the investor's home state or by mutual agreement of the parties.

Conditional Consent Provisions. In contrast to unconditional consent provisions, a host state's Investment Code offer to submit disputes to arbitration may be conditional to the extent that it requires a separate implementing agreement between the host state and the investor or the performance of certain acts or fulfilment of certain conditions. The Code may also limit the guarantee of international arbitration to certain classes of investors or certain classes of investments – the determination of whether an investor or investment is eligible for membership of the "class" rests solely with the host state or its subdivisions or agencies. In the context of Article 25(1) of the ICSID Convention, there is no unilateral standing offer by the host state to submit disputes to ICSID – an offer that could be accepted by the investor at any time, either before or after a dispute arises. Satisfaction of the consent requirement under Article 25(1) of the Convention is thus subject to a separate implementing agreement, performance of the acts or fulfilment of the conditions prescribed by the host state's investment promotion legislation.

The Investment Incentive Code of Liberia, for instance, provides certain incentives for an "approved investment project" – defined in the Code as "an investment project in respect of which an investment incentive contract has been signed by the Government of the Republic of Liberia and the Sponsor."[75] Section 3 of the Code lists the priority sectors of the economy; an investment in one or more of those sectors qualifies as a "approved investment project" eligible for the incentives. To be granted the incentives provided in the Code, a prospective investor is required to submit a final plan describing the investment project and the incentives requested.[76] The prospective investor is also required to submit a draft incentive contract, which if approved becomes part of the investment incentive contract.[77] The Code stipulates that an investment incentive contract shall be negotiated and signed by the Government of Liberia with the sponsor of an "approved investment project".[78] Dispute settlement procedures are not included in the list of incentives. However, there is nothing in the Code that bars a prospective investor from including dispute settlement procedures in his desired list of incentives or guarantees which he is required under the Code to submit along with his investment proposal (failure to do this will jeopardize his right of recourse to ICSID arbitration or any other arbitration procedure).[79] In other words, dispute settlement by a neutral forum can only result from a negotiated agreement of the parties for an "approved project". In *Phillipe Gruslin v. Malaysia,*[80] the Tribunal held that that the Respondent's consent was not established as required by Article 25(1) of the ICSID Convention because the Inter-Governmental Agreement (the IGA) between Belgium and Malaysia required that the investment be made in an "approved project".[81]

The "approved investment project" status in the Liberian Investment Incentive Code is markedly similar to the "Certificate of Status Investment" under the Foreign Investment Act of Namibia.[82] The holders of such certificates are entitled to international arbitration only if they indicate this preference when the certificate is about to be issued. If an investment is an eligible investment as defined by the Act, the Minister of Trade and Industry, subject to the provisions of the Act, may categorize the investment as "Status Investment" and issue a "Certificate of Status Investment" in respect thereof.[83] The "Certificate of Status Investment" can only be issued to a foreign investor in respect of an eligible investment of "a value of not less than an amount which the Minister [of Trade and Industry] may determine from time to time by notice in the *Gazette* for this purpose."[84]

The issuance of the Namibian "Certificate of Status Investment" entitles the holder (the foreign investor), *inter alia,* a guarantee of international arbitration for the settlement of *two classes* of disputes: the amount of compensation for expropriation and the validity or continued validity of the Certificate.[85] The Act provides for the Minister to notify the foreign investor to whom a Certificate is to be issued so that he can elect to settle the two classes of dispute by international arbitration; and if he chooses international arbitration, UNCTIRAL Arbitration rules at the time the Certificate was issued should apply, "unless by agreement between the Minister and the foreign national to whom the Certificate is issued, another method of settling the dispute has been chosen and the Certificate so provides."[86] Section 13(3) stipulates that "A Certificate which makes provision for international arbitration *shall constitute the consent of the holder of the Certificate and the Government* to submit to arbitration…"[87] The investment promotion laws of Rwanda and Uganda are other examples of laws that refer to "license" and "certificate of registration" respectively, as constituting consent to submit to international arbitration if the said "license" or "certificate of registration" contains an arbitration clause.[88]

Yet, other than an investment license or certificate, other legislative provisions may require an *ad hoc* agreement between the parties to submit disputes to ICSID or an alternative arbitral forum. Apparently in response to the *SPP* case, Egypt enacted a new investment law in 1989,[89] Article 55 of which makes it abundantly clear that submission of disputes to ICSID or any of the alternative methods listed therein requires the parties' agreement.[90] Other investment promotion legislations that require the parties' agreement to submit disputes to ICSID or to alternative neutral arbitral tribunals include those of Uganda,[91] Senegal,[92] Rwanda,[93] Mozambique,[94] The Gambia,[95] Mauritania,[96] and Tanzania.[97] Recently, the implications of the dispute settlement provisions of the 1997 Tanzania Investment Act concerning the right of the investor to submit disputes to arbitration were considered by an ICSID tribunal in *Biwater Gauff (Tanzania) Limited v. United Republic of Tanzania*.[98] Section 23(2) of the Tanzania Investment Act provides:

> A dispute between a foreign investor and the [Tanzania Investment] Centre or the Government in respect of a business enterprise which is not settled through negotiations may be submitted to arbitration in accordance with any of the following methods *as may be mutually agreed by the parties,* that is to say:
>
> (a) in accordance with arbitration laws of Tanzania for investors;
> (b) in accordance with the rules of procedure for arbitration of the International Centre for the Settlement of Investment Disputes;
> (c) within the framework of any bilateral or multilateral agreement on investment protection agreed to by the Government of the United Republic of Tanzania and the Government of the country the investor originates.[99]

The Certificate of Incentives issued by the Tanzania Investment Centre (TIC) to the investor (the Claimant) when the investment was made referred to the above quoted Section of the Tanzania Investment Act on dispute settlement. The Claimant argued that by virtue of Section 23(2), which was confirmed in the Certificate of Incentives, further consent of the host state was not required to elect any of the dispute settlement options. Rather, Section 23(2)(b) in particular constitutes a unilateral standing offer to submit a dispute to ICSID jurisdiction.[100] The Tribunal rejected the Claimant's interpretation of the dispute settlement options in Section 23(2)(a)-(c), pointing out that the dispute settlement options are conditioned by the words "*as may be mutually agreed by the parties*".[101] The Tribunal found that:

> In the present context, these words are naturally read as meaning that a dispute may be referred to any one of the three options, but only depending upon the agreement of the parties. In other words, a subsequent agreement between the parties is required — which is very different from a standing unilateral offer which simply requires an acceptance by the investor.

Indeed, there is no other language at all in Section 23 to suggest a standing unilateral offer by the Republic.[102]

The Tribunal further posited that if the Claimant's interpretation were accepted, no sensible meaning could be given to the words *"as may be mutually agreed by the parties"* and that even if the optional language of "may" were construed as a mandatory "shall", "there would still be no existing consent by the Republic..."[103] With respect to the Certificate of Incentives, the Tribunal held that it did not contain any separate consent because it simply referred back to the dispute settlement provisions of the Tanzania Investment Act.[104]

Thus the dispute settlement provisions in the Investment Codes of African states and other developing countries are diverse. The host state may provide a list of dispute settlement options to be agreed between the parties which may simply be referenced in an investment certificate. If the dispute settlement provisions in the Investment Code require a further implementing agreement of the parties or any other condition, mere reference to them in the investment certificate does not transform them into a standing offer to submit disputes to international arbitration. At the time of planning the investment, a prudent investor should examine the dispute settlement provisions in the host state's investment law and if they are unfavorable, seek to modify them in the investment license. For instance, if the dispute settlement options in the host state's Investment Code are subject to a mutual agreement of the parties, the investor could select one of the options and require that the state express its consent to submit disputes to that arbitral forum in the investment license.

Investment Codes and the Exception to the Nationality of a Juridical Person Under Article 25(2)(b) of the ICSID Convention.

The ICSID Convention is designed for the settlement of investment disputes between a Contracting State and a national of another Contracting State. For purposes of ICSID jurisdiction, Article 25(2) outlines the eligible nationalities for natural and juridical persons. In relation to a natural person, Article 25(2)(a) defines a "national of another Contracting State" as:

> ...any natural person who had the nationality of a Contracting State other than the State party to the dispute on the date on which the parties consented to submit such dispute to conciliation or arbitration as well as on the date on which the request was registered pursuant to paragraph (2) of Article 28 or paragraph (3) of Article 36, but does not include any person who on either date also had the nationality of the Contracting State party to the dispute...

This definition excludes a natural person who had the nationality of the Contracting party to the dispute on the date of consent and on the date of registration of the request for arbitration. Thus ICSID will not have jurisdiction if a natural person has dual or multiple nationality including the nationality of the Contracting State party to the dispute.[105] However, a natural person who is "a national of another Contracting State" will have standing in proceedings before the Centre, even if he concurrently possesses the nationality of another Contracting State or a non-Contracting State. In other words, the Convention only requires that a natural person must be a "national of another Contracting State", irrespective of whether he also has the nationality of another Contracting State or of a non-Contracting State. As long as one of the nationalities is not that of the Contracting State party to the dispute, the jurisdictional requirement relating to a natural person would, in all probability, be met even if all the nationalities were effective at the crucial dates. For instance, in *Eudoro A. Olguín v. Republic of Paraguay*,[106] the Claimant, a dual national of Peru and the United States, initiated ICSID arbitration pursuant to the Paraguay-Peru BIT. One of the grounds for the Respondent's objection to the jurisdiction of the Centre was that the Claimant had the nationality of United States in addition to his Peruvian nationality and that he resided in the United States. The Tribunal held that even though the Claimant held both Peruvian and United States nationalities and was resident in the United States he was entitled to treaty protection because he held a valid and effective Peruvian nationality.[107]

With regard to the nationality of a juridical person, the *Barcelona Traction Case* is authority for the proposition that in international law, the nationality of a corporation is determined by the place of incorporation or registered office.[108] A company that is incorporated in accordance with the domestic legal system of a state possesses the nationality of that state, and a state cannot be sued internationally by its own national.[109] In developing countries, particularly African states, foreign investors are often required by the laws of the host state to carry out their business through locally incorporated subsidiaries. This is often the case with respect to oil and gas and other natural resources investments where the foreign investor may be mandated by law to enter into a joint venture with the host state or a state corporation. For instance, Section 2(2) of the Nigerian Petroleum Act provides that "a license or lease under this Section may be granted only to a company incorporated in Nigeria under the Companies and Allies Matters Act or any corresponding law".[110] In such situations, a locally incorporated company would be excluded from the Centre's jurisdiction because it is not "a national of another Contracting State". Hence the exception to corporate nationality pursuant to the second clause of Article 25(2)(b) of the Convention:

any juridical person which had the nationality of a Contracting State other than the State party to the dispute on the date on which the parties consented to submit such dispute to conciliation or arbitration *and any juridical person which had the nationality of the Contracting State party to the dispute on that date and which, because of foreign control, the parties have agreed should be treated as a national of another Contracting State for the purposes of this Convention.* (Emphasis added)

Article 25(2)(b) thus uses the criteria of "incorporation" and "control" in determining the nationality of juridical persons for purposes of ICSID jurisdiction. The first criterion relies on customary international law rule on corporate nationality, so that the Centre's jurisdictional requirement is met if the corporation is a "national of another Contracting State". The second clause of Article 25(2)(b) departs from traditional principles of international law on corporate nationality by making an exception for a foreign-owned but locally incorporated company, which would otherwise have no *locus standi* before the Centre.[111]

For a foreign-owned but locally incorporated company to be an eligible party to ICSID proceedings, the host state and the company must specifically agree to treat the company as "a national of another Contracting State", "because of foreign control". The agreement required under Article 25(2)(b) in case of a foreign-owned but locally incorporated company is different from the "consent in writing" under Article 25(1). The latter provision establishes the Centre's basic and general jurisdiction, while the former extends the Centre's jurisdiction to the exceptional case of a foreign-controlled but locally incorporated company that would otherwise be a national of the Contracting State party to a dispute. If it is determined that the nationality of a juridical person is that of the Contracting State party to the dispute, the question arises as to whether the parties have agreed to treat the locally incorporated company as a national of another Contracting State as a result of foreign control.

ICSID jurisprudence has not established a bright-line test for the undefined term "foreign control" or the form of agreement required to establish ICSID jurisdiction pursuant to the second clause of Article 25(2)(b). In general, ICSID Tribunals have found or presumed the objective existence of "foreign control" in cases where the foreign shareholding of a locally incorporated company was between 51%[112] and 100%.[113] But the Tribunal did not find "foreign control" in *Vacuum Salt Products Limited v. Government of the Republic of Ghana.*[114] In this case, a Greek national (Mr G.S. Panagiotopulos) owned 20% of the shares of Vacuum Salt Products Limited, a company incorporated under the laws of Ghana. The Claimant alleged *inter alia* both a breach and progressive expropriation of its contractual rights to develop a salt production and mining company in Ghana.[115] It also alleged a "continual violation" by Ghana of a lease agreement between Vacuum Salt and Ghana dated January 1988 and "a predecessor agreement", ultimate repudiation of the 1988 lease agreement and "its expropriation of the business and property of Vacuum Salt."[116] On the question of jurisdiction *ratione personae*, the Claimant argued that although Vacuum Salt was a corporation organized under the laws of Ghana, in the lease agreement the parties agreed that because Vacuum Salt was controlled by a Greek national, it should be treated as a foreign corporation pursuant to the second clause of Article 25(2)(b) of the Convention. In its objections to the jurisdiction of the Tribunal, Ghana asserted that the conditions of Article 25(2)(b) of the Convention (agreement premised on foreign control) were not satisfied. It argued that the Claimant was a Ghanaian company which "is not foreign-controlled and there had been no agreement between the parties that it should be treated as a national of another Contracting State."[117] The Tribunal considered whether there was an agreement and whether such an agreement was indeed "because of foreign control" within the meaning of the second clause of Article 25(2)(b). Notwithstanding Panagiotopulos' 20% shareholding, the Tribunal examined the facts and the evidence to ascertain whether he was in control. The Tribunal declined jurisdiction over *Vacuum Salt* because, according to the Tribunal: "…the entire proceedings, even if viewed in the light most favorable to the Claimant, are instinct with the sense that Mr. Panagiotopulos, for all his admitted talents, was not in any sense "in charge"".[118] The Tribunal distinguished *Vacuum Salt* from the previous ICSID Awards in *Klöckner*,[119] *LETCO*,[120] and *Amco Asia*[121] as follows:

> These cases are distinguishable from the instant case in that in none of them was the issue of consent separated from that of foreign control. In each of them the objective existence of foreign control was presumed, in particular because foreign shareholding was 100 percent (or, in one case, 51 percent).[122]

Like the term "foreign control", the form agreement required by Article 25(2)(b) is not entirely clear. Unlike Article 25(1) which requires written consent, the Convention does not specify the form of agreement required under Article 25(2)(b) – express or implied agreement. The Convention only provides that because of foreign control, the parties "have agreed" to treat a locally incorporated company as a national of another Contracting State. The form of agreement required by Article 25(2)(b) was a central issue in *Holiday Inns v. Morocco*.[123] At issue were four companies incorporated in Morocco which were wholly owned subsidiaries of Holiday Inns. The Government of Morocco (the Respondent) contested the jurisdiction of ICSID on the ground that the companies were juridical persons of Moroccan nationality and that it had never consented to treat them as "nationals of another Contracting State."[124] In the Respondent's view, "...a State's consent to international adjudication of disputes with its own nationals is an act of such impact and importance as to deserve unequivocal expression".[125] The Claimants contended while Article 25(1) requires written consent, there is no particular form with regard to the special situation under Article 25(2)(b). It was enough, the Claimants argued, that the parties "have agreed" to treat a juridical person, because of foreign control, as a national of another Contracting State.[126] The Tribunal interpreted the requirement of Article 25(2)(b) restrictively and declined jurisdiction over the four locally incorporated subsidiaries. The Tribunal stated:

> The question arises, however, whether such an agreement must be expressed or whether it may be implied. The solution which such an agreement is intended to achieve constitutes an exception to the general rule established by the Convention, and one would expect that parties should express themselves clearly and explicitly with respect to such a derogation. Such an agreement should therefore normally be explicit. An implied agreement would only be acceptable in the event that the specific circumstances would exclude any other interpretation of the intention of the parties, which is not the case here.[127]

Although the Tribunal was cautious in its approach, it did leave the door open for an implied agreement where "the specific circumstances would exclude any other interpretation of the intention of the parties." Subsequent ICSID tribunals have interpreted the provision expansively to the effect that the mere insertion of arbitration clause in an investment contract may be sufficient evidence of the parties' intention to treat a locally incorporated as a national of another Contracting State because of foreign control. In *Klöckner*,[128] the Tribunal posited:

> The insertion of an ICSID arbitration clause by itself presupposes and implies that the parties were agreed to consider SOCAME [a locally incorporated subsidiary] at the time to be a company under foreign control, thus having the capacity to act in ICSID arbitration. This is an acknowledgement, which completely excludes a different interpretation of the parties intent. Inserting this [ICSID arbitration] clause in the establishment agreement would be nonsense if the parties had not agreed that, by reason of the control then exercised by foreign interests over SOCAME, said agreement could be made subject to ICSID jurisdiction.[129]

Likewise in *LETCO*, the Tribunal concluded that the inclusion of an ICSID clause in the Concession Agreement was enough to imply an agreement by the parties to treat LETCO as a national of another Contracting State:

> When a Contracting State signs an investment agreement, containing an ICSID arbitration clause, with a foreign controlled juridical person with the same nationality as the Contracting State [the Contracting State party to the dispute] and it does so with the knowledge that it will only be subject to ICSID jurisdiction if it has agreed to treat the company as a juridical person of another Contracting State, the Contracting State could be deemed to have agreed to such treatment by having agreed to the ICSID arbitration clause. This is especially the case when the Contracting State's laws require the foreign investor to establish itself locally as a juridical person in order to carry out an investment.[130]

It is submitted that as a general rule, the second clause of Article 25(2)(b) of the ICSID Convention requires an express agreement of the parties to treat a locally incorporated company as a national of another Contracting State because of foreign control. This is because the consent required under Article 25(1) is different from the agreement to treat a locally incorporated company as a national of another Contracting State. The agreement required under Article 25(2)(b) is a deviation from or an exception to the principles of international law to the effect that a sovereign State cannot be sued before an international tribunal by its own national(s). Such an agreement cannot be implied by the mere insertion of ICSID arbitration clause in an investment contract. As Professor Lalive cautioned:

> …consent to international arbitration between a state and a juridical person which is, legally or formally speaking, its 'national' needs to be unequivocal and not open to doubt. Too liberal an interpretation of Article 25(2)(b) would hardly contribute to a wider acceptance by states of ICSID arbitration and, therefore, to the protection of foreign investors. It is up to the latter to take all necessary precautions whenever the creation of a 'local' legal person (wholly or partly owned) is required or decided upon.[131]

However, in exceptional circumstances, the facts and circumstances of a particular case may compel a tribunal to make such inference. For instance, a host Ssate's domestic investment law may define "foreign control" only in terms of the percentage of a foreign investor's shareholding. However, a foreign investor may be a *de facto* controller of the investment even if he is not the majority shareholder. Under this scenario, an arbitral tribunal could rightly infer the host state's intention to treat a locally incorporated company as a national of another Contracting State because of foreign control.

Investment Codes and the Exception to the Nationality of a Juridical Person Under the Second Clause of Article 25(2)(b)

With very few exceptions, Investment Codes of African states that provide for ICSID arbitration generally do not extend it to locally incorporated but foreign-controlled companies. In the very few Investment Codes that deal with the subject, two legislative techniques are apparent: locally incorporated but foreign-controlled companies may directly be included in the host state's unilateral, standing offer to submit disputes to ICSID arbitration, or else the definition of a "foreign investor" may include a company incorporated under the laws of the host state, a majority of whose shares are owned by foreigners. With respect to the three post-conflict states discussed above, only the Investment Code of the DRC and its Mining Code[132] deal with the exception envisaged by the second clause of Article 25(2)(b) of the ICSID Convention. The identical provisions of Article 38 of the Investment Code[133] and Article 319 of the Mining Code require that in accepting the offer to submit disputes to ICSID, the foreign investor should include juridical persons of Congolese nationality which he controls. The relevant part of Article 38 of the DRC Investment Code provides:

> …If an investor has carried out an investment through…a company of Congolese rights that he controls, the parties agree that such company as far as [the ICSID Convention] is concerned, has to be considered as a citizen of another Contracting State.[134]

Other Investment Codes do not extend ICSID jurisdiction directly to foreign-controlled local companies but "a foreign investor" is defined in some Investment Codes to include foreign-controlled juridical persons constituted according to the laws of the host state. Examples include the Investment Codes of Mozambique, Uganda and Namibia. Under Section 1 of the Namibia Act, "a foreign national" means:

(a) a person who is not a citizen of Namibia;

(b) a company incorporated under the laws of any country other than Namibia;

(c) *a company incorporated within Namibia in which the majority of the issued share capital is beneficially owned by foreign nationals within the meaning of this definition.*[135] (Emphasis added)

The restriction of the meaning of "foreign control" of locally incorporated companies by reference only to the percentage of foreign shareholding raises the important question of whether an ICSID tribunal is bound by such a definition in determining "foreign control" pursuant to the second clause of Article 25(2)(b) of the Convention. As discussed above, there is no bright-line test either in the Convention or in ICSID jurisprudence for ascertaining "foreign control", although tribunals have found "foreign control" in the obvious cases where the foreign shareholding were more than fifty percent.[136] In the *Vacuum Salt*[137] case, however, the foreign investor owned only twenty percent of the shares of the locally incorporated company. The Tribunal stated that "foreign control" under the second clause of Article 25(2)(b) "does not require or imply any particular percentage of shareholding". After considering all the facts and circumstances of the case, the Tribunal found held that there was no "foreign control", but not necessarily because of the twenty percent shareholding; rather, as the Tribunal put it, "...Mr. Panagiotopulos, for all his admitted talents was not in any sense "in charge.""[138] The Tribunal would have reached a different conclusion if it had found that Mr. Panagiotopulos was "in charge" notwithstanding his twenty percent shareholding. In oil and gas and other natural resources development joint ventures between developing countries and multinational corporations, it is not uncommon for the government to own a majority of the shares while the foreign investor is the *de facto* controller and operator of the joint venture. This is because the expertise and the technology, operational and managerial skills can only be provided by the foreign investor. In such joint venture arrangements, majority ownership and "control" are different. The arbitral tribunal in *Anaconda v. Overseas Private Investment Corporation (OPIC)*[139] expressed this distinction as follows:

> ...In general, "control" as applied to corporate operations is an elusive term, dealing as it sometimes does with the degree of influence in fact or potentially exerted by some persons within a complex structure over a multitude of actions taken by many others. In differing legal contexts different aspects of that influence may assume greater or lesser importance; sometimes actually exercised control is more important than potential but dormant control and sometimes the reverse is true...[140]

The case concerned the nationalization of the Claimants' mining concession by the government of Chile, as a result of which the government became the majority shareholder. The government also appointed four members of the Board of Directors while Anaconda had three members. The central question before the Tribunal was whether Anaconda had continued "control" of its copper mining investment in Chile after the Chilean government had acquired 51% of the company. The Tribunal observed:

> …Although Codelco [the Government corporation] could, if it desired, exercise authority over policy matters through its legal control of the Board of Directors, Anaconda had the power to propose mining development plans and personnel decisions to the board (on which Codelco had 4 and Anaconda 3 members). In short, while the board could reject the plans proposed it could not develop its own alternatives. Dividends and other financial and accounting matters were entrusted to Anaconda and Anaconda had a veto power over some essential matters…[141]

After reviewing the facts and circumstances of the case, particularly the management arrangements, the Tribunal concluded:

> …On the evidence, it is clear that …Anaconda retained de facto control in the sense that operations continued to be carried on in the same way as before, by the same personnel—with a handful of exceptions—as before, through substantially the same practical chain of command as before, and pursuant to the same plans as before. It is true that the majority of the board, representing the 51% stock interest now held by Codelco, had the power to interfere with or veto management plans and policies favored by Anaconda. Taken together, Codelco's powers amounted to de jure control of a sort on a policy level and, had it chosen to exercise those powers, it might have at least stalemated the situation at the mines…[142]

An international tribunal applying international law is not strictly limited to foreign shareholding as the only indicator of "foreign control" as is the case with the Investment Codes of Uganda, Mozambique and Namibia, if the facts and circumstances of the case prove otherwise. However, an international tribunal may look into municipal law of a country as facts which if proven can evidence the intention of the State concerned – in this case as evidence of the host state's intention to treat a locally incorporated company as a national of another Contracting State "because of foreign control".[143]

Summary and Conclusion

From the perspective of a prospective investor, the domestic investment law of Liberia is less than satisfactory in relation to the guarantee of the investor's access to a neutral forum for the settlement of investment disputes. Liberia's Investment Incentives Code, the country's only publicly available

135

legislation relating to incentives and guarantees to foreign investors, does not include dispute settlement among the guarantees to foreign investors. The Code outlines the available incentives to foreign investors who meet certain eligibility criteria specified there under. In 2006, the World Bank through its Foreign Investment Advisory Service (FIAS) carried out a field investigation of Liberia's investment climate.[144] A Report that was published thereafter recommended, *inter alia*, the enactment of an Investment Code that would include necessary investor guarantees such as expropriation clauses and the guarantee of international arbitration for settlement of foreign investment disputes.[145] Liberia apparently implemented this recommendation by enacting an Investment Code in 2007.[146] It cannot however be ascertained whether the guarantees to foreign investors under the new Investment Code meet the standard of best international practice as the law has not been made public.

On the other hand, under the Investment Codes of the DRC and Sierra Leone, the investor is guaranteed the option of a neutral arbitral forum for the settlement of disputes. However, it is pertinent to point out that under the Investment Code of Sierra Leone, the state's unilateral, standing offer to submit disputes to a neutral arbitral forum is somewhat limited to UNCITRAL Arbitration, since the other options could only arise either by a BIT or a negotiated dispute settlement agreement between the parties. In comparison to the foreign investment laws of Sierra Leone and Liberia, the dispute settlement provisions of the 2002 DRC Investment Code are far-reaching vis-à-vis ICSID jurisdiction. Its dispute settlement provisions are better suited for marketing the DRC as an investment destination and for mitigating, to a considerable extent, the volatility and instability of foreign investment in a post-conflict environment. The DRC Investment Code explicitly addresses two important requirements of ICSID jurisdiction: consent to ICSID arbitration under Article 25(1) and the exception to the nationality of a juridical person pursuant to the second clause of Article 25(2)(b) of the Convention. Article 38 of the DRC Investment Code and Article 319 of its Mining Code themselves embody the state's unequivocal consent to submit investment disputes to ICSID. For purpose of ICSID jurisdiction, the provisions also contain a guarantee by the state to treat a locally incorporated company as a "national of another Contracting State" because of "foreign control" as required by Article 25(2)(b) of the Convention. This unilateral, standing offer can be accepted by the foreign investor even before the investment and after a dispute arises by filing a Notice of Arbitration.

The strengths and weaknesses of the dispute settlement provisions notwithstanding, the next question that arises relates to the legal certainty and predictability of the guarantee of international arbitration in the host state's

Investment Code. This question is important because the investment climate of a state, particularly a post-conflict state, must be understood as referring not only to the present but to the investor's "legitimate expectations" in the future, i.e. the basic and legitimate expectations that were taken into consideration by the investor in making the investment. In other words, if an investor relied on the host state's guarantee of a neutral arbitral forum for the settlement of disputes in making the investment, then he has a legitimate expectation that the host state will act consistently by not arbitrarily revoking that guarantee. But in reality, the Host State has the sovereign right to change its laws if it so desires, with the result that the offer to submit disputes to a neutral arbitral forum may be withdrawn before it is accepted by the foreign investor – if the investor had not accepted the offer before the investment was made. This is exemplified by the recent Investment Codes of Kenya and Cameroon which, unlike the ones that they repealed, do not provide for dispute settlement by international arbitration[147] Indeed, the dispute settlement provisions in the repealed Investment Code of Cameroon were very similar to the dispute settlement provisions under Article 38 of the Investment Code of the DRC. Thus, as Professor Sornarajah points out:

> The situation of the foreign investor in a host state contains an inequality. The host State has the legislative power to change the rules of the game at any time. The expectations with which the foreign investor entered the state may be undermined at any stage.[148]

The point being made here is that the Investment Codes of the post-conflict states discussed above do not have a stability provision against future adverse legislative changes affecting the unilateral, standing offer to settle disputes by international arbitration, assuming the offer has not been accepted before a dispute arises. For post-conflict state seeking to attract foreign investment, a further legislative assurance is imperative to preserve the guarantee of international arbitration in the event of adverse legislative changes. *Rumeli Telekom A.S. & Another v. Republic of Kazakhstan*[149] is very illustrative. In addition to its Article 27(2) & (3) which provided for the state's advance consent to submit disputes to ICSID, Article 6(1) of the 1994 Foreign Investment Law (FIL) of Kazakhstan specifically granted protection to foreign investors against adverse legislative changes for a period of ten years from the date the investment was made, or for the entire duration of a contract exceeding ten years entered into with authorized state bodies.[150] The law was repealed before the dispute arose. The Claimants argued that notwithstanding the repeal of the law, ICSID had jurisdiction by virtue of Article 6(1) which preserved the offer to submit disputes to ICSID.[151] The Claimants also argued that they had accepted the offer to submit disputes to

ICISD by filing their Request for Arbitration.[152] The Respondent took the opposite view, and argued that the consent to submit disputes to ICSID jurisdiction was no longer valid because the FIL had been repealed.[153] According to the Respondent, Article 6(1) could only apply if the investor had accepted the offer of ICSID arbitration in writing while the legislation was still in force;[154] since the FIL had been repealed before the filing of the Request for Arbitration, the law could not be a valid basis to establish ICSID jurisdiction.[155] The Tribunal concluded, and rightly in this author's view, that the offer to submit disputes to ICSID jurisdiction was still valid because Article 6(1) of the FIL protected the rights of the investor against adverse legislative changes for ten years or for a longer period if stipulated in a contract.[156] The Tribunal held that the Respondent had consented to ICSID jurisdiction on the date the law came into force (December 28, 1994) and that the Claimants gave their consent by filing their Request for Arbitration.[157]

A stability clause in the Investment Codes of post-conflict states, similar to Article 6(1) of the FIL of Kazakhstan, is imperative in attracting foreign investment. For investors to commit their capital resources in a post-conflict state, such a stability clause in the Investment Code will go a long way in reassuring them of the continued guarantee of dispute settlement by a neutral arbitral tribunal while they seek to realize their investments.

Notes

[1]   Investment Code, national investment law or domestic investment law are used interchangeably in this paper. In 2002, the DRC enacted a new investment code and a new mining code. Other countries that have enacted new investment codes or other legislation relating to foreign investment include Sierra Leone (2004), Rwanda (2005), Angola (2003), Cameroon (2002), Madagascar (2007), and Mauritania (2003).

[2]   Established by the *Multilateral Investment Guarantee Agency Convention (MIGA Convention)*, October 11, 1985. Available at <http://www.miga.org/quickref/index_sv.cfm?stid=1583> (Last visited June 30, 2008).

All three post-conflict States considered in this paper are parties to the MIGA Convention. MIGA provides insurance for foreign investments against political, currency and other risks, particularly in post-conflict and high risk States. The objectives and purposes of the Agency are articulated in Article of the MIGA Convention as follows:

The objective of the Agency shall be to encourage the flow of investments for productive purposes among member countries, and in particular to develop member countries, thus supplementing the activities of the International Bank for Reconstruction and Development (hereinafter referred to as the Bank), the International Finance Corporation and other international development finance institutions.

To serve its objective, the Agency shall:

• issue guarantees, including coinsurance and reinsurance, against non-commercial risks in respect of investments in a member country which flow from other member countries;
• carry out appropriate complementary activities to promote the flow of investments to and among developing member countries; and
• exercise such other incidental powers as shall be necessary or desirable in the furtherance of its objectives.

See generally, *MIGA in Conflict-Affected Countries*; <http://www.miga.org/documents/post_conflict.pdf>. In 2005, the Agency provided political risk insurance cover to Anvil Mining Limited of Toronto, Canada, for its mine in the Democratic Republic of Congo; see News Release: Anvil Mining Limited Secures Political Risk Insurance from World Bank Agency for Mine in the DRC; available at: <http://www.anvilmining.com/files/2005May04MIGAPoliticalRisk Insurance.pdf> (Last visited June 15, 2008)

3   See generally, Paul Comeaux & Stephan N. Kinsella: *Protecting Foreign Investment Under International Law: Legal Aspects of Political Risk* (Dobbs Ferry, New York: Oceana Publications, 1997)

4   To this day, violence continues in the eastern DRC despite the peace agreement. See, "DR Congo: Peace Process Fragile, Civilians at Risk" (Human Rights Watch Report, January 29, 2008), available at: <http://www.hrw.org/english/docs/20 08/07/28/congo19486.htm> (Last visited July 15, 2008). In 1993, the warring factions in Liberia signed a ceasefire agreement but the conflict continued for many more years because any of the warring factions chose to disregard any ceasefire/peace agreement which they had signed. See "Warring Factions in Liberia in Peace Accord" *New York Times* (July 18, 1993), online: <http://query.nytimes. com/gst/fullpage.html?res=9F0CE7D9133FF93BA25754C0A965958260>   (Last visited August 2, 2008). For a comprehensive documentation of the various efforts to   resolve   the   Liberian   conflict,   visit   <http://www.c-r.org/our-

work/accord/liberia/commentary.php >. DRC and Sierra Leone also experienced similar situation.

5   See for example, *Kaiser Bauxite Co. v. The Government of Jamaica*, 1 ICSID Reports, 296. In this case, Jamaica entered into bauxite Mining Agreement with the investor. The agreement contained a "no further tax" clause. After the host state had unsuccessfully sought more revenues from the investment, it increased the tax, in violation of the "no further tax" clause. See also, J.T. Schmidt, "Arbitration Under the Auspices of the International Centre for Settlement of Investment Disputes (ICSID): Implications of the Decision in Alcoa Minerals of Jamaica, Inc. v. Government of Jamaica," (1976) 17 Harvard Int'l L.J. 90. For the oscillation of developing countries between privatization and nationalization, *see*, Amy L. Chua, "The Privatization-Nationalization Cycle: The Link Between Markets and Ethnicity in Developing Countries," (1995) 95 Columbia L.R. 223.

6   *The Investors' Guide to Liberia*. Available at: <http://www.nic.gov.lr/doc/INVESTOR%20GUIDE2.pdf>

7   According to UNCTAD, as of June 1, 2006, DRC had concluded twelve BITs but only four have entered into force (with France (1975), Germany (1971), Switzerland (1973) and United States (1989). As of June 1, 2007, Liberia had concluded four BITs, only three of which have entered into force (France (1982), Germany (1967) and Switzerland (1964). There is no indication that the remaining BIT with Belgium and Luxembourg has entered into force. Sierra Leone has concluded three BITs (with China, Germany and the United Kingdom) but only its BIT with Germany (1966) has entered into force. Available at: <http://www.UNCTAD.org/Templates/Page.asp?intItemID=2344&lang=1.

8   Also known as *The Washington Convention*, March 18, 1965. The text of the Convention and the Report of the Executive Directors are together *reprinted* in (1966) 4 I.L.M 524. The three post-conflict States considered in this chapter are Contracting States to the ICSID Convention. See generally, Christoph Shreuer, *The ICSID Convention: A Commentary*, 2d ed. (Cambridge, England: Cambridge University Press, 2009).

9   This chapter is focused mainly on ICSID because the three post-conflict States discussed in this chapter have ratified the ICSID Convention. Moreover, ICSID is the most popular forum for settlement of foreign investment disputes as is evident in the increasing number of cases administered by the Centre. See,

ICSID, *Annual Report*(2008), online: <http://icsid.worldbank.org/ICSID/Front Servlet?requestType=ICSIDPublicationsRH&actionVal=ViewAnnualReports#>

[10]   Pursuant to Article 25(1) of the Convention, the jurisdiction of ICSID is subject to fulfilment of the following four conditions: (a) there must be a legal dispute; (b) arising directly out of an investment; (c) between a Contracting State (or its constituent subdivision or agency designated to the Centre) and a national of another Contracting State; and (d) the parties must have consented in writing to submit the dispute to the Centre.

[11]   See generally, E. Beveridge, "Taking Control of Foreign Investment: A Case Study of Indigenization in Nigeria," (1991) 40 Int'l & Comp. L.Q. 302; T. Biersteker, *The Political Economy of Indigenizatgion: Multinationals, The State and Local Capital in* Nigeria, (Cambridge, MA, USA: MIT Press, 1987; L.L. Hood, "Nationalization and Indigenization in Africa," (1976) 14 J. Modern African Studies, 427.

[12]   The leading text on Africa and international arbitration is Amazu .A. Azouzu, *International Commercial Arbitration and African States: Practice, Participation and Institutional*, (Cambridge: Cambridge University Press, 2001). *See also* M. Sornarajah, The International Law on Foreign Investment, 2d ed. (Cambridge: Cambridge University Press, 2004).

[13]   See Jan Paulsson, "Third World Participation in International Investment Dispute," (1987) 2 ICSID Rev-F.I.L.J. 19 at 21): "It may be true that in the beginning of this century and until the 1950s, arbitrations conducted by various international tribunals or commissions evidenced bias against developing countries — or rather territories." See also M. Sornarajah, "Power and Justice in International Law," (1997) 1 Singapore J. Int'l & Comp. L. 28.

[14]   *See generally,* M. Sornarajah, *The Pursuit of Nationalized Property* (Dordrecht, Netherlands: Martinus Nijhoff, 1986).

[15]   U.N. General Assembly Resolution 3171, U.N. GAOR, 28th Session, December 17, 1973 on Permanent Sovereignty Over Natural Resources, *reprinted in* (1974) 13 I.L.M. 238. The resolution referred to and reaffirmed an earlier Resolution 1903 of the same title. U.N.G.A. Res. 3201, U.N. GAOR, 29th Session, May 1, 1974, "Declaration on the Establishment of a New International Economic Order" and U.N. G.A. Res. 3281, U.N. GAOR, 29th Session, December 12, 1974, on Charter of Economic Rights and Duties of States, reprinted in (1975) 14 I.L.M. 251.

16   The legal effect of Article 2(2)(c) of CERDS was considered in *Texaco Overseas Petroleum Co. & California Asiatic Oil Co. ("TOPCO") v. Government of the Libyan Arab Republic*, (1978) 17 I.L.M. 29. The sole arbitrator, Professor Dupuy, held inter-alia, that Article 2(2)(c) can only be regarded as a *de lege ferenda* formulation, "which even appears *contra legem* in the eyes of many developed countries," because of the lack of connection between the procedure of compensation and international law as well as the designation of municipal law as the sole applicable law. See generally, C.N. Brower & J.B. Tepe, Jr., "The Charter of Economic Rights and Duties of States: A Reflection or Rejection of International Law?" (1975) 9 Int'l L. 295; R.W. Cox, "Ideologies and the New International Economic Order: Reflections on Some Recent Literature," (1979) 33 Int'l Org. 257; J.K. Gamble, Jr. & M. Frankowska, "International Law's Response to the New International Economic Order: An Overview," (1979) 9 Boston College Int'l & Comp. L.R. 257; E.J. De Aréchaga, "State Responsibility for the Nationalization of Foreign Owned Property," (1978-79) 11 N.Y.U. J. Int'l L. & Pol. 179; B.H. Weston, "The Charter of Economic Rights and Duties of States and the Deprivation of Foreign-Owned Wealth," (1981) 75 American J. Int'l L. 437.

17   See generally, M. Bedjaoui, *Towards a New International Economic Order* (New York: Holmes & Meier, 1979)..

18   For an analysis of the failure of the NIEO, see T.W. Wälde, "A Requiem for the New International Economic Order: The Rise and Fall of Paradigms in International Economic Law and a Post-Mortem with Timeless Significance," in G. Hafner et al. eds., *Liber Americorum: Professor Ignaz Seidl-Hohenveldern in Honour of His 80th Birthday* (The Hague, Netherlands; Boston, Mass: Kluwer Law International, 1998).

19   Professor Lipson summarized the rationale for the shift as follows: "Historically, contingent circumstances have, as always, played a role in this shifting environment. LDC debt problems, in particular, have helped sweeten the incentives for foreign direct investment. For several years, when the Euro-credit markets were eager lenders, the largest (and most creditworthy) LDCs could fund their development programs without direct investments. They could rely heavily on state-owned corporations, which borrowed abroad to finance their expansion. But the combination of heavy borrowing, high real interest rates, and a global recession changed all that…The result was predictable: most LDCs were forced to reschedule their debts. No longer able to borrow freely, they have tried to attract direct investments as an alternate source of long-term capital"; see Charles

Lipson, *Standing Guard: Protecting Foreign Capital in the Nineteenth and Twentieth Centuries* (Berkeley: University of California Press, 1985), p.24.

20   For the changing attitude of Latin America to foreign investment protection, *see generally* P. Peters & N. Schrijver, "Latin America and International Regulation of Foreign Investment: Changing Perceptions," (1992) 39 Netherlands Int'l L.R. 355; G.L. Sandrino, "The NAFTA Investment Chapter and Foreign Direct Investment in Mexico: A Third World Perspective," (1994) 27 Vanderbilt J. Transnat'l L. 259.

21   See generally, W. Baer & M. Birch, "Privatization and the Changing Role of the State in Latin America," (1992) 25 N.Y.U. J Int'l L. & Pol. 1; R. Ramamurti, "Why are Developing Countries Privatizing?", (1992) 23 J. Int'l Bus. Stud. 225.

22   See generally, J.W. Salacuse, "BIT by BIT: The Growth of Bilateral Investment Treaties and Their Impact on Foreign Investment in Developing Countries," (1990) 24 Int'l L. 655; K.J. Vandevelde, "The Economics of Bilateral Investment Treaties," (2000) 41 Harvard Int'l L.J. 469; K.J. Vandevelde, "U.S. Bilateral Investment Program: The Second Wave," (1993) 12 Michigan J. Int'l L. 621.

23   Examples include DRC's National Agency for the Promotion of Investment (ANAPI), Sierra Leone Investment and Export Promotion Agency, National Investment Commission of Liberia (NIC), Nigeria Investment Promotion Commission (NIPC), Ghana Investment Promotion Centre (GIPC), Tanzania Investment Centre (TIC), Uganda Investment Authority, etc. For a comprehensive listing of investment promotion agencies, visit the website of World Association of Investment Promotion Agencies (WAIPA): Available at: <http://www.waipa.org/members.htm>

24   The effectiveness or otherwise of these agencies in fulfilling their mandate is not within the scope of this chapter.

25   Examples include Article 6 of the 2002 DRC Investment Code (30 days), Section 6(2) of the 2004 Sierra *Leone Investment Promotion Act* (seven working days) (hereinafter Sierra Leone Act), Section 14(4) of the 1991 *Uganda Investment Code* (seven days), Section 20(2) of the 1995 *Nigerian Investment Promotion Commission Act* (NIPC Act) (fourteen working days), Section 22(2) of the 1994 *Ghana Investment Act* (five working days).

26   See generally, A.A. Fatouros, *Government Guarantees to Foreign Investors* (New York: Columbia University Press, 1962).

27 A good example is the Investment Incentives Code of Liberia which outlines various incentives and guarantee granted to foreign investors, the eligibility for and duration of such incentives.

28 Liberia's Investment Incentives Code lists the priority sectors for which investors may be granted incentives. The Investment Code of the DRC list three investment regimes, with different sets of applicable incentives, Other examples of countries that list priority sectors include Namibia, Nigeria, and Ghana.

29 See for example, Article 26 of DRC Code, *supra* note 23, Section 11 of Sierra Leone Act, *supra*, note 23, Section 22 of Tanzania Investment Act (TIA), Section 25 of NIPC Act, *supra* note 23, Section 28 of Ghana Act, *supra* note 23, Section 27 of Uganda Code, supra note 23.

30 Ibid; see Article 38 of DRC Code, Section 16 of Sierra Leone Act, Section 26 of NIPC Act, Section 29 of Ghana Act, Section 23 of TIA, Section 28 of Uganda Code, Article 319 of the DRC Mining Code, Article 12 of the 2004 Senegal Investment Code, Article 25 of the 1993 Mozambique Code.

31 M. Sornarajah, *The Pursuit of Nationalized Property*, supra note 14.

32 Ibid

33 See P. Weil, "The State, the Foreign Investor and International Law: The No Longer Stormy Relationship of a Ménage a Trois," (2000) 15 ICSID Rev-F.I.L.J. 401–16. Article 25 of the DRC Code; *supra* note 23, guarantees "fair and equitable treatment in conformity with the principles of international law".

34 For a commentary on the ICSID Convention, see generally, Christoph Schreuer, *supra* note 8; A. Broches, "The Convention on the Settlement of Investment Disputes Between States and Nationals of Other States," (1972) 136-II Recueil des Cours, (hereinafter, "The Convention"); P.F. Sutherland, "The World Bank Convention on the Settlement of Investment Disputes," (1979) 28 Int'l & Comp. L.Q., 367; I.F.I. Shihata, "The Settlement of Disputes Regarding Foreign Investment: The Role of the World Bank with Particular Reference to ICSID and MIGA," (1986) 1 American J. Int'l L. & Policy, 97.

35 Paragraph 9 of The Report of the Executive Directors of the World Bank states that the Convention is: "prompted by the desire to strengthen the partnership between countries in the cause of economic development. The creation of an in-

stitution designed to facilitate the settlement of disputes between States and foreign investors can be a major step toward promoting an atmosphere of mutual confidence and thus stimulating a larger flow of private international capital into those countries that wish to attract it…", *see Report of the Executive Directors on the Convention on the Settlement of Investment Disputes Between States and Nationals of Other States*, (1956) 4 I.L.M. 524, 525.

36 See I.F.I. Shihata, "Towards a Greater Depoliticization of Investment Disputes: The Role of ICSID and MIGA," (1986) 1 ICSID Rev-F.I.L.J. 1; (noting that prior to ICSID, investment disputes were highly politicized and led to frequent exercise of diplomatic protection, sometimes followed by the use of force). *See also, History of the Convenion* (Vol. II), p. 273.

37 Article 27(1) provides: "No Contracting State shall give diplomatic protection, or bring an international claim, in respect of a dispute which one of its nationals and another Contracting State shall have consented to submit or shall have submitted to the arbitration under this Convention, unless such other Contracting State shall have failed to abide by and comply with the award rendered in such dispute".

38 *See generally*, S.J. TOOPE, *Mixed International Arbitration: Studies in Arbitration Between States and Private Persons* (Cambridge: Grotius, 1990).

39 This includes the parties' agreement on the expenses incurred in connection with the arbitration proceedings. Thus Article 61(2) provides that "in the case of arbitration proceedings the Tribunal shall, except as the parties otherwise agree, assess the expenses incurred by the parties in connection with the proceedings…"

40 Article 25(1)

41 *Ibid*

42 Article 45(2). See generally, S.C. Schreuer, *supra* note 8; M. Hirsch, *The Arbitration Mechanism of the International Centre for the Settlement of Investment Disputes* (Dordrecht, Netherlands: Martinus Nijhoff, 1993).

43 *See Lanco International Inc. v. The Republic of Argentina*, (2001) 40 I.L.M 457; where an ICSID Arbitral Tribunal reiterated the exclusivity of ICSID arbitration in the

absence of an express provision requiring the exhaustion of local administrative or judicial remedies).

[44] See Article 25(4). Pursuant to this Article, the government of Ecuador notified the Centre on December 4, 2007 that it will not submit to the jurisdiction of the Centre disputes arising from oil and gas and mining investments; < http://icsid. worldbank.org/ICSID/Index.jsp> (Last visited, August 2, 2008). Under Article 71 of the Convention, any Contracting State may denounce the Convention altogether; such denunciation becoming effective six months after receipt of the notice. Pursuant to this Article, Bolivia denounced the Convention on May 2, 2007 and the denunciation became effective six months thereafter on November 3, 2007. However, by virtue of Article 72, such denunciation does not affect preexisting consent to ICSID jurisdiction.

[45] See generally, G.R. Delaume, "ICSID Arbitration and the Courts," (1983) 77 American J. Int'l L. 784. In general, courts have deferred to ICSID jurisdiction. See *Attorney General of New Zealand v. Mobil Oil New Zealand et al*, (1987) 2 ICSID Rev-F.I.L.J. 491; (a New Zealand High Court stayed proceedings pending ICSID decision on jurisdiction)

[46] Article 53(1).

[47] A Broches, "Awards Rendered Pursuant to the ICSID Convention: Binding Force, Finality, Recognition, Enforcement, Execution," (1987) 2 ICSID Rev-F.I.L.J. 287; S. Choi, "Judicial Enforcement of Arbitration Awards Under the ICSID and New York Conventions," (1996) 28 N.Y.U. J. Int'l L. & Pol. 175.

[48] Article 52(1) specifies the five grounds on which the award may be annulled. The grounds are far narrower or limited than the non-enforcement grounds under the New York Convention on the Recognition and Enforcement of Foreign Arbitral Awards of 1958. *See* S. Choi, *Ibid*

[49] See, N. Nassar, "Internationalization of State Contracts: ICSID, The Last Citadel," (1997) 14 J. Int'l Arb. 185.

[50] Report of the Executive Directors, *supra* note 8, paragraph 23; A. Broches, "The Convention", *supra* note 34, 351-352; C. Schreuer, *supra* note 8, 193; Carolyn B. Lamm, "Jurisdiction of the International Centre for Settlement of Investment Disputes," (1991) 6 ICSID Review-F.I.L.J. 462

51 *Id*, para. 24.

52 *Tradex Hellas S.A. v. Republic of Albania*, (Award on Jurisdiction, December 24, 1996), (1999) 14 ICSID Review-F.I.L.J. 161, 186-187. (Hereinafter the *Tradex* case).

53 See generally, A.R. Parra, "Provisions on the Settlement of Investment Disputes in Modern Investment Laws, Bilateral Investment Treaties and Multilateral Instruments on Investment," (1997) 12 ICSID Review-F.I.L.J. 287.

54 Negotiated settlement of disputes is a common feature of virtually all the Investment Codes. The Investment Codes of Angola (2003), Libya (1997), and Cameroon Investment Charter (2002) do not contain provisions on international arbitration. *See*, A.P. Mutharika, "Creating an Attractive Investment Climate in the Common Market for Eastern and Southern Africa (COMESA) Region," (1997) 12 ICSID Review-F.I.L.J 237.

55 For instance, Section 28(1) of Uganda Code refers to "a licensed business enterprise."

56 DRC Investment Code, *supra*, note 25.

57 *Ibid*. However, Article 319 of the Mining Code is slightly different to the extent that it does not include an express stipulation that the State's consent "is hereby granted by this article as far as the DRC is concerned". *See* DRC Mining Code, *supra* note 30.

58 The 1986 Code, which the present Code repealed, uses the phrase 'a separate instrument'.

59 *Supra*, note 52

60 *Law No. 7764 of November 2, 1993, Law on Foreign Investment of the Republic of Albania*. All references to this law are as referenced by the arbitral tribunal in the *Tradex* case.

61 *Ibid*, p. 173-174.

62 *Ibid*.

63   *Ibid,* p. 189-190. The tribunal found that the 1993 law protected investments that
      were made prior to its enactment.

64   This is further subject to the Sierra Leone-UK BIT coming into force. See *supra*
      note 7. Article 8(1) of UK-Sierra Leone BIT states: "Each Contracting Party
      hereby consents to submit to the International Centre for the Settlement of In-
      vestment Disputes (hereinafter referred to as "the Centre") for settlement by
      conciliation or arbitration under the Convention on the Settlement of Investment
      Disputes between States and Nationals of Other States…"

65   Italics for emphasis. Under Section 26(2) of the Nigerian Act, the investor choose
      from (a) in the case of a Nigerian investor, the rules of procedure for arbitration
      as specified in the Arbitration and Conciliation Act; or (b) in the case of a foreign
      investor, within the framework of a BIT or multilateral agreement on investment
      to which Nigeria and the investor's home State are parties; or (c) any other
      national or international machinery for dispute settlement agreed on by the par-
      ties. *See generally,* K.U.K. Ekwueme, "Nigeria's Principal Investment Laws in the
      Context of International Law and Practice", (2005) 49 J. African Law

66   Section 29(3) of Ghana Investment Act provides: "Where in respect of any
      dispute, there is a disagreement between the investor and the Government as to
      the method of dispute settlement to be adopted, the choice of shall prevail". Sec-
      tion 26(3) of the Nigerian Act provides: Where in respect of any dispute, there is
      disagreement between the investor and the Federal Government as to the
      method of dispute settlement to be adopted, the International Centre for Settle-
      ment of Investment Dispute Rules shall apply." See also Article 7(2)(c) of the
      2003 Investment Code of Mauritania: "…and an *ad hoc* arbitration court which,
      absent any other arrangement between the parties to the dispute, will be set up
      in accordance with the rules of arbitration of the United Nations Commission on
      International Trade Law."

67   *Southern Pacific Properties (ME) Ltd & SPP Ltd. v. The Arab Republic of Egypt,*
      Decision on Jurisdiction, 14 April, 1988, 3 ICSID Reports, 131 (hereinafter the
      SPP case or the Pyramids case).

68   *Law No. 43 of 1974 Concerning the Investment of Arab and Foreign Capital and the*
      Free Zones.

69   *Supra* note 67, para. 73.

70 *Ibid*, para. 116. See, G.R. Delaume, "The Pyramids Stand— The Pharaohs Can
    Rest in Peace," (1993) 8 ICSID Review-F.I.L.J 231; W.L. Craig, "The Final Chapter
    in the Pyramids Case: Discounting an ICSID Award for Annulment Risk," (1993)
    8 ICSID REV. 264. For a different view on legislative consent to ICSID arbitra-
    tion, see, J. Fouret, "Denunciation of the Washington Convention and Non-
    Contractual Investment Arbitration: "Manufacturing Consent" to ICSID Arbitra-
    tion," (2008) 25 J. Int'l Arb. 71.

71 Award of 24 January 2003, 10 ICSID Reports, 3 (hereinafter the *Zhinvali* case).

72 All references to the 1996 Georgia Investment Law are from the Award of the
    Tribunal.

73 *Supra* note 71, para. 335. Other options provided by the law are ICSID Addi-
    tional Facility and UNCITRAL procedures.

74 *Ibid*, para. 342.

75 Investment Incentive Code of Liberia (1973). In late 2009, a Liberian government
    official, Mr. Roosevelt Gould informed me that a new Investment Law was be-
    ing debated at the Liberian legislature. He could not give me a copy of the draft
    bill for the obvious reason that it had not been passed into law.

76 Section 2 of the Code.

77 *Ibid*.

78 Section 3(5)

79 Liberia recently entered into a Mining Concession with Acelor-Mittal which
    reportedly contained an ICSID arbitration clause.

80 5 ICSID REPORTS, 483

81 *Ibid*

82 An Act to Make Provision for the Promotion of Foreign Investments in Namibia
    (1990). For a commentary on the Act, see S.C. Vasciannie, "The Namibian For-
    eign Investment Act: Balancing Interests in the New Concessionary Era," (1992)
    7 ICSID Review-F.I.L.J. 114.

83 Section 4 of the Act.

84 *Ibid*, Section 5(1)

85 Section 13(1)(a) & (b).

86 Section 13(1) & (2).

87 Emphasis added.

88 Article 33 of *Rwandan Law No. 26/2005 of December 12, 2005*, Relating to Investment and Export Promotion and Facilitation, refers to "Certificate of Registration" (hereinafter Rwandan Code or Law). Section 28(3) of *Uganda Investment
Code, 1991*, provides: "The license in respect of an enterprise may specify the
particular mode of arbitration to be resorted to in the case of a dispute relating
to that enterprise, and that specification shall constitute the consent of the Government, the authority or their respective agents and the investor to submit to
that mode and forum or arbitration." See also Section 29(3) of The Gambia Investment Promotion Act, 2001.

89 *Law No. 230 for 1989 Promulgating Investment Law*, English text *reprinted* in (1989)
4 ICSID REV. 376.

90 Article 55 provides that: "Without prejudice to the right to resort to Egyptian
Courts, investment disputes related to the implementation of the provisions of
this Law may be settled in the manner to be agreed upon with the investor. The
parties concerned may also agreed to settle such disputes within the framework
of the agreements in force between the Arab Republic of Egypt and the investor's home country, or within the framework of the Convention on the Settlement of Investment Disputes between States and Nationals of Other States to
which the Arab Republic of Egypt has adhered to by Law No. 90 for 1971, subject to the terms and conditions, and in the instances where such agreements do
apply. It may further be agreed to settle the disputes referred to above through
arbitration before the Regional Center for International Commercial Arbitration
in Cairo." For a comment on Egypt's new law, see, B.P. Marchais, "The New Investment Law of the Arab Republic of Egypt," (1989) 4 ICSID REV., 297.

91 Section 28(2), Uganda Code, *supra* note 25.

92 *Supra*, note 30.

[93] *Law No. 26/2005 of 17/12/2005 Relating to Investment and Export Promotion and Facilitation* (Rwanda Code).

[94] Article 25(2), Mozambique Code, *supra* note 30.

[95] Section 29(2), The Gambia Investment Promotion Act (2001).

[96] Article 7(2), Investment Code of Mauritania, 2003. However, paragraph (c) of Article 7(2) provides that if the parties cannot agree on a dispute settlement method, the dispute will be settled by "an *ad hoc* arbitration court" in accordance with UNCITRAL Arbitration Rules.

[97] Section 23(2), Tanzania Investment Act, 1997.

[98] Award of July 24, 2008. Available at: <http://icsid.worldbank.org/ICSID/FrontServlet> (hereinafter the *Biwater* case).

[99] Emphasis added.

[100] The *Biwater* case, *supra* note 98, para. 255.

[101] *Ibid*, para. 329. Original italics.

[102] *Ibid*.

[103] *Ibid*, para. 332

[104] *Ibid*, para. 336.

[105] See, *Champion Trading Company & Others v. Arab Republic of Egypt* (Decision on Jurisdiction, October 21, 2003). Available at: <http://icsid.worldbank.org/ICSID/FrontServlet >. The individual claimants were dual nationals of Egypt and the United States. The Tribunal held that it had no jurisdiction over the three individual claimants because in addition to their United States nationality, they possessed the nationality of the Contracting State party to the dispute i.e. Egypt. See, C.F. Amerasinghe, "Jurisdiction Ratione Personae under the Convention on the Settlement of Investment Disputes Between States and Nationals of Other States," 251 (1974-75) 47 BRITISH YRBOOK INT'L LAW, 227; stating that if one of the nationalities is that of the Contracting State party to the dispute, "neither agreement on the part of the host State nor the fact that the nationality

of another Contracting State was the 'effective' nationality nor the fact that the host State was aware of the fact that the person had its nationality nor any other fact would normally assist to give the Centre jurisdiction".

106 Award of July 26, 2001. Available at: <http://icsid.worldbank.org/ICSID/ FrontServlet >

107 *Id*, paras. 61-2.

108 *Barcelona Traction Light & Power Company*, (1970) I.C.J. 3. *See also, Autopista Concesionada de Venezuela, C.A. (Aucoven) v. Bolivarian Republic of Venezuela* (Decision on Jurisdiction, September 27, 2001). Available at: <http://icsid. worldbank.org/ICSID/FrontServlet>, para. 107: "According to international law and practice, there are different possible criteria to determine a juridical person's nationality. The most widely used is the place of incorporation or registered office..."

109 *See generally*, I. Seidl-Hohenveldern, *Corporations in and under International Law* (Cambridge, England: Grotius Publications Limited, 1987).

110 *Petroleum Act (Cap. 350, Laws of the Federation of Nigeria*, 1990). See generally, S. Wallace, "The "Juridical Architecture" of ICSID Arbitration Under International Petroleum Agreements (and in Other Complex Situations)," (2003) 18 ICSID Review-F.I.L.J. 412.

111 For a detailed examination of ICSID jurisprudence on Article 25(2)(b), see A.A. Asouzu, "A Review and Critique of Arbitral Awards on Article 25(2)(b) of the ICSID Convention," (2002) 3 J. World Inv. 397, (hereinafter "A Review and Critique").

112 *Klöckner Industrie—Anlagen GmbH & Others v. United Republic of Cameroon & Société Camerounaise des Engrais* (Award of October 21, 1983), 2 ICSID Reports, 3 (51% foreign ownership). See, J. Paulsson, "The ICSID Klöckner v. Cameroon Award: The Duties of Partners in North-South Economic Development Agreements," (1984) 1 J. Int'l Arb. 145.

113 *Liberian Eastern Timber Corporation (LETCO) v. The Government of the Republic of Liberia*, (1987) 26 ILM 647 (100% foreign ownership); *Amco Asia et al v. The Republic of Indonesia* (Award on Jurisdiction, September 25, 1983), (1984) 23 I.L.M. 351 (100% foreign ownership); *Aucoven, supra*, note 106 (75% owned by a juridical

person of US nationality and the remaining 25% held by the parent company, a juridical person of Mexican nationality).

[114]   Award, February 16, 1994. Available at: <http://icsid.worldbank.org/ICSID/FrontServlet> (hereinafter *Vacuum Salt*)

[115]   *Ibid*, para. 2

[116]   *Ibid*

[117]   *Ibid*, para. 12

[118]   *Ibid*, para. 53.

[119]   *Supra* note 112

[120]   *Supra* note 113

[121]   *Supra* note 113

[122]   *Vacuum Salt, supra* note 114, para. 31.

[123]   The unpublished Award is discussed by P. Lalive, "The First World Bank Arbitration (Holiday Inns v. Morocco— Some Legal Problems," *reprinted* in I ICSID Reports, 645.

[124]   *Ibid*, 660-661.

[125]   *Ibid.*

[126]   *Ibid*

[127]   *Ibid*, 663.

[128]   *Supra,* note 112

[129]   *Ibid*, para. 16.

[130]   *LETCO v. Liberia, supra* note 113 at 653.

131 P. Lalive, *supra* note 123 at 663.

132 *Supra*, note 30

133 *Supra* note 25

134 *Supra*, note 25. *See* Article 319 of the Mining Code which provides in relevant part as follows: "Upon issuing a mining or quarry title, the holder gives his consent to [ICSID] arbitration pursuant to [the ICSID Convention], and both on his own behalf and that of his affiliated companies. He also accepts that such affiliated company should be considered as a "National" of another Contracting State".

135 Namibia Act, *supra*, note 80. .See also Article 1(q) of Mozambique Code, *supra* note 28; defines a Foreign person as: any individual whose nationality is not Mozambican, or in the case of a corporate person, the company originally formed under the legislation of another country, *or which, having been formed in the Republic of Mozambique under Mozambican laws, has more than 50% (Fifty percent) of the respective share capital held by foreign persons...*" (Emphasis added). Section 9(1) of Uganda Code, *supra*, note 23: "In this Code, "foreign investor" means: (a) a person who is not a citizen of Uganda; (b) *a company, other than a company referred to in subsection 2, in which more than 50 percent of the shares are held by a person who is not a citizen of Uganda;* (c) a partnership in which the majority of partners are not citizens of Uganda. (Emphasis added)

136 *Supra*, notes 112 & 113 and the accompanying text

137 *Supra*, note 114.

138 *Ibid*, para. 53

139 *Anaconda Company & Chile Copper Company v. Overseas Private Investment Corporation* (Award of Arbitral Tribunal of American Arbitration Association, July 17, 1975), (1975) 14 I.L.M. 1210.

140 *Ibid*, para. 14.

141 *Ibid*

142 *Ibid*, para. 28

143   See, *Certain German Interest in Polish Upper Silesia,* PCIJ Series A, No. 7, p. 19; *Elettonica Sicula SpA (ELSI),* (1989) ICJ Reports, 15, 73-4 . Ian Brownlie, *Principles of Public International Law* 6d ed. (Oxford; New York: Oxford University Press, 2003), 36-9; M.N. Shaw, *International Law* 5d ed., (Cambridge: Cambridge University Press, 2003), pp. 124-7.

144   See, *Liberia: Mini-Diagnostic Analysis of the Investment Climate,* March 2006 (Report of Foreign Investment Advisory Service (FIAS)). <http://www.ifc.org/ifcext/fias.nsf/Content/FIAS_Resources_Country_Reports>

145   *Ibid,* p.10.

146   Some provisions of the new Investment Code are highlighted in the news report titled: *New Investment Code Prohibit Discrimination,* <http://www.bilaterals.org/article.php3?id_article=11632>

147   Examples of new Investment Codes that no longer contain dispute settlement provisions are: Investment Promotion Act of Kenya (2004); Cameroon Investment Charter, *supra,* note 52, Angola Basic Investment Law (2003).

148   M. Sornarajah, *The Settlement of Foreign Investment Disputes* (The Hague; Boston: Kluwer Law International, 2000), p.14.

149   ICSID Award, July 29, 2008. Available at: <http://ita.law.uvic.ca/documents/Telsimaward.pdf>

150   *Ibid,* paras. 220-1

151   *Ibid*

152   *Ibid,* para. 222.

153   *Ibid,* para. 308

154   *Ibid*

155   *Ibid*

156   *Ibid,* paras. 332-3

157 *Ibid*, para. 334. *See* also para. 335: "Besides Article 6(1), it is also well established in international law that a State may not take away accrued rights of a foreign investor by domestic legislation abrogating the law granting these rights. This is an application of the principles of good faith, estoppel and *venire factum proprium*". *See* also, M. Sornarajah, *The International Law on Foreign Investment, supra* note 12 at 112: "…there is the view that guarantees that are held out to foreign investors do have legal implications, despite regime changes. It is suggested that these guarantees have the effect of indicating a willingness on the part of the State to refer disputes that arise from the foreign investments attracted by the guarantee to an international rather than a national tribunal for settlement…"

Chapter 5

Towards Mechanisms for Assessing the Impacts of Foreign Direct Investment Law and Policy in Post-Conflict Rwanda

Ibironke T. Odumosu·

Introduction

Depending on the description attached to the term "conflict" in Rwanda – the civil war of the early 1990s, the genocide, attempted insurgencies and the impacts of the crisis in the African Great Lakes region – 'post-conflict Rwanda' could be a reference to different periods in recent history. Considered from the end of the genocide in 1994, which coincided with the cessation of the civil war of the early 1990s, Rwanda has been a post-conflict society for over thirteen years. The relatively lengthy period of time since the end of hostilities has afforded Rwanda ample time to adopt legal and policy frameworks to restructure its economy, including the private investment regime, but not necessarily enough time to meaningfully measure the impact of the frameworks. This essay engages in a two-pronged analysis of the measures established to promote and protect foreign direct investment (FDI) in Rwanda. It examines the legal and policy measures that have been adopted and commences a discussion on mechanisms for assessing the impacts of these measures on the post-conflict investment regime and on Rwandans.[1]

While it is still considered a poor country, some commentators regard Rwanda as a post-conflict success having made considerable efforts at rebuilding its economy since 1994.[2] Rwanda's recent incidence of violent conflict colours assessments of its post-conflict economic policies. Post-conflict Rwanda inevitably undergoes constant reassessment through the lens of its crisis of the early 1990s. Many conflicts in Africa are identified with the quest for economic gain or at least reprieve from economic hardship, and Rwanda is no exception. However, while economic factors loom large in many internecine conflicts in postcolonial African states, identity crises and clashes also constitute primary causes of conflict. In his stellar work on the Rwanda crisis, Mahmood Mamdani suggests that the crisis cannot be understood without an engagement with the political identities that were both subjects and causes of the conflict.[3] Beyond the cultural and grievance analyses that Mamdani and some political scientists offer,

economists suggest profit/greed explanations for rebellion.[4] In a modifica-
tion of their earlier work on greed as explanation for civil wars, Paul Collier
and Anke Hoeffler suggest that rebellion may be explained in terms of
opportunities.[5] The economic analysis of the incidence of conflicts from an
opportunity perspective relies on indicators like available finances for
rebellion, the opportunity costs of rebellion, and military advantage arising
from atypically weak armed forces of the government of the day, while high
levels of inequality among the population is an example of the grievance
explanation.[6]

Collier and Hoeffler assert that their opportunity thesis is consistent
with both the economic focus on greed as a motivation for conflict and the
grievance explanation, on the condition that "perceived grievances are
sufficiently widespread to be common across societies and time."[7] The
opportunity explanation can incorporate both profit-seeking and non-profit
seeking rebel groups. Thus, Sambanis argues that it is difficult to see
"greed" and "grievance" as competitive explanations of rebellion.[8] Indeed,
the factors that contributed to the Rwanda civil war and genocide were
"multiple" and "complex".[9] Beyond a quest for resources, the Rwanda civil
war was also a quest for citizenship. The conflict essentially had social
undertones as well as economic triggers. The crisis was a culmination of
dissatisfaction with complex socio-economic and political factors.[10] And
some of these factors continue to underlie Rwanda's landscape, suggesting a
cautious approach to the assessment of Rwanda's post-conflict FDI laws and
policies.[11] Because of the complexity of the factors that drove the conflict,
there is a need for sustained engagement with the potential impact of FDI
policies and activities that form part of post-conflict restructuring.[12] Such
engagement suggests the adoption of a perspective on private investment
that is not only investor-friendly and growth focused, but possesses the
potential to account for the socio-economic dynamics of Rwandan society.

Essentially, just as the Rwanda crisis cannot be entirely explained in
terms of greed or even opportunity, the behaviour of economic actors in the
post-conflict climate might not be reducible to a single greed explanation.
After all, theories that have been developed to explain the incidence and
continuation of conflict cannot necessarily translate, in wholesale form, to
explanations of the motivation for post-conflict economic activities. Even if
there exists a remote possibility that conflict theories could offer some
insight into post-conflict economic climates, arguably, because huge reserves
of natural resources are absent in Rwanda, the 'greed' or 'opportunity' thesis
may not exhaustively explain FDI inflows into post-conflict Rwanda. However, this observation depends on the weight that is attached to tangible and
intangible resources. While natural resources are tangible resources that
might fuel greed in both conflict and post-conflict circumstances, laws and

policies that give free rein to foreign investors in terms of entry, establishment, tax holidays and other incentives might be regarded as intangible "resources" that could support the greed, so to speak, of economic actors or create opportunities for investment in post-conflict countries.

Yet, although the incidence and history of conflict inform post-conflict economic policies and activities, the explanations for conflicts are not necessarily synonymous with post-conflict determinants of FDI and its impact on the socio-economic landscape. Here, the focus is twofold – the motivations for investment, and the impact of FDI laws and policies on the economy and society. The twofold nature of these assessments that resonate throughout this essay represents a focus on opportunities for investors as well as addressing the concerns that citizens might have. First, with regard to investors in Rwanda, it is not easy to read the picture on the basis of conflict theories of greed or opportunity, especially in the absence of major FDI determinants like natural resources. By a simulation (an unsatisfactory one) of conflict explanations, however, one could argue that a non-resource rich state like Rwanda could create "opportunities" that investors might seek to exploit in the form of intangible resources highlighted in the preceding paragraph, thereby enhancing the *quantity* of FDI within its territory. Second, with regard to the society, socio-economic and political grievances continue to some extent post-conflict, and in accordance with prudent policy and law-making, these factors and the impact of FDI should be accounted for in the government's post-conflict initiatives. Hence the dynamics of Rwanda's post-conflict society suggest the need for measures that address the *quality* of FDI as well. Basically, even though post-conflict states are assessed on the basis of their past conflict, and in spite of the possibility of drawing uncomfortably from conflict theories, economic explanations for conflict do not translate effectively in post-conflict situations. Conflict theories cannot effectively provide mechanisms for assessing post-conflict dynamics, and they were not developed to accomplish this purpose. As a result, there arises a need for paradigms that explain the legal and policy frameworks driving FDI regimes in post-conflict countries.

This chapter engages in a discussion of Rwanda's FDI regime in light of the need for establishing mechanisms for assessing post-conflict FDI measures. The chapter's discussion of the nature and contents of the laws and policies that drive post-conflict private investment in Rwanda is situated within the broader, although mostly implicit framework of pre-conflict/conflict economic factors that conflict theories seek to explain.[13] It engages in this assessment on the understanding that regard for history, economic experiences, and the country's peculiarities should inform the adoption of a post-conflict private investment regime specifically tailored to the country's needs and aspirations. The chapter's modest agenda is to discuss and raise questions about the feasibility of a general investment regime that is prescribed for other countries at this time in Rwanda's history. In addressing this agenda, it outlines the multifaceted framework that the government has adopted – on the international, regional and domestic levels – and offers suggestions for a further research agenda on mechanisms for assessing FDI law and policy, focusing on the peculiarities of Rwandan society. That research agenda draws largely on a difference between assessments based on FDI inflows (quantity) and those based on a sustainable private investment regime (quality).

Determinants of Foreign Direct Investment in Post-Conflict Rwanda

In spite of the Rwandan Government's efforts at reconstruction, it is completely legitimate to raise questions about Rwanda's attractiveness as an investment destination. Generally, factors that further the decision to invest in a particular country include the geography of the region, abundant reserves of natural resources, available infrastructure, human capital, costs of transport, population, access to international markets, size of domestic and/or regional markets, macroeconomic and political stability, and legal frameworks and policies that investors consider favourable.[14] Rwanda does not score well with many of these determinants,[15] especially given the significant deterioration of infrastructure and loss of skilled labour during the conflict years.[16] Yet, several arguments are advanced in favour of Rwanda as a viable investment destination. The country's situation as a "virgin territory" for investors, the stability in government, the low level of corruption and crime, and Rwanda's potential to serve as a hub for market access to the East African region's 120 million consumers, are some of those investor-friendly determinants that Rwanda possesses.[17] In addition to these, a visible factor that has taken centre-stage in the Rwandan landscape is the government's adoption of legal and policy instruments as mechanisms for attracting FDI.

The stigma of being a post-conflict society that is viewed with suspicion by observers (even if such suspicion is somewhat unfounded) and the desire to correct such impressions propel the Rwandan government towards a proactive stance on its economy. However, it appears that a major factor driving Rwanda's turn to policy in order to attract FDI stems partly from the country's lack of substantial reserves of mineral resources.[18] By 2005, in spite of what may be considered as economic or political instability in these countries, Egypt, Nigeria and South Africa were among the top five African destinations for FDI, partly because of their significant natural resource reserves.[19] It is reported that even war-torn Iraq still has about seventy international firms registering to compete for tenders to exploit its oil reserves.[20] While Rwanda lacks the traditional FDI determinants in the form of substantial reserves of natural resources that could fuel *greed* pre-, during and post-conflict, it has adopted reforms that conform to conventional international financial institutions' (IFIs) prescriptions for accelerating economic growth in Third World countries. However, it would be inaccurate to depict the general reforms as completely new to Rwanda. In fact, one of the criticisms of the World Bank and the International Monetary Fund (IMF) in relation to the Rwanda conflict was the role that structural adjustment policies, which *inter alia* fostered liberalization, played in exacerbating economic hardship during the conflict in the early 1990s.[21]

In spite of the criticisms of the impact of IFI-led policies during its conflict, what Rwanda lacks in natural resources that may attract FDI it seeks to make up for in active investment promotion and in the adoption of legal and policy reforms that are considered favourable to FDI. And the country is not alone in the adoption of these legal and policy frameworks. Since the turn to economic liberalization by many African countries in the wake of the structural adjustment policies of the 1980s and 1990s, there has been a belief led by IFIs that some policies could account for increased investment flows. IFIs and some foreign investors often view these liberal investment policies as factors that contribute to the promotion and protection of FDI.[22] Largely, the international economic order, especially IFIs, other donor agencies, and major transnational corporations operate on a perception that there are "good" and "bad" investment policies.[23] Major international economic actors identify liberal investment policies as the *acceptable* model of ordering in the global economy. Hence, small economies that do not conform to this model in competing for FDI perceive that they will be losers in the global economy and in the competition for FDI in an age where such investment has become the major source of external finance for many economies.

As a result, Rwanda's reform of its investment regime in conformity with the dominant FDI wisdom, especially given the absence of many FDI determinants in the country, is not entirely surprising. Meanwhile, the impacts of legal reforms in attracting FDI are not entirely certain. Some commentators suggest that stable policy frameworks contribute to the decision to invest in a country,[24] whereas others consider that there is no empirical research to support a proven *uniform* sensitivity of investors to the effectiveness of legal systems.[25] While this essay's aim is not to (dis)prove the point that laws and policies may attract FDI, it can be noted that although FDI inflows to Rwanda remain modest, some tangible FDI flows have occurred and interviewed investors assess Rwanda as investment friendly.[26]

Rwanda's investment policies are only one of the reforms that accompanied the liberal macro-economic structures that the government established.

FDI-friendly policies transcend a single focus on FDI. They extend to the establishment of general macroeconomic reforms, ranging from trade liberalization and tax reforms (to income, corporate and other taxes) to market-driven interest rates and competitive exchange rates. These policies emphasize enhanced institutional capacity in the form of a functioning and independent judiciary, and investment promotion agencies that depart from excessive bureaucracy. The policies presuppose a state that is active in promoting and protecting investment but passive in regulating the activities of private investors. Essentially, these policies require a deregulated investment regime.

If nothing else, adoption of these legal and policy measures contributes to the rhetoric of Rwanda's success. They affect the perception of IFIs and some investors towards the country as a place that is interested in restructuring characterized by a free market economy and deregulation of the investment regime. An examination of Rwanda's investment regime in the next part of this essay reveals a multifaceted regime but one that generally reflects willingness to attract FDI; a regime that is not substantially different from the FDI regime of societies that have not experienced recent conflict. The appropriateness and sustainability of these measures in a post-conflict state with Rwanda's peculiar dynamics is an issue that is yet to be rigorously examined and hence gives cause for healthy scepticism. Thus, the concluding part of this chapter commences a discussion of some issues that require consideration in this regard.

Rwanda's Legal Regime for Private Investment

In July 2000, Rwanda's Ministry of Finance and Economic Planning published a Vision Statement for the Country, called "Vision 2020."[27] The document acknowledged the country's "deeply unsatisfactory social and economic situation." Vision 2020's "major aspiration" is Rwanda's transformation into a middle-income economy.[28] One of the six pillars of the Vision statement involves the active "development of an efficient private sector spearheaded by competitiveness and entrepreneurship."[29] A perusal of Vision 2020 reveals a major challenge in the interconnectedness of its pillars. Thus, although private sector led development is a separate pillar, it is dependent on, and in fact rides on the pillars of infrastructure development, human resource development, and security and political stability, which may all contribute to the promotion of private investment.

In furtherance of its short-term goals of promoting macroeconomic stability and a private sector-led economy, the government has expended resources in the development of policies that could foster trade liberalization and privatization, attract foreign investors and encourage investment in services, as well as tax reforms.[30] The government limits its excursion into the realm of private investments in a truly liberal fashion and tries to withdraw itself as much as is possible from that realm. Its roles are mostly related to the promotion of "good governance" and transparency, the establishment of the legal and commercial framework, the promotion of the entry and establishment of FDI, and the delivery of the infrastructure necessary to facilitate private investment activities.[31]

Prior to 1994, Rwanda's reliance on private sector investment was negligible.[32] The country mostly relied on development aid. At that time, aid was larger than both investment from the private sector and exports combined.[33] Professor Uvin asserts that to the international community, pre-genocide Rwanda was "a model developing country, in which government and citizens were actively, wisely, and successfully committed to development."[34] Yet, Rwanda "never attracted large amounts" of FDI, even though the FDI inflows were larger in the 1980s than in the 1970s.[35] In the post-conflict era, Rwanda is once again committed to the development agenda, this time with a broader focus on private investment. However, as Uvin notes there was a major contradiction between being a "model" developing country and a social catastrophe. In this regard, several commentators have examined the contribution of World Bank and IMF policies to the catastrophe that Rwanda suffered.[36] The earlier failure of the *usual* trade liberalization, privatization and currency devaluation policies in the face of economic hardship makes observers who take history into account wary of FDI and trade liberalization policies that engage the socio-political impacts of such policies as mere rhetoric.

Thus, this essay does not pretend that Rwanda's reconstruction process and challenges are merely economic "problems" that FDI can solve. It examines with the utmost caution the policies and legislation that promote private investment as only one of the multiple ways in which the country is being rebuilt. It recognizes the many pitfalls that could assail this initiative – the baggage of history, the potential impact of the turn towards aggressive private-sector led development on the majority of the population who continue to be rural dwellers, the challenges of redistribution, the danger of crowding out local investment, the inadequate attention to important social sectors that could complement investment, among others – and in that light, engages in an analysis of the investment climate.

As a background to the discussion of the laws and policies that are the focus of this essay, the next section offers an overview of the major themes that drive Rwanda's investment climate, while the following sections discuss the legal and policy mechanisms that Rwanda subscribes to at the international, regional and domestic levels. While multifaceted, they do not adequately capture Rwanda's economic and social peculiarities as a post-conflict society, and could conveniently apply in any East African country that has not recently encountered civil war. Again, it reflects the need for commentators to turn sustained attention to paradigms that define and have the capacity to assess investment regimes in post-conflict states.

Overarching Themes

 Rwanda's legal reform of its private investment regime draws on several broad themes and forms part of a broader macroeconomic restructuring. Two primary themes – liberalization and privatization – run through Rwanda's private investment regime. Liberalization informs the policies at all levels – international, regional and domestic – while by its nature, privatization has been one of the tools that the government has adopted to foster its commitment to a private sector-led economy. These two themes are interdependent and are integral parts of each other. So interdependent have they been in Rwanda's private investment climate that privatization of state-owned enterprises has accounted for a significant amount of the FDI flows to the country.[37]

Liberalization. The adoption of a liberal economic regime is not new to Rwanda, and neither is the country alone in the pursuit of liberal investment policies.[38] The liberalization of domestic FDI regimes is a common occurrence,[39] and experts suggest that further liberalization will continue to play a huge role in attracting FDI.[40] Rwanda's Vision 2020 clearly shares this view when it states that "it will be necessary to pursue an open, liberal trade regime, minimizing barriers to trade as well as implementing policies to encourage foreign direct investment."[41]

Pursuant to the country's liberalization of its investment regime, the *Law Relating to Investment and Export Promotion and Facilitation* ("*Investment Code*"), which is the primary instrument that regulates private investment, does not screen or restrict the entrance and establishment of investment in Rwanda, neither does it preclude investment in any sectors of the economy.[42] However, by virtue of article 8 of the Investment Code, the Rwanda Investment and Export Promotion Agency ("RIEPA") – the Government agency that promotes and facilitates the entry and establishment of private investment in Rwanda – reserves the right to 'select' and 'authorize' an investor to exploit a scarce resource. RIEPA actively promotes the establishment of investments in Rwanda. The institution seems open to a myriad investment avenues to boost the country's post-conflict economy. In addition to domestic laws, Rwanda's participation in international and regional institutions and agreements like the World Trade Organization (WTO) and the Common Market for Eastern and Southern Africa (COMESA) further enhances its mission of investment liberalization.

Rwanda seeks to strike a balance between pure economic reform and social policies. After all, this is the 21st century, a time when the world has turned its attention to the intersection between the economy and subjects like the environment and labour, even if such relationships are essentially uneasy ones. Thus, Rwanda subscribes to the principles of sustainable development in its laws.[43] The preamble to the *Organic Law Determining the Modalities of Protection, Conservation and Promotion of Environment in Rwanda* ("*Environmental Law*") reveals an insightful trend in the Government's attention to the protection of the environment.[44] Four of the international environmental conventions listed in that preamble were authorized for ratification on the same day in December 2003, while all but one of the other seven listed international conventions are of post-conflict origin. This picture of post-conflict ratification of environmental conventions at the same time that the government adopted an active stance towards investment promotion seems to confirm that the government accepts that sound environmental laws might not be a deterrent to a buoyant investment climate. In fact, the *National Investment Strategy* regards agricultural development – the "engine of primary growth" – and the environment as different sides of the same coin owing to the fragile nature of the soil and the need for soil protection.[45] Also, "sustainable environmental and natural resources management" form one of the three "cross-cutting" issues of Vision 2020, in addition to gender equality and science and technology.[46] The *Environmental Law* as well as the Investment Code requires that projects undergo an Environmental Impact Assessment (EIA) prior to their implementation.[47]

For all the promising focus on environmental protection in the books, the interest in private investment appears paramount in practice. The Environmental Law is an organic law that in Rwanda requires other laws for its implementation, and many of these other laws have not been enacted.[48] Even though the Environmental Law purported to establish the Rwanda Environmental Management Authority (REMA), compared to RIEPA, REMA is invisible.[49] In addition, the Ministry of Lands, Environment, Forestry, Water and Mines barely has sufficient information on its website compared to the websites that host information on the economy.[50] These facts reveal that the commitment towards restructuring *is* principally a commitment towards the economy, while effectively neglecting the reality that for most of the population, sound environmental practices might aid in curbing deforestation, soil erosion and land degradation. Ironically, adequate attention to these issues in Rwanda's case does not necessarily undermine the economy, in fact it can boost the livelihoods of many of the rural population and might reduce economic grievances in post-conflict Rwanda.[51]

Unlike the Environmental Law, Rwanda's *Law Establishing the Labour Code* ("*Labour Code*") is not an organic law. The *Labour Code* applies to all employees in the country regardless of nationality, ensuring that the labour rights of expatriates and other non-Rwandan employees are protected.[52] It includes provisions that guarantee health and safety at work,[53] outlaw forced labour,[54] and proscribe child labour.[55] In order to foster its liberal investment policies, the government very recently adopted a policy that eliminates the requirement of work permits for foreigners with at least a Master's Degree, in order to facilitate its capacity building.[56] However, this policy does not preclude the requirement of residence permits for foreigners and affords the government, like other governments around the world, the opportunity to continue to account for the number of people within Rwanda's borders.

Apart from these general laws, in a bid to make itself attractive to FDI, Rwanda does not legally mandate performance requirements in terms of local content requirements or technology transfer, although it strongly suggests and encourages foreign investors to use available local materials and to transfer technology and expertise.[57] It adopts a very flexible stance on the entry and establishment of FDI. In sum, with regards to the contents of the laws, it is difficult to suggest that there is a race to bottom – in this case, the reduction of environmental and labour standards – in a bid to foster a liberal investment climate. However, the assessment might not be the same with regards to the implementation of the environmental laws. Several arguments could support the absence of effective implementation of these laws, one of which is insufficient resources, and another, the perennial race to the bottom.

Privatization. Vision 2020 incorporates a comprehensive privatization policy as one of its key components. The government actively pursues a privatization policy in the belief that promoting macroeconomic stability and wealth creation from the private sector would reduce dependence on foreign aid. It launched its privatization programme with the enactment of *Law No. 2 on Privatization and Public Investment* of March 11, 1996. And the government continues to maintain privatization as a key element of its economic reform. In this regard, Vision 2020 states that:

> The Government of Rwanda will not be involved in providing services and products that can be delivered more efficiently by the private sector. It is, therefore committed towards a comprehensive privatization policy that will help reduce costs and prices and widen consumer choice. The State will only act as a catalyst; ensuring that infrastructure, human resources and legal frameworks are geared towards stimulating economic activity and private investment.[58]

Rwanda's privatization policy does not discriminate against local or foreign investors.[59] It proceeds on the basis of private sector-led growth as articulated in Vision 2020. The implementation of the privatization policy is well under way and foreign investors are active participants in the process.[60] UNCTAD and the ICC note that in 2004 and 2005, proceeds from privatization constituted about half of the FDI inflows into Rwanda.[61] Privatizations in the telecommunications sector have formed some of the largest in Rwanda. These figures are not surprising since telecommunications investors are often regarded as one group of investors that invests in volatile post-conflict regions.[62]

So far, the Rwandan Government has not encountered major challenges with its privatization scheme, although it has repurchased some privatized entities owing to the private investors' failure to honour their commitments.[63] However, because of the unrest that has accompanied the privatization of essential services in other places, including neighbouring Tanzania, it is legitimate to raise issues about Rwanda's preparedness for public backlash and the availability of institutional mechanisms that may address potential or real disadvantages of privatization. In this regard, Rwanda's post-conflict economic policies have been more concerned with the amount of FDI that flows from privatization, without adequately contemplating the attendant downsizing of labour in privatized enterprises, potential rises in prices that may accompany privatizations, and the means for addressing these impacts on the population.

While the twin pillars of liberalization and privatization drive Rwanda's domestic private investment climate, the international and regional frameworks are mostly informed by the liberalization theme. Liberalization at the domestic, regional and international levels are synonymous and as the subsequent sections of this essay will demonstrate, they are driven by essentially identical principles, even if the exact mechanisms adopted differ.

The International Framework

Introduction. Rwanda is a member of several international organizations that contribute to the promotion and protection of FDI. The country became a member of the WTO in 1996 and was a contracting party to the General Agreement on Tariffs and Trade from 1966. It is also a member of the International Centre for Settlement of Investment Disputes (ICSID), having deposited instruments of ratification in 1979. Although Rwanda has not been a respondent to any dispute submitted to ICSID, this position might change shortly, given the increased number of Rwandan agreements and laws that allow recourse to arbitration under the auspices of ICSID.[64] A member of the World Bank's Multilateral Investment Guarantee Agency

(MIGA), Rwanda is also a founding member of a similar initiative, the African Trade Insurance Agency (ATI).[65]

The contents of these international instruments shape Rwanda's private investment climate to a significant extent because ratified international agreements and treaties supersede Rwandan domestic law, including organic laws, but are ranked below the Constitution.[66] By implication, international economic agreements that the government has ratified take pre-eminence over domestic legislation and policies, and could trump local policies that are well tailored to the needs of the Rwandan people and economy. As discussed in the fourth section of this part of the essay, investors may initiate claims against the Government of Rwanda based on these international instruments. The reality of the domestic force attached to international economic instruments heightens the need for a rigorous engagement in treaty negotiation processes to ensure that only those treaties that contribute positively to the well-being of Rwandan people are concluded. However, power dynamics highly influence these negotiations, and especially in the case of bilateral investment treaties (BITs), the host state invariably shoulders all but a few of the burdens and responsibilities in exchange for an unenforceable *promise* of investment flows. Surely, the international balance of power encourages a suspicious stance, or at best a cautious stance, towards the assessment of these bilateral international agreements on Rwanda's socio-economic wellbeing.

Bilateral Investment Treaties. Rwanda has concluded few BITs. Instead, the country's investment promotion mechanisms have mostly centred on regional and domestic initiatives. By 1 July 2007, UNCTAD had a record of four Rwandan BITs.[67] In its immediate post-independence era, the Government of Rwanda concluded BITs with Switzerland and Germany in 1963 and 1967 respectively. It concluded a BIT with Belgium and Luxembourg in 1983 and another with Mauritius in 2001. The most recent BIT was signed on 19 February 2008, when Rwanda's President Paul Kagame and the US President George W. Bush signed the United States-Rwanda Bilateral Investment Treaty.[68] The treaty will enter into force after ratification and approval by the Rwandan parliament and the US Senate. While the contents of the treaty have not been made public, news releases suggest that it includes the "regular" features of contemporary BITs, although it is difficult to draw conclusions without a text, as BITs vary widely even though their general contents may appear similar.

The United States-Rwanda BIT seeks protection for foreign investors in the host states through non-discrimination provisions, legal assurances that investors may freely transfer investment related funds, and the establishment of a scheme for the payment of prompt, adequate, and effective compensation in the event of expropriation. There are also provisions enshrining transparency in the host states' governance scheme and the now common opportunity to have recourse to investor-state arbitration for the settlement of investment disputes between investors and the host state.[69]

Given that there is some US FDI in Rwanda, the United States-Rwanda BIT and its contents might be put to the test on either the investment promotion or the protection level. It remains to be seen, however, whether this BIT will contribute significantly to the level of US FDI flows into Rwanda.

The Regional Framework

Compared to the international framework, the regional mechanism for FDI promotion and protection is more visible in Rwanda's investment climate. Like the international instruments discussed in the preceding section, regional treaties also trump domestic – ordinary and organic – laws in Rwanda. The East African sub-region is composed of countries that share similar historical heritages, somewhat similar economic challenges, and similar perceptions on policies that may attract FDI. The institutional mechanisms by which these countries have sought to jointly address their challenges are discussed in this section.

(a) The *East African Community* ("EAC"/"Community") is a regional intergovernmental organization that includes the Republics of Burundi, Kenya, Rwanda and Uganda and the United Republic of Tanzania. Rwanda acceded to the *Treaty Establishing the East African Community* ("*EAC Treaty*") on June 18, 2007 and became a member on July 1, 2007.[70] In terms of economic integration, the Community established a Customs Union in 2005. It is undertaking negotiations for the establishment of a Common Market by 2010 and a Monetary Union by 2012.[71] By virtue of article 8(4) of the *EAC Treaty*, "Community organs, institutions and laws... take precedence over similar national ones on matters pertaining to the implementation" of the Treaty. It echoes the provisions of the Rwandan Constitution on the prevalence of treaties and international agreements over ordinary and organic domestic laws.

In terms of the immediate effect of the EAC on Rwanda's economy and on private investment in the country, the Customs Union involves a progressive internal tariff elimination that culminates in zero tariffs by January 1, 2010.[72] However, except for Tanzania, in the short term Rwanda's economic relationship with the other EAC members might not change significantly because it already interacts with these countries under the umbrella of COMESA.

(b) The *Common Market for Eastern and Southern Africa* (COMESA) is an economic community that promotes economic integration through the mechanisms of trade and investment in Eastern and Southern Africa.[73]

Rwanda is one of the founding signatories to the *Treaty Establishing the Common Market for Eastern and Southern Africa* ("*COMESA Treaty*"), which was concluded in 1993.[74] While the COMESA regime incorporates multiple economic integration mechanisms – like the COMESA Free Trade Area and the bid to eliminate tariffs among COMESA members, and the COMESA Customs Union – the *Investment Agreement for the COMESA Common Investment Area* (CCIA) ("*COMESA Investment Agreement*") is the COMESA instrument most relevant to this essay.[75]

In a fashion similar to Rwanda's domestic private investment themes, the *COMESA Investment Agreement* clearly emphasizes a broad objective of establishing a "more liberal and transparent investment environment" among COMESA states. It also seeks to increase the "free flow" of investment into the region from both COMESA and non-COMESA sources.[76] Like many contemporary investment agreements, the COMESA Investment Agreement adopts a broad definition of investment. For COMESA, investment includes current and future investment. Specifically, the ramification of investment that the agreement contemplates includes tangible property and related property rights, intellectual property rights and concessions.[77] Both natural and juridical COMESA investors and investments are the subject of many of the provisions and protections of the Agreement.

Article 3 of the COMESA Investment Agreement anticipates the extension of national treatment to COMESA investors by 2010 and the opening up of all economic activities to COMESA investors by the same date. Rwanda had adopted this projected position of the CCIA on national treatment in its Investment Code before the COMESA Investment Agreement was concluded. Through the provisions of the Agreement, there is a general encouragement to COMESA states to further internationalize their investment regimes. For example, article 6 suggests that members should accede to the ICSID Convention and the MIGA Convention among others. Article 6(e) curiously urges accession to "any other multilateral agreement designed to promote or protect investment" irrespective of the contents of such agreements and their implications for COMESA states. In addition to the openness towards further internationalization of COMESA states' investment regimes, the international trend towards transparency also resonates throughout the Agreement.[78]

In what purported to be a departure from most contemporary investment agreements, one of the objectives of part two of the COMESA Investment Agreement is the balancing of rights and obligations between investors and COMESA states.[79] Nevertheless, the Agreement falls short of the realization of such a 'balancing' endeavour. It mostly reads like traditional investment agreements that create rights (without much attention to obligations) in favour of foreign investors and reaffirm the duties of host states. The only

clear provision in the COMESA Investment Agreement on investor obligation reiterates COMESA investors and investments' obligation to comply
with applicable domestic measures in their host COMESA states. That single
provision does not suffice to substantiate the claim in article 11 that the
Agreement seeks to balance rights and obligations between investors and
COMESA states.[80]

The balance of the Agreement establishes the obligations of COMESA
states through mechanisms requiring fair and equitable treatment in accordance with the customary international law standard, the guarantee that
capital may be repatriated, national treatment which applies at both establishment and post-establishment phases, and most favoured nation (MFN)
treatment.[81] The Agreement also adopts the "prompt and adequate compensation" standard in the event that investments are expropriated or where the
state adopts measures tantamount to expropriation on a non-discriminatory
basis and in the public interest.[82] Depending on the text and interpretation of
other agreements, by virtue of the MFN provision in article 19 of the
COMESA Investment Agreement, non-COMESA investors may be entitled
to the extensive establishment and post establishment rights available to
COMESA investors, which might make the results of the Agreement rather
unsustainable.

The COMESA Investment Agreement dedicates an entire section to elu-
cidating the methods for settling both state-state investment disputes and
investor-state disputes.[83] The dispute settlement mechanisms are important
for several reasons, one of which is the not negligible fact that investor-state
dispute settlement mechanisms have attained prominent status as tools for
implementing investment agreements. In addition, the historical pattern
suggests that problems surrounding investment agreements and their
implications for the parties involved, especially Third World states and their
peoples, are usually brought to the fore of international attention when
disputes arise. The dispute settlement part of the COMESA Investment
Agreement includes the now common provisions on negotiation and mediation, domestic dispute settlement in a court of competent jurisdiction in the
host COMESA state, and international mechanisms like dispute settlement
under the UNCITRAL Arbitration Rules, the ICSID Convention and the
ICSID Additional Facility Rules.[84] It also institutionalizes the recent trend
towards the publication of arbitration documents, public hearing and *amicus
curiae* participation.[85]

As is usual with contemporary investment agreements, the COMESA
Investment Agreement adopts the traditional model of recourse to arbitration where the foreign investor is the only party seized of the ability to
initiate international arbitral proceedings, without a corresponding right in
the host state. However, this format is not necessarily optimal considering

that the COMESA Investment Agreement envisages investor obligations, albeit in very limited terms.[86] Nevertheless, in a departure from the strict one-way model of traditional investment arbitration, but without going as far as institutionalizing state-investor dispute settlement, article 28(9) allows COMESA states to raise breaches of investor obligations as a counterclaim or set-off. Had the Agreement addressed the balance in the investor-state and state-investor dispute settlement dynamic, perhaps, it might have been able to substantiate the claim that it balances rights and obligations between investors and host states.

The COMESA Investment Agreement is a rather detailed agreement, largely similar to contemporary investment agreements that have been heavily criticized for their imbalance between rights and obligations. The Agreement tries to address this issue but did not pay enough attention to it to be able to claim that it establishes some meaningful balance. Thus, even though the COMESA Investment Agreement could have achieved a historic change in the world of investment agreements, it failed to seize the opportunity to be a uniquely "Made in Africa" agreement that takes the vulnerability of African peoples and economies into account and also protects them as much as it protects foreign investment. It essentially suffered from the myopia that fosters belief in a system that deifies FDI because such investment may provide the capital that fuels a domestic economy. It focuses on investment promotion without adequate corresponding regard for the potential impact of FDI or the impact of a lopsided focus on investor rights on vulnerable peoples and economies.

The Domestic Framework

Investing in post-conflict zones presents both opportunities and risks.[87] The opportunities lie *inter alia* in the near absence of concrete regulatory mechanisms. Paradoxically, the unsatisfactory state of regulatory institutions and mechanisms constitutes a major risk, in addition to the volatility of the country's post-conflict state. Rwanda's situation is somewhat complex as it has been designated "post-conflict" for over a decade. It has had enough time to formulate comprehensive investment policies, and has indeed formulated those policies. If there is a perception that regulation in the traditional sense is absent in Rwanda, it is not for lack of an opportunity to formulate such policies, but is due to conscious adoption of an essentially deregulated and liberalized investment regime. Still, the government retains the role of investment promoter and facilitator and establishes institutions to fulfil these roles.

Institutional Mechanisms

Even though the Government of Rwanda emphasizes its limited role in private investments, it recognises the importance of a stable state and government for the economy. Hence, the first pillar of Vision 2020 is national reconstruction and a "capable state."[88] However, by comparison with other sectors, the state's visibility in private investment is curtailed. On its part, this chapter adopts the view that institutions do matter. For, if a post-conflict country is to truly restructure its socio-economic climate, it cannot take its institutional development for granted.

Several government agencies are responsible for the promotion of private investments in Rwanda. The Privatization Secretariat assumes a direct role in relation to private investments because of its work in making erstwhile state-owned facilities available to private sector bidders.[89] Other agencies like the Immigration Service perform incidental roles including the issuing of relevant visas and work permits. And the central government retains its role in providing the necessary infrastructure and public investments that boost the establishment of private investments that fuel the economy.[90]

Most prominent among the relevant institutions is the RIEPA, which is an agency charged with the promotion and facilitation of private investment in Rwanda. The Rwanda Investment Promotion Agency (RIPA) was established in 1998 by the then investment legislation.[91] It is one of the government's earliest enduring post-conflict mechanisms to make Rwanda an investment destination of choice. In 2005, RIPA's mandate was extended to include exports, hence, the name change to the Rwanda Investment and Export Promotion Agency (RIEPA). RIEPA also assumes the role of the government agency responsible for registering investments. In a bid to reduce bureaucratic bottlenecks, in May 2004 the government adopted a relatively simplified process of registration and what the RIEPA refers to as the "One Stop Center" or the "Red Carpet Service for Investors", where investors may conclude multiple administrative applications in a few days.[92] Although Rwanda retains RIEPA and other institutions, it operates a largely deregulated investment climate in order to attract FDI.

(a) The Investment Code provides the basic regulatory framework for local and foreign investments in Rwanda. The Code guarantees national treatment for foreign investors.[93] Except, perhaps, for the dichotomy in minimum capital requirement (USD$100,000 for local investors and USD$250,000 for foreign investors), the legislation does not differentiate significantly between local and foreign investments.[94] It proceeds in consonance with Vision 2020 and the National Investment Strategy's dual focus on encouraging FDI and at the same time recognizing that "a local-based business class remains a crucial component of development."[95] In fact, on incentives and facilities, the Investment Code expressly adopts the position that foreign and Rwandan investors will be treated in the same manner.[96]

Nevertheless, the Investment Code defines local and foreign investors as separate categories. The Code sometimes adopts provisions that apply specifically to each category. Preempting the COMESA Investment Agreement's requirement that prescribes national treatment by 2010, Rwanda's Investment Code treats COMESA investors as local investors, even though they are not, strictly speaking, Rwandan investors.[97] Apart from the ability to qualify for recognition and protection under the Investment Code with a smaller minimum capital, when assessed qualitatively the Code does not seem to serve locals better than foreigners. However, qualification as an investor in either of the local or foreign categories is instructive for determining incentives that private investors may be entitled to under Rwandan law.

In keeping with the liberalization and deregulation models, the Investment Code does not mandate the registration of investment projects. Article 3 of the Investment Code provides for the registration of investment projects, but not in absolute terms.[98] Even the revocation of a certificate of registration does not hinder the continued operation of an investment enterprise in Rwanda.[99] However, from the perspective of a private investor, non-registration might not be feasible given that many incentives and benefits under the Investment Code are reserved for registered investments. In addition, the COMESA Investment Agreement only applies to investments that are registered pursuant to the laws of a COMESA member state.[100] Thus, even though there are hardly any restrictions on the entry of FDI into Rwanda, under the COMESA Investment Agreement the government retains some mechanisms for keeping track of the number of investments to which it extends protection and incentives.

Most fiscal incentives in the Investment Code are tax incentives. For long-term investors, stability and certainty of the tax regime are perhaps just as important as the incentives. While the effectiveness of tax incentives in attracting FDI may be questioned, these incentives could form, in part, the basis for the argument that post-conflict states, like any other state, might exploit the *greed* of businesses. Investors are able to consider the legal regime and incentives available at several destinations and decide where to invest. Indeed, this is not a new phenomenon as many ships have been registered under flags of convenience for almost a century in order to avoid heavy taxes. One of the dangers in trying to exploit the greed of businesses in this manner is that a foreign investor may establish FDI in a country for the purpose of benefiting from incentives without any significant attachment to the country and without contributing to the sustainability of the country's economy. It is at this point that it becomes necessary to distinguish between investment flows and real contribution to socio-economic fulfilment. Many commentators assessing Rwanda's investment climate are fixated with the amount of FDI that flows or does not flow into the country without adequate attention to the quality of such FDI. Thus, one of the questions for a further research agenda that this essay suggests in the concluding part concerns rigorous assessment of the quality of FDI that is established in Rwanda and the adoption of legal and policy mechanisms that address this issue. For Rwanda does not seek FDI just for its sake but in order to fuel its post-conflict economy. Fortunately, there is some basis for the commencement of this discussion with the requirements outlined in articles 3 and 24 of the Investment Code.[101]

The tax incentives that Rwanda offers are quite broad. Registered investors – both local and foreign – are entitled to exemption from value added tax that is levied on goods and services imported in accordance with their certificates of registration.[102] Still on indirect taxes, annex 1 to the Investment Code details incentives that the government offers to investors which import certain goods. For example, registered investors that import machinery and raw materials are exempted from import duties.[103] In one of the rare instances in the Investment Code where foreign investors are entitled to tax incentives that are unavailable to local investors (on account, in this case, of the very nature of the incentive), a foreign investor or an expatriate working for a registered investment enterprise is exempted from duties on personal property, household property and one personal car.[104] Investors operating in a free economic zone (FEZ) are also entitled to the importation of goods, machinery, equipments and raw materials free of duty.[105]

Annex 2 to the Investment Code provides a comprehensive list of incentives offered in relation to direct income tax, including available investment allowance, training and research expenses, and export commodities and services.[106] Specifically, for example, investors that employ Rwandans are entitled to profit tax discounts depending on the number of Rwandans in their employment and the length of time that they are employed. Whereas business profit is taxable at the rate of thirty per cent, some investments, including some operating in free trade zones, may be entitled to the payment of a zero per cent corporate income tax and a non-taxed repatriation of their profits to other countries.[107] FEZs in Rwanda include export processing zones, free trade zones, and "single enterprise[s] considered as export processing zone[s]."[108] RIEPA authorizes investors' operation in a FEZ, and has the responsibility for the organization and management of the FEZs.[109] The ability of some investors operating in a free trade zone to operate at a zero per cent income tax rate (with tax free repatriation of profits) has been criticized for being "excessive" and running the risk of being unsustainable, because it may attract investors that operate in Rwanda for the sake of the incentives and without any significant economic ties to the country.[110]

Rwanda also offers a constitutionally guaranteed inviolable right to private property, subject to expropriations in the public interest upon payment of compensation.[111] *Organic Law No. 08/2005 of 14/07/2005 Determining the Use and Management of Land in Rwanda ("Land Law")* reiterates the constitutional provisions on the right to private property. It specifically articulates the position that both local and foreign investors may enjoy "full rights of ownership of land".[112] The Land Law allows the state to grant "ownership" rights in the nature of a lease for a period not exceeding ninety-nine years.[113] Such rights are transferable gratuitously, and by sale, lease or mortgage.[114]

In staying true to its intention of being a liberal instrument, the Investment Code also includes mechanisms for the protection of FDI. Again, this is one of the points of separation between local and foreign investment in the Investment Code. While it is difficult to justify the difference in the treatment of local and foreign investors on investment protection, some of the mechanisms, like ICSID arbitration and conciliation, are by their nature only available to foreign investors. Although the Investment Code does not address investment protection for local investors, a Rwandan investor may have recourse to local courts, and a COMESA investor (which is a local investor by virtue of the Investment Code) may have recourse under the mechanisms established under the COMESA Investment Agreement.

Like many of the other provisions in the Investment Code, the mechanisms for the protection of foreign investment apply only to registered investment enterprises.[115] In article 30, the Code incorporates the prompt and adequate compensation in foreign convertible currency and free repatriation standard that (foreign) investors have come to expect, in the event of expropriation.[116] Notably, this provision does not expressly refer to foreign or local investors, but simply to investors. But a holistic reading of the chapter, including the headings, suggests an exclusive application to foreign investors, and may be the subject of various interpretations. Such a purported application of article 30 exclusively to foreign investors is problematic on several levels. First, local investors may not feel as protected as their foreign counterparts because they are not included in the law on compensation, and if the arguments on the negative impacts of expropriation translate into practice, they might not be as willing to invest in the country. On this note, it is pertinent to recall that the private sector, including local small businesses and family businesses, is the second largest employer of labour in Rwanda.[117] Second, on a conceptual level, such an approach does not resonate with the government's resolve to promote local as well as foreign investment but reflects a bias in favour of foreign investment. Third, under the Investment Code, local investors include COMESA investors, which form a not negligible percentage of the investors in Rwanda. These investors require investment protection like those investors categorized as "foreign". True, COMESA investors might benefit from investment protection under the COMESA Investment Agreement, but a COMESA investor might choose to refrain from engaging a regional mechanism and prefer to proceed under local legislation. Essentially, the arrangement of investment protection mechanisms under a heading that captures only foreign investment reflects the inherent magnification of everything foreign that plagues many parts of Africa and undermines much needed local capacity and incentive.

Dispute resolution mechanisms applicable to disputes between foreign investors and the government range from amicable negotiation and arbitration to litigation before Rwandan courts.[118] The international investor-state arbitration mechanisms that are incorporated into most international investment agreements are available under the Investment Code. Thus, even though the Rwandan Government has not concluded many BITs, it remains susceptible to the heated debates that have surrounded investment arbitration in the late 20th and early 21st centuries. By virtue of article 32 the Investment Code, an investment dispute may be resolved on the basis of the contents of, and through procedures included in, any bilateral or multilateral agreements that Rwanda has concluded with the foreign investor's home state (thereby not precluding the application of the UNCITRAL Rules, where applicable) and through the mechanisms established under the ICSID Convention. The ICSID Convention requires mutual consent by the parties, which might be articulated in several ways. Such consent may be included in domestic legislation, in investment contracts, and in investment treaties.[119] By article 33 of the Investment Code, the Rwandan Government's consent to arbitration under the auspices of ICSID is included in the certificate of registration of the investment enterprise.

On the domestic, regional and international levels, Rwanda has, or is party to, an assortment of sophisticated investment promotion and protection laws and policies. It proceeds on the basis of a liberal access to FDI in a bid to reconstruct its post-conflict economy. However, in order to achieve even the basic mission of complying with the positions articulated in Vision 2020 and the National Investment Strategy, there is a dire need to fully integrate local investment and investors into the corpus and to reappraise the quality of the investment projects established in the country. More importantly, the policies and especially the omissions (for example on protection of local investment) suggest that the country might not necessarily be dancing to the beat of its own drums but to that of another. Rwanda has experimented with the IFI and foreign investors' model of investment policies. Even if some might argue that the situation is not ideal, the government has created an investor-friendly climate through the instrumentality of its laws and policies in a bid to attract FDI. To draw from the earlier discussion on the rather unsatisfactory simulations of conflict theories in post-conflict situations, in its bid to enhance peace within its territory Rwanda has created "opportunities" that investors may seek to exploit. Now it is time that the country assessed its FDI model and its contribution to Rwanda's socio-economic fulfilment, and on the basis of that assessment, perhaps, began to contemplate a framework that is truly made in Rwanda for Rwandans. The following conclusion offers some thoughts on urgent questions and on a future research agenda, with the caveat that for some issues, the future is now.

Conclusion: Measured Successes, Cautionary Notes, and a Research Agenda

It is undeniable that Rwanda has made admirable progress from the state in which it was in 1994. It has truly emerged as a country with a clear commitment to economic restructuring after a crisis that cost awful losses of human life at a speed unprecedented in recorded history, losses of infrastructure, and even loss of reputation and confidence. The discussions in this chapter have engaged a single part of the attempts at rebuilding the country's economy – the legal and policy framework for FDI promotion and protection in the country. This concluding part seeks to frame issues for further discussions and research on mechanisms for assessing the impacts of the type of investment regime that Rwanda has adopted. It extrapolates from the preceding discussions and commences discussion of suggestions for a further research agenda in terms of the country's next steps in developing its private investment regime, in a manner that accounts for its peculiarities.

Before outlining the suggestions for a further research agenda, some comments on the potential contributions of economic policies, broadly speaking, to peace-building in conflict zones or the avoidance of conflict are in order. Generally, mechanisms for assessing FDI laws and policies have not formed a significant part of post-conflict research. In addition, the contributions of these policies to peace-building are not exactly clearly mapped out. For example, several founding members of the COMESA Treaty – Burundi, Democratic Republic of Congo, Somalia, Sudan, and Uganda – have all suffered conflict despite the efforts of economic integration that the Treaty offered. True, reprieve from economic hardship contributes to the reduction of economic grievances that may partly trigger violent conflicts. However, these policies may not substantially alter the incidence of conflicts if they do not alleviate the plights of citizens or are not tailored to address their concerns. As a result, in framing a research agenda, experience supports a focus on the impacts of the policies on the local population, and not only on their potential to attract FDI.

First on the research agenda is the pertinent issue of the determinants of success. It raises the "who", "what" and "how" questions. The questions help focus and frame the context and location of Rwanda's investment regime. From whose perspective has Rwanda achieved success in its investment regime – the Rwandan people and/or government, foreign investors, IFIs or other international observers? On what basis and by what standards are Rwanda's legal and policy reforms being measured – is the adoption of policies that IFIs and some foreign investors deem acceptable sufficient, or is there a "higher" standard of local accountability? What exactly is the measure of success – the amount of FDI flows (quantity) or the increased welfare of Rwandans (quality)? How is the contribution of FDI to the livelihoods of the people of Rwanda and the rule of law measured – is it in terms of GDP, reduced economic and political grievances, or general human development? These are some of the principal questions that are relevant to any meaningful assessment of Rwanda's investment regime. They form the background for further research on the robust welfare enhancing capabilities of Rwanda's investment regime.

Second, even though it might contradict the liberal economic stance that Rwanda has adopted, the country's place and time suggest the need for a *visible* and *active* democratic state. Such a state is an embodiment of multiple factors. It is visible and active in terms of charting a private investment course for the country in consultation with the people. The people of Rwanda have to own the policies that drive their economy. The state has to be visible and active in terms of prioritizing the needs of Rwandans above the dictates of international economic trends, so that if a policy is not in consonance with Rwanda's socio-economic well-being, the government will not adopt it. Such a state is a Rwandan state with functioning institutions that drive confidence in the investment sector without administrative bottlenecks, yet does not bargain with the well-being of the population in the competition for foreign capital. In this case, other agencies have to be just as visible as RIEPA. RIEPA's prominent position in the country's economic landscape is not in itself problematic. However, inadequate focus on other agencies betrays a lopsided focus on one sector of the country's socio-economic fabric. As discussed earlier, REMA requires visibility in order to fulfil the promises of environmental protection in the Investment Code. It requires an active role in order to foster a sustainable use of agricultural lands that serve the economic interests of Rwanda's majority rural population.

Further, a visible and strong democratic state is thr right one for the formulation and execution of policies of wealth redistribution in a country with a large rural population where agricultural jobs still tend to predomi-nate.[120] Such a state with this focus is especially necessary in a post-conflict society like Rwanda that suffered a crisis arising partly from economic grievances and needs to continue to avoid fuelling conflicts between differ-ent groups in the country.[121] Experience has taught that the market alone cannot address the multifaceted issues that dominate Rwanda's socio-political climate. Even in Nigeria, whereas the Niger Delta is home to sig-nificant amounts of FDI, it is also the most unstable part of the country.

Perhaps a deregulated investment regime and a redistributionist state are incompatible, and Rwanda has to make a choice between these two somewhat competing policy choices.[122] Perhaps it is (im)possible to combine these two concepts at the point where Rwanda is situated in terms of its history and economic status. These issues require further research, in a manner that contemplates and incorporates Rwanda's specific peculiarities and not on a general level that formulates a grand theory about investment protection and wealth redistribution. Admittedly, redistribution by a visible and active state is an issue to which answers might not be located solely in the realm of law, or in any one discipline for that matter, but in a combina-tion of interdisciplinary allegiances.

Third, Vision 2020 and the National Investment Strategy propose a bal-anced focus on foreign and local investment. However, as demonstrated in the third part of this essay, legal provisions seem to favour FDI above local investment, especially in terms of investment protection. And, in the In-vestment Code, local investment includes investment from neighbouring COMESA states. These legal rules discount the fact that local investors are part of group that forms the second largest employer of labour in Rwanda and, given COMESA investors' familiarity with the region, there is a strong presence of COMESA investors. If nothing else, their potentials suggest a need for a balanced incentive and investment protection scheme. In addi-tion, in the view of some scholars history reveals that developed countries engaged in systematic discrimination between local and foreign investors.[123] At the time that these now industrialized countries sought to develop their economies, they required technology transfer, joint venture arrangements, performance requirements and other mechanisms like restrictions on entry of foreign investment that are now considered inconducive to attracting foreign investment in much of the Third World. Professor Chang's interpre-tation of these historical surveys suggests that countries move in the direc-tion of further liberalization and non-discrimination as an *outcome* of economic development and not necessarily as a *cause* of development, that is, in order to develop their economies.[124] Of course, generalizing these issues will read against the grain of this essay. Thus the interaction between local and foreign investment in Rwanda's particular context requires dedicated investigation. Inquiries into the potential impacts of the one on the other, for example the possibility of FDI crowding out local investments, cannot but be beneficial for the formulation of policies that enhance the well-being of the country.

Finally, after establishment of a regime that the international financial community deems acceptable, it is time to query the economic, social, political and environmental sustainability of these policies that Rwanda has been credited as being economically savvy for adopting. Several of these questions have been the subject of general debate but would serve Rwanda well if they were examined in light of the country's past and present experiences. Thus, it is not new to question the contribution of FDI to economic growth and economic development. An extension of the analysis to Rwanda specifically, and an examination of how the country has fared with current FDI. might be helpful. Beyond the growth question, a common question queries FDI's contribution to the promotion of socio-economic and human development. The United Nations Development Programme's (UNDP) *Human Development Report 2007/2008* ranks Rwanda 161 out of 177 countries on the Human Development Index.[125] While Rwanda's ranking might not be particularly shocking, Nigeria, one of the countries with the highest levels of FDI flows in Africa, was ranked in the 158th position in the same report, demonstrating that FDI cannot on its own make a country socially sustainable. Hence, the need for a system that welcomes FDI but with the sort of cautious enthusiasm that takes a bigger social picture into account.[126] That wider social picture assumes a higher magnitude in post-conflict societies. Such a bigger picture might dictate the application of themes other than those that Rwanda has relied on. But, until that time when we proffer responses to the inquiries noted in this conclusion, it is important to exercise caution in labelling Rwanda's investment regime a success story because it has adopted policies and legal frameworks that some international actors consider ideal.

Even if the explanations for conflict and their economic ramifications are not conclusive, conflict theories are relatively well advanced. A major assignment with regard to Rwanda and other post-conflict states (especially those without significant reserves of natural resources) is to develop mechanisms for explaining the establishment of FDI in these states and, even more important, to develop mechanisms for assessing the positive as well as the negative impacts of FDI law and policy on post-conflict states. Generalizations may be inappropriate, so each state might have to be addressed separately. However the information garnered from one might inform assessments of the other, without defining it.

Notes

* The author would like to thank Natasha Affolder, Ljiljana Biukovic, Jalia Kangave and Richard Oppong for their comments on earlier versions of this chapter.

1 This essay does not attempt to outline the number of investments that Rwanda has attracted. For a (non-exhaustive) list of foreign investors in Rwanda and outlines of the stories of several foreign investors and their experiences with the Rwanda investment climate, see United Nations Conference on Trade and Development & International Chamber of Commerce, *An Investment Guide to Rwanda: Opportunities and Conditions, October 2006*, UNCTAD/ITE/IIA/2006/3 (New York and Geneva, United Nations, 2006) [UNCTAD & ICC].

2 UNCTAD & ICC, *ibid*. at 1.

3 Mahmood Mamdani, *When Victims Become Killers: Colonialism, Nativism, and the Genocide in Rwanda* (Princeton, New Jersey: Princeton University Press, 2001), chap. 1. On explanations for the conflict, see pp. 196-202.

4 See H.I. Grossman, "A General Equilibrium Model of Insurrections" (1991) 81 *American Economic Review* 912; J. Hirshleifer, *The Dark Side of the Force: Economic Foundations of Conflict Theory* (Cambridge, England: Cambridge University Press, 2001).

5 Paul Collier & Anke Hoeffler, "Greed and Grievance in Civil War" (2004) 56 Oxford Economic Papers 563. Collier and Hoeffler's thesis in this work revises their earlier work. See Paul Collier & Anke Hoeffler, "On the Economic Causes of Civil War" (1998) 50 Oxford Economic Papers 563.

6 Collier & Hoeffler, "Greed and Grievance" *ibid.*, at 565-570, 588.

7 *Ibid.*, at 589.

8 He notes: "Greed and grievance are often alternative interpretations of the same phenomenon; they are shades of the same problem. Indeed, we often see more political greed and economic grievance than the other way around. ... if state failure or government illegitimacy turns domestic politics into a near-anarchic world, then what Collier and Hoeffler call "greed" is really synonymous to the pursuit of survival. Civil war may be a response to either greed or grievance, but most often it is the result of both." Nicholas Sambanis, "Conclusion: Using

Case Studies to Refine and Expand the Theory of Civil War" in Paul Collier & Nicholas Sambanis eds, *Understanding Civil War: Evidence and Analysis* (Vol. 1: Africa) (Washington: World Bank, 2005) 303 at 329.

9   Peter Uvin, *Aiding Violence: The Development Enterprise in Rwanda* (Connecticut: Kumarian Press, 1998) 3. See also Karen Ballentine & Jake Sherman eds, *The Political Economy of Armed Conflict: Beyond Greed and Grievance* (Boulder, Colorado & London, England: Lynne Rienner Publishers, 2003).

10   See Uvin, *ibid.*, chapter 4, for a concise statement of some of the economic and political crises that contributed to the Rwanda crisis.

11   See generally, Filip Reyntjens, "Rwanda, Ten Years on: From Genocide to Dictatorship" in Steffan Marysse & Filip Reyntjens eds, *The Political Economy of the Great Lakes Region in Africa: The Pitfalls of Enforced Democracy and Globalization* (Basingstoke, Hampshire, UK; New York: Palgrave Macmillan, 2005) 15.

12   A lot of the work on the economies of post-conflict societies has been on aid. See for example, Paul Collier & Anke Hoffler, "Aid, Policy and Growth in Post-Conflict Societies" (2004) 48 *European Economic Review* 1125. See also, Jean A.P. Clement ed., *Post-Conflict Economics in Sub-Saharan Africa: Lessons from the Democratic Republic of Congo* (Washington, DC: International Monetary Fund, 2004).

13   For an assessment of features of legal systems like predictability and efficiency, and their impacts on attracting foreign investment, see Amanda Perry, "An Ideal Legal System for Attracting Foreign Direct Investment?: Some Theory and Reality" (1999-2000) 15 *American University International Law Review* 1627.

14   V.N. Balasubramanyam, "Foreign Direct Investment in Developing Countries: Determinants and Impact" in Organisation for Economic Co-operation and Development, *Global Forum on International Investment: New Horizons for Foreign Direct Investment* (Paris: OECD, 2002) 187.

15   UNCTAD, *Investment Policy Review: Rwanda* (New York & Geneva: United Nations, 2006) 17 states succinctly: "The small size of the economy, its rural nature, the low level of human capital, the poor quality of infrastructure and landlocked position, high operating costs and limited proved natural resources mean that Rwanda lacks the main drivers of foreign investment by major transnational corporations (TNCs) that may be in search of resources, markets or internationally competitive centres of production."

16 The government has and continues to make considerable effort at rebuilding its infrastructure and developing local skilled labour, while also seeking to attract foreign experts. In a survey on investor perspectives, UNCTAD and ICC note that the main difficulty of doing business in Rwanda stems from the cost of production – the landlocked nature of the country and the cost of energy. See UNCTAD & ICC, *supra* note 1 at 56.

17 *Ibid.*, at 1.

18 It is estimated that Rwanda has 60 billion cubic metres of renewable methane gas in Lake Kivu. See Unit for the Promotion and Exploitation of Lake Kivu Gas, http://www.upegaz.gov.rw/. A Canadian company, Vangold, recently received rights to explore for oil in Rwanda. See "Rwanda: Canadian Firm Starts Oil Exploration," (November 7, 2007) *The New Times,* Kigali. Rwanda also exports commercial crops, especially coffee and tea.

19 UNCTAD, *Prospects for Foreign Direct Investment and the Strategies of Transnational Corporations, 2005-2008* (New York & Geneva, United Nations: 2005) 30.

20 "Foreign Firms Seek Iraq Oil Deals" (February 18, 2008), Global Policy Forum, http://globalpolicy.org/security/oil/2008/0218foreignfirms.htm. Yet, others suggest that some oil giants are declining invitation to inspect existing oil fields. The chief executive of one of the big five oil companies is quoted as saying that before investing in Iraq, he would like to see some of the legal mechanisms discussed in this essay, and other factors, including a "contract system, arbitration, physical security and social cohesion" in place. See Steven Mufson, "A Crude Case for War?" *Washington Post,* March 16, 2008, p. B01.

21 See Michel Chossudovsky, *The Globalization of Poverty: Impacts of IMF and World Bank Reforms* (London & New Jersey: Zed Books; Halifax, Nova Scotia: Fernwood Publishing, Australia: Pluto Press; Cape Town: Institute for Policy and Social Research; 1997) 111-122.

22 For the view that proactive policies and reforms may generate the interests of foreign investors in a country, see Jacques Morisset, "Foreign Direct Investment in Africa: Policies also Matter" in OECD, *Global Forum on International Investment, supra* note 14 at 167.

23 See Department for International Development, *Eliminating World Poverty: A Challenge for the 21ˢᵗ Century,* White Paper on International Development Pre-

sented to Parliament by the Secretary of State for International Development, UK, November 1997, para. 3.28. Referring to the conditions for attracting private investment to developing countries, the DFID stated that "the *right* domestic policies and conditions in these countries, including political stability, transparent and accountable government and the prevention of corruption" are crucial to attracting and retaining private investment. (Emphasis added.) See also, World Bank, *World Development Report 1997: The Role of the State in a Changing World* (New York: Oxford University Press, 1997) 30-38, especially at 33 where the Report states that "[g]ood policies by themselves can improve results."

24   Morriset, *supra* note 22; Balasubramanyam, *supra* note 14, at 192-194.

25   Amanda Perry, "Effective Legal Systems and Foreign Direct Investment: In Search of the Evidence" (2000) 49 Int'l & Comp. L.Q. 779, esp. at 796.

26   Some of the investment opportunities that made news in 2007 and early 2008 were Chinese investments in the telecommunication and information technology (IT) sectors. Rwandatel, the major provider of land telephone lines in Rwanda and Huawei Technologies, concluded an $US35 million expansion contract in February 2008. See RIEPA, "Rwandatel to Invest $35 million in Network" (February 15, 2008), http://www.rwandainvest.com/spip.php?article 415. LAP Green Networks, a subsidiary of the Libyan African Portfolio, acquired 80 per cent of the shares in Rwandatel in 2007. On investment in IT, see RIEPA, "Chinese Invest Big into IT" (August 15, 2007), http://www.rwanda invest.com/spip.php?article387. See UNCTAD & ICC, *supra* note 1 for accounts of investors expressing satisfaction with several facets of Rwanda's investment law and policy, including the tax regime and registration procedures. These investors largely assess the investment climate as "positive and encouraging."

27   Republic of Rwanda, Ministry of Finance and Economic Planning, Rwanda Vision 2020 (Kigali, July 2000).

28   *Ibid.* at 3.

29   *Ibid.*

30   *Ibid.*, at 9-10.

31   Rwanda, Ministry of Finance and Economic Planning, *National Investment Strategy* April 27, 2002 (Updated June 4, 2002), para. 29 [*National Investment Strategy*].

32   Uvin, *supra* note 9 at 40-41.

33   *Ibid.*

34   *Ibid.*, at 40. On page 42, Uvin notes that Rwanda "was the image of a country ... faced with daunting economic and demographic challenges but endowed with a government that followed the right policies, the fruits of which the hardworking population enjoyed." Statistically, the amount of FDI that flowed to Rwanda was once higher than those of many of its East African neighbours. See UNCTAD & ICC, *supra* note 1 at 3, 15.

35   UNCTAD, *Investment Policy Review, supra* note 15 at 17.

36   Chossudovsky, *supra* note 21; International Panel of Eminent Personalities, *Report on the 1994 Genocide in Rwanda and Surrounding Circumstances (Rwanda: The Preventable Genocide)* (2001) 40 I.L.M. 141.

37   UNCTAD & ICC, *supra* note 1 at 3.

38   Prior to the conflict of the early 1990s, the country operated one of the most liberal economies in sub-Saharan Africa and was one of the "three most advanced countries" in the region (although it had its fair share of mountainous economic problems). See Uvin, *supra* note 9 at 46 & 48.

39   UNCTAD notes that in 2003, forty per cent of African countries further liberalized their foreign investment regimes. See UNCTAD, *Prospects for Foreign Direct Investment and the Strategies of Transnational Corporations, 2004-2007* (New York & Geneva, United Nations: 2004) 8.

40   *Ibid.*, at 47.

41   Vision 2020, *supra* note 27 at 19.

42   Law No. 26/2005 of 17/12/2005 ["*Investment Code*"]. Although the Investment Code does not include explicit provisions on restrictions or prohibition of investment in any sector, UNCTAD & ICC credit RIEPA as a source for the posi-

tion that the "manufacture and dealing in narcotic drugs and firearms, including ammunition and explosives is prohibited." See UNCTAD & ICC, *supra* note 1 at 57.

43   It is conceded that the definition of sustainable development is a problematic subject. See article 4(C)(1) of *Organic Law N° 04/2005 of 08/04/2005 Determining the Modalities of Protection, Conservation and Promotion of Environment in Rwanda* (*"Environmental Law"*) for the definition that the Rwanda *Environmental Law* adopts.

44   *Ibid*.

45   *National Investment Strategy, supra* note 31, paras. 78-81.

46   Vision 2020, *supra* note 27 at 4 & 19-20.

47   *Environmental Law, supra* note 43, arts. 67-70; *Investment Code, supra* note 42, arts. 3 & 22.

48   See article 93 of the Rwandan Constitution. Government of Rwanda, Kigali, *Constitution of the Republic of Rwanda* (June 4, 2003) [*"Rwandan Constitution"*]; UNCTAD & ICC, *supra* note 1 at 51.

49   See article 65 of the *Environmental Law, supra* note 43.

50   See http://www.minitere.gov.rw/.

51   On ecosystems and wellbeing in Rwanda, see Carissa Wong, Marlene Roy, Anantha K. Duraiappah, *Connecting Poverty & Ecosystem Services, A Series of Seven Country Scoping Studies: Focus on Rwanda* (UNEP & IISD, 2005).

52   *Law No. 51/2001 of 30/12/2001 Establishing the Labour Code* [*"Labour Code"*], art. 2.

53   *Labour Code, ibid*, arts. 132-138.

54   *Labour Code, ibid*, art. 4.

55   *Labour Code, ibid*, art. 11.

56   RIEPA, "Government Scraps Work Permit for Masters Degree Holders" (February 18, 2008) http://www.rwandainvest.com/spip.php?article416. Public Service Minister, Professor Manasseh Nshuti, however, notes that "after Rwandans develop capacity", the doors could be closed and every foreigner would be required to pay for work permits.

57   *Investment Code*, supra note 42, arts. 3 & 24.

58   Vision 2020, *supra* note 27 at 15. At page 9, Vision 2020 also notes that the "[g]overnment will desist from providing services that the private sector can deliver more efficiently and competitively."

59   See *Ministerial Order No 007/03/10/MIN of 07/08/2003 Determining Procedures for the Privatisation of Public Services and Enterprises and for the Selling of Government Shares and Partnership Shares in Semi-Public Companies.*

60   For a list of some of the privatized entities, see Rwanda Privatization Secretariat, http://www.privatisation.gov.rw/documents/privatisation_status.pdf.

61   UNCTAD & ICC, *supra* note 1 at 51.

62   *See Antonio Carvalho & Samia Melhem,* Attracting Investment in Post-Conflict Countries: The Importance of Telecommunications, Archived Discussion, May 2005 *(Washington DC: The World Bank Group) (noting that "in the two years after the fall of the Taliban in Afghanistan, private investors poured $130 million into telecommunications. In October 2003 when three, two-year phone licenses came up for bid in Iraq, more than 200 company consortia submitted bids.") See also Antonio Carvalho, "Sierra Leone and Rwanda: Sequencing ICT in Post-Conflict/Low-Capacity Countries Undergoing Decentralization" (Washington DC: The World Bank Group, March 2005).*

63   Several privatizations have been reversed. For example, the Rwandan Government bought back Rwandatel, the privatized telecommunication company, after the deal broke down when the government accused Terracom Communications – the American company that bought Rwandatel – of failing to honour its commitments. See Bosco Hitimana, "Rwandatel, Huawei in $35m Deal," (February 18, 2008) *East African Business Week*. James Manyaneza, "Rwanda: President Explains Dane Associates Deal" (March 1, 2007), *The New Times* (Kigali), reported that the government terminated the management contract it concluded with Lahmeyer International on Electrogaz, the country's power and water utility. The government also recovered three formerly privatized hotels

when the purchasers did not respect the contract. See Rwanda, Privatization Secretariat, "Privatized Companies" (Ministry of Finance and Economic Planning, 2005) 3.

64   *Convention on the Settlement of Investment Disputes between States and Nationals of Other States*, 18 March 1965, (1965) 4 I.L.M 532 [*ICSID Convention*].

65   *Convention Establishing the Multilateral Investment Guarantee Agency* (October 11, 1985), (1985) 24 I.L.M. 1605 [*MIGA Convention*]; *Agreement Establishing the African Trade Insurance Agency* (May 18, 2000, as amended on July 28, 2006), http://www.africa-eca.com/download/Agreement(English).pdf.

66   *Rwandan Constitution, supra* note 48, art. 190.

67   UNCTAD, "Country-Specific Lists of BITs," http://www.UNCTAD.org/Templates/Page.asp?intItemID=2344&lang=1.

68   RIEPA, "United States-Rwanda Bilateral Investment Treaty" (February 19, 2008) http://www.rwandainvest.com/spip.php?article421. Rwanda and the United States concluded a Trade and Investment Framework Agreement on June 7, 2006.

69   *Ibid.*

70   EAC, "About EAC," http://www.eac.int/about_eac.htm; *Treaty Establishing the East African Community* (November 30, 1999), http://www.eac.int/treaty.htm. Rwanda is also member of the African Economic Community. See *Treaty Establishing the African Economic Community* (June 3, 1991), (1991) 30 I.L.M. 1245.

71   "About EAC," *ibid.*

72   See article 11 of the Protocol on the Establishment of the East African Customs Union (March 2, 2004), http://www.eac.int/EAC_CuctomsUnionProtocol.pdf.

73   See *Treaty Establishing the Common Market for Eastern and Southern Africa* (November 5, 1993), (1994) 33 I.L.M. 1072. Current members of COMESA are Burundi, Comoros, Democratic Republic of Congo, Djibouti, Egypt, Eritrea, Ethiopia, Kenya, Libya, Madagascar, Malawi, Mauritius, Rwanda, Seychelles, Sudan, Swaziland, Uganda, Zambia, and Zimbabwe.

74 *Ibid.*

75 *Investment Agreement for the COMESA Common Investment Area* (May 23, 2007), http://www.comesa.int/ [*COMESA Investment Agreement*]. By article 37, the *COMESA Investment Agreement* will enter into force when it is signed and ratified by at least six members.

76 *COMESA Investment Agreement, ibid.*, art. 2(a).

77 *COMESA Investment Agreement, ibid.*, art. 1(9).

78 See for example, article 4 of the *COMESA Investment Agreement, ibid.*

79 *COMESA Investment Agreement, ibid.*, art. 11.

80 For a model agreement that adopts a wider view of investor obligations, see Howard Mann *et al., IISD Model International Agreement on Investment for Sustainable Development: Negotiators' Handbook* (Winnipeg, Manitoba: International Institute for Sustainable Development, 2nd ed., 2006).

81 *COMESA Investment Agreement, supra* note 75, arts. 14-19. By virtue of article 18 of the Agreement, COMESA states may wholly or partially exclude some economic activities from national treatment.

82 *COMESA Investment Agreement, ibid.*, art. 20.

83 *COMESA Investment Agreement, ibid.*, arts. 26-31.

84 United Nations Commission on International Trade Law (UNCITRAL) Arbitration Rules, approved by the UN General Assembly, 15 December 1976, (1976) 15 I.L.M. 701; *ICSID Convention, supra* note 64.

85 For an overview of these mechanisms, see Ibironke T. Odumosu, "Revisiting NGO Participation in WTO and Investment Dispute Settlement: From Procedural Arguments to (Substantive) Public Interest Considerations" (2006) 44 *Canadian Yearbook of International Law* 353.

86 See Jan Paulsson, "Arbitration without Privity", 10 ICSID Rev.–FILJ 232 (1995).

87 See Virginia Haufler, "The Private Sector and Governance in Post-Conflict Societies" in Derick W. Brinkerhoff ed., *Governance in Post-Conflict Societies* (London, New York: Routledge, 2007) 143.

88 Vision 2020, *supra* note 27 at 3. The realization of this pillar in practice has not been without criticism as some commentators consider the current Rwandan government a dictatorship, even though it purports to be a democratically elected government. See Reyntjens, *supra* note 11.

89 See Privatization Secretariat, http://www.privatisation.gov.rw/eng/indexe.htm.

90 Public investment is a central feature of Rwanda's *National Investment Strategy*. See *supra* note 31.

91 Law No. 14/98 of 18/12/1998.

92 See RIEPA, "One Stop Center: Red Carpet Service for Investors" http://www.rwandainvest.com/spip.php?rubrique16. It includes services from RIEPA (investment certificates), Immigration (visas), the Ministry of Public Service and Labour (work permits), Customs (exemption of some imported goods from customs duties), and the Company Registry (incorporation of companies).

93 *Investment Code, supra* note 42, art. 7.

94 *Investment Code, ibid.,* arts. 2(5) & (11).

95 Vision 2020, *supra* note 27 at 15.

96 *Investment Code, supra* note 42, art. 7.

97 *Investment Code, ibid.,* arts. 2(5) & (11). So far, Rwanda is the only COMESA state that accords the status of "local" investor to COMESA investors and their investments in extending national treatment to these investors and investments.

98 For the procedures for registering an investment, see articles 3 & 5 of the *Investment Code, ibid.*

99 *Investment Code, ibid.,* art. 11.

100 *COMESA Investment Agreement, supra* note 75, art. 12.

101   Article 3 of the Investment Code, which addresses the contents of an application for investment registration, includes criteria that require investors to state the number of employees, prospects of technology transfer, locally sourced inputs to be used in the project and so on. Nevertheless, the article does not mandate a certain number of employees, neither does it insist on technology transfer, rather, it refers to the *prospects* of such transfer. Article 24 of the Investment Code also includes similar provisions for operating in a Free Economic Zone. This article explicitly suggests the "creation of linkages within the economy." The COMESA Investment Agreement seeks to address this phenomenon in its definition of the concept of "substantial business activity" in article 1. The Agreement states: "The concept of 'substantial business activity' requires an overall examination, on a case-by-case basis, of all the circumstances, including, *inter alia*: (a) the amount of investment brought into the country; (b) the number of jobs created; (c) its effect on the local community; and (d) the length of time the business has been in operation." One of the ambiguities of the provision is that it is subject to interpretation on all its criteria. Thus, one wonders whether the creation of one job will suffice or whether an investment must create at least about five jobs to be considered a substantial business activity, or what exactly, "effect on the local community" would mean in the almost infinite number of possibilities that could exist.

102   *Investment Code, supra* note 42, art. 17.

103   *Investment Code, ibid.*, Annex 1, art. 1. See also article 182 of *Law No. 21/2006 of 28/04/2006 Establishing the Customs System* ("*Customs Law*").

104   *Investment Code, ibid.*, Annex 1, art. 2. The Investment Code also includes provisions on immigration and work permits that are not applicable to local investors. See article 21 of the Investment Code.

105   *Investment Code, ibid.*, Annex 1, art. 6.

106   These tax incentives are offered to holders of certificates of registration. *Investment Code, ibid.*, art. 18.

107   See article 41 of *Law No 16/2005 of 18/08/2005 on Direct Taxes on Income*, which attaches the tax relief and exemptions to operations in a free trade zone and foreign companies headquartered in Rwanda.

108   *Investment Code, ibid.*, art. 2(7). See also articles 149-160 of the *Customs Law, supra* note 103.

109   *Investment Code, ibid.*, arts. 24-26.

110   UNCTAD, *Investment Policy Review, supra* note 15 at 41. The volume suggests that "better targeted investments" aimed at promoting specific investments that Rwanda needs might be more appropriate.

111   *Rwandan Constitution, supra* note 48, arts. 29-30. See also articles 3-6 of *Organic Law No. 08/2005 of 14/07/2005 Determining the Use and Management of Land in Rwanda* [*Land Law*].

112   *Land Law, ibid.*, art. 6.

113   *Land Law, ibid.*, art. 24.

114   *Land Law, ibid.*, arts. 33-34.

115   *Investment Code, supra* note 42, chap. XII.

116   *Investment Code, ibid.*, art. 30

117   UNCTAD & ICC, *supra* note 1 at 24-25.

118   *Investment Code, supra* note 42, arts. 31-34.

119   Consent to arbitration before ICSID may be given in several ways and not all references to ICSID in domestic legislation and international agreements are tantamount to consent. See Aron Broches, "Bilateral Investment Treaties and Arbitration of Investment Disputes" *in* Jan C. Schultz & Albert Jan van den Berg eds, *The Art of Arbitration: Essays on International Arbitration: Liber Amicorum Pieter Sanders 1912-1982* (Deventer, Netherlands; Boston: Kluwer Law and Taxation Publishers, 1982) 63.

120   90 per cent of Rwanda's population engages in subsistence farming. See Wong *et al., supra* note 51 at 3.

121   In Margit Bussmann, Gerald Schenider & Nina Wiesehomeier, "Foreign Economic Liberalization and Peace: The Case of Sub-Saharan Africa" (2005) 11 EJIR

Ibironke T. Odumosu

551 at 560, the authors note that "[i]f policy-makers do not take the redistributive effects of foreign economic liberalization into account, they risk fostering social tensions."

122 See Upendra Baxi, *The Future of Human Rights* 2nd ed. (New Delhi: Oxford University Press, 2006) 249.

123 See Ha-Joon Chang, "Regulation of Foreign Investment in Historical Perspective" (2004) 16 *European Journal of Development Research* 687. See generally, Ha-Joon Chang, *Kicking away the Ladder: Development Strategy in Historical Perspective* (London: Anthem, 2002).

124 Chang, "Regulation of Foreign Investment," *ibid.*

125 United Nations Development Programme, *Human Development Report 2007-2008, Fighting Climate Change: Human Solidarity in a Divided World* (Basingstoke, England & New York: Palgrave Macmillan, 2007) 247.

126 This bigger social picture continues to be relevant for Rwanda like many post-conflict societies because of the tendencies that tensions might trigger the resumption of hostilities. BBC, "Genocide Hatred Lingers in Rwanda Schools," February 19, 2008, http://news.bbc.co.uk/2/hi/africa/7246985.stm; BBC, "Rwandans Still Divided Ten Years On," http://news.bbc.co.uk/2/hi/africa/3557565.stm.

Chapter 6

Transitional Commercial Law and Foreign Direct Investment in Afghanistan: A Case Study

Patricia J. McCall

Introduction

Afghanistan is a country with a turbulent history and a complex ethnic mix. Its modern political and legal state has its foundations in 1747 when Ahmed Shah Durrani was elected king by a "Loya Jirga" or "assembly" of the southern tribes. The Afghan throne changed hands as the Persians, Russians and British vied to control the buffer state between their respective empires. Once the monarchy was abolished in 1973 Afghanistan entered a short period of relative democratic peace prior to the Soviet invasion in 1979. After a protracted insurrection by Afghan jihadists supported by a coalition of foreign powers, the Soviet Union withdrew in 1992 leaving a vacuum filled by warring tribal factions. These factions included an extreme Islamic religious movement calling themselves Taliban. The Taliban finally wrested control of Kabul in 1996 and set about enforcing an extreme and brutal version of Islamic and Pashtun law. In 2001, the Taliban were deposed by a coalition of foreign powers, and with the support of the international community prominent Afghans met in Bonn in Germany to agree on a constitution and legal framework by which a democratically elected government could govern the country.

Since the nomination of an interim president by Loya Jirga the international community has been assisting the government to reform and in many cases create the necessary judicial, political and economic institutions and processes required to enable efficient government. Justice, the rule of law and law enforcement have historically been weak and moreover characterized by a system of complex layers, ranging from a formal state-led legal system to customary law and informal systems of dispute resolution.

In 1964, a new constitution provided for a Constitutional Afghan Monarchy based on the separation of executive, legislative, and judicial authorities. Prior to this, the powers of the state and legal framework had been entrusted to the King. Almost a decade after the new constitution was enacted the monarchy of King Mohammed Zahir Shah was replaced by military coup in 1973. The constitution of 1964 was abolished, and the

Republic of Afghanistan was officially created. The Afghan Grand National Assembly (Loya Jirga)[1] adopted a new constitution in February 1977, but that was abrogated in 1978 and the Democratic Republic of Afghanistan was founded by means of another coup and was governed by the Afghan Revolutionary Council.[2] The 1970s witnessed more political and economic upheavals. In 1979, the political landscape was once again changed with the invasion of the Soviet military in December 1979, to shore up the pro-Soviet government formed in 1978. Throughout the years of the Soviet-aligned government, the country's legal framework took on a more Marxist nature. A new constitution was established in 1987 changing the name of the country back to the Republic of Afghanistan and reaffirming its non-aligned status. The new constitution acted to strengthen the position of president, and permitted other parties to participate in government. This government was short-lived as the nationalist Islamic Mujahideen rebels did not recognize the Soviet-backed regime. In 1989, the Soviet forces were forced to withdraw and the adoption of a multiparty Islamic-oriented Constitution began in 1990. The socialist government of Afghanistan lasted only two years and was overthrown by the Mujahideen in 1992. Subsequently Afghanistan was proclaimed an Islamic State and elections took place in which Professor Burhannudin Rabbani was elected President.

On September 27, 1996, President Rabbani and the other ruling members of the Afghan Government were displaced by members of the fundamentalist Islamic Taliban ("students of Islam") movement. The Taliban eventually took control of 90% of the country, leaving only a small northern enclave in the hands of opposition "Northern Alliance" forces. After the attacks on the United States on September 11, 2001, the US-led coalition, Operation Enduring Freedom (OEF), entered Afghanistan on October 2001, with the aim of defeating the Al-Qaeda network deemed to be responsible for the events of September 11. The operation took less than two months and resulted in the removal of the Taliban from Kabul, forcing them to retreat to the southwestern Afghanistan and Pakistan border areas. On December 5, 2001, a UN-sponsored Afghan peace conference was held in Bonn, as noted earlier. The conference approved a broad agreement for the establishment of a six-month interim authority, the Afghanistan Interim Administration (AIA), which would govern the country. The AIA Chairman, Hamid Karzai, and his cabinet took office on December 22, 2001. The conference resulted in the Bonn Agreement calling for the convening of a Constitutional Loya Jirga within eighteen months in order to adopt a new constitution for Afghanistan.

The Bonn Agreement outlined the priorities and framework for reconstruction and reform as well as outlining the formation of the Interim Afghanistan Authority. Additionally, the United Nations Security Council approved an international force, the International Security Assistance Force (ISAF), which deployed in the capital, Kabul, and the surrounding areas. In March 2002, the United Nations mandated the United Nations Assistance Mission in Afghanistan (UNAMA) with the task of assisting the interim government in implementation of the Bonn Agreement.

The Bonn Agreement was signed by representatives of the Northern Alliance and technocrats and intellectuals in power at the time of the former King, Zahir Shah, many of them who fled when the King was deposed in 1973. Several other smaller Afghan tribal groups from border areas near Pakistan and Iran were also included. It created a framework for a broad agreement of a multi-party pluralistic government. Its goal was to create a new constitution and its first act was to agree upon an interim legal framework that would be adopted prior to the constitution's completion. The interim framework included:

(i)   The Constitution of 1964; a) to the extent that its provisions are not inconsistent with those contained in this agreement, and b) with the exception of those provisions relating to the monarchy and to the executive and legislative bodies provided in the Constitution; and

(ii) existing laws and regulations, to the extent that they are not inconsistent with this agreement or with international legal obligations to which Afghanistan is a party, or with those applicable provisions contained in the Constitution of 1964, provided that the Interim Authority shall have the power to repeal or amend those laws and regulations.[3]

Since 2001, rule of law reform and private sector development have been critical aspects of the government's reform policy. Significant policy developments include: the National Policy Development Framework which created in 2002 provided overall policy direction; the Afghanistan development budgets which elaborated on sectoral development and resource allocation; and the Berlin Conference in 2004 which further set out the reconstruction and the development agenda and priorities.[4]

Objective of the Case Study

This case study focuses on rule of law reform in post-conflict Afghanistan in order to evaluate the relevance of utilizing third-country jurisdictions to provide enhanced legal stability for investment in post-conflict areas. United Nations Conference on Trade and Development (UNCTAD) and the United Nations University (UNU) seek to create new approaches and to develop guidelines for business transactions in and around zones of armed conflict.

The objective of the overall project is to evaluate the potential applicability of existing global international conventions and agreements in conflict-related areas when government authority is insufficient for the conduct of normal commercial activities or where it is non-existent. In these circumstances, the study will evaluate the potential applicability of alternate functional laws and regulations and methods by which the gap in national rule of law can be temporarily closed. The project will explore the extent to which current international law, regulation, guidelines, voluntary corporate social responsibility standards, and similar principles of good business practice can form part of a framework for the conduct of business in these circumstances.[5]

As part of the overall framework or analysis, this paper seeks to study the circumstances in Afghanistan regarding the post-conflict Rule of Law framework. The study has these main objectives:

1. To briefly review the process by which the Afghanistan judiciary is being reformed and provide an overview of the lessons learned;
2. to provide supporting background information to efforts to create a mechanism for transitional commercial law in the initial post-conflict phase;
3. to outline examples of either successful investments and/or lost opportunities due to the lack of rule of law and;
4. to provide a summary of main obstacles faced in Afghanistan and provide initial recommendations for improvement.

This case study aims to understand how a third party mechanism may be applicable in post-conflict areas, notably in Afghanistan, and in the absence of such a mechanism, what are the implications and consequences for the country and its people. Afghanistan has withstood decades of war, ravaging both the physical and the structural infrastructure of the country. The country's entire foundations, ranging from economic development to political and judicial frameworks, are in the process of being reformed and adapted to the new post-Taliban era government of Hamid Karzai. This study aims to shed light on the conditions present for investment and how a transitional commercial law mechanism could have possibly supported further investment in the country post-conflict.

Judicial Reform

Background. With no apparent functioning nationwide judicial system, many municipal and provincial authorities in Afghanistan rely on some interpretation of Islamic law and traditional tribal codes of justice. With years of conflict and regimes that ranged from royal and communist to socialist and Islamic, the legal system has been adapted several times, creating multiple layers of interpretation.

The Bonn Agreement of December 2001 called for the establishment of a Judicial Commission to rebuild the domestic justice system in accordance with Islamic principles, international standards, the rule of law, and Afghan legal traditions. The agreement initially raised hopes of a strong foundation, although shortly after the signing the reinstatement of several warlords as key political leaders led to doubt as to the real effective power of the agreements.[6] Since the agreement, international agencies and Afghan institutions have focused on laying the foundation of a strong legal and regulatory framework; however, the process is long and arduous and continues to be plagued by delays and disputes.

The formal system over the last twenty years has been influenced greatly by both Western influences (mainly French), moderate Islam and radical Marxism. These reflect the varying political powers of the times, the state systems versus Shariah law, the Marxist government during the Soviet invasion followed by an Islamic system under the Mujahideen and Taliban regimes. Additionally, in many rural areas even to this day, a system of informal justice and traditional institutions prevails based on systems of *jirga* and Shariah law. The informal systems do often offer greater access and speedy dispute resolution, but often conflict with Afghan legal norms and with international standards of human rights.[7] The new transitional authority in 2001 and the ensuing Afghan Transitional Authority have recognized the need to incorporate the international standards in the legal system.

The current framework is a mixture of Shariah laws, existing laws from the 1964 constitution and new laws to complement the system. The independent Judicial Commission of Afghanistan was enacted to oversee the development of the new system in 2001 as part of the Bonn Agreement. The system was enacted to allow for the top Afghan and international lawyers to review the current system and comment on the appropriate new system for the country.

The new constitution, enacted in January 2004, used the constitution of 1964 as its foundation, but amended many components. The constitutional Loya Jirga adopted the constitution after much work by the Karzai government to revise and amend it through the commission.[8]

Despite continued reforms, the judicial system in Afghanistan is complex, predominantly informal and characterized as lacking any formal structure that is routinely practiced. Courts have historically been run in a chaotic manner and lack sufficient numbers of highly qualified and learned lawyers and judges able to interpret the various laws on the books. The laws have been adapted by different regimes, and the relevance and applicability of the existing laws and jurisdiction is often unclear.[9]

Courts have been historically ill-equipped and mismanaged and continue to be so. Not only has there been little attention to the physical structure and the administrative staff but additionally, owing to decades of war, the access to statutes and associated legal materials is often difficult to achieve.[10] The Ministry of Justice and the University of Kabul do not have a full collection of the main statutory laws.

The country is undergoing a massive nation building exercise. The new constitution is creating a new rule of law, an institutional framework, and governance structures as well as executive and judicial bodies. The reform includes an independent judiciary, a human rights commission, a national army and police force to ensure security and economic independence, and financial sector reforms at the Ministry of Finance and the Central Bank. The changes are sweeping and substantial and understandably have been fraught with setbacks and delays.

Lessons Learned. The importance of the Rule of Law in transition cannot be overemphasized. In fact, in Afghanistan's case, studies suggest that the Bonn Agreement did not fully emphasize and give critical importance to the firm and resolute establishment of the Rule of Law:

> "not only is the establishment of the Rule of Law of fundamental import-
> ance to the transition from conflict to stable governance but also that is not
> merely a subset of the all-important achievement of security. A lack of
> strategy results in negative impacts in a range of dimensions: criminal,
> commercial social and political...the Rule of Law is the key to making the
> government and its institutions real, present, credible and legitimate to the
> people of Afghanistan."[11]

Afghanistan's rule of law reform program was multi-tiered and multi-donor, and was and continues to be fraught with challenges. The Bonn Agreement provided for the creation of the Judicial Reform Commission (JRC), the Constitutional Commission and the Human Rights Commission. The Constitutional Commission was established in 2003 to draft a new constitution for the Constitutional Loya Jirga.[12] Likewise the Afghan Independent Human Rights Commission (AIHRC) was set up in 2002 to investigate and monitor human rights abuses as well as educate the public on Human Rights.

The JRC, established in November 2002, initially was composed of 12 prominent Afghan legal experts. It was mandated to "rebuild the domestic justice system in accordance with Islamic principles, international standards, the rule of law and Afghan legal traditions". As the JRC was mandated only

to propose strategies, the importance of the JRC in creating strong relationships with the administrative bodies, the Supreme Court, the Ministry of
Justice and the Attorney General's office cannot be underestimated.[13]

The JRC convened working groups on various segments of the law and
has been moderately successful to date in lobbying for certain laws to be
enacted. At the Rome Conference in 2002, the international community and
the Afghan government pledged support to the reconstruction and reform
of the judicial system;

> "The development of a fair and effective justice system in Afghanistan is a
> vital requirement to meet the needs of the Afghan people and to protect
> their human rights, with special consideration for the most vulnerable sec-
> tions of society, to ensure peaceful dispute resolution, to promote good
> governance....an effective justice system is essential not only for successful
> development of Afghan society as a whole, but also to achieve lasting peace
> and security in Afghanistan".[14]

There are several areas of judicial and rule of law reform that have provided stumbling blocks to expeditious and comprehensive reform:

- Donor Coordination and Strategy: Donor-led assistance and delays in
  financing are cited as key factors in the slow pace of reform. The lead
  donor role for rule of law was given to Italy and critics have been skep-
  tical of the ability of one country to manage such a role.[15] The process
  also required strong donor coordination amongst all players in the rule
  of law process, which did not occur for a myriad reasons.[16] Additionally, often competing donor agendas impeded progress and timely
  recommendations leading to a stalemate on working group conclusion.
  Consistent communication with the Afghan government and a full
  understanding of local laws, customs and culture is a necessity in creating a cohesive and strong system. One example cited was the early
  persistence of the lead donor to enact a monocratic court system that
  requires one judge instead of a three court judge system – something
  vehemently opposed by both the JRC and Afghan legal reform experts.[17]
- Overlapping and Conflicting Legal Framework: The diverse history of
  Afghanistan is reflected in the legal framework; while the constitution
  of 1964 acts as a foundation, the legal framework often has overlapping jurisdictions, laws and regulations, and amendments that are ambiguous as to legal status, as well as a commercial law that reflects a
  system primarily dependent on the state and therefore lacking in private sector laws. Many of the laws are from the communist era or the

early monarchy, and thus the vast quantity of new legislation needed is also an impediment to swift progress. A World Bank report in 2005 estimates that there are over 200 laws considered by the government to be high priority and waiting to be passed, and for many of the laws that have been enacted, enforcement is a major problem.

- Judicial Capacity: the ability of the existing judicial institutions to both function administratively and adapt to new laws, procedures, best practice and donor coordination is severely restrained. Again, experts argue that there was also an initial insufficient allocation of resources for both technical assistance to the institutions and training of existing lawyers and judges.[18]

- JRC: The nature of the JRC was such that the effectiveness rests in its ability to cooperate and coordinate with the other institutional bodies, the Ministry of Justice and the Supreme Court as well as with the international donors.[19]

- UNAMA: UNAMA has also been criticized for its role in supporting the rule of law process and the JRC.[20] It was mandated, under the Bonn Agreement, to support and to assist the JRC in carrying out its mandate. The UNAMA rule of law component is criticized for being understaffed and lacking resources and capacity to provide technical assistance to the JRC. Amnesty International, early on in the process, in August 2003, called for the strengthening of UNAMA's role including strengthening of staff levels, and for an expert on international human rights law to be included to ensure human rights are incorporated in all activities of the process.

- Corruption: Given the resurgence in opium production in the last two years and coupled with the alleged corruption, mainly focused on the Ministry of Interior, widespread corruption is cited as a major constraint to constructive reform of the rule of law. Eradication efforts set forth by the government have often led to undesired results of strengthening key warlords and drug trade players.[21] The corruption attributed to the drug industry has an impact on the perception of corruption within the entire governmental apparatus.

Understanding the tremendous challenges, the JRC is currently focusing on four major areas: law reform; assessment and development of technical, logistical and human resources; review of the structure and functions of the justice system and the division of labor among its various components; and legal aid and access to justice.

Transitional Law

A relevant case study for transitional commercial law in Afghanistan is the use of an interim criminal procedures law in Afghanistan. The lead donor on legal reform enacted an interim rule of law for criminal procedures which became the foundation for the formation of the Afghan criminal code. The new interim code of criminal procedures was promulgated into law by presidential decree in February 2004.[22]

The interim code and Italy however came under pressure as the code was heavily influenced by strong foreign political pressure and was prepared by Italian officials with the help of US military lawyers with very little input from Afghan justice institutions.[23] The Italians planned to introduce the system in specific areas of the country where they deemed courts not to be functional and criminal procedures most needed.

While the interim code has had some success and has led to improvements in the Afghan criminal code system, there are several areas for improvement:

- Inadequate coordination with Afghan institutions: inadequate consultation with existing Afghan systems and experts leading often to recommendations and codes that are not appropriate for Afghan context. For example, the code mandated that an accused can only be held for 48 hours, by which time sufficient evidence should be collected and analyzed for validity. Afghan experts argued that 48 hours was not sufficient in the Afghan context owing to the lack of tools available to prosecutors and/or lawyers for such a process. The AIHRC, while concerned with a lengthy period, supported a 72-hour holding period to take such restraints into account. Such examples have also led to certain jurisdictions and practitioners not using the code at all, given its irrelevance in some areas.
- Lengthy implementation: The length of time to enact the Afghan code was substantial; the interim code played a role in providing a frame of reference and guide to formation of a new criminal procedure code.
- Insufficient dissemination of information: The interim code was not sufficiently broadcast to judges, lawyers and administrative within Kabul and in the provinces. Often provinces were completely unaware of the new code and tools for implementation, and therefore it was not adhered to.
- Insufficient Iinstitutional capacity: The current institutions were unable to absorb code and procedures; where the code was sufficiently communicated insufficient resources were allocated to training judges, lawyers and the population on the process and their rights under the

new code. Critics cite the lead nation, Italy, for providing insufficient technical assistance to the judicial system regarding the interim code.[24] The donors,in addition, did not understand fully the tools available in the Afghan system and adapt the enforcement of the code to the tools readily available within the system.

- Poor donor coordination: Poor coordination amongst donors in regards to capacity building related to the interim code also undermined the success of the project.

Transitional Commercial Law. The need for a new commercial code, investment laws and functional dispute resolution system in regards to commercial law was recognized early on by the lead donor, Italy, as well as other donors and the Afghan government. The American Bar Association, in collaboration with the JRC and the other Afghan agencies, in early 2002 produced a report *Filling the Vacuum: Prerequisites to Security in Afghanistan.* The report was based on a previously completed in-country fact-gathering mission. In early June 2002, in partnership with International Resources Group and with funding from the US State Department, ABA-Asia distributed 1,000 copies of key Afghan codes to justice sector officials in Afghanistan. This project helped ensure that justice sector officials have access to the laws governing their operations.

The Afghan Embassy in Washington established the Private Sector Development Task Force for Afghanistan with the objective to "support Afghanistan with a set of principles, objectives and opportunities to accelerate development of a private enterprise-driven market economy".[25] One of the priorities for promoting a market economy, as set out by the government of Afghanistan, was the rule of law. The Center for International Management Education partnered with ABA program on the Afghanistan Transitional Commercial Law Project. The project recognized the need for rule of law as it relates to investment and providing an attractive investment climate. According to the documents of the project ,"The Project aimed to recommend a set of transitional commercial laws or a "Transitional Code of Commerce." The Transitional Code of Commerce will incorporate, to the extent possible, existing Afghan law and will be drafted to comport with international standards. Since the Transitional Code of Commerce is meant to "fill in the gaps" while the judicial system is being re-organized, the goal is to complete the review and recommendation process as quickly as possible."[26]

Additionally, the objectives of the program were to "provide an adequate means of enforcement for the Transitional Code of Commerce," and "the Project will recommend that for the short term, a system of private arbitration be established to resolve disputes involving commercial transactions. Until the courts have been reformed to the point that consistent and impartial enforcement of awards is in evidence, the Project will recommend the adoption of a decree that would require the Ministry of Justice and Afghan courts to enforce the arbitration awards without discretion. After completing this Project, CIME and ABA-Asia plan to work with the Judicial Commission and the Ministry of Justice in Afghanistan to reform other areas of the law and judicial system."[27] The project worked on compiling first the existing Afghan laws relating to commercial law, and formed working groups to address several areas including law on private and domestic investment, contract law, property law, customs, trade and financial sector law, laws on employment, bankruptcy and registration, and corporate and partnership laws.

The program had successes and failures as a result of a myriad influences including poor donor coordination, the lack of influence of the working groups and the JRC with the other institutional bodies, inadequate capacity in the Afghan system, and a reform agenda that was already extremely full and slow. A notable success was the input the program had on the new Private Investment Law enacted in 2004, which supports private investment with a series of reforms.

A notable criticism of the rule of law reform process is the lack of political will that may have accompanied the commercial law reform; there was a focus predominantly on criminal justice and civil and political rights at the expense of support for reforms in other areas including administrative reform (dealing with license and permits), land and registration systems, the state of the financial system and other non-state justices systems.

These areas of reform, such as administrative reforms, are often overlooked in immediate post-conflict situations; many practitioners argue they are just as important,

> but they rarely attract the attention of rule of law reformers because they are seen as vaguely, if at all, connected to rule of law. It is argued here that they are. The rule of law is a systemic concept which expands the full breadth and the full width of state institutions and is a concept for how to best organise a state and a state's relationship to its citizens. To secure the principle of legality in relation to public procurement can be just as vital a reform strategy for state-building as fair criminal law trials. It is not argued here that the international community should pick and choose between projects and programs, but to treat rule of law as a holistic concept.[28]

Despite progress in legal reform, serious shortcomings persist. Studies indicate that Afghanistan could benefit from a new private investment law and that serious shortcomings exist in the new law that was passed in 2002. Furthermore, the insurance and business organizations laws have yet to be fully implemented and further regulation in land titling and registration are key barriers to investment.[29] These formal changes to the legal system are only one part of the equation – continuous investment in the infrastructure and the skills of the legal economy are needed, and more lawyers, judges and clerks with a strong educations and legal background are needed, as well as enforcement mechanisms that are transparent and viable.

Additionally, the legacy of war and criminal activity over the last quarter century has led to human rights abuses in the country that continue to occur today. The history of war and poverty and religious fanaticism has affected Afghan women and continues to present itself in human rights abuses and even death. The Bonn Agreement authorized the use of an independent human rights commission for Afghanistan, although the agreement is notably silent on issues of accounting for past justices and transitional justice. This area is not the focus of this paper, so it will not be discussed in detail here. The Afghan Human Rights Commission, formed in 2002, is working on issues such as human rights education, monitoring and investigations, women's human rights and transitional justice.

The Economy

Background. Conflict over almost a quarter of a century has also left the Afghan economy in ruins as warring factions and outside governments have used the land as a battleground for proxy wars and ideological battles. The country's inability to have a sustained period of peace has led to a severely damaged economy that now relies heavily on the opium trade to support its revenue base, despite government efforts to clamp down on the trade. The economy has been primarily a war economy, relying on the maintenance of military power and military supplies as the driver for the economy. This has led to a lack of solid infrastructure development or economic growth in diversified areas of manufacturing and services as, and has produced a generation of leaders and workers lacking severely in education and vocation skills.[30]

Post-conflict Afghanistan has, however, made some marked improvements, driven by the government's drive to improve the institutional structure of both the ministries as well as the legal system, aimed at providing security, rule of law and stability. In addition to the new constitution, there were elections in 2005 to elect the president and a parliament. However, the government and the economy are still very fragile and insurgencies outside the Kabul area threaten to not only bring economic insecurity but political instability as well.

Afghanistan is a low-income country with a population of over 24 million people and one of the lowest GDP per capita in the world at $270/capita.

There is a large informal economy, mainly in the opium trade, that augments this, but the underlying economic weakness and poverty persist. The economy is, however, growing. The International Monetary Fund (IMF) estimates that the official (non-opium) gross domestic product (GDP) grew by an average of 22.5% between 2002 and 2004. It estimates 7.5% growth in 2005 and 14% in 2006. Investment is high at around 22% of GDP, indicating the incredible need for infrastructure and development. The bulk of the investment remains public sector and driven by international aid rather than private investment.[31]

Other reforms have been completed or are ongoing, including tax code restructuring in 2004, currency reform in 2003, and the rationalization of customs tariffs. Additionally, the country has been working toward increased participation globally, has signed several bilateral trade agreements, and is moving toward WTO status in the next five years. However, a large part of the GDP is informal, with agriculture making up the largest share. In 2003 illicit production of opium accounted for over one third of GDP, and in 2005-6 the number is expected to grow to 50 per cent.

The production of opium has increased dramatically over the last several years owing to several factors, including a lack of alternative sources of income, increased corruption, and centralization of the drug trade which has acted to increase production, and various other socio-economic reasons.[32] This paper will not address specifically the opium economy, nor the myriad reasons why the country is producing more opium than in the last two decades, but will address several supporting factors including a lack of rule of law, corruption and the lack of alternative avenues for investment.

Private Sector Investment. Given the rise in opium production, the government is keen to encourage and support private sector development, as evidenced by several initiatives including the new banking laws, more licenses issued for private banks, and the establishment of the Afghanistan Investment Support Agency (AISA), which acts to facilitate foreign investment and administrative processes. AISA acts as a "one-stop shop" for investors and was created to handle the registration, licensing and promotion of new investments in Afghanistan.

With over 80% of the economy in informal activities, mainly agriculture and small family run businesses, the importance of creating a conducive investment climate cannot be overstated. The government has been keen to push forward the privatization process and has had some success, but most of the post-conflict business has been centralized in telecoms and construction, not unusually for a post-conflict economy.[33] In addition to construction and telecoms, industry includes bottling, plastics and packaging.

Attracting resources and talent from overseas Afghans as well as other foreign investors has been a focus of the government. According to a survey conduced in 2005 by the World Bank over 20% of firms sampled are owned by investors who returned after the Taliban era. Attracting money for private investment has been difficult given the security situation, and most investors tend to invest alongside the government or the donors. While attracting foreign investment has been difficult, the survey did show that domestic firms are adding to their capital stock, with nearly 70% of the firms investing in new equipment in the last year.[34]

Security is a prerequisite for investment, and for foreign investment this requirement is almost always heightened. However, in a survey conducted last year by the World Bank Group, the three biggest constraints to business were access to electricity, access to land and the widespread corruption in the country. While responses differed by region, the three constraints mentioned above were by far the most often cited, with security further down the list. This can be explained to some extent by the government's success in select cities in disarming militias and increasing the police force. Moreover, many firms have learned to adapt to the environment by co-opting the militias and warlords as well as government officials to ease the security burden.[35] It follows then that corruption would be cited as a key constraint. The report states that "corruption is endemic in Afghanistan and adds to the uncertainty facing investors, especially foreign investors or returning Afghans who do not understand the system. Nearly 58 percent of surveyed firms cited corruption as a major or severe problem." The WB report also cites infrastructure in Afghanistan as among the worst in the world, including access to power, telecoms and transport. Additionally, there is a massive supply of overseas Afghan money sitting in Dubai, estimated to be around $5bn, but unfortunately much of it has remained outside the country.

In addition to these constraints, the report highlights the absence of a clear legal framework as a key barrier to investment, mentioning that many of the basic laws for private investment are simply missing.[36]

"Firms mostly use informal mechanisms, including force, to resolve disputes and enforce property rights. There are no formal alternative dispute resolution mechanisms such as arbitration or mediation. The formal court system suffers from a lack of qualified legal professionals, no method to hold judges accountable, and reportedly endemic corruption. Consequently, businesses do not rely on the formal judicial system. Only 3 of the 338 firms surveyed reported using the commercial courts to settle a payment dispute in the past two years. Many managers do not understand the benefits of a strong and efficient legal system and, given the arbitrary enforcement and lack of effective courts, do not spend much time worrying about it. Only 10 percent of the survey sample survey sample mentioned the legal system as a major or severe constraint. However, good laws, effectively enforced, are essential to encourage large-scale investment, especially by foreign investors and returning Afghans."

- World Bank Group. *Investment Climate Assessment: Afghanistan*. December 2005

Economic growth in Afghanistan has accelerated but still remains heavily supported by illegal growing of opium, accounting for over 50% of the combined licit and illicit GDP. GDP per capita is estimated to be around $350/capita including the opium economy. This reliance on opium and the drug economy has not only undermined the real economy, but also increased levels of corruption and undermined the rule of law reform process. With the economy plagued by what is not only an informal economy, but one driven by opium, problems affecting rule of law, legal frameworks, institutional capacity and access to land, infrastructure and finance are all consistently identified barriers to investment. While domestic investment is increasing, it is mainly fuelled by international aid as well as businesses that have key ties and networks with local warlords and militia. This is not a sustainable solution for both domestic and foreign investment. In order to thrive and create a fully functioning forma economy, Afghanistan must move toward a regulated and transparent economy.

Corruption, a major impediment to business and investment, must be curtailed and addresses at the highest levels of government. Indicative of this situation are the recommendations put forward by the World Bank in its *Investment Climate Assessment* in December 2005; the report recommends four categories of actions for accelerating private sector development:

1. Improve access to inputs: firms need factors of production, notably finance, land, skilled labor and physical utilities and infrastructure, including power, water, telecoms, roads and ports;
2. Clarify and strengthen property rights by creating a sound legal, judicial, and regulatory framework for investment;
3. Improve the flow of information: When market players lack information about market opportunities and trends, quality of products, availability of resources, and government policies and regulations, they become dependent on informal contacts for information;
4. Improve the provision of business services: The government needs to put in place a policy and regulatory framework to facilitate private investors.

Despite the remarkable challenges that the Afghanistan economy is facing, the country has succeeded in attracting some foreign investment. The economy continues to grow rapidly, by an estimated 7.5 % in 2005 and an estimated 14% in 2006.[37] Studies have noted an increase in both the services and goods available in the country and the entry of a few multinational corporations.

The main foreign investors in the last several years have been in the transport and logistics sector (DHL), food processing (Coca Cola), banking (Standard Chartered Bank, National Bank of Pakistan), telecommunications (Roshan and AWCC), tourism (Hyatt Hotels and Serena Hotel), and trade (Toyota Motors and Alcatel). The largest investors since 2002 have come from Turkey, followed by Germany, India and Pakistan. The telecommunications sector has by far attracted the most investment, standing at almost $200m.[38]

Investment Projects in Afghanistan

Sector Investment	(in US$ M)	Direct Employment
Construction	389	54,800
Services	213	4,300
Industry	150	21,000
Agro Business	6.4	535
Total	758	80,635

Source: World Bank 2005

There have been notable success stories of investment in Afghanistan, and research indicates that each company had a particular success, notably in the legal structure area, for specific reasons. For this project, I conducted interviews of each of the following investors in the Afghan economy below as well as other private sector participants. The following are brief descriptions of the businesses as well as conclusions drawn on experience post conflict investment.

Case Studies

The methodology used in this study follows the guidelines of the project. A survey was conducted by the author in person with each of the companies listed. The author met with the CEO's or senior management of each company on three occasions and reviewed the following data with external reviews to confirm the data. The interview consisted of a set of questions on areas including the legal framework, customs, tax, infrastructure and the financial sector, in order to gauge the experiences of starting a business in post-conflict Afghanistan as well as the ongoing operational situations.

The major findings of the study are listed below by category. For the most part, the respondents shared similar challenges and often addressed such challenges in similar ways, by directly approaching the ministries and officials responsible, rather than using the cumbersome court system to rectify complaints and/or legal issues. The summary is not exhaustive but highlights the most pertinent information in regards to the status of the commercial law system and the impact of a lack of rule of law on investment in the country.

Legal Framework and Commercial Law. Each company indicated that during the process of undertaking its investment activities, including registration, licensing, securing local and foreign legal representation, and other legal aspects, the existing commercial law and codes were extremely difficult to interpret, understand and enforce if the law was applicable. The investors surveyed chose to invest despite such situations, both because they were able to negotiate contracts at high levels of governments, which provided some reassurance as to the recourse they might have, and because all the respondents said that given the post-conflict nature of the economy, the lack of commercial law was expected and the desire to invest and return to their country outweighed the perceived risks. Roshan, the one company surveyed that did not have an overseas Afghan driving the investment, was able to import its best practices learned in other such situations and work with the Government of Afghanistan (GoA) to implement contracts and agreements that they felt comfortable with. Again, each company was acutely aware of the lack of recourse and the opaque nature of the existing laws but the prospects for early market entry and relations with the senior government altered their risk appetite.

Roshan, the largest investor in Afghanistan, is backed by the Aga Khan foundation and took on its role as a foreign investor fully aware of the shortcomings of the commercial law. Roshan worked closely with the government to implement best practice, drawing upon its experiences in other post-conflict countries. It worked closely with the authorities to explain the private sector concerns and policy advice on customs, tax, land and fiscal reform. Roshan, also backed by the Asian Development Bank, was able to invest and justify its risk management because of its long experience in such areas as well as its strong shareholder base capable of influencing policy and instating best practice in many areas. Clearly, smaller or less influential foreign investors would not have such ability and confidence in a post-conflict environment as Roshan and its backer the Aga Khan foundation. Without the clear ability to have access to top officials and support best practice, other investors would surely find the risk too high for investment post-conflict.[39]

The private investment law was important in supporting investment, as well as the banking law; however, several private sector investors cited the continued lack of progress on other areas including[40] labor, corporate law, land and property administration and insurance law, bankruptcy law, secured transaction law and business organizations. In 2007, several key laws were enacted but there continued to be a backlog of key commercial laws governing commerce that had not been approved through the GoA. The status of key laws then included: corporation law, approved in January 2007; partnership law, January 2007; commercial arbitration law, January 2007; commercial mediation law, January 2007; contracts law, pending; agency law, pending; standards law, pending; copyrights law, pending; mortgage and secured transactions law, pending; and negotiable instruments law, pending.

Owing to a lack of uniform commercial code and process and a lack of capacity of the court system, up to 90% of the commercial disputes are resolved informally. This increases the risk associated with contracts and acts as a deterrent to investment. Investors cite a lack of qualified lawyers locally to conduct business transactions, and with very few disputes adjudicated in the formal system, transparency and recourse remain major barriers to investment.

Tax and customs regulations were cited by all respondents as key impediments to investment, and all were affected by changes in these regulations. The driving factor of early investment in Afghanistan was the attractive tax holiday of eight years granted by the GoA, specifically the MoF (Ministry of Finance), for both domestic and foreign investment. Subsequently, the GoA retracted the benefits and imposed income and business receipts tax on the corporations. Similarly, there were several rounds of customs tariffs changes that were not expected by the companies and changed their underlying profitability. Specifically, the cost of importing raw materials changed significantly, which affected each company's ability to forecast equipment procurement and cost. The impact is substantial: in absence of a clear and consistent framework for tax and customs rates, investors are unable to accurately forecast business inputs and costs. A regulatory environment that is either unclear or unreliable acts a deterrent to investment and prohibits existing investors from re-investing and/or increasing levels of investment.

There were concerns also over *infrastructure*. The lack of critical infrastructure and the legal framework surrounding the sector was a common concern for all the investors surveyed. Clarity of ownership, transfer process and security of property transactions were serious issues for each company and continues to be issues. While each company negotiated with the GoA to secure land, ongoing uncertainty as to property rights and clear ownership regulations is an ongoing liability for companies.

Critical services such as water and electricity are lingering issues that continue to effect daily operations. Upon investment each company projected that the proper legislation and subsequent provision of these services would ensue in due course; no company expected to be completely supplying its own electricity and water five years later in 2007. This continues to put a high cost burden on each company and is a key variable in decisions to make further investments. The World Bank cites regulation and perceptions of regulatory risk as key impediments to the sector's provision of electricity. The paper recommends potential government guarantees to mitigate the risk of changes in the law, failure to meet contractual payment obligations, obstruction of the arbitration process, expropriation and nationalism and other regulatory matters.[41]

Corruption is endemic within the government and the judicial system. Corruption not only acts as deterrent to investment by raising the cost and uncertainty of the investment but also acts to stall rule of law reform by reinforcing corrupt policies and administrative practices. With the economy still plagued with increasing levels of opium production, the centralization of the opium trade and the endemic perception that the government institutions are not addressing the issues and are in fact part of the problem, corruption and criminalization remain a major obstacle to sustainable investment. All companies cited significant levels of corruption in the country as barriers to investment. Each experienced corrupt practices to varying degrees but it is clear that the prevalence of "informal payments" is still a major issue in the country.

Case Study: Telecom Development Company Afghanistan Limited: Roshan

Roshan is the largest wireless services provider in Afghanistan, with over 1 million subscribers in 2006. It is an international consortium led by the Aga Khan Fund for Economic Development (AKFED) and includes Monaco Telecom International (MTI), the US-based MCT Corp and Alcatel. The company moved into Afghanistan in 2004 and used its extensive network and experience of AKFED in other countries to develop its business in Afghanistan. The total investment is approximately $120 million over the next decade, with the AKFED investing over $400m in the country, including the Serena Kabul Hotel.[42]

The story has been one of the highlighted success stories of Afghanistan, with mobile phone penetration rising to an estimated 6.9% in 2006.[43] The investment in the sector has led to rapid penetration gains as well as providing a key success story for the Afghan government, and has been instrumental in encouraging the government to support the private sector.

Roshan commenced operations with a license granted by the GoA. In 2003, there were two licensed operators, Roshan and Afghan Wireless Communications Company (AWCC). The Ministry of Communications (MoC) worked closely with the management of Roshan and the GoA to establish the proper regulatory framework from the outset. The MoC effectively governed the sector, although a telecom law was not passed in Afghanistan until December 2005.

The decision by Roshan to invest in Afghanistan stems from the shareholders' vast experience in dealing in both conflict zones and developing markets. As the Aga Khan Development Network is familiar with such environments and additionally positioned itself as a key investor, the company was able to assess the risk environment and feel confident it had enough influence to certain regulatory risk factors and work with the GoA to implement best practice.

The sector was regulated by the MoC and the GoA. Prior to the enactment of the telecom law, the sector was governed by the Telecom Regulatory Board (TRB). Since commencing operations, Roshan has constantly struggled to accelerate the pace of regulatory reform while consistently pushing for best practice. Roshan played a critical role in the development of the private sector by investing in the infrastructure of the country while also applying international best practice in its operations, as well as working with the MoC and the GoA to implement best practice through their framework.

While there are a myriad operational activities that pose problems, this case study will address the legal and commercial law aspect. As mentioned,

Roshan, as one of the first foreign investors, came to Afghanistan when there was a minimal framework for investment. As a result, one of the most significant issues for Roshan has been one of consistency and transparency of laws in Afghanistan.

The company's activities are covered by the Investment Agreement under the MoF in 2003, which included clauses on customs law, income tax and other areas of operations. The company has its license from the MoF and its regulatory responsibilities were outlined from 2003 by the MoC, outlined in its draft policy on telecommunications. From early on the MoC committed itself to "engage private investment to the greatest extent possible" and to "introduce market liberalisation".[44] The ability of Roshan to thrive in this environment was greatly enhanced by the decision by the MoC and GoA to allow the private sector to operate relatively openly and freely in the sector with the support of the GoA as needed.

In 2005 the telecom law came into force, but the regulatory mechanism was not formal. The license came from the MoC and MoF, both of whom had internal advisors and worked closely with the AKDN and their legal advisors. Most of the legal work was done outside the country with international lawyers. Roshan now has two local lawyers. It was very difficult to use outside lawyers to work with domestic law.

However, there were, and continue to be, instances of reversal of policies and lack of clarity on the part of the regulators. An example is the Income Tax Law of 2005, which invalidated the 2003 agreement Roshan had signed. Then the GoA changed it in 2006. The financial basis for Roshan's investment was the 2003 law which declared the customs duty on telecoms imports to be 5%, but then it was increased; this remains a major issue, the unreliability of policy regarding taxes and customs. Additionally, under the agreement with the MoF in 2003, Roshan had signed income tax agreements that effectively granted a tax holiday to the company under certain guidelines. In 2005, however, the GoA introduced a 10% tax on telephone services. The explanation given by the GoA was that in 2003 the MoF did not have the authority to conclude such an agreement, only the cabinet could grant such incentives. This clearly had a great impact on Roshan as the calculations of its return on investment and initial supporting reasons for investment were being altered. In total, the change increased the tax burden of the sector to 20%. After months of negotiations the effective rate was decreased to 14.5%, and while this indicated the willingness of the GoA to support the sector, the change in regulation despite provisions of signed contracts sets a worrying precedent for the sector.

If Roshan had decided to appeal to the courts, the process would most likely have been lengthy and too costly. Furthermore, its license was granted through the MoF and although there was a clause providing for international arbitration provision, the contract was only enforceable in Afghan courts.

When the new investment law was approved by cabinet in 2006, Roshan considered an appeal to the international arbitration arena, but again it would have to be settled in the Afghan courts. Now, under the Private Investment Law, the company can dispute a ruling under the World Bank arbitration rules or in international arbitration courts, but according to Roshan, this is only feasible if it is a major issue, as the cost in both time and fees is high. Thus for minor issues it is only feasible to do so under Afghan Law – which is not an optimum solution owing to the lack of enforcement capacity and transparency. There was a lack of capacity to solve these types of issues that are not critical enough to go to the international courts, such as expropriation. Thus, effectively, as the Afghan courts are unable to handle such cases, there is effectively no dispute resolution in the country.

Notably, for an interim commercial law system to be effective should one have existed, Roshan argues that it would have been helpful only if there was the capacity to resolve cases in the assigned courts and the ability of the local officials to enforce judgments. Instead, to resolve issues, Roshan would go to the MoC and the Aga Khan Development Network (AKDN) for assistance to open doors, as it is the largest investor in the country. The new Investment Agreement of 2006 allows for disputes to be settled under English law, and under the new Telecom Law of December 2005, the sector can appeal to the private sector tribunal under the banking law. The problem is that the tribunal does not exist yet under the Banking Law. Thus there was still in 2007 no actionable method to resolve domestic dispute issues.

Securing local financing was not a pressing issue for Roshan as the initial capital expenditure was financed by founding shareholders loans and it made successful share issues in 2005 and 2006. It used the ADB and IFC for guarantees.

Security, however, is a major issue for Roshan daily. The impact comes from risks to the company's property, including 500 base stations, as well as the high cost of providing safety to its employees. An important consideration is that when Roshan entered Afghanistan there was no legal framework for provision of security, and the government is still trying to regulate the sector. The company arranged for its security via private arrangements and uses private security companies, both domestic and international. While Roshan does not foresee any legal issues, again private companies are at risk because of a changing regulatory environment and the use of retroactive policy is not unprecedented. There has been pressure from NGOs for further increased regulation of private security companies and they are now coming under more scrutiny. Changes to the legal framework may leave the company with unexpected liabilities.

Roshan has provided insurance based on international best practice and international policies as the services are unavailable in Afghanistan. Its ability to provide insurance is limited as the cost of provision from international companies is very high.

Access to land has been very important to Roshan both for operations as well as for collateral for financing. The procurement of land is onerous in Afghanistan, with clarity on ownership of existing land, terms of lease, length of lease and transfer lacking in most cases. Zoning and planning have also been an issue for the company. Initially the length of the lease was three years, but it has increased to 5-10 years. Electricity is a main constraint for business in Afghanistan, and for Roshan this means generating all of its own electricity through private generators.

When Roshan launched its operations there was no functioning labour law. The law was enacted in 2006. Again, Roshan drew upon international best practice and experience in other countries to establish a framework for labour contracts and agreements. Additionally, Roshan was a pioneer in best practice policies as well as corporate social responsibility, including providing staff with medical clinics, ongoing educational training and pension entitlements, as well as best practice in termination policies.

Roshan invested in Afghanistan despite all these uncertainties and the endemic problem of corruption – there is no clear anti-corruption policy that is uniformly implemented – as it had, through the AKDN, vast experience in other post-conflict areas and countries that are difficult regulatory environments such as Kosovo and countries in Africa. It has been profitable and the market surprised it on the upside with subscriber numbers and returns.

Concerns remain over security and consistency of laws – the worry that a law can be changed at any time and the lack of enforceability of laws. The issue is also one of institutional capacity – will the judiciary be able to understand the laws, test the laws, interpret them and enforce them? There needs to be both the political will to do so and the capacity.

Case Study: Coca-Cola Beverages Afghanistan

Coca-Cola established distribution and manufacturing facilities in Afghanistan starting in 2002. The Gulzar family and company negotiated with Coca-Cola immediately after the end of the Taliban era to represent the company in the country. The Gulzar family has been in business in Afghanistan since 1940 and has been conducting trade and business since the 1960s. Started in Jalalabad in 1965 with a textile company, the company is now involved in several industries in Afghanistan. In 1975 Habib Gulzar took over the family business. During the wars of 1979-2001 they did not operate in the country directly but facilitated trade from Dubai and globally; no direct investment was done in the country during that period.

In 2002, the company decided to invest once again in the country. It was approached by Coca-Cola in 2001 to be the distributor of the product in Afghanistan as it already was in Pakistan. The family, eager to invest directly in the country, put forward a proposal to not only distribute the product in the country but to produce it in the country as well.

In 2003, Coca-Cola decided that a factory in the country was viable and approached the Ministry of Commerce to assist it alongside investment from the Gulzar family. At the time the Minister of Finance, Ashraf Ghani, and the Ministry of Industry, as well as the US ambassador Khalizad, were of great assistance and eager to ease the entry of such multinational players into the country.

The deal was negotiated through the Ministry of Commerce, the US embassy and the company. The main factor influencing the investment of $25m by the Gulzar company was a desire to do something for their home country. Studies indicate that there is a strong desire in post-conflict situations for citizens living abroad to return and assist in the reconstruction of the country. A World Bank study found that 33% of respondents to a survey put the desire to help the country and Afghan patriotism as the primary reason for investing.[45]

Despite expected lower returns on their investment than what they would have received in other countries, the Gulzars chose to invest over $25m. Influencing their decision were the eight-year tax holiday and the support of the US embassy and the GoA, which helped allay the risks in terms of accessibility to the government.

Upon signing of the agreement, the factory was built on land procured from the government and the company commenced with first distribution, then production. Customs duties at the time seemed transparent and at that time the investors were unaware that electricity and water supply problems would be serious impediments to their business and profitability. The factory required land, procured from the government, electricity, provided by the company's private generators, and water coming from the company as well. There were no provisions from the government for security, nor a framework for regulation; security was handled privately by the company.

One of the major drivers for investment was the eight-year tax holiday that the government was giving to all investors in the country, both domestic and foreign. This greatly influenced the return profile and the comfort to the investors in terms of an investor-friendly government. In addition, agreement on customs duties was a key factor in determining their return on investment. However, the inconsistency of the application of customs duties and regulation has been a serious issue for the company.

Initially the duty was 2.5% on imports of the Coca-Cola finished product and 5% on imports of raw materials to produce the product. Thus as producers they were selling at a price that was not competitive. In January 2006, the company appealed to the GoA for an increase in import duty for finished goods, and in June 2006 the MoF changed the duty, although only after a hard fought battle. Not unexpectedly, traders dealing in beverage products lobbied against the change. In addition to the duties, there was also dumping from international sellers. There was no clear anti-dumping regulation and thus the company had little recourse except to lobby the GoA.

The protective tariff was increased to 20% but other issues arose. There was speculation that the traders were actively under-invoicing their sales and that thus the true effective rate was around 10%. The company cites continuing issues with the enforcement and transparency of duties; with other beverage producers, it lobbied the GoA to address such issues. The company feels the situation was exacerbated by the lack of clarity and inconsistency of the laws and their application, but also by the poor enforceability of the laws and poor communication of them to all producers and traders.

The profitability of the company is not public information, but the company indicates that the costs were much higher than had been even conservatively estimated. Higher costs are mainly due to the high cost of electricity, supplied by the company, and water and security. The company insists it needs to increase the volume of production in order to maintain a profitable business. It is a positive sign that the company plans to increase investment and add another production line at the cost of $10m.

Electricity, as noted, is provided by the company internally. It was required to purchase its own generators: three 2.5 mw machines. The company still depends on its own generators. The company procured its security staff through a firm that was referred to its by the Ministry of Interior.

Case Study: Tolo TV

Tolo TV was started by Moby Capital Partners, run by Saad Mohseni and his brothers Zaid and Jahid. The brothers, Afghan-Australians living in Australia, decided in 2002 to return to Kabul and explore business opportunities. Their initial idea was to invest in a wide range of sectors, although upon arrival they decided to initially focus on media; specifically TV and radio stations. Their vision became a new private sector radio and television station for the Afghan people, one that they knew, despite all the critics, the Afghan people would appreciate and support. Moby Capital now has interests in media throughout the country, reaching over 8 million Afghans daily through TV programs, magazines and radio stations.

Tolo received initial funding from USAID, which helped the funding process considerably. The USAID component was in funding only, so that all company operating activities and legal and regulatory work were done by the company independently. The regulatory system at the time of launch was under the control of a monopoly provider, Radio TV, which was until then the only TV station. This was therefore the only mechanism to grant licenses to new entrants that existed post-Taliban. Tolo TV had to receive a license from that body, i.e. the competitor. Eventually, the Ministry of Information and Culture was given the authority to grant new licenses; the Ministry of Commerce controlled the licenses for the frequency.

A major issue for Tolo TV was that the regulatory process was not transparent; there were such issues as the role of the RTA and the Ministry of Commerce in allocating frequency. Each entity sent conflicting messages as to the jurisdiction of its regulation, and it was often unclear which regulator controlled which contracts.

Tolo TV was relatively comfortable with the civil law system in Afghanistan as it is similar to that in Australia. However, the founders are very open when they say that they entered the market with a leap of faith in terms of confidence in both the regulatory environment and the recourse they would have in many of their contracts. At the time, there were no competitors as there were not many who believed a private radio station would be successful; thus they seized the opportunity despite serious shortcomings in the legal and regulatory framework for media and investment.

Driving factors for investment for the company are similar to those in other case studies, including the attractive tax holidays and customs regulations. As with other investors, such as Roshan and Coca-Cola, the tax system has impacted the company greatly. The tax holiday of eight years was overturned and now the effective tax rate on profits is 20% and 2% of sales; it is not a value added tax and therefore cannot be directly passed on to the consumer. This change in policy, of course, affected profitability enormously. There was also an issue with customs tariffs, as capital equipment was initially imported at 7%, but this was subsequently brought down to 4% and again increased to 10%, all in the space of one year. These changes had a considerable impact on the ability of the company to keep equipment up to date, given the need for repairs, and have often led to permanent damage to equipment.

The company moved forward with its plans despite such obstacle, as it recognised Afghanistan was a new market and Tolo TV knew the GoA well, which allowed it to mitigate some risks.

Other barriers to investment cited include a very high registration fee for new businesses, with informal estimates ranging up to $10,000 for AISA although officially AISA states the fee is $1,000. There was a lack of engagement of the private sector when determining such a framework, which is in part due to lack of experience in dealing with the private sector in the government, on account of the communist past. Additionally, there are, despite efforts by donors, no effective business associations that effectively communicate the private sectors concerns

There was no clear labour law when the company started operations and therefore it set its own best practice standards. In 2006, a new labour law was created, but it is often seen as draconian by the private sector because of its aggressive termination regulations. It is also often unclear as to the responsibilities for previous contracts. There is also a clear lack of local expert Afghan lawyers to understand the laws and help companies adhere to them. As Tolo TV started in 2002, AISA was not there when it arrived and thus it did not have an agency to assist it with such issues.

Land again was an issue for Tolo TV, as it was for other companies. The lack of clarity about land ownership, transaction law and ongoing property rights added to the uncertainty regarding the purchase. Tolo TV used a local lawyer to navigate the system. As much of the land is owned by the government, the negotiations are complex and bureaucratic. Since the formation of AISA, the process has been simplified somewhat, but still there are ongoing issues of lease terms and length.

Electricity provision is extremely expensive for the company as it is entirely by private generators. Again, the legal framework for energy provision is not the main constraint to the provision of electricity provision, but the World Bank cites regulation and perception of regulatory risk as major risk factors for potential investors.[46] Tolo TV suffered loss of equipment due to power surges and has to supply its own electricity to prevent such occurrences.

Again, security is a major concern for Tolo TV. Its security requirements are provided by private security firms. There was no guidance from the government as to approved security firms, and the arrangements were completed on a case by case basis through local procurement of security officers and organizations.

From the start, like the other companies in the survey, Tolo TV made it a clear company policy early on not to participate in any actions that might be construed as informal or similar to a bribe. In a political environment where this is commonplace this is not as uncomplicated as it may sound. Additionally, there was no agency created to make complaints when a company encounters corrupt practices, such as an anti-corruption office.

Conclusion

In 2001, Afghanistan was faced with the overwhelming task of reconstructing itself as a modern, cohesive and viable democratic state. It was immediately clear that rule of law reform would be critical to ensuring economic and private sector development. The process began with the Bonn agreement; since then several laws and regulations have been enacted and implemented with some success, but many critical laws have yet to be developed. The commercial rule of law reform process has been hindered by both systemic issues and external factors including:

- Problems over prioritizing of reform: While rule of law reform was prioritized from the start, the emphasis on and attention to the process were eventually lessened because of the other urgent needs of the country, such as security. Often the process was fragmented and slowed down by competing donor agendas and competing areas of reform, such as security. There was an under-appreciation for the extent to which the rule of law issue permeates all other aspects of society and development;
- Lead donor structure of reform: Rule of law reform was championed by a lead donor, Italy. This approach led to competing strategies on rule of law, a narrow approach to reform, over-reliance on one nation to provide guidance and funding for reform, and a fragmented process as other countries' agendas on rule of law reform were pursued independently;
- Lack of consistency in training: Legal advisors were assigned for specific training initiatives and their assignments in country were often short-term, indeed as short as two weeks to one month. Trainers rotated frequently and this led to inconsistency in training methods, content and delivery.
- Insufficient communication of new policies and laws: a critical factor which lessened awareness of, and therefore compliance with, new laws and regulations both in Kabul and elsewhere.
- Limits to institutional capacity: given the fractured layers of the legal system, the reform process at times was too complex for the existing institutions and did not fully complement the inherent strengths. The capacity and potential of existing legal structures should have been more carefully documented before Bonn, and the reform processes tailored accordingly.

Businesses in Afghanistan face many hurdles to investment including: inconsistent reform policies, such as the tax reform policy that was applied inconsistently and/or changed without prior notice; the absence of a labor law that outlines fair and consistent practices across all sectors and industries; a lack of financing for small and medium size businesses; an underdeveloped banking system; security issues affecting among others staff, customers and the tangible assets of the company; an absence of clear land zoning and ownership laws to support business activity; and insufficient infrastructure such as water, telecom and road transport networks.

The implementation of a transitional commercial rule of law could feasibly play a significant role in alleviating some of the challenges to attracting and retaining both foreign and domestic investment through:

- providing a transparent legal framework giving a country the opportunity to develop its own set of commercial laws without time pressures and/or competing foreign and domestic interests;
- supporting an internationally accepted framework that would underpin immediate post-conflict investment in the country, such as investment in roads, water, electricity and telecoms, and would lay the foundation for further investment;
- providing clear guidance on certain commercial transactions as well as supporting mediation and arbitration of potential disputes;
- a transparent campaign that is consistent and widespread to effectively communicate the new laws, in all the local languages and cities, which would improve public awareness;
- working closely with existing institutions, utilizing their capabilities to support legal reform, in a process led and driven by Afghans, and providing long-term and focused technical assistance to the judiciary to strengthen its capacity to both enact and implement legal reform;
- a consistent and cohesive donor strategy and transparent and full accountability of the lead donor. Delays in donor financing, short-term assignment of technical experts, and competing donor strategies often hampered the development of the judicial reform process. The strategy should be cohesive and consistent and yet flexible enough to react to changing conditions. It should be based on a long-term holistic approach to rule of law reform whilst addressing short term pressing issues. The interrelationship between the economy, civil society, security and rule of law needs to be considered when outlining the process and roadmap for reform.

In 2001, Afghanistan's complex society was faced with restructuring its political system, economic institutions and building the infrastructure necessary to support the economy. Years of war, fractured domestic political parties and differing reform priorities from within the government and from outside the country have had an impact on the economic growth of the country and the investment climate. As mentioned in the case studies, a transitional commercial rule of law could have laid the foundation for inward investment earlier in the reconstruction phase. A clear investment framework could act to attract more investment and support sustainable economic growth. The transitional rule of law process in Afghanistan had some successes, but its implementation lacked consistency and cohesiveness and was weakened by competing donor agendas and a flawed communications strategy. A holistic approach to transitional law implementation focused on leveraging existing institutional capacity and maximizing donor coordination and lead donor accountability, as well as ensuring the effective dissemination of information, could increase the impact of such a program.

Notes

1   A *Loya Jirga* (General Assembly) is a traditional Afghan body dating from the 18th century. The assembly, which generally meets to appoint new leadership, determine national policy, or draft a constitution, last met in 1977.

2   http://jurist.law.pitt.edu/world/afghanistan.htm

3   Sources: U.S. State Department; *CIA World Factbook*; wire service reports.

4   Scimitar Global Ventures, *Afghanistan; A Critical Land Bridge for Regional Economic Cooperation*. May 2006.

5   Ibid.

6   Ali Wardak, *"Building a Post-war justice system in Afghanistan,"* Crime, Law and Social Change, 2004.

7   Ibid.

8   United States Institute of Peace, *Establishing the Rule of Law in Afghanistan*. March 2004

9   Ibid.

10   International Commission of Jurists, *Afghanistan's Legal System and its Compatibility with International Human Rights Standards*, 2002.

11   Center for Humanitarian Dialogue. *Assistance to Justice and the Rule of Law in Afghanistan; A strategic analysis*, February 2004.

12   Ibid.

13   Ibid.

14   Final Statement of Rome Conference on Justice in Afghanistan. December 2002.

15   Center for Humanitarian Dialogue. *Assistance to Justice and the Rule of Law in Afghanistan; A Strategic Analysis*, February 2004.

16   Ibid. Also interviews conducted January 2007 with various representatives of the rule of law reform including USAID, UNAMA, AISA and the private sector.

17   Ibid. Including statements that the lead donor had a flawed and uniformed understanding of the three-judge system and the necessity for such – given there is no jury in Afghan justice. After much lobbying and resistance by the JRC, the system now has three judges and Italy's insistence on an inquisitorial framework has been rejected.

18   Ibid.

19   Ibid – interviews suggest continued lack of coordination and/or agreement on objectives and priorities. Furthermore, donor led agendas often clashed not only with the JRC agenda but with each other, creating further delay in implementation.

20   Ibid and Amnesty International Report. *Afghanistan: Establishing the Rule of Law*. August 2003.

21   UNODC and World Bank Group. *Afghanistan's Drug Industry*. December 2006.

22   United States Institute of Peace, *Establishing the Rule of Law in Afghanistan*. March 2004.

23   Ibid.

24   Interviews conducted with Commissioner of AIHRC, UNAMA, and USAID. January 2007.

25 ABA Asia Law Initiative. January 2003. http://www.abanet.org/abaasia/projects/afghanistan .shtml

26 Ibid.

27 Ibid

28 Richard Sannerholm, "Beyond Criminal Justice: Promoting Rule of Law in Post-conflict Societies".

29 World Bank Report. *Investment Climate Assessment; Afghanistan.* December 2005.

30 Wardak, Ali "Building a Post-war Justice System in Afghanistan." *Crime, Law and Social Change.* 2004.

31 World Bank Group. *Investment Climate Assessment: Afghanistan.* December 2005.

32 United Nations Office on Drugs and Crime and the World Bank Group. *Afghanistan's Drug Industry.* 2006.

33 World Bank Group. *Investment Climate Assessment: Afghanistan.* December 2005.

34 Ibid.

35 Ibid.

36 Ibid.

37 IMF. December 2005.

38 World Bank Group. *Benchmarking FDI Opportunities.* 2005.

39 Interview with AISA CEO indicates that indeed in 2002 several foreign investors came to Afghanistan and owing to lack of transparency, commercial codes, enforcement and security found the risk levels of investment too high to invest. Only in 2006 did AISA see a resurgence of investment in the country. January 2007.

40 World Bank Group. *The Investment Climate in Afghanistan: Exploiting Opportunities in an Uncertain Environment.* December 2005.

41 World Bank Group. *Access to Energy.* June 2007.

42 Scimitar Global Ventures. *Afghanistan: A Critical Land Bridge for Regional Cooperation.* May 2006.

43 The Enabling Environment Conference. Government and the Private Sector working together to create the Afghan telecommunications industry. June 2007.

44 Ibid.

45 *The Investment Climate in Afghanistan.* December 2005.

46 World Bank Group Study. *Lack of Access to Energy.* June 2007.

Chapter 7

FDI in the Economic Transformation of the Post-civil war Economies of Angola and Mozambique

Estelle Bierman and Henri Bezuidenhout

Introduction

Angola and Mozambique were both Portuguese colonies, and before the guerrilla wars against colonial rule broke out, foreign investment was sharply restricted by Portugal. After armed struggles began in Angola (1961) and Mozambique (1964), measures were taken to encourage foreign investment, especially in the area of mineral extraction and manufacturing. New foreign investment and industrial production laws had been implemented by 1965 and this resulted in a sharp increase in private foreign investment in Angola and Mozambique. However, these investment policies implemented by Portugal were designed to increase Portugal's share in these countries' economies and did not seek investments that might lead to Angola and Mozambique's eventual economic self-sufficiency (El-Khawas, 1974:21-22).

Both these countries regained their independence from Portugal in 1975, leaving both with grim economic conditions. According to the United Nations Development Programme (UNDP) and the World Bank (cited by Mayer, 1990:463), all economic sectors in Angola recorded significant decreases in production, of up to 100 per cent, between 1974 and 1976. Extensive damage to infrastructure also had a significant negative influence on the economy (FDR & LOC, 1989; UNCTAD & ICC, 2001:2). In Angola, bridges, roads, and transport vehicles were severely damaged and most undamaged vehicles were taken out of the country by Portuguese refugees. This caused the distribution system to collapse and essential food and other supplies could not reach some parts of the country. A significant part of the economy also collapsed when Portuguese settlers, including highly skilled workers and government and economic development administrators, left the country (FRD & LOC, 1989). In Mozambique a similar situation emerged, leading to the wrecking of installations and equipment, which paralyzed the country's economy (Mayer, 1990:463).

There were long periods of civil war in Angola and Mozambique after their independence, adding to the economic and social damage already suffered. Mozambique's civil war ended in 1992 with the signing of the

General Peace Agreement, while Angola's war only ended in 2002 with the defeat of the armed opposition party, the National Union for the Total Independence of Angola (UNITA), and the death of its leader, Dr Jonas Savimbi (Sidaway & Simon, 1993:6; UNCTAD & ICC, 2001:6, Da Gama, 2005:1). After their respective wars, the economic conditions of Angola and Mozambique were dire (FDR & LOC, 1989).

These two countries have since revolutionised their policies and incentives to attract more foreign direct investment (FDI). The objective of foreign direct investment is to obtain a lasting interest in an entity resident in the host country. The lasting interest implies the existence of a long-term relationship between the direct investor and the enterprise in the host country, and a significant degree of influence on the management of the enterprise. Direct investment involves both the initial transaction between the two entities and all subsequent capital transactions between them and amongst affiliated enterprises, both incorporated and unincorporated (OECD, 1999:7-8).

Most African countries experience a shortage of investment capital and are thus aware of the importance of FDI for bridging this gap (Loots, 2000:1), as well as for economic growth and development, because of its distinctive combination of tangible and intangible assets (UNCTAD & ICC, 2001:2). Since both these countries are classified as least developed countries (LDCs), it is unsure whether FDI may have a net positive or negative influence on them as host countries (Da Gama, 2005:39). A more comprehensive explorative analysis of the relationship between FDI, economic growth and human development will however be made in the next section. Although FDI represents the largest portion of all international capital flows to middle-income developing countries since the 1990s, the flows to low-income countries were smaller. These countries also, usually, receive more foreign aid than FDI (Perkins *et al.*, 2006:415). The global, regional and country-specific distribution of FDI inflows since 1980 will be analysed more profoundly below.

The main aim of this paper is to evaluate whether FDI assists in the rebuilding and development of a country after a period of conflict. Therefore, the role that FDI plays in the economic growth of post-conflict zones in Africa is investigated, particularly examining the case of Angola and Mozambique. This is done by (i) discussing the relationship between FDI, economic growth and human development, (ii) analysing the distribution of global FDI among developing countries and in Africa generally, as well as Angola and Mozambique in particular, (iii) exploring the investment focus areas in Africa and more specifically in Angola and Mozambique, (iv) analysing the main motives for FDI in Angola and Mozambique, (v) examining the separate FDI policies of these countries, and (vi) exploring their overall investment climates. To wrap up this paper, several policy recommendations for Angola and Mozambique will be given, with regard to studies on other developing and least developed countries (LDCs). First the theory regarding the relationship between FDI, economic growth and human development are briefly discussed; this will serve as a foundation for the rest of the chapter.

The Relationship between FDI and Economic Growth

The relationship between FDI and economic growth is a controversial subject, with many studies contradicting one another on whether a relationship exists. White (1992; cited by Jansen, 1995:197) concludes that a majority of the studies were affected by statistical and theoretical problems, which led to unreliable results. Therefore, the question should rather be whether an increase in capital flows would increase the level of investment and economic growth at all. According to Jansen (1995:197) the majority of cross-country studies have seen an increase in growth. A brief review of the different schools of thought on whether FDI influences growth and development or not, and whether growth may influence FDI in return, follows below, and then the two channels through which FDI is claimed to influence growth are detailed.

Controversial views on the FDI-Growth Relationship

According to Lim (2001:9) there tends to be a positive correlation between FDI and economic growth, as deduced from recent empirical work conducted at an economy-wide level. However, it is argued that the host country must have obtained a certain level of development to be able to absorb the new technology, as it is evident that higher-income developing countries experience the most significant positive influence on economic growth. Kosack and Tobin (2006:213) agree that the influence of FDI on economic growth, as well as human development, will depend on the type of FDI a country receives, as well as the country's ability to absorb the benefits brought by FDI.

Li and Liu (2005:404) conclude that an endogenous relationship between FDI and economic growth exists, which has been evident since the mid-1980s for developing and developed countries. Upon inclusion of FDI directly in the growth model, they find FDI significant, and two interactive terms of FDI, FDI with human capital[1] and FDI with the technology gap,[2] also proved significant (Li and Liu, 2005:404). The first interactive term was significant and positively related to growth, while the second interactive term demonstrated a significant negative influence on growth. Hansen and

Rand (2006) also confirm a strong causal link between FDI and GDP for thirty-one developing countries. This positive link is also relevant over the long term, where the fixed-effects model with country-specific time trends is used.

UNCTAD (2005:4) also finds that there is an overall stable and positive relationship between GDP growth and FDI flows, and that the availability of investment capital (generated by corporate profits of loans) affects FDI on the supply side. This is in turn affected by the local economic conditions, including economic growth. On the demand side, it is argued that expand-ing foreign markets lead TNCs to invest more, and gloomy markets, on the other hand, inhibit TNCs.

According to Chowdhury and Mavrotas (2006), a bi-directional causality between FDI and growth for Malaysia and Thailand can be found. Their findings for Chile however confirmed that the direction of causality runs from economic growth to FDI, and not, as conventional views hold, from FDI to economic growth. This must be considered in developing policies to enhance FDI, in order to increase economic growth, since economic growth itself is a crucial determinant of FDI (UNCTAD, 2007a).

Theoretical Relationship between FDI, Economic Growth and Human Development

Kosack and Tobin (2006) provide a practical illustration of the relationships between FDI, human development and growth. Figure 1 represents their findings regarding these relationships. Firstly the relationship between economic growth and human development will be discussed regarding Figure 1; then the influence of FDI on growth and human development will be analysed.

Figure 1:   The relationship between FDI, economic growth and human development

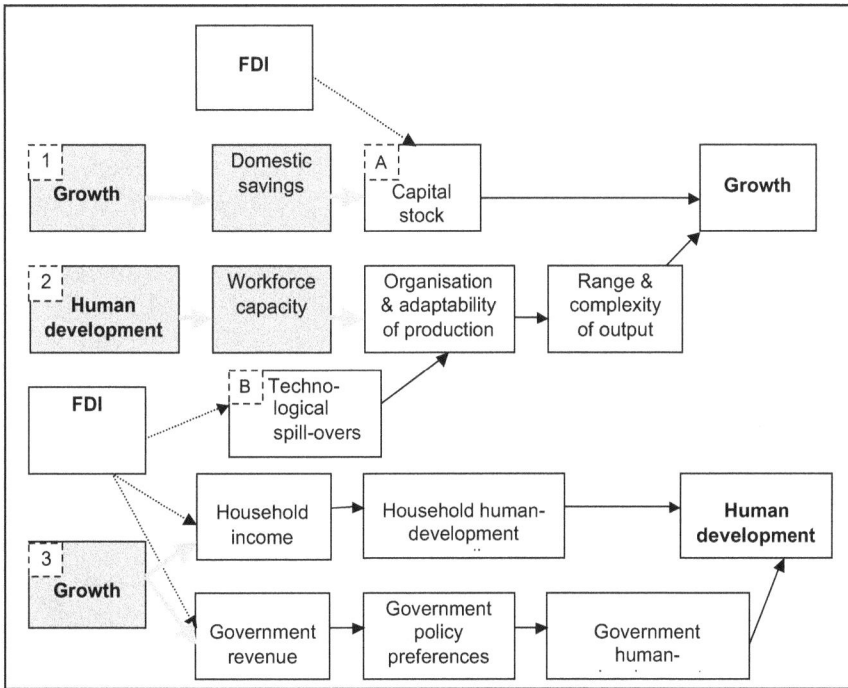

Source: Kosack & Tobin (2006:214)

Relationship between Economic Growth and Human Development

Firstly, economic growth may just lead to a further increase in economic growth, without improving human development. The increase in income may increase domestic savings, ultimately leading to increased capital stock. The increased capital stock may in turn increase the productivity, therefore contributing to further growth (Kosack & Tobin, 2006:208-209).

Secondly, Kosack and Tobin (2006:208) argue that human development may contribute to economic growth by an increase in the capacity of the workforce, which leads to a change in the organisation and adaptability of production, as well as the range and complexity of output. Overall, increased human development may lead to increased national income *via* social capital and the policy environment, amongst other things.

Thirdly, economic growth may contribute to human development by its direct positive influence on household income and government revenue. Increased government revenue may be reinvested further in human development, depending on government policies and priorities; and increased household income may be reinvested by households in their own develop-ment, for example health, education and welfare (Kosack & Tobin, 2006:208).

Influence of FDI on Economic Growth and Human Development

Foreign direct investment's contribution to economic growth mainly takes place through two channels: directly through an increase in capital stock (A) and the subsequent capital flows, and indirectly through its spill-over effect (B; Lensink & Morrissey, 2006:479). The influence of FDI on economic growth *via* these to channels will subsequently be discussed. Regarding the influence of FDI on human development, Kosack and Tobin (2006:212) argues that FDI may contribute to human development as well, but only if it is able to increase household income or tax revenue. This issue will not be discussed in more detail, as this falls beyond the scope of this paper.

Direct Influence on Capital Stock. Todaro (2000:582-583) recognises FDI's role in filling the gap between the available domestic savings and the tar-geted level of investment. Foreign direct investment forms part of private investment, and thus increases total private investment. Local private in-vestment and FDI are likely to be determined by the same factors, reflecting the investment climate of the host country. New FDI projects may invite complementary local investments to provide intermediary products for TNCs, or to use the products and services produced by TNCs. It is also likely that total private investment will be more than the FDI inflows re-ceived. This may be because only a part of the total investment project is financed by foreign equity capital, and local financial institutions finance the remainder (Jansen, 1995:196 & 199). The relationship between FDI and capital stock is positive, but the question now is what the relationship be-tween FDI and economic growth is.

How investment relates to economic growth is summarised by Jansen (1995:197). He states that an increase in FDI inflows is likely to have a posi-tive effect on growth. The perceived positive relationship between capital inflows, investment, and growth is the central tenet behind the two-gap (or three-gap) models. The traditional two-gap model states that all capital inflows will be used to finance investment, but Griffin (1970; cited by Jansen, 1995:197) argues that not all capital inflows will be used to finance invest-ment, and that some part of it will be consumed (decreasing domestic sav-ings). The net effect will be an increase in investment of less than the increase in capital inflows.

Indirect Influence through Spill-over Effects. Increased capital inflows may indirectly affect the growth efficiency of an investment, because FDI usually consists of a package of capital, technology, management skills, marketing channels, and other elements. This type of capital flow promotes the transfer of technologies and may increase productivity, although these effects may be difficult to measure (Jansen, 1995:197). There are a number of ways in which spill-overs through FDI can occur:

- Firstly, spill-overs can occur when a local firm copies the new technology brought to the country through a TNC (imitation channel; Lensink & Morrissey, 2006:479).
- Secondly, a spill-over may occur when local firms have to use their current technology and resources more efficiently, or obtain more effective techniques, in order to respond to greater competitive pressures coming from a TNC (competition channel; Lensink & Morrissey, 2006:479). However, according to Harrison (1996, cited in Lim, 2001:4), FDI may have an adverse effect in the short run by decreasing the market share of local firms, but with a chance for positive spill-over effects over the long term.
- Thirdly, spill-overs can take place when a person starts their own firm or takes employment elsewhere in the country, after receiving training by an affiliate in a new technique or technology (labour spin-offs and turnover channel; Miyamoto, 2003:34).
- Fourthly, the linkages between a TNC affiliate and its local suppliers and customers are an important channel for spill-overs (vertical linkages channel; Miyamoto, 2003:34). Local firms' productivity may be improved through TNCs (Lim, 2001:3): (i) assisting potential suppliers in setting up their production facilities; (ii) setting high standards for their potential suppliers to achieve, but also ensuring potential suppliers have the means to do so; (iii) training these suppliers also on managerial and organisational skills; and (iv) assisting suppliers in expanding their clientele basis, including other foreign affiliates.

As mentioned above, the controversial results of empirical studies on the relationship between FDI and economic growth may be due to the fact that the results are country specific. The mechanisms through which FDI influences growth may also differ across countries, and the existence of reverse causality from growth to FDI in present in many countries (Duttaray, Dutt & Mukhopadhyay, 2008).

Kosack and Tobin (2006) concluded from their empirical study on the influence of FDI and aid on economic growth and human development that FDI does have a significant influence in highly developed countries, but a slight negative influence in countries with low levels of human capital. However, the reason for this may be that the low level of human capital in a developing country does not contribute to the absorption of FDI into that country's economic development. Unfavourable government policies may also inhibit the absorption and effectiveness of FDI in that country.

Vu (2008), on the other hand, conducted a study on the influence of FDI on endogenous growth in Vietnam by testing the effect of FDI indirectly on growth via labour productivity. The results showed that FDI has a significant positive effect on labour productivity and economic growth, although the effect is not equally distributed among the different economic sectors. Although the influence of FDI on growth is country specific, the results for Vietnam may be true for other developing countries such as Angola and Mozambique.

According to El-Khawas (1974:24), the importance of FDI to economic growth was evident in his study of Angola and Mozambique, conducted just before their independence. The empirical analysis of whether FDI has contributed to economic growth in the post-conflict era of these countries falls beyond the scope of this paper and only the theoretical influence of FDI on economic growth is of concern. In the next section, the global distribution of FDI, as well as the distribution amongst developing countries generally and Angola and Mozambique specifically, is analysed.

Distribution of Foreign Direct Investment

To support this paper's argument, a thorough analysis of the distribution of FDI around the world, and especially to developing countries, is needed. The distribution of FDI to Africa, in comparison to the other developing regions, is analysed, and the distribution of FDI, specifically to Angola and Mozambique, is the focus point of the paper.

Figure 2 plots the FDI inflows to developed countries, developing countries, and South-East Europe and transition economies. It is evident that developing countries' share in FDI inflows is still minimal, but has steadily grown since 1980. FDI inflows to developing countries increased on average, but decreased from the middle of 2000 to the end of 2002, whereafter they increased at a higher rate than before. Africa in particular received the smallest part of FDI flows to developing countries, while Latin America received the greatest portion (see Figure 3).

Figure 4 demonstrates how Angola's FDI inflows increased significantly during the late 1990s and early 2000s. FDI flows decreased sharply from 2003 and turned negative in 2005. They were still negative in 2006 and even more negative in 2007. According to (2007b:36), this negative inflow was due to the acquisitions of ongoing oil exploitation and refinery projects (previously owned by foreign TNCs) by the government-owned oil company, Sonangol. It is not clear why these acquisitions took place, but according to Sonangol (2008), one of its corporate goals is to constitute new companies and acquire all or part of the capital of an established company in the pursuit of its social objective. If the voting capital is obtained in its totality or majority, it is also the goal of Sonangol to establish coordination, as well as economic and financial direction and the business development of the said company.

Figure 2: FDI inflows to the world, 1980-2007

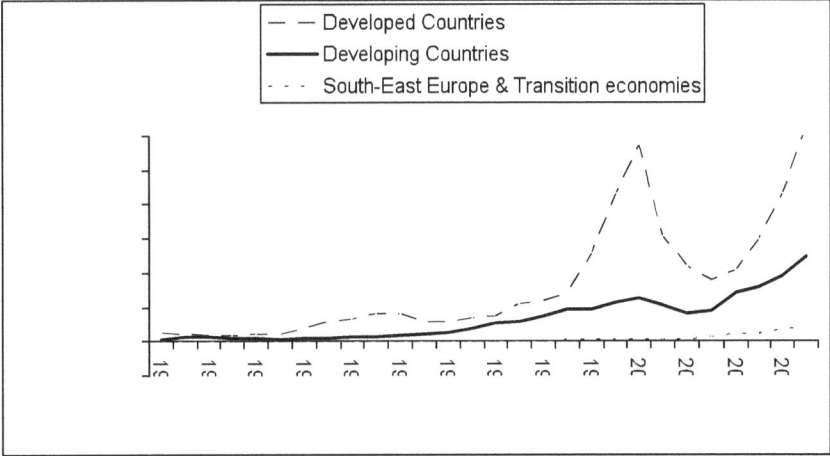

Source: UNCTAD (2009).

Figure 3: FDI inflows to developing countries, 1980-2007

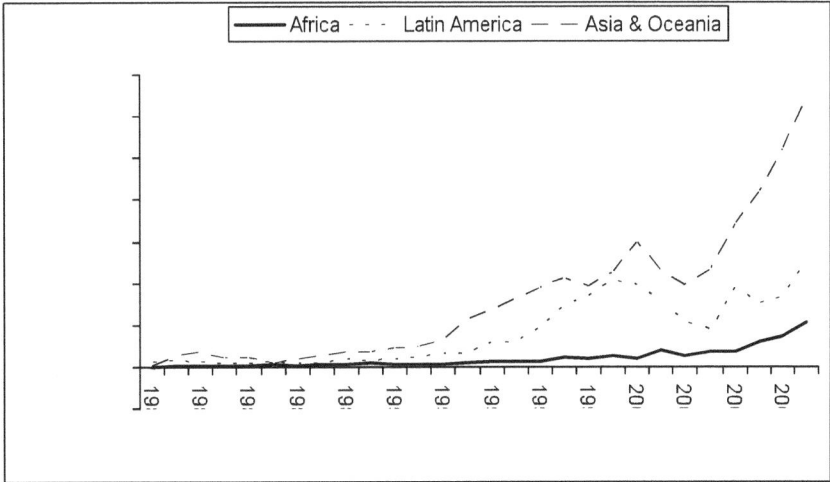

Source: UNCTAD (2009).

Figure 4:   FDI inflows to Angola and Mozambique, 1980-2007

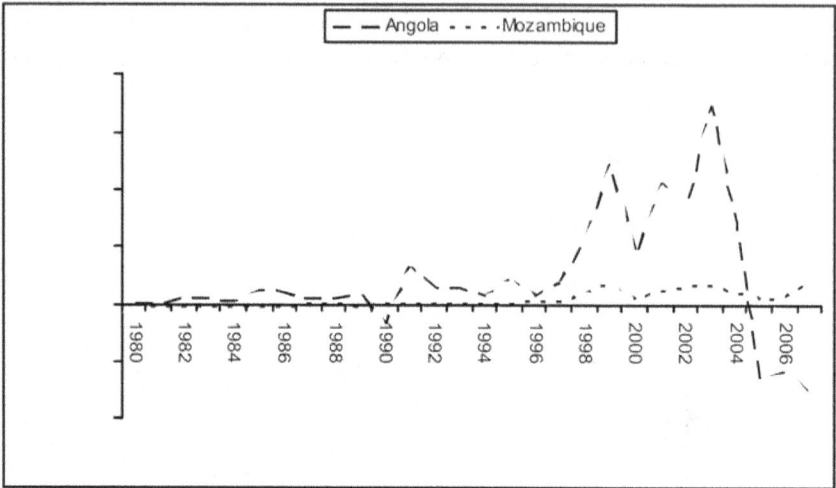

Source: UNCTAD (2009).

It is also evident that Angola generally receives more FDI than Mozambique, except for Angola's negative inflow of FDI in 1990, 2005, 2006 and 2007. Mozambique is systematically attracting more FDI. While Mozambique was amongst the top 10 recipients of FDI in Africa for 2007, Angola was one of two African countries which reported a negative FDI inflow in 2007. The steep increase in the FDI inflows to Mozambique in 2007 was due to the increased investment in the aluminium industry, as a result of the bigger demand for its products in China (UNCTAD, 2008b:41).

Since Angola's economy is oil-dependent, Figure 5 plots the FDI inflows to Angola against annual crude oil production, annual crude oil exports and the number of crude oil producing wells, to compare trends. According to Figure 5, the trend of FDI inflows is generally the same as oil production, export and producing wells trends, although other indefinite factors also had an influence on FDI inflows. In 1990 FDI inflow was negative, and according to Figure 5, the number of producing wells slightly decreased in 1990. This may have caused the extraction of foreign capital out of Angola.

The available data on the production of diamonds for 2001-5 were also compared to FDI inflows into Angola, as it is the second most important natural resource in the country, but no conclusive comparisons could be made between them.

Figure 5:   FDI inflows to Angola versus its crude oil production, exports and producing wells, 1980-2006

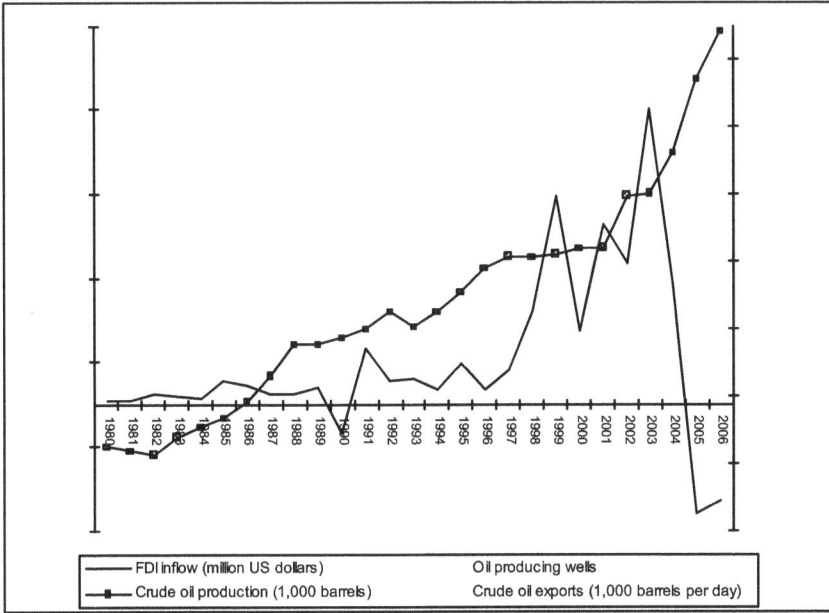

Source: OPEC (2007) & UNCTAD (2009)

When FDI inflows are expressed in terms of the GDP of that country (see Figure 6), the picture does not change much. Angola still received higher FDI proportionately to GDP.

Surprisingly, both Angola and Mozambique proved to attract FDI above their potential, according to UNCTAD's (2007b:14) matrix of inward FDI performance and potential for 2006. This matrix classifies countries into four categories according to their FDI performance and FDI potential: (i) Front-runners: countries with high FDI potential and performance; (ii) Above potential: countries with low FDI potential, but strong FDI performance; (iii) Below potential: countries with high FDI potential, but low FDI perform-ance; and (iv) Under-performers: countries with low FDI potential and performance. Angola and Mozambique both fell in the second category. However, according to the latest inward FDI performance and potential index of 2008 (UNCTAD, 2008b:13), which is based on the 2007 FDI data, Angola and Mozambique fell in the fourth category as under-performers. Their FDI potential remained low, but their FDI performance decreased (as is evident in Figure 4).

Figure 6:   FDI inflows per GDP, 1980-2007

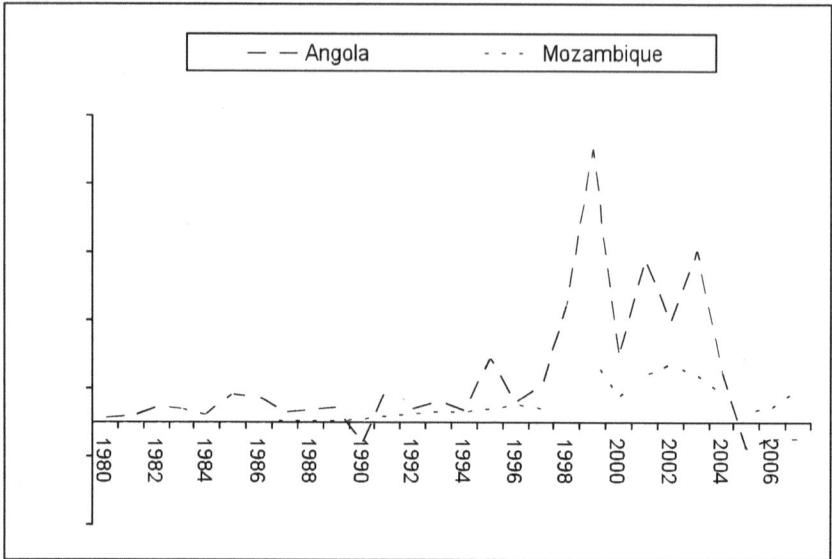

Source: UNCTAD (2009) and World Bank (2008a).

In Figure 7 the FDI inflows per GDP of Angola and Mozambique are compared with those of Southern Africa counterparts (South Africa and Botswana), two developing countries with a high FDI inflow (China and Brazil), and the average for developing economies.

In 1992, Angola and Mozambique received a greater percentage of FDI in total GDP than the average developing country. Their Southern Africa counterparts (South Africa and Botswana) received almost zero per cent FDI proportionately to their GDPs. Brazil received less FDI expressed in terms of GDP than the average developing country, while China received the most, although very comparable to Angola.

In 2002 the FDI inflows proportionately to GDP were significantly higher than in 1992 for all the countries. Angola, Mozambique and Botswana were well above the average for developing countries, with Angola receiving the most and Botswana the least FDI proportionately to GDP. South Africa still lagged far behind these countries and also had smaller FDI inflows proportionately to its GDP than the average developing country. China and Brazil received similar percentages of FDI proportionately to GDP and these were higher than the average for developing countries. However, they received less than Angola and Mozambique.

Figure 7:   FDI inflows per GDP for 1992,[3] 2002[4] and 2007

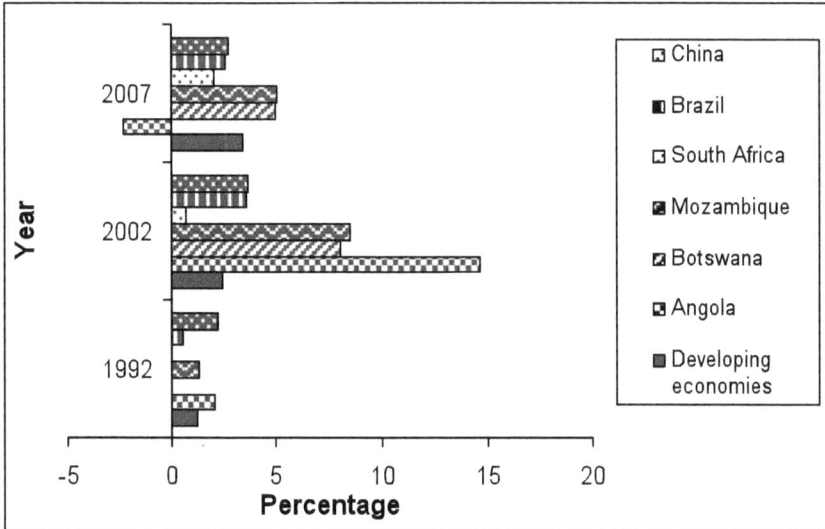

Source: UNCTAD (2009) and World Bank (2008a).

In 2007 Angola had a negative FDI inflow as percentage of its GDP for reasons mentioned earlier on in this section. Mozambique's FDI inflow per GDP was also lower than in 2002, but exceeded the average for developing countries. Botswana's FDI per GDP was slightly less than Mozambique's, and South Africa received significantly smaller FDI inflows per GDP. China and Brazil received less than the average for developing countries, and Mozambique.

To conclude this section, it may be summarised that developing count-ries are receiving an increasing portion of global FDI inflows, but that Afri-can countries still receives the smallest proportion of that amount. Angola performed well up until 2004, but has since reported a negative inflow of FDI. Mozambique's FDI inflows have slowly, but surely, increased since 1998. According to the matrix of inward FDI performance and potential, Angola and Mozambique performed above their potential according to 2006 FDI data, but underperformed according to the 2007 FDI data. When these two countries' FDI inflows as a percentage of their GDP are compared with those of their Southern African partners and other developing countries, Mozambique received a greater value of FDI inflows proportionate to its GDP than the rest. Angola, however, scored a negative inflow of FDI pro-portionate to its GDP. Yet, both of these countries still have unexplored opportunities for FDI, and in the next section the investment focus areas of

Africa, in specific, and Angola and Mozambique, in particular, will be investigated.

Investment Focus Areas

This section elaborates on the different investment focus areas of Africa, and more specifically, Angola and Mozambique.

Africa. According to UNCTAD (2008a:28-29), the long-term prospects for FDI in Africa are promising for investments in raw-material value-chain activities. The recent changes in the US African Growth and Opportunity Act (AGOA) may also increase further diversification into textile processing. It is also expected that FDI in oil, gas and other minerals will remain robust in the medium term, but that FDI in the manufacturing sector will increase in the long-term. This would be due to the implementation of new initiatives, such as the African Investment Incentive Act (AIIA) by the United States Government (under the AGOA initiative), that could contribute to the region's FDI attractiveness.

According to UNCTAD (2007b:82), investments in extractive industries make up the majority of FDI flows to many low-income countries, especially those in Africa. It is, however, evident that most of these countries lack the capacity to transform those FDI flows into broader development gains. Figure 8 represents the Human Development Index (HDI) ratings of Angola, Mozambique, Botswana, South Africa, Brazil and China. According to UNCTAD (2007b:82) Angola was among the top five sub-Saharan African host countries of inward FDI stock in 2005 and among the top four sub-Saharan oil exporters, but Angola's human development performance has been disappointing, as it scored only 0.4 on the most recent HDI.

From Figure 8 it is also evident that Mozambique's HDI trend is close to Angola's. When compared with the HDI values of their Southern Africa counterparts (South Africa and Botswana), and two developing countries with a high FDI inflow (China and Brazil), Angola's and Mozambique's HDI ratings are far lower than their Southern African counterparts, whose ratings are still lower than those of China and Brazil.

The inability of many African countries to utilise the gains from transnational corporation (TNC) participation in export-oriented resource extraction is regularly referred to as the 'resource curse' (UNCTAD, 2007b:93). Sachs and Warner (1997; cited by UNCTAD, 2007b:94) found a negative relationship between natural-resource-based exports and economic growth during the period of 1970 to 1990. According to UNCTAD (2007b:94), these results were confirmed by Auty (2001) and Mikesell (1997).

However, it was suggested by Moore (2000; cited by UNCTAD, 2007b:94) that political under-development, and not resource abundance in itself, may be the root of the poor performance of mineral-rich countries. According to UNCTAD (2007b:82 & 94), the revenue from mineral extraction is often wasted through weak governance, and not invested in projects that promote sustainable development. Thus, the role of foreign direct investment as a driving force for development, made especially in the extractive industries, should be reconsidered.

Figure 8:   Human Development Index (HDI) value, 1987-2005

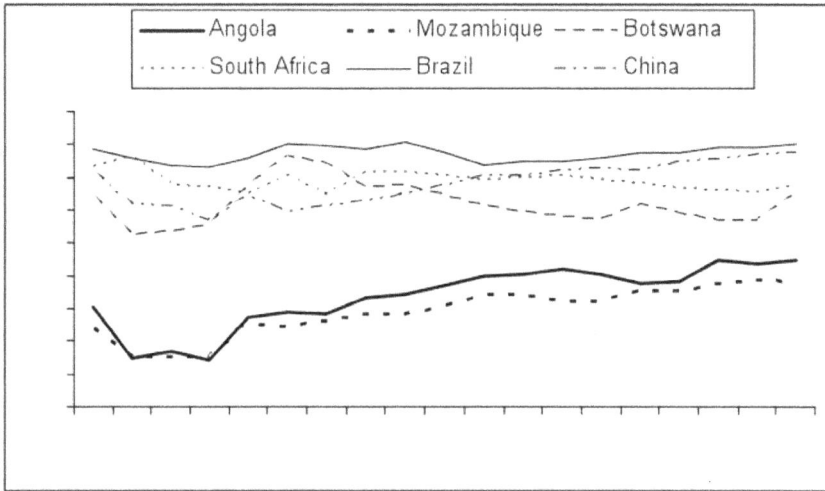

Source: UNDP (2008)

Firstly, it must be noted that mineral extraction is primarily an export-oriented activity with significant potential for income generation, but the opportunity for employment creation and local linkages is restricted. Secondly, this activity creates substantial threats to the host country's environment and may have undesirable social repercussions. Thirdly, mineral resources are exhaustible and frequently of strategic and geopolitical importance. Consequently, government involvement tends to be high, especially in the case of oil and gas. Unfortunately, LDCs cannot generally obtain the financial resources needed for capital-intensive investments, either from national government-owned enterprises or from national private firms. Therefore, they are prompted to attract investments from TNCs or to borrow from a lender equipped to agree to the high risk brought about by such investment (UNCTAD, 2007b:92). The FDI policies and respective investment climates of Angola and Mozambique will be discussed below.

The substantial FDI made in infrastructure, in recent years, under the regional integration scheme may have resulted from the New Partnership for Africa's Development (NEPAD) initiative in infrastructure (UNCTAD, 2008a:28-29). NEPAD's (2006:1) collaboration with the Regional Spatial Development Initiatives (SDI) Programme aims to enhance the economic growth and development prospects of high potential areas across Africa.

Originally, the SDI Programme focused on the facilitation of investment-led growth on a number of South African development corridors, by enhancing their attractiveness for investment, mainly through the provision of infrastructure. The early success of the Maputo Development Corridor, an initiative to rehabilitate the trade route between South Africa and Mozambique, led to the investigation and launch of numerous SDI projects. These include the Lubombo SDI (South Africa, Mozambique and Swaziland), the Bas-Congo SDI (Democratic Republic of Congo (DRC), Republic of Congo and Angola), the Mtwara Corridor (Southern Tanzania, Northern Mozambique, Southern Malawi and Eastern Zambia), the Lobito Corridor (Angola, DRC, Zambia), the Kinshasa-Luanda-Windhoek-Johannesburg Corridor (South Africa, Namibia, Botswana, Angola, DRC, Republic of Congo), the Great East Africa "Barrier Reef" (Kenya, Tanzania, Mozambique), the Shire-Zambezi Waterway (Malawi and Mozambique), the Beira Corridor (Mozambique to Zimbabwe and Zambia), and the Nampula Corridor (Mozambique to Malawi and Tanzania). Not all of these have however been implemented. Through these projects, the attractiveness of Angola and Mozambique for investment may be improved by the elimination of bureaucratic, administrative and institutional impediments to trade and investment (NEPAD, 2006:2-3, 31, 39, 42-43 & 48-50; Bain, 2009).

Angola. Angola's integration into the Southern African Development Community (SADC) offers investors easier access to the main markets in Southern Africa, including South Africa and 13 other member countries (UNCTAD & ICC, 2001:1). The increased market size makes Angola more attractive to TNC's wanting to locate here.

Regarding special endowments, Angola's remarkable deposits of diamonds, petroleum and iron ore have always attracted foreign investors (El-Khawas, 1974:24). Angola's economy is mainly dependent on its oil production, but according to Eisenstein (2007), Angola's government-owned diamond company (Endiama) is urging foreign companies to join it as partners to diversify Angola's oil-dependent economy. It is believed that Angola is only exploring 40 per cent of the territory believed to have potential for diamond mining.

According to UNCTAD (2008b:60), Petrobras, Brazil's national oil company, has recently joined forces with Eni (from Italy) to explore African bio-fuel sources for export to Italy, and is currently looking to work in partnership on the construction of bio-diesel plants in Angola and Mozambique, as well as in Brazil.

According to the *Africa Investor* magazine (2007:48), a construction boom has been likely in Luanda since 2007, because of the ports, railways, roads and bridges that were being restored. Angola's industry Minister also encouraged foreign investors to help with these restorations, including the restoration of telecommunications systems and power plants. Agriculture is also an important focus area for the government and can pose great investment opportunities. According to *The Africa Report* magazine (2009a:132), thousands of kilometres of roads are currently being built in Angola and new ports are scheduled to be built in Luanda, Lobito, Cabinda and Porto Amboim from 2009 on.

According to Da Gama (2005:1 & 35), civil construction, tourism, mining, petroleum and fisheries are the most attractive investment focus areas in Angola. Da Gama (2005:35) also lists other potential areas of investment such as water and electricity, transport, industry, education and health. In 2006 some foreign investment took place in the banking and telecommunications sector, adding these to the list of potential areas of investment (UNCTAD, 2007b:38).

Mozambique. Although Mozambique's market size is small, its integration into the SADC offers investors there (as in Angola) easier access to the main markets in southern Africa. Agriculture (especially the cultivation of cashews, cotton, tobacco, and sugar) and fishing and aqua-culture (especially prawns and shrimp) are two pillars on which the Mozambican economy stands. Other potential areas for investment include the related agroprocessing industries, manufacturing, financial services, export-processing (specifically for cashews and aluminium), transport and the related services regarding transport (UNCTAD & ICC, 2001:1).

Mozambique has immense energy resources, in terms of both hydropower and natural gas (Bjorvatn, Kind & Nordas, 2001:18). Owing to the country's favourable location, rich endowment of renewable energy, untapped mineral wealth and market-oriented policies, Mozambique has attracted some significant manufacturing and mineral-exploration projects recently. The Mozambique Aluminium smelter project (MOZAL) is certainly one of the most prominent projects (UNCTAD & ICC, 2001:1). According to Bain (2009), MOZAL has contributed the most to GDP in recent years, followed by the sugar industry.

The beauty of the country has also created the opportunity for tourism, and even with the presence of infrastructural constraints, opportunities in the areas of game, adventure and coastal resorts exist (UNCTAD & ICC, 2001:1). According to Bain (2009) several schemes are already underway, such as the Tourism Anchor Investment Programme, which aims to secure up to US$ 1 billion worth of investment by the International Finance

Corporation (IFC) in the tourism industry, in light of the 2010 soccer World Cup to be held in South Africa.

The construction industry also creates abundant investment opportunities. The world's largest steel company, ArcelorMittal South Africa (AMSA), opened its Trem de Varao rolling mill in Maputo in May 2008, and also plans a greenfield bar and mill plant. Extensive investments in the Moatize coking coal project are also forecast, and the South African oil company SASOL aims to double its import of gas through the pipeline that stretches from Mozambique to South Africa (Bain, 2009).

According to UNCTAD (2008a:9), Mozambique's primary sector FDI increased from 2.4 per cent of total FDI inflows in 2001 to 62.2 per cent in 2006. This increase was due to investments made in mining and quarrying. Secondary sector FDI decreased from 76 per cent in 2001 to 30.9 per cent in 2006, and tertiary sector FDI decreased from 21.7 per cent in 2001 to 6.9 per cent in 2006. Overall, Bain (2009) expects that FDI will increase by 30 per cent until 2012, with forecasts of US$ 450 million for this year, compared with US$ 430 in 2008. Foreign direct investment is expected to increase up to US$ 560 million in 2011.

In the next section, the motives of foreign investors aiming to invest in Angola and Mozambique will be briefly discussed.

Motives for Foreign Direct Investment

According to Dunning (1993:57-59) and Salvatore (1995:374), the classification of FDI according to motives results in four types of FDI: resource-seeking FDI, market-seeking FDI, efficiency-seeking FDI, and asset-seeking FDI.

Resource-seeking FDI occurs when TNCs are motivated to invest abroad in order to acquire particular resources at a lower real cost than could be obtained in the home country (should they be obtainable at all). The incentive for this type of investment is to make the TNC more profitable and competitive in the markets it serves. There are three main types of resource-seeking FDI: FDI seeking physical resources, FDI seeking unskilled or semi-skilled labour, and FDI to firms seeking technological capabilities, management or marketing expertise, and organisational skills (Dunning, 1993:57).

The first type of resource-seeking FDI seeks physical resources, such as minerals, raw materials, and agricultural products. Foreign direct investment in the service industry may also intend to exploit location-bound resources, such as tourism, car rentals, oil drilling, construction, and medical and educational services. Transnational corporations may want to engage in this type of FDI to minimise their costs and to obtain security of supply sources. Natural resource-based industries, such as petroleum, minerals and agricultural production, are popular for investment. Investment in these types of activities is usually very capital-intensive and is predominantly negotiated directly with the host government (in order to make it a partner in the investment; Perkins *et al.*, 2006:418).

The second type of resource-seeking FDI seeks unskilled and semi-skilled labour that is highly motivated and can be employed at a low cost. Transnational corporations involved in the manufacturing or the service industry are the most likely to seek cheaper labour than what is available in their home countries. The products manufactured using cheaper labour are then usually exported to other countries, in particular to industrialising countries. Host countries may set up free trade areas or export processing zones to attract this kind of FDI (Dunning, 1993:57).

The third type of resource-seeking FDI is motivated by firms in host countries seeking to acquire advanced technologies, management or marketing expertise, as well as organisational skills from other enterprises abroad (Dunning, 1993:57).

Resource-seeking FDI has previously been, and remains, an important part of FDI for developing countries, but not for the rest of the world. The relative decline of resource-seeking FDI may not only be attributed to natural resources forming part of a declining share of global output, but also to FDI giving way to other arrangements for attracting resources to a country, such as joint ventures, non-equity engagements with foreign investors, and arms'-length trade relations when host countries are no longer inhibited in terms of capital or technical skills (Nunnenkamp, 2001:11).

According to UNCTAD (2007b:34), natural resources drove the increase in FDI in Africa in 2006. Earlier it was concluded that both Angola and Mozambique focus investment primarily on natural resources, such as raw materials, minerals, agricultural resources and tourism. Therefore, it may be assumed that the FDI in Angola and Mozambique is mainly of the first type of resource-seeking FDI.

Since the independence of Angola and Mozambique, their policies towards FDI have become more attractive. A summary of some of the most important FDI policy changes of Angola and Mozambique in recent years follows.

Foreign Direct Investment Policy in Angola

Since these two countries' independence in 1975, Angola has implemented several investment laws. The first investment code implemented was Law no. 10/79, the second was Law no. 13/88 and the third was Law no. 15/94. Like the previous laws, the law of 1994 still created a barrier for foreign investment, because of its bureaucratic principles and the substantial time that was needed to obtain approval for a new investment in Angola (Da Gama, 2005:2-3).

The introduction of the Basic Law of Private Investment (Law no. 11/2003) revolutionised private investment in Angola, through (i) encouragement for both domestic and foreign investment, (ii) offering of tax and custom incentives, (iii) a simplified investment application process, and (iv) a reduction of the minimum amount of investment capital required (Da Gama, 2005:2-4). Investment in the special zones, namely the oil, diamond and financial sectors, is governed by specific legislation (ANIP, 2003), the discussion of which falls beyond the scope of this paper.

The first improvement under this law is that all types of private investment (either national or foreign) are allowed, provided that they do not go against the current legislation and legal procedures. The second improvement is the offering of tax and custom incentives. All income generated within the borders of the country is subject to the Angolan tax legislation, but for investments that are located in a special development zone, or are nationally beneficial, specific tax reductions of up to 50 per cent for periods of up to 10 years, and tax exemption for a period of three to five years, are granted. For profits and dividends to be remitted out of the country, for the first five years only 50 per cent of the tax value, before the recovery of the capital, is taxed. After this period, 100 per cent of the tax value is taxed. In addition, reinvested private investment profits and dividends are exempted from the payment of capital gains taxes. The investment application process is simplified, while lastly, the minimum amount of investment capital required was reduced to US$ 50,000 (for national investors) and US$ 100,000 (for foreign investors) (Da Gama, 2005:11, 14 & 18).

Although Angola has signed several bilateral investment agreements,[5] it has not approved or implemented any of these agreements (USDS, 2008). Up until 2006 no double taxation treaties (DTTs) were signed (UNCTAD, 2008a:26).

Foreign Direct Investment Policy in Mozambique

Mozambique's latest law on investment was adopted in 1993: Law no. 3/93. Subsequently amendments were passed: (i) Decree no. 14/93 and (ii) Decree no. 36/95 (USDS, 2007). The law aims to promote the equal treatment of national and foreign investors and provide guarantees and incentives regarding (a) protection of property rights, (b) the remittance of funds abroad, and (c) tax and customs incentives (Mozambique, 1993).

According to UNCTAD (2007b:39), Mozambique implemented some tax reductions in 2006 in order to promote foreign investment. Mozambique is generally in compliance with the World Trade Organisation's (WTO) Trade-

Related Investment Measures (TRIM) obligations. Mozambique offers tax reductions of up to 80 per cent, and additional incentives include special tax benefits granted to investors for the rehabilitation or expansion of operations, valid for the period after tax reductions. For investments in new equipment, the construction of civil mechanisms, and agricultural infrastructure, an immediate total exemption for five years is allowed. Customs exemptions also exist when investors import capital equipment and raw materials (USDS, 2007).

Mozambique had also signed 21 BITs and three DTTs up until 2006 (UNCTAD, 2008a:26), with countries including South Africa, which is Mozambique's biggest trading partner and the largest cumulative source of its FDI (USDS, 2007). According to the regulations of Law no.3/93, the minimum amount of investment capital required is currently US$ 5,000 (for national investors) and US$ 50,000 (for foreign investors), figures lower than the minimum amounts required in Angola (Mozambique, 1995).

However, Mozambique recently introduced a regulatory measure less favourable to the country's FDI attractiveness. In 2007, foreign shares in local companies were restricted to minority holdings, and foreign investors were banned from becoming managers, administrators and directors of companies (UNCTAD, 2008b:44). However, amidst the tightening policy environment, the country is expected to continue on its forecast route of robust growth, high FDI inflows and donor support for poverty reduction (*The Africa Report*, 2009b).

In the next section, the overall investment climate of Angola and Mozambique is discussed with regard to the general indicators of an investment climate, and their individual attributes. Firstly, the general indicators regarding an investment climate will be explored, and then Angola's and Mozambique's investment climates will be discussed in more detail.

Overall Investment Climate

General Indicators

The general indicators which are used to evaluate a country's investment climate are divided into (i) social political indicators, (ii) good governance indicators, and (iii) economic indicators. These indicators for Angola and Mozambique are yet again compared with their Southern African neighbour countries, South Africa and Botswana, and China and Brazil.

Table 1 summarises the investment climate indicators. In general, the higher the value of an indicator, the more favourable, and the opposite is true when countries are ranked against other countries.

Table 1: **Investment climate indicators of Angola, Mozambique, South Africa, Botswana and Brazil (latest data)**

Country:	Angola	Mozambique	South Africa	Botswana	Brazil	China
Social Political Indicators[6]:						
HDI (0=worst; 1=best)	0.4	0.4	0.7	0.7	0.8	0.8
HDI rank (out of 177 countries)	162	172	121	124	70	81
Corruption Perception Index (0=worst; 10=best)	2.2	2.8	5.1	5.4	3.5	3.5
CPI Rank (out of 180 countries)	147	111	43	38	72	72
Good Governance Indicators[7]:						
Voice and Accountability	15.9	47.1	68.8	61.5	59.1	5.8
Political Stability	28.4	57.2	51.0	78.4	36.5	32.2
Government Effectiveness	11.4	40.3	74.9	73.0	52.6	61.1
Regulatory Quality	16.5	31.6	65.5	65.0	53.4	45.6
Rule of Law	6.7	29.0	57.1	70.0	43.3	42.4
Control of Corruption	6.3	35.3	67.1	79.7	52.2	30.9
Economic Freedom Indicator (0=worst; 10=best)	4.2	6.2	6.8	7.2	101	86
Economic Freedom rank (out of 141 countries)	138	91	60	38		
Economic Indicators[8]:						
					189.3	1311.8
Population (millions)	16.6	21.0	47.4	1.9	$4,044	$1,598
GDP per capita (US Dollar)	$1,069	$330	$3,562	$4,423	2.0	10.0

continued on next page

Growth rate percentage	15.0	6.0	4.0	1.0	20.8	11.0
FDI Stocks percentage GDP	23.3	65.3	31.1	10.8	1.8	2.6
FDI Flows percentage GDP	-2.4	2.1	-1.3	-3.1		
Trade percentage of GDP	112.0	89.0	63.0	84.0	26.0	72.0
Final consumption expenditure % GDP	50.0	87.0	83.0	48.0	80.0	47.0
Inflation	12.0	13.0	5.0	12.0	4.0	1.0
Gross national investment per GDP	87.8	89.9	97.9	93.7	97.2	100.4
Current Account Balance percentage of GDP	24.0	-9.0	-6.0	18.0	1.0	9.0
Labour force participation rate	84.0	84.0	66.0	59.0	72.0	82.0
Exchange rate with US dollar	80.0	25.0	7.0	6.0	2.0	8.0

Overall it can be concluded that Angola and Mozambique have less attractive investment climates that the two Southern African counterparts examined, and far worse investment climates than Brazil and China. Mozambique scores more favourably on the social political indicators (except the HDI ranking) and good governance indicators. However, Mozambique scores less favourably regarding the economic indicators.

It may be suggested that Angola has a less stable political environment but a more stable economic environment, while Mozambique has the more stable political environment. Angola's unique natural resource endowment with oil and diamonds, as well as its high GDP growth rate, may make Angola a more attractive investment destination than Mozambique. However, the question is whether this endowment and economic condition of Angola are enough for sustainable investment. As was mentioned above, Moore (2000; cited by UNCTAD, 2007b:94) suggests that political underdevelopment may be the root of the poor performance of mineral-rich countries, regarding their attraction of investment among other things. Therefore, it may be suggested that a country with a more stable political environment (like Mozambique) will attract more sustainable FDI over the long term than a country with a less stable political environment (like

Angola). What makes Angola unique is its rich natural resource endowment and current favourable economic environment. This may be a reason why Angola received greater amounts of FDI than Mozambique, but these flows were more volatile and may become smaller than Mozambique's over the long term.

Angola's Investment Climate

According to the US Department of State (USDS, 2008), Angola offers high returns to investors, but also great risks. The increasing oil and diamond production, together with the serious infrastructure restoration that followed the end of the civil war in 2002, creates increasing business opportunities (USDS, 2008).

The Angolan business environment is also said to be one of the most complex in the world, because of the corruption, the under-developed financial system, and high on-the-ground costs. A big drawback in the business environment is the time it takes to obtain the proper permits and business licences to operate in Angola (USDS, 2008). According to the World Bank's (2008a:2) *Doing Business in 2009* report, Angola scored an overall ranking of 168 out of 181 countries. Its lowest rankings were in the categories of (i) enforcing contracts (179th), (ii) employing workers (174th), and (iii) registering property (173rd). Companies familiar with the Angolan business environment frequently have an advantage over foreign investors, and the Promotion of Angolan Private Entrepreneurs Law favours locally-owned companies in the tendering of goods, services and public works contracts with the Angolan government (USDS, 2008). According to the 2009 *Index of Economic Freedom* (THF, 2009a) published by the Heritage Foundation, Angola scores an overall value of 47 and a value of 20 in the category of investment freedom, where zero indicates the lowest freedom and 100 indicates the most freedom. The global average for this category was 48.8, indicating that Angola does not have a very free investment environment.

Local access to foreign exchange and facilitated remittance and transfer of funds are improving increasingly, owing to the changes in economic and financial policies. Since 2004, the Central Bank has loosened controls and bank service time has now been reduced from several months to a matter of hours. Although the Investment Law no. 11/2003 guarantees the repatriation of profits for officially approved foreign investment, and the Central Bank Order 4/2003 allow investors to remit funds through local commercial banks, the Bank must still authorise the repatriation of profits and dividends in excess of US$ 100,000. The Central Bank also reserves the right to momentarily suspend the repatriation of dividends or impose repatriation in instalments, should immediate repatriation negatively influence the country's balance of payments (USDS, 2008).

A few specific performance requirements exist for foreign investments. These include the encouragement of localisation and the use of Angolan suppliers for goods and services. Foreign investors can however set up fully-owned subsidiaries in many sectors, although they are usually encouraged, but not obliged, to employ local partners. The oil and diamond sectors are also forced, for example, to deliver infrastructure and social services to benefit local communities, for example constructing schools, equipping hospitals, or financing micro-credit projects. The government also supports downstream investments in facilities such as refineries and diamond processing (USDS, 2008).

China played, and is still playing, an important role in the Angola's post-conflict reconstruction through its financial and technical assistance that brought to life over a hundred projects in the subject matters of energy, water, health, education, telecommunications, fisheries, and public works. China's partnership with Angola shifted to one based on economic interest after the conflict ended in 2002 (Campos & Vines, 2008:1, 3).

In 2004, a strategic partnership was established between the governments of Angola and China to finance infrastructure investments. Angolan infrastructure was in serious need of rehabilitation after the civil conflicts, and so Angola made an agreement with China. This agreement stated that Angola would receive a US$ 2 billion oil-supported loan for the rehabilitation and development of their infrastructure from EximBank (Export-Import Bank of China), in exchange for supplying China with a secure flow of oil. It is too early to assess the efficiency of the Angola-China arrangement, especially to evaluate it against other approaches. However, the cooperation between these two countries has since 2004 been characterised by frequent bilateral visits of important state officials (UNCTAD, 2008b:127; Campos & Vines, 2008:3).

According to the US State Department (USDS, 2008), better governance, more effective rule of law, and less corruption are important to lower the investment risk and provide greater assurance, especially to foreign investors. The overall tendency for key players in the economy to be corrupt and the lack of accounting information published have only fuelled the suspicion of investors. However, the government has started to publish financial information and guarded against non-budget expenditure since 2006, to obtain greater transparency. Angola is also part of NEPAD, which provides a peer review on each country's good governance and transparency. Following the audit law approved in 2002, Angola is also inviting major international accounting firms to perform regular audits of Angola's largest public companies – though this cannot be enforced comprehensively, owing to the lack of professional accounting oversight institution (USDS, 2008).

In conclusion, the greatest barriers for investment in Angola include the difficult business environment, the risk existing regarding the repatriation of profits, the localisation of investment projects, corruption and the lack of transparency. Da Gama (2005:27-30) adds other barriers not discussed in this section: interests charged against the investment; a high illiteracy rate which make the acquisition of qualified labour, and even more so qualified labour that speaks both Portuguese and English fluently, difficult; epidemic diseases, such as the Marburg virus in Angola; and uncertain power supply.

Mozambique's Investment Climate

According to Bain (2009), it is relatively easy to invest in Mozambique compared to investing in other African countries. The government has begun to remove the negative influence of bureaucracy and the remnants of the country's colonialist and socialist history. According to Morisset (2000:1, 17), Mozambique has succeeded in attracting increasing FDI through improvements in its business environment since the 1990s. These improvements include (i) liberalisation of trade, (ii) initiation of an attractive privatisation plan, (iii) modernising of mining and investment codes, (iv) taking up of international agreements on FDI, (v) developing of a small number of priority projects that had multiplier effects on their other investments, and (vi) an image-building endeavour in which political figures, such as the nation's president, participated. The relatively large inflows of FDI during the 1990s may have been due to the 'catch-up' effect when it is easy to attract new investments in the initial recovery phase. Therefore, sustained improvements to the business climate are vital to increasing FDI flows.

According to Morisset (2000:17) there is room for improvement, especially in the areas of infrastructure, transport costs and human capital. In the 2009 *Index of Economic Freedom* (THF, 2009b), Mozambique scored an overall value of 55.7. This is higher than Angola's score of 47, but improvement is possible. Mozambique scored a value of 50 in the category of investment freedom, which is a lot higher than Angola's score of 20. In Mozambique foreign and local capital are usually treated equally and most of the sectors in the economy are open to foreign investment.

As in Angola, business registration procedures can be problematic, and those who are unfamiliar with the country and the Portuguese language face bigger challenges (USDS, 2007). According to the World Bank's (2008b:2) *Doing Business in 2009* report, Mozambique scored an overall ranking of 141 out of 181 countries. Its lowest rankings were in the categories of (i) employing workers (161st), (ii) dealing with construction permits (153rd), and (iii) registering property (149th).

As for Angola, a few specific performance requirements exist for foreign investments made in Mozambique. These requirements are built into mining concessions and management contracts, and even into the sales contracts of privatised entities. When investments are made in partnership with the government, certain conditions must be met in order for the investor's project to continue. Other requirements include the numerous criteria for permits, approvals and clearances, resulting in a lengthy process of doing business. This creates the opportunity for corruption, and as a result, bribes are often requested to aid transactions. Despite political declarations issued repeatedly to put a stop to corrupt practices, bribery still prevails (USDS, 2007).

In conclusion, the most noticeable barriers to foreign investment in Mozambique include the existence of bureaucracy; difficulties in the business environment; the numerous requirements set up in contracts and the lengthy business processes resulting in corruption. According to UNCTAD & ICC (2001:2), inadequate infrastructure; limited administrative capacity, including the labour law and regulations regarding labour relations, and the law on land occupancy that only allows a non-tradable lease for up to 50 years;[9] and the lack of qualified labour may be added to the list of barriers.

In the following section, potential policy changes are proposed for the areas in Angola and Mozambique that need to be improved, in order to stimulate their FDI inflows. This is done with regard to studies on other developing and least developed countries (LDCs).

Policy Recommendations

In the previous section several elements that inhibit FDI inflows to Angola and Mozambique were brought to attention. By investigating several studies on other developing countries and LDCs, valuable policy lessons may be identified to apply to Angola's and Mozambique's cases.

Considering several studies on the influence of FDI in LDCs, UNCTAD (2007c:41) concluded that there little evidence exist that FDI significantly contributes to technological capability accumulation in LDCs. This limited contribution is not a result of insufficient openness to foreign investors, because substantial policy changes have been implemented since 1980 and there was a steady growth in FDI from the 1990s. Rather, it is a result of the type of TNC integration into host countries economies', the sectoral distribution of FDI, the priorities of policies endorsed by LDCs, and the insufficient absorptive capacity of these countries. Therefore, following the recommendations of UNCTAD (2007c:42) for LDCs, Angola and Mozambique should implement active policy initiatives to reap some of the technological spillovers attributed to the presence of TNCs in a host country, and also introduce policies aimed at maximising the development and technological learning impact of foreign investment.

Science, technology and innovation (STI) policies form part of these policies and aims to promote technological development. In LDCs this policy should be focused on technological catch-up with more technologically advanced countries, through technological learning and innovation, where firms apply the new knowledge (UNCTAD, 2007c:51). In 2008 UNCTAD released its first STIP review of Angola, but no such review has yet been issued for Mozambique that we are aware of.

According to the STI policy review for Angola (UNCTAD, 2008c:72), the government is aware that:

- There exists the need to diversify the economy, and that the allocation of resources should be adjusted and shifted towards the agriculture and manufacturing sectors.
- Innovation should be demand-driven and the development of capacity in STI and in private sector development should be equally open and encouraging.
- Improvements are needed in the operation of the country's innovation system and in its building blocks to reach these aims.

According to UNCTAD (2008c:72-73), the implementation of STI policies is well in progress in certain areas, especially in the area of creating a favourable framework for an effective innovation system. This is being done through the rehabilitation of physical infrastructure, the expansion of fundamental education, financing and business support schemes for small and medium enterprises (SMEs), and regulatory reforms.

In other areas, policies are under-developed in terms of STI objectives, and/or implementation mechanisms, especially in the areas of electricity supply, health, and, to a minor degree, manufacturing and agriculture. However, this STIP review is only aimed at contributing towards the development of a national strategy – although, where sector policies are still insufficiently well defined to identify STI needs, the development of a practical national STI strategy may be difficult (UNCTAD, 2008:73). UNCTAD (2008c:73) therefore recommends that a national framework strategy for STI development should be created, in line with the national system of innovation (NSI) approach, to institute the general principles for the formulation of STI policies in central sector and cross-sectoral policies.

According to UNCTAD (2007c:66), the Republic of Korea has achieved an extraordinary rate of economic growth and poverty reduction through its rapid capital accumulation and technological change, associated with increasing employment and rising labour productivity. Therefore, the STIP of the Republic of Korea can serve as an excellent example for Angola and Mozambique. According to UNCTAD (2007c:66), the Republic of Korea adopted technology policies aimed to accelerate the acquisition of technological capabilities. During the early stage of catch-up, both their trade and financial policies proved to be the most important policies to stimulated demand for technology. Changes in the trade policy included a combination of tariff protections, export promotion, protection for the domestic machinery industry to enable capital goods to be imported at international prices, and the financing of these purchases by supplier's credits (which carried lower rates of interest than those on the domestic market).

Early substantial investment in human development was essential to the Republic of Korea's acquisition, distribution, and improvement of technology. Overall, the country strongly promoted research and development (R&D) in both the public and the private sector. The government opened up to foreign direct investment and relaxed foreign licensing, encouraged domestic firms to increase their competitiveness, and revised intellectual property laws to prevent imitative product development (UNCTAD, 2007c:66).

According to UNCTAD (2008b:xx), the provision of good quality infrastructure is a necessity for economic and social development. It is considered one of the main requirements necessary for developing countries to accelerate or maintain the rate of their development and achieve the Millennium Development Goals (MDGs) set by the United Nations. Unfortunately, a considerable financing gap exist between the potential investment needs of developing countries in infrastructure and the quantities being invested by governments, the private sector and other stakeholders. On average (according to World Bank estimates) developing countries invest an annual 3 to 4 per cent of their GDP in infrastructure, but an estimated investment of 7 to 9 per cent is necessary to achieve broader economic growth and poverty reduction goals. Therefore, FDI is necessary to fill this financing gap and eventually contribute to economic growth and development.

Musila and Sigué (2006) explore the strategies needed to accelerate FDI flows to Africa and focus particularly on the NEPAD programmes. One of NEPAD's goals is to achieve and sustain an average GDP growth rate of at least 7 per cent per annum, so as to reduce the share of Africans living in poverty by half, amongst other things. Significant investments in the various sectors of African economies are however needed in order for these countries to reach this goal. Since Africa's share of FDI flows to developing countries is still mediocre, strategies need to be implemented for Africa to attract a higher share of FDI. In general, African countries should establish and maintain political and macroeconomic stability and a policy environment favourable for investment. In addition, strategic marketing approaches should be used to (i) target selected FDI, and (ii) invent sustainable and competitive positioning strategies that can match the interests of investors in a free market.

According to UNCTAD (2007b:39), a change in the regulatory frameworks or improvement in the investment climate may not be enough to attract greater FDI into the manufacturing sector and generate the expected benefits from it. Because Angola and Mozambique have small local markets, investment in their manufacturing sector must be supported by appropriate export markets. Natural resources (abundant in Angola and Mozambique) may promote export-oriented FDI, but may not provide a sufficient basis for sustainable economic growth (UNCTAD, 2007b:39), because natural resources only provide rent for as long as they last and are in demand. Therefore, according to Nwokeabia (2007; cited by UNCTAD, 2007b:39), resource-exporting countries may eventually face stagnant prices and the risk of specializing in products that may become outdated, if their FDI is not accompanied by technological and skills development.

ShuMing (2006:69) suggests that post-conflict counties should focus on improving their governance quality and property protection in order for them to promote FDI inflows. The reason for this is that potential foreign investors are concerned about personal security, property security and legal infrastructure.

According to UNCTAD and ICC (2001:2), Mozambique is a formidable example of a LDC whose government is gradually removing the constraints to development, as it is aware of the importance of the private sector, and especially FDI, to sustainable economic growth. Its more stable social and political environment also contributes to improving FDI. Therefore, this country will remain a prime investment location in Africa.

Angola and Mozambique can learn from these different policies implemented by and recommended to LDCs, developing countries and African countries specifically. The most important policies that they can implement, considering the example of those implemented by the Republic of Korea (UNCTAD, 2007c:66), are (i) the promotion of extensive public and private investment in human capital, to address the shortage of skilled labour; and (ii) the encouragement of both private and public R&D to improve their countries' technological capabilities. They should also promote infrastructural investment (UNCTAD, 2008b), both local and foreign, as this is necessary for a country to build a stable economic framework. As post-conflict countries, Angola and Mozambique can also focus on establishing a good quality of governance, sufficient property protection (ShuMing, 2006), and macroeconomic stability (Musila & Sigué, 2006), as these are important factors to restore integrity and faith in a country. Angola and Mozambique should also focus on implementing a strategic marketing plan for their countries (Musila & Sigué, 2006), to provide for the individual needs of potential foreign investors. It may also be wise for them to concentrate their efforts to promote export-oriented FDI (UNCTAD, 2007b), as this may provide a more sustainable source for economic growth and development than resource-seeking FDI.

In order for African countries, including Angola and Mozambique, to attract more FDI, and in order for FDI to assist in a virtuous cycle of economic growth, job creation, and rising income, the GBPC (2005:34) suggests that countries develop targeted public- and private-sector initiatives that link industry, education, human capital, and institutional capacity. Foreign direct investment can be stimulated indirectly by governments, through initiatives that subsidise industries and encourages training and skills development.

Furthermore, it is important for countries to reinforce the linkages between their export sectors and the rest of their economies, by giving thought to physical infrastructure, production capacity, and institutions that encourage private investment (UNCTAD, 2006:xix). Foreign direct investment can also be stimulated directly through improved incentives, such as favourable tax regimes and repatriation policies.

Conclusion

After Angola and Mozambique gained their independence in 1975, long periods of civil war followed, leaving their respective economies in distress. Over the years their FDI policies have become more inviting to foreign investors, as they realised the importance of FDI for their countries. The main aim of this study was to determine whether FDI contributed to economic growth in these post-conflict zones.

First, the relationship between FDI and economic growth was discussed. Although conflicting arguments exist about this relationship, the hypothetical positive influence that FDI might have on growth was evaluated. The two possible channels through which FDI may influence growth were identified as a direct channel – through an increase in capital stock and the subsequent capital flows – and an indirect channel, through its spill-over effects. These two channels were discussed in reference to Kosack & Tobin's (2006:213) illustration of the relationship between FDI, economic growth and human development. Nevertheless, it was concluded that the type of FDI that a country attracts, as well as the capacity of a country to absorb the positive effects of FDI, will determine whether FDI will have a positive or negative influence on growth.

Secondly, the distribution of FDI, both globally and regionally, was explored, and it is evident that developing countries, and especially Africa, received the smallest portion of global FDI. Angola's and Mozambique's FDI inflows have increased since 1990, but have been quite volatile. Angola started to record a negative FDI inflow from 2005, owing to the acquisitions of ongoing oil exploitation and refinery projects by Sonangol. However, Angola generally received more FDI than Mozambique from the 1980s. It was suggested that a country with a more stable political environment (like Mozambique) will attract more sustainable FDI over the long term than a country with a less stable political environment (like Angola), which can explain the volatility in FDI flows to Angola. When FDI is expressed in terms of GDP, it is evident that Angola and Mozambique received more FDI proportionately to GDP in 1992 and 2002 than the average developing country. However, Angola received less than the average developing country in 2006, while Mozambique received more.

Thirdly, the investment focus areas of Africa, and more specifically Angola and Mozambique, were discussed. Angola has remarkable investment potential in civil construction, tourism, mining, petroleum and fisheries, while Mozambique's agriculture, mineral exploitation, and fishing and aquaculture, as well as the related agro-processing and export-processing industries, are the areas with the most investment potential. It was therefore suggested that Angola and Mozambique mainly attract resource-seeking FDI.

Fourthly, regarding FDI policies, it was concluded that both Angola and Mozambique's policies are becoming less restrictive to foreign, as well as local, investors. This is particularly due to tax and customs incentives. However, some barriers to FDI still exist and the most important of these are (i) political instability, (ii) administrative burdens, (iii) bureaucracy, (iv) corruption, and (v) a lack of qualified labour. It was concluded that Angola has a less stable political environment, but a more stable economic environment, while Mozambique has the more stable political environment. Whether Angola's unique natural resource endowment with oil and diamonds and high GDP growth rate make Angola a sustainable more attractive investment destination than Mozambique is a question.

Fifthly, the overall investment climates of Angola and Mozambique were evaluated, by (i) referring to the general indicators which are used to evaluate a country's investment climate, and (ii) the individual qualities of each. With regard to (i) social political indicators, (ii) good governance indicators, and (iii) economic indicators, it was concluded that Angola and Mozambique have less attractive investment climates than South Africa and Botswana, and far worse investment climates than Brazil and China. Mozambique scores more favourably on the social political indicators (except the HDI ranking) and good governance indicators. However, Mozambique scores less favourably regarding the economic indicators. It was also concluded that both Angola and Mozambique have to improve their business environments and address the lack of skilled labour. Angola has to improve its transparency and repatriation policy, while Mozambique needs to work on its labour and land laws.

Lastly, some policy recommendations were made for Angola and Mozambique, in reference to the findings in other studies. These recommendations include the following: (i) the promotion of extensive public and private investment in human capital, to address the shortage of skilled labour; (ii) the encouragement of both private and public R&D to improve their countries' technological capabilities; (iii) the promotion of infrastructural investments to build a stable economic framework; (iv) the establishment of a good quality of governance; (v) sufficient property protection; (vi) macroeconomic stability; (vii) the implementation of a strategic marketing plan to provide for the individual needs of potential foreign investors; and (viii) the promotion of export-oriented FDI (UNCTAD, 2007b), as this may provide a more sustainable source.

Notes

[1]   The level of secondary school attainment is used as a proxy for human capital (Li & Liu, 2005:396).

[2]   The technology gap: $GAP_{i,t} = (\gamma\max - \gamma_{i,t})/\gamma_{i,t}$ where $\gamma\max$ is the GDP per capita of the United States and $\gamma_{i,t}$ is the various countries' GDP per capita (Li & Liu, 2005:396).

[3]   In 1992 the civil war ended in Mozambique.

[4]   In 2002 the civil war ended in Angola.

[5]   Including Italy, Germany, Portugal, South Africa, and the United Kingdom (USDS, 2008).

[6]   The HDI data were obtained from UNDP (2008) and the corruption perception data were obtained from Transparency International (2008).

[7]   All data obtained from World Bank (2008b), except the economic freedom indicator and rank, which were obtained from Fraser Institute (2008).

8   FDI data were obtained from UNCTAD (2008b) and the rest from the World
     Bank (2008a).

9   It creates additional problems for the financial sector, because the title cannot be
     used as credit collateral (UNCTAD & ICC, 2001:2).

References

AFDB & OECD (African Development Bank & Organisation for Economic Co-
     Operation and Development). 2008. 'Angola.' *African economic outlook*, :121-136,
     May. http://www.oecd.org/dataoecd/3/49/40568599.pdf Date of access: 12 Jan.
     2009.

AFDB & OECD (African Development Bank & Organisation for Economic Co-
     Operation and Development). 2008. 'Mozambique.' *African economic outlook*,
     :459-474, May. http://www.oecd.org/dataoecd/13/6/40578303.pdf Date of access:
     12 Jan. 2009.

Africa Report, The. 2009a. 'Angola: a vote for more boom times.' *The Africa Report*,
     (14):130-132, Dec. - Jan.

Africa Report, The. 2009b. 'Mozambique: Frelimo's tightening noose.' *The Africa
     Report*, (14):138, Dec. - Jan.

ANIP (National Private Investment Agency, Angola). 2003. 'Basic private investment
     law: law 11/03 of 13th of May 2003.' http://www.iie-angola-us.org/legislation.htm
     Date of access: 1 July 2008.

Bain, J. 2009. 'Mega-projects: mega-Mozambique.' *The African Investor* (26), Jan-Feb.
     http://www.africa-investor.com/article.asp?id=4270 Date of access: 21 Jan. 2009.

Bjorvatn, K., Kind, H.J. & Nordas, H.K. 2001. 'The Role of FDI in Economic Devel-
     opment' (working paper no.62/01, Dec.). Bergen: Foundation for Research in
     Economic and Business Administration. 27 p.

Campos, I. & Vines, A. 2008. 'Angola and China: a pragmatic partnership' (working
     paper presented at a CSIS conference, Mar.). http://www.csis.org/media/csis/
     pubs/080306_angolachina.pdf *Date of access: 26 Jan. 2009.*

Chowdhury, , A. & Mavrotas, G. 2006. 'FDI and Growth: What Causes what?' *World Economy*, 29(1):9-19, Jan.

Da Gama, A.N.P. 2005. 'FDI in Angola: Constraints Encountered by Investors in the Angolan Territory, Advantages and Implications of FDI to Angola.' Minithesis: University of Western Cape.

Del Castillo, G. 2001. 'Post-conflict Reconstruction and the Challenge to International Organizations: the Case of El Salvador.' *World Development*, 29(12):1967-1985.

Dunning, J.H. 1993. 'Multinational Enterprises and the Global Economy.' Wokingham: Addison-Wesley. 687 p.

Duttaray, M., Dutt, A.K. & Mukhopadhyay, K. 2008. 'Foreign Direct Investment and Economic Growth in Less Developed Countries: an Empirical Study of Causality and Mechanisms.' *Applied Economics*, 40(15):1927-1939.

Dynes, M. 2007. 'Investment Climate Update: Clear-cut Opportunity.' *The African Investor*, (17):48-49, July-Aug.

Eisenstein, Z. 2007. 'Angola wants foreign investors for diamond sector.' http://africa.reuters.com/business/news/usnBAN63551.html Date of access: 25 July 2008.

El-Khawas, M.A. 1974. 'Foreign Economic Involvement in Angola and Mozambique.' *A Journal of Opinion*, 4(2):21-28, Summer.

FDR & LOC (Federal Research Division and Library of Congress). 1989. 'Economic Problems and the Implementation of Socialist Policies. (*In* Collelo, T., *ed. Angola: a Country Study*. Washington, DC) http://memory.loc.gov/frd/cs/aotoc.html Date of access: 29 Jul. 2008.

Fedderke, J.W. & Romm, A.T. 2006. 'Growth Impact and Determinants of Foreign Direct Investment into South Africa, 1956 – 2003.' *Economic Modelling*, 23:738-760.

Fraser Institute. 2008. Economic freedom of the world dataset. http://www.freetheworld.com/2007/2007Dataset.xls Date of access: 5 July 2008.

GBPC (Global Business Policy Council). 2005. *FDI Confidence Index*. Alexandria, Va: A.T. Kearney. 40 p. http://www.atkearney.com/shared_res/ pdf/FDICI_2005.pdf Date of access: 1 Sept. 2007.

Hansen, H. & Rand, J. 2006. 'On the Causal Links between FDI and Growth in Developing Countries.' *World Economy*, 29(1):21-41, Jan.

Jansen, K. 1995. 'The Macroeconomic Effects of Direct Investment: The Case of Thailand.' *World Development*, 23(2):193-210.

Kosack, S. & Tobin, J. 2006. 'Funding Self-sustaining Development: the Role of Aid, FDI and Government in Economic Success.' *International Organization*, (60):205-243, Winter.

Lee, G. 2006. 'The Effectiveness of International Knowledge Spillover Channels.' *European Economic Review*, 50:2075-2088.

Lensink, R. & Morrissey, O. 2006. 'Foreign Direct Investment: Flows, Volatility, and the Impact on Growth.' *Review of International Economics*, 14(3):478-493.

Li, X. & Liu, X. 2005. 'Foreign Direct Investment and Economic Growth: An Increasingly Endogenous Relationship.' *World Development*, 33(3):393-407.

Lim, E.G. 2001. 'Determinants of, and the Relation between, Foreign Direct Investment and Growth: A Summary of the Recent Literature' (working paper no. 01/175, Nov.). Washington, DC: International Monetary Fund. 27 p.

Loots, E. 2000. 'Foreign direct investment flows to African countries' (research paper no. 0011, Oct.). Johannesburg: Randse Afrikaans University. 19 p.

Mayer, J. 1990. 'Development Problems and Prospects in Portuguese-speaking Africa.' *International Labour Review*, 129(4):459-478.

Miyamoto, K. 2003. 'Human Capital Formation and Foreign Direct Investment in Developing Countries' (working paper no. 211, July). Paris: Organisation for Economic Co-operation and Development. 46 p.

Morisset, J. 2000. 'Foreign Direct Investment in Africa: Policies also Matter' (working paper no. 2481, Nov.). Washington, DC: World Bank. 20 p.

Mozambique. 1993. Law on investment 3 of 1993. http://www.cpi.co.mz/e107_files/downloads/lawinv.pdf Date of access: 20 July 2008.

Mozambique. 1995. Regulation of the investment law (approved by decree 14 of 1993, with changes approved by decree 36 of 1995 incorporated). http://www.cpi.co.mz/e107_files/downloads/lawregul.pdf Date of access: 20 July 2008.

Musila, J.W. & Sigué, S.P. 2006.'Accelerating Foreign Direct Investment Flow to Africa: from Policy Statements to Successful Strategies.' *Managerial Finance,* 32(7):577-593.

NEPAD (New Partnership for Africa's Development). 2006. 'An indicative assessment to determine prospects for a NEPAD spatial development programme.' http://www.nepad.org/2005/reports/SDScopingReport30-03-06Part1_en.pdf Date of access: 25 July 2008.

Nunnenkamp, P. 2001. 'Foreign direct investment in developing countries: What policymakers should not do and what economists don't know' (discussion paper no. 380, Jul.). Kiel: Kiel Institute for the World Economy.

OECD (Organization for Economic Co-Operation and Development). 1999. 'OECD benchmark definition of foreign direct investment.' 3rd ed. http://www.oecd.org/dataoecd/10/16/2090148.pdf Date of access: 19 July 2007.

OPEC (Organization of Petroleum Exporting Countries). 2007. *Annual Statistical Bulletin* (web version). http://www.opec.org/library/Annual%20Statistical%20 Bulletin/interactive/FileZ/Main.htm Date of access: 19 July 2008.

Perkins, D.H., Radelet, S. & Lindauer, D.L. 2006. *Economics of Development.* 6th ed. New York: Norton. 864 p.

Ramirez, M.D. 2006. 'Is Foreign Direct Investment Beneficial for Mexico? An Empirical Analysis, 1960 – 2001.' *World Development,* 34(5):802-817.

Salvatore, D. 1995. *International Economics.* 5th ed. Upper Saddle River, NJ: Prentice-Hall. 778 p.

Shuming, L. 2006. 'A Study of Some Most Important Policies for Developing Countries to Attract Foreign Direct Investment Successfully.' Reno: University of Nevada. (Thesis – M.A.) 77 p.

Sidaway, J.D. & Simon, D. 1993. 'Geopolitical Transition and State Formation: the Changing Political Geographies of Angola, Mozambique and Namibia.' *Journal of Southern African Studies (special issue),* 19(1):6-28, Mar.

Sonangol. 2008. Corporate goals and vision. http://www.sonangol.co.ao/wps/por-tal/!ut/p/c1/04_SB8K8xLLM9MSSzPy8xBz9CP0os3gDC2NnH0NjAxdHA38Pb1N DHwsjAwjQDwfpAKrAARwNoP-JoJjgjTMAqb-JpiFfeJQgu7-eRn5uqX5CdHeRR7qgIAPl6kyE!/dl2/d1/L2dJQSEvU Ut3QS9ZQnB3LzZfMDgzQ0wxMzBEQTBPSEs1MUk4MjAwMDAwMDA!/ Date of access: 28 July 2008.

THF (The Heritage Foundation). 2009a. 'Index of economic freedom: Angola.' http://www.heritage.org/index/country/Angola Date of access: 13 Jan. 2009.

THF (The Heritage Foundation). 2009b. 'Index of economic freedom: Mozambique.' http://www.heritage.org/index/country/Mozambique Date of access: 13 Jan. 2009.

Todaro, M.P. 2000. *Economic Development.* 7th ed. New York: Addison-Wesley Long-man. 783 p.

Transparency International.2008. 'Corruption perception index 2008.' http://www.transparency.org/policy_research/surveys_indices/cpi/2007 Date of access: 5 Jul.2008.

UNCTAD & ICC (United Nations Conference on Trade and Development and International Chamber of Commerce). 2001. *An Investment Guide to Mozambique: Opportunities and Conditions.* New York: United Nations. 79 p.

UNCTAD (United Nations Conference on Trade and Development). 2005. *GIPA: Prospects for Foreign Direct Investment and the Strategies of Transnational Corpora-tions, 2005-2008.* Geneva: UNCTAD. 74 p.

UNCTAD (United Nations Conference on Trade and Development). 2006. 'World Investment Report – FDI from Developing and Transition Economies: Implica-tions for Development.' Geneva: UNCTAD. 340 p. http://www.unctad.org/ en/docs/wir2006_en.pdf Date of access: 5 Feb. 2007.

UNCTAD (United Nations Conference on Trade and Development). 2007a. 'The investment compass.' http://compass.unctad.org Date of access: 12 Sept. 2007.

UNCTAD (United Nations Conference on Trade and Development). 2007b. *World Investment Report: Transnational Corporations, Extractive Industries and Develop-ment.* New York: United Nations Publications. 323 p.

UNCTAD (United Nations Conference on Trade and Development). 2007c. *The Least Developed Countries Report 2007*. New York: United Nations Publications. 221 p.

UNCTAD (United Nations Conference on Trade and Development). 2009. 'Foreign direct investment statistics (FDIStat) database.' http://stats.unctad.org/fdi/Report Folders/ReportFolders.aspx Date of access: 25 Jan. 2009.

UNCTAD (United Nations Conference on Trade and Development). 2008a. *World Investment Directory 2008*, volume X Africa. New York: United Nations Publications. 726 p.

UNCTAD (United Nations Conference on Trade and Development). 2008b. *World Investment Report 2008: Transnational Corporations, and the Infrastructure Challenge*. New York: United Nations Publications. 411 p.

UNCTAD (United Nations Conference on Trade and Development). 2008c. *Science, Technology and Innovation Policy (STIP) Review of Angola*. New York: United Nations Publications. 101 p.

UNDP (United Nations Development Programme). 2008. 'Human Development Reports.' http://hdr.undp.org/en/reports/ Date of access: 3 July 2008.

USDS (U.S. DEPARTMENT OF STATE). 2007. 'Investment climate statement: Mozambique.' http://www.state.gov/e/eeb/ifd/2008/100991.htm Date of access: 12 Jan. 2009.

USDS (U.S. DEPARTMENT OF STATE). 2008. 'Investment climate statement: Angola.' http://www.state.gov/e/eeb/ifd/2008/100819.htm Date of access: 12 Jan. 2009.

Vu, T.B. 2008. 'Foreign Direct Investment and Endogenous Growth in Vietnam.' *Applied Economics*, 40(9):1165-1173.

WORLD BANK. 2008a. 'Doing business in 2009 - Angola.' http://www.doing business.org/Documents/CountryProfiles/AGO.pdf Date of access: 10 Jan. 2009.

WORLD BANK. 2008a. 'World Development Indicators (WDI)' online. http://web. world-bank.org/WBSITE/EXTERNAL/DATASTATISTICS/0,,contentMDK:20398986~m enuPK:64133163~pagePK:64133150~piPK:64133175~theSitePK:239419,00.html Date of access: 3 July 2008.

WORLD BANK. 2008b. 'Doing business in 2009 – Mozambique.' Date of access: 10 Jan. 2009.

WORLD BANK. 2008b. 'Governance matters 2008: worldwide governance indicators, 1996 – 2008.' http://info.worldbank.org/governance/wgi/sc_country.asp Date of access: 5 July 2008.

Chapter 8

FDI Policies in Times of Conflict: The Case of Colombia

Philippe De Lombaerde and Luis Jorge Garay

Introduction

This chapter looks at how open FDI policies have been put in place in Colombia since the beginning of the 1990s and assesses their effectiveness. The beginning of the 1990s marks an important moment in Colombian modern history when a peace process with the M-19 and some other insurgent groups was concluded, a new Political Constitution was adopted, and a new (open) economic model was implemented, known as the *apertura* programme.

Unfortunately, the moment, although historic, did not mean a definitive turning point in the course of the conflict. The conflict even intensified and only recently are there signals (and objective indications) that the intensity is again decreasing. Whether this brings us closer to its end is a possibility (and a hope for the Colombians) but depends on a combination of factors.

Section two presents the main features of the (still ongoing) conflict in Colombia, whereas section three illustrates the linkages between the internal management of the conflict by the different governments and the formulation and conduct of external policies, including external economic policies and diplomacy. Section four then presents the development of FDI policies, followed by an assessment of their effectiveness. For that purpose, we will look at the relative capacity of Colombia to attract FDI, the direct measurement of the cost of the conflict to the economy and investment levels, and finally, the impact of FDI on growth and development. Section five concludes.

The Colombian Conflict

Colombia is a country known by a long tradition of political violence. It is worth mentioning that at the beginning of the 20th Century (1899-1902) Colombia suffered a violent confrontation on a national scale between the two traditional political parties, the Liberal and Conservative parties, commonly known as the "War of a Thousand Days". This episode constituted a precedent for a new period of political confrontation between these parties during the early 1950s (1948-55), called *"La Violencia"*. As mentioned by CSIS (2007): "A plethora of factors drove the violence, ranging from the traditional struggle in Colombian history between federalism and central authority, to religious factors, party loyalty, local politics, economic advantage, and personal vendettas. Following a rare period of military rule, the Liberals and Conservatives entered into the "National Front" coalition agreement which allowed them to alternate in the presidency between 1958 and 1974 and return the country to a semblance of internal peace."

In the 1960s the current constellation of the conflict emerged, when two armed groups were formed: the Revolutionary Armed Forces of Colombia (FARC) and the National Liberation Army (ELN). FARC was created in 1966 after government forces attacked a leftist rural militia, aligned with the Liberal Party, during the *La Violencia* period. It has been the most successful over time, dedicated to rural insurgency. Soon thereafter, pro-Castro university students founded the ELN and several other insurgent groups also sprouted up. The Colombian army nearly eliminated the ELN by the mid-1970s and kept the FARC on the defensive in isolated rural areas.

A third important guerrilla movement, the M-19, and several smaller groups laid down their arms in 1990, and many of the members of these groups are currently active politicians.

When the guerrillas became stronger in terms of number of militants, regional coverage and income, rural large landowners formed armed "self-defense" groups against them. These became the precursors to the paramilitary forces of the late 1980s and 1990s. In fact the paramilitary (self-defense) groups originated at the end of the 1970s, but only in the late 1980s were they transformed up to the point that by the mid-1990s they had already cartelized in a representative organization, involving most of these groups, known as the United Self-Defense Groups of Colombia (AUC). These groups built their strength on their connections with the drugs trade in the second half of the 1980s. It was only after they had gained this power that they began to develop a political agenda.

During the last two and a half decades illicit drugs have financed the insurgent FARC and the far-right AUC to a large degree. For this reason drug trafficking is a crucial determinant of the Colombian conflict.

At the beginning of the present decade, estimates of FARC's strength, in terms of numbers of combatants, fluctuated between 15,000 and 20,000. Although figures are obviously not too reliable, it is not impossible that by 2008 the number had halved owing to the combined effect of casualties and desertios (Wieland 2008a). ELN at one stage numbered 5,000 combatants, but is also believed to number far fewer today.

At the beginning of 2005 and after 18 months of negotiations with the Uribe government, at least in principle some 30,000 paramilitary fighters were demobilised, including the AUC chiefs, but the facts have demonstrated that the paramilitary maintain their networks with drug traffickers and keep intact their illegal assets, particularly in rural Colombia.

The Colombian conflict is difficult to categorize (McLean 2002).[1] It could be said that, at least initially, it belonged to what Rogers (2002) has called the category of "anti-elite insurgencies and rebellions often stemming from the development of radical social movements" as a result of socio-economic divisions. Ethnic, religious or (sub-) nationalist drivers are indeed absent in the Colombian case. It is, or has seemed, not inconceivable, in one of the more pessimistic scenarios, that the internal conflict might gradually move towards a so-called "complex regional conflict" (Buzan, 1991).

To fall within the definition of a civil war, a conflict, apart from being predominantly internal, should show two additional characteristics: a remarkable scale and a sufficient level of socialization. The scale of the conflict was initially, and until the 1980s, very limited. According to a common criterion for characterizing civil wars – causing a minimum of 1,000 conflict-related casualties per year – the Colombian conflict was not a civil war for many years (Singer and Small, 1982). After the intensification of the conflict from the end of the 1980s the number of annual casualties began rising above 1,000. Restrepo *et al.* (2003) estimate an annual average of about 3,150 conflict-related casualties in the 1988-2002 period. However, according to the State Failure Task Force (Gurr, 1998), the conflict should still not be characterized as a civil war, but rather as a guerrilla war of considerable intensity (causing between 1,000 and 10,000 political casualties per year).

The predominant view appears to be that the conflict does not demonstrate remarkable levels of socialization. Although it objectively affects the majority of the population in some way or another, especially the people who have been displaced by force and violence from their rural properties, amounting to a total of 3.5 million medium and small farm owners – equivalent to almost 8% of the Colombian population – the illegal armed groups have not succeeded in mobilizing important sectors of the population and polarizing society (Posada, 2001). It would therefore not be accurate to call the Colombian conflict a civil war (Pizarro, 2002; cf. Ramírez Tobón 2002). The moderate levels of socialization of the conflict are linked to its apparent coexistence with relatively solid institutions and a considerable degree of state legitimacy. It is on this basis an a-typical conflict, when placed in a global and comparative perspective[2].

The long duration of the conflict contributes to its complexity, because elements of auto-sustainability, like action-reaction patterns and the institutionalization of violence as a way to settle differences, have been generated. The conflict has acquired new characteristics over the last decades. On the one hand, there was a move from a "war of guerrillas" to a "war of positions". On the other hand, the modes of financing of this "war" have changed and increased in volume, owing to increasing involvement with the illegal drugs trade and the rise of the so-called extortion and kidnap "industry". This corroborates Collier's analysis of civil wars over the period 1965-99 and his conclusion that the financial viability of organizations in conflict, often related to the existence of natural resources, is a major variable in explaining the existence of today's conflicts (Collier, 2000).

At this point, it is worth stressing, as argued by the Crisis Group (2005), that "[t]he prospect for bringing an end to Colombia's armed conflict would also be much increased if demand for drugs could be reduced in the large US and European consumption centres, since this would cut the profit margin of the armed groups as well as international drug trafficking organisations. To achieve this, ... [t]hey should also examine urgently whether harm reduction measures" are needed.

The Shaping of External Policies in Times of Conflict

Traditionally, Colombia has maintained close ties with the United States. In fact, Colombia received considerable US assistance under the Alliance for Progress program of the 1960s.

Later a major US plan of cooperation with Latin America and the Caribbean was launched in Miami in 1994 at the Summit of the Americas in the presence of 34 Heads of State of the hemisphere. The approved Action Plan included as main objectives: strengthening democracy through, among others, combating the problem of illegal drugs and related crimes and eliminating threat of internal and international terrorism; promoting prosperity through economic integration and free trade; eradicating poverty and guaranteeing sustainable development.

This Plan follows the postulates of the Washington Consensus in the area of economics, in particular in promoting free trade and investment, economic integration and free markets, and stresses political purposes like the strengthening of democracy and action against illegal drugs, related crimes and terrorism. The latter political objective corresponds to one of the most acute problems commonly stressed by the US public opinion. Precisely, these problems became even more emphasized by the people after the attacks of September 11, 2001.

Unfortunately, Colombia is probably the American country which confronts the most serious crisis related to illegal drug trafficking and internal terrorism. It is worth remembering that since 1997 the FARC and the ELN have been on the US State Department's list of international terrorist organisations; the AUC was included on 10 September 2001. All three are also on the similar European Union list (Crisis Group, 2003). At the same time, Colombia has been the first supplier of cocaine to the US market.

For these reasons Colombia has been a natural partner country to the US in promoting and applying the Agenda and Plan of Action of the Americas. In fact, since early 1990s Colombia and the other Andean countries, except Venezuela, have been enjoying unilateral tariff reductions from the US as recognition of the combat against drug trafficking in their countries. This is an application of the principle of international cooperation between consumer and producer countries of illegal drugs. This cooperation was reinforced in the case of Colombia at the end of the 1990s with the US Congress' approval of the so-called Plan Colombia. In September 1999 the Colombian president announced an ambitious "Plan for Peace, Prosperity, and the Strengthening of the State" commonly known as *Plan Colombia*. The plan laid out strategic objectives over a six-year period, including as a target: "[to] reduce the cultivation, processing and distribution of narcotics by 50 percent." Key objectives included counter-drug efforts; neutralizing the drug economy; strengthening the armed forces and police; providing alternative development opportunities to coca cultivation; eradicating illicit crops through aerial spraying. The budget of Plan Colombia for six years was estimated around $7.5 billion, $4 billion to be provided by Colombia and $35 billion basically from the US (CSIS, 2007). The Plan has been continued under the presidency of Álvaro Uribe, renamed *Plan Patriota*.

According to the UNDP, underlying this strategy is the belief that "the end of drugs would mean the end of the (armed) conflict (and) the end of the conflict would bring the end of the drug business" (UNDP, 2003:306). This is part of the logic behind both aerial spraying of coca and poppy crops under Plan Colombia and President Uribe's Democratic Security policy (Crisis Group, 2003).

Therefore, the special role played by Colombia in the Hemispheric Plan of Action being promoted by the US is clear. Obviously it imposes serious constraints on the autonomy of the Colombian government. In fact, the international agenda of Colombian governments, and to an important extent their internal agenda, consult the main guidelines of the US international agenda, and especially its hemispheric agenda. It is not fortuitous that Colombia is considered as the American country most aligned with US interests.

It was in this geopolitical context that Colombia developed its FDI policies.

FDI Policies

The Reorientation of FDI Policies, Apertura, and the 1991 Constitution

Until the end of the 1980s, Colombia adhered to the common Andean foreign investment regime as established by Decision 24 of the Council of the Cartagena Agreement in 1971.[3] The principle elements of this regime were the following:

- Obligatory authorization and registration of each investment project by the competent national authority;
- Prohibition of FDI in infrastructure, communications, electricity, public services, waste collection, and the financial sector;
- Restrictions on the authorization of FDI in those sectors where foreign firms would enter to compete with the domestic ones;
- Prohibition of takeovers of existing national firms, except for very specific circumstances like, for example, risk of bankruptcy.
- A principle of forced and programmed transformation of foreign companies into national or mixed companies in a time span of 15 years (the rule) or 20 years (the exception);[4] for existing companies, foreign participation to be brought down to a maximum of 85% within three years, and a maximum of 55% within ten years; new companies should have as a minimum 15% of national capital at the moment of their creation;
- Non-application of trade preferences derived from the Agreement to goods produced by foreign companies, for those companies that fail to comply with the programmed ownership transformation plan;
- Restriction of access to official long-term credits for foreign companies;
- Free repatriation of utilities up to 14% of the invested capital,[5] and free repatriation of capital (De Lombaerde and Pedraza, 2005).

Colombia implemented this Decision through Decree-Law 1900 of 1973, and complemented it with the "Exchange Statute" (Decree 444 of 1967). The latter decree established strict exchange controls and intervention mechanisms for FDI and in other areas.

A confluence of factors in the 1980s led to a reorientation of FDI policies in the region. Countries faced massive capital outflow and sharp foreign exchange restrictions. In addition, it became clear that the integration process, as a development strategy, showed poor results (Reina and Zuluaga, 1998).

Decision 220 of 1987 replaced Decision 24 and related decisions. It gave each country a degree of autonomy in the design of its FDI policies. The requirements according to which foreign firms could associate themselves with local firms and benefit from the trade liberalization program were made more flexible. The list of restricted industries for FDI was abolished and it was left for each member state to take measures related to profit remittances.[6]

By the end of the 1980s and the beginning of the 1990s, the Andean region adopted a new development model based on the opening up (*"apertura"*) of the economy and the implementation of structural reform programs. It was in this context that investment regimes, foreign capital markets and exchange markets were liberalized (OECD, 1999; Agosín, 1996; Anzola, 1997).

Decisions 291 and 292 adopted in 1991 by the Andean countries liberalized the FDI regime and eliminated the discrimination between foreign and national investors. Goods produced by foreign firms were entitled to fully benefit from the trade liberalization program.

The Andean rules left the individual countries with the possibility to further deepen the liberalization of the FDI regime. Colombia decided to reform its legislation in 1991 (Law 9 of 1991 on the Exchange Regime, further regulated by the Statute of Foreign Investment, Resolution 51 of 1991). The government sought to attain three related objectives: (i) to substantially reduce restrictions to FDI, (ii) to actively promote foreign investment, and (iii) to manage political risks (Hommes *et al.*, 1994:71-78).

The liberalization of the Andean investment regime practically coincided with the adoption of a new Constitution in Colombia. After a Constituent Assembly, in which delegates participated of the M-19 and other smaller guerrilla groups who laid down their arms, the new Political Constitution was adopted in 1991. The new Constitution was quite ambitious and included several innovations, such as the strengthening of economic and social rights, the incorporation of an economic liberalization and integration agenda, the reform of the judicial sector, and the decentralization of the state. Of special relevance for the new FDI regime were articles 13 (right to equality), art. 58 (right to private property), art. 100 (rights of foreigners), art. 333 economic freedom), and art. 334 (role of the state in regulating the economy).

The Current Investment Regime

Decree 2080 of 2000 sought to further expand FDI, facilitating capital mobility and simplifying administrative procedures, especially in the area of financial investment and the operation of investment funds in Colombia (Cubillos and Navas, 2000; De Lombaerde and Lizarazo, 2001). The principles of the current foreign investment regime are: equal treatment, universality, automatic nature, and stability (box 1).[7] The only obligation for most of the FDI is registering before the central bank (Banco de la República) (DNP, 2001).

Direct foreign investment is defined as an investment made to: (i) "acquire interests, shares, corporate quotas, bonds required to be converted into shares or any other contribution representing an interest share in the capital stock of a company; (ii) acquire rights in autonomous equities created through a merchant trust contract as a means to develop a company or for the purchase, sale and management of interest shares in companies not registered in the National Record of Securities and issuers; (iii) acquire real estate, stock certificates in real estate securitization processes or real estate funds, through either public or private offers, (iv) acquire contributions through deeds and contracts when such deeds and contracts do not represent a direct interest share in the company's capital and the returns generated by the investment depend on the company's profits. That is the case of technological transfer, collaboration, concession, administrative service and licensing contracts; (v) make investments in branches created in Colombia by foreign corporations, investing in the branch's capital or as a supplementary capital investment (additional to the assigned capital); and (vi) acquire participations in private capital funds" (Proexport, 2008:5-6).

With respect to investment promotion and the management of political risk, Colombia has entered a number of international agreements. These are, on the one hand, the bilateral investment treaties (BITs), covering both promotion and protection, signed with a number of countries since the early 1990s, including the UK, Italy, Peru, Cuba (1994), Chile (2000), Spain (2005), Guatemala and Switzerland (2006) (Table 1).[8] In addition, Colombia is covered by the Overseas Private Investment Corporation (OPIC) since an Exchange of Notes on 3 April 1985 between the Colombian and US governments (Restrepo Uribe, 1997:16-20).

On the other hand, Colombia is a member of the Multilateral Investment Guarantee Agency (MIGA), a World Bank agency, since 1994 (Law 149 of 1994) and of the International Centre for the Settlement of Investment Disputes (ICSID) since 1995 (Law 267 of 1995)[9].

Box 1: Principles of current Colombian foreign investment regime

Equal treatment: Foreign investments are treated the same as national investments. Therefore, the imposition of discriminatory conditions or treatments that may imply more favorable conditions for foreign investments are not admitted;

Universality: Foreign investment is welcome in all sectors of the economy, except in the following cases: (i) activities in the area of national defense and security; (ii) management, processing and disposal of toxic hazardous or radioactive waste not produced in the country; (iii) concessionaries of open television services, where foreign investment may not exceed 40% of the concessionary's corporate capital; (iv) private security and vigilance companies.

Automatic nature: Foreign investment does not require prior authorization, except when made in the above-mentioned special regimes, as well as investments in the financial sector, which in some cases require the prior authorization of the Financial Superintendence. Investments in the hydrocarbon and mining sector as well as portfolio investments are subject to a special regime for which investors must normally apply.

Stability: Investment reimbursement and profit remittance conditions in force on the date on which investments are registered may not be modified in any way that may be detrimental to the investor, except on a temporary basis, when the country's international reserves fall below the three-month imports mark.[10]

Source: Proexport (2008:4-5).

Table 1:   BITs signed by Colombia, as of 1 June 2008

Partner country	Date of signature	Date of entry into force
Chile	25 January 2000	-
Cuba	16 July 1994	-
Guatemala	5 June 2006	-
Italy	9 March 1994	-
Peru	26 April 1994	21 March 2004
Spain	9 June 1995	-
	31 March 2005	22 November 2007
Switzerland	17 March 2006	-
United Kingdom	9 March 1994	-

Source: Lizarazo (1997); UNCTAD Investment Instruments Online [www.unctad. org] (last visited 6 Nov. 2008).

Effectiveness of FDI Policies in Times of Conflict

There are different ways of approaching the effectiveness of FDI policies in a context of conflict. One approach is to look at FDI inflows in a comparative perspective and attribute possible underperformance to the existence of the conflict. Another approach is to try to measure the direct impact (i.e. cost) of the conflict in terms of investment and FDI. The reverse side of this relationship is the contribution of FDI to peace or conflict. The effectiveness of FDI policies can further be measured not only in terms of FDI inflows but also in terms of the contribution of attracted FDI to growth and development. The complex interactions between the variables involved are shown in the (simplified) figure 1, together with the expected signs of the relationships. The three different approaches mentioned and the interactions will be discussed in the subsequent sections.

Figure 1:   Interactions between conflict, FDI and growth

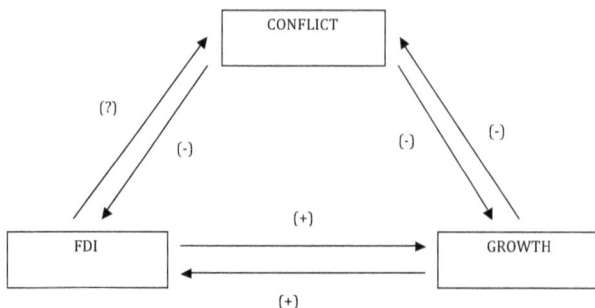

FDI Inflows in Comparative Perspective

The drastic changes in the FDI regimes in Latin America have had a visible impact on FDI inflows from the rest of the world (table 2).[11] If we compare the second half of the 1980s with the second half of the 1990s, FDI inflows as a percentage of GDP, almost doubled in CAN. Colombia is the exception here, probably ascribable to the continuation and even accentuation of the conflict, combined with drugs related terrorism. The figure for Chile is relatively high but stable. This is explained by the fact that Chile had already liberalized its FDI policy in the 1970s. Argentina is a similar case.

Table 2:   FDI Inflows in Latin America (% of GDP)

	1985-1990	1995-2000
Andean Community (CAN)	1.08	1.96
Bolivia	*0.71*	*4.57*
Colombia	*2.70*	*1.61*
Ecuador	*1.31*	*1.79*
Peru	*0.17*	*2.21*
Venezuela	*0.28*	*2.00*
CARICOM	0.71	3.16
CACM	1.55	1.22
MERCOSUR	0.73	1.37
Mexico	1.68	1.59
Chile	3.76	3.69

Source: Stein *et al.* (2002:225).

From the UNCTAD figures of FDI inflows over a longer time period (1985-2007) (annexes 1-3), the following can be observed. For most of the years, Colombia shows higher figures for FDI inflows as a percentage of gross fixed capital formation (GFCF) than the average for South America. A clear upward shift is observable from 1996 onwards. From then on, the figures are systematically higher than 10%. 2005 was a peak year, when Colombia showed the highest proportion of FDI in GFCF in South America (42%). Inward FDI stocks as a percentage of GDP in 2007 are slightly higher than the figure for South America.

UNCTAD developed a methodology to assess inward FDI potential, FDI performance, and their relationship through a series of indicators (Box 2). Table 3 shows that Colombia's potential continuously worsened in the 1990s, with the exception of the final years, and that it stabilized in the present decade at relatively low levels.[12] The performance picture is different, however. The adverse potential has only partly been translated in low performance and the current performance levels are (again) comparable to the levels of the beginning of the 1990s. The combination of both indexes in a matrix classifies Colombia in recent years systematically as "low potential" but in most of the years as a country that is performing "above potential" (Figure 2).

Box 2: UNCTAD Inward FDI Potential and Performance Index Methodology

The UNCTAD Inward FDI Potential Index (POT$_i$) monitors the joint evolution of a set of variables that are likely to affect the decision to investment in the country by foreign investors. The index is calculated as an unweighted arithmetic average of the normalized values of 12 variables. These are:

- GDP per capita,
- Rate of GDP growth over the previous ten years,
- Share of exports in GDP,
- Number of (mobile) telephones per 1000 inhabitants,
- Commercial energy use per capita,
- Share of R&D spending in GDP,
- Share of tertiary studies in the population,
- Country risk,
- World market share of exports of natural resources,
- World market share of imports of parts and components for automobiles and electronic products,
- World market share of exports of services,
- Share of world FDI inward stock.

The UNCTAD Inward FDI Performance Index (PER$_i$) monitors inward FDI in a particular country relative to its relative economic importance.

It is calculated as: PER$_i$ = (FDI$_i$ / FDI$_w$) / (GDP$_i$ / GDP$_w$)

Where: FDI$_i$ = FDI inflows in country i; FDI$_w$ = world FDI inflows; GDP$_i$ = GDP in country I; GDP$_w$ = world GDP.

Source: www.unctad.org (last visited 19 Nov. 2008)

Table 3: **Colombian scores on UNCTAD's FDI Potential and Performance Indexes**

Period	POTi			PERi		
	Rank	N	Score	Rank	N	Score
1988-1990	58	140	0.141	42	140	1.106
1989-1991	56	140	0.147	45	140	1.428
1990-1992	71	140	0.170	52	140	1.695
1991-1993	71	140	0.172	50	140	1.956
1992-1994	80	140	0.166	48	140	1.981
1993-1995	86	140	0.173	65	140	1.437
1994-1996	86	140	0.163	57	140	1.782
1995-1997	100	140	0.149	39	140	2.403
1996-1998	90	140	0.164	38	140	2.179
1997-1999	89	140	0.162	61	140	1.354
1998-2000	86	140	0.159	82	140	0.706
1999-2001	101	140	0.146	78	140	0.736
2000-2002	101	140	0.144	69	140	0.953
2001-2003	103	140	0.132	64	140	1.317
2002-2004	104	141	0.135	69	140	1.450
2003-2005	97	141	0.136	41	141	2.813
2004-2006	94	141	0.148	41	141	2.487
2005-2007	-	-	-	44	141	2.144

Note: POTi scores are between 0 (lowest potential) and 1 (highest potential); PERi scores greater than 1 point to countries receiving more FDI than its relative economic weight would suggest; scores below 1 point to the opposite.

Source: www.unctad.org (last visited 19 Nov. 2008)

Another way of assessing the impact of the conflict on the levels of inflowing FDI is to estimate its cost in terms of production and investment levels, in general, and FDI, in particular. However, whereas Colombian scholarship has been quite active on this front, both at the methodological level and with respect to actual estimations, separate estimations for aggregate FDI do not seem to be available. The macro-economic cost estimates range between 0.5 and 7.4 % of GDP (table 4). These estimates mostly concentrate on direct costs, as the indirect costs like foregone investments are more difficult to estimate. Only in recent studies like Pinto *et al.* (2005) are indirect costs treated, but not in an exhaustive way. The figures might therefore well underestimate actual economic costs.

Figure 2:   Colombia's position in UNCTAD's matrices of inward FDI performance and potential

		FDI performance	
		High	Low
FDI Potential	High	*"front runners"* 1990	*"below potential"*
	Low	*"above potential"* 1995 2002 2003 2005 2006	*"under-performers"* 2001 2004

Source: www.unctad.org (last visited 19 Nov. 2008)

Table 4:   Estimations of the economic cost of the Colombian conflict

Study	*Results*
Rubio (1995)	Direct cost of illegal activities en terms of lost growth: 2% of GDP in 1993
Granada and Rojas (1995)	Cost of armed violence: 4.2% of annual GDP (1991-1994)
Trujillo and Badel (1998)	Cost of urban violence: 2.1% of annual GDP (1991-1996) Total cost of armed violence: 2.4% of annual GDP
Echeverry, Piraquive and Salazar (1999)	GDP below long-term average. Investment needed to reach peace: 8% of GDP
Londoño and Guerrero (1999)	Costs of criminal activities (direct material losses: 6.4% of GDP Costs of violence (loss of productivity and investment): 2% of GDP
Echeverry, Salazar and Navas (2001)	Loss of annual growth of production due to armed violence and its long-term trajectory: around 0.5% of GDP
Pinto, Vergara and Lahuerta (2005)	Estimated total cost of conflict: 7.4% of GDP in 2003 (direct costs: 88%; indirect costs: 12%)

Source: Pinto, Vergara and Lahuerta (2005).

The Economic Cost of the Colombian Conflict

This is also suggested by more recent survey results among employers, showing thus a contrasting view indicating that foregone FDI, and indirect costs in general, could be far more important than macro-economic studies suggest. According to Rettberg's survey results (Rettberg, 2008), indirect costs are perceived as far more important than direct costs, and lost business opportunities (including those involving foreign partners and FDI) are ranked as the most important cost category (table 5). Earlier results from a survey targeted at executives of foreign companies operating in the Andean region (Vial, 2002) also pointed to the very negative evaluation of (transport) security conditions in Colombia from an investor point of view.

As indicated before (figure 1), the opposite relationship, referring to the extent to which FDI contributes to peace or conflict, is a more ambiguous relationship and will not be further elaborated here.[13]

Table 5: **Ranking of perceived direct and indirect costs by Colombian private sector (survey results)**

Rank	Cost	Type of cost	Average score
1	Lost business opportunities	Indirect	0.399
2	Increased expenditure on insurance policies	Indirect	0.378
3	Increased expenditure on security	Indirect	0.374
4	Lost sales due to damages in distribution and transportation networks	Indirect	0.339
5	Delays in product delivery	Indirect	0.331
6	Lost sales due to changes in markets and demand	Indirect	0,279
7	Threats	Direct	0.062
8	Extortion	Direct	0.041
9	Lost sales due to plant closures	Direct	0.036
10	Attacks against companies	Direct	0,029
11	Attacks against workers	Direct	0.029

Source: Rettberg (2008:26).

FDI and Growth

There are good theoretical arguments in favor of (promoting) FDI inflows. These foreign investments can contribute to enhancing competitiveness of the domestic economy, technical change and innovation, more competition, higher exports and so on.

As far as we can see, there is no clear econometric evidence available that shows, at the macro-level, the specific contribution of FDI inflows on economic growth in Colombia. There is some evidence on trade liberalization, but it appears to have negligible (although positive) effects on growth (Perilla Jiménez, 2006).

There is however some micro-level evidence. For example, productivity indicators of foreign and domestic companies have been compared, using firm-level data from the DANE Annual Manufacturing Survey (AMS) for the 1995-99 period. Labour productivity, capital/labor ratios, unit remuneration, and the unit labor costs have been calculated (annex 4).[14] [15] The results are shown as ratios of the average indicator for the foreign firms over the average for the local firms.[16] A value of 2.0 for labor productivity, for example, indicates that the foreign affiliates obtained productivity levels twice as high as the competing local firms. The general conclusion is that foreign affiliates are more productive than local ones. Foreign affiliates are more capital intensive than local firms, which confirms previous studies on Colombia's manufacturing industry (Misas, 1993; Agudelo and Silva, 1996). Likewise, foreign affiliates show higher average levels of labor productivity. Only for the leather sector do local firms seem to be more productive than their foreign counterparts. Foreign affiliates also exhibit higher unit remuneration, consistent with Misas' observations (Misas, 1993). Finally, foreign owned companies operate with lower unit labor costs than local companies.

This general result of higher productivity levels for foreign affiliates suggests that there might be scope for positive productivity spillovers. In De Lombaerde and Pedraza (2005) we tested the hypothesis of positive spillovers using firm-level data from the Superintendencia de Sociedades (Superintendence of Companies) for the period 1995-2000. The information from this source was accounting information, therefore it was necessary first to calculate the economic variables to be included in the econometric model.[17]

Starting with an initial sample of about 2,000 firms, owing to problems of availability and consistency of the data, finally 1,533 manufacturing firms were selected. Foreign firms were defined as those firms that register a fraction of foreign ownership superior to 0%.[18] This discrimination was done using the same data source. According to this definition, 23% of the firms in the sample were called "firms with FDI" or "foreign firms", the remaining 77% "local firms".

Using the AMS criteria to classify the companies by size, 19% are considered as large companies (≥ 200 employed), 47% as medium-sized (51-199 employed), and 34% as small (10-50 employed). The most important subsectors (ISIC Rev 2) represented in the sample were: Pharmaceuticals (18.44% of total number of companies), Industrial Chemical Substances (8.07%), Food

(7.49%), Plastic Products (7.49%), and Metal Products, except Machines and Equipment (6.34%). Of the 346 firms with FDI, the majority (65.5%) shows a majority stake for foreign capital (> 50% of assets).[19] The representativity of the sample is relatively high. The 1,533 firms represent on average 65% of total sales registered in the AMS for the 1995-99 period.

The econometric model that was estimated is similar to those estimated by Haddad and Harrison (1993), Aitken and Harrison (1999), and Barrios (2000). A log-linear production function was estimated, in which the production level is modelled as a function of its inputs (capital and labor) and variables that measure the presence of FDI within the firm and in each manufacturing subsector. Answers to two questions were sought: (i) Is foreign ownership of a firm positively associated with its productivity?, and (ii) Is foreign ownership in a sector related to productivity levels of local firms competing in the same sector through positive spillover effects?

On the one hand, the coefficient capturing FDI at the firm level suggests that an increase of foreign ownership in a firm, from 0 to 100%, increases its production in 0.03%. However, the coefficient is not statistically significant, so that there is very weak evidence that firms that receive FDI benefit from it. The low value and lack of statistical significance of the variable is surprising, given the evidence of superior productivity of foreign affiliates (mentioned earlier). Nevertheless, other empirical studies also revealed mixed and unclear results. For example, whereas the value for this coefficient was 10.5% and statistically significant for Venezuela, in Spain it was 0.1% and not significant.[20]

One possible explanation for these differences in the results might be related to the differences between the type of samples that were used. As we mentioned before, our sample of firms controlled by the Superintendencia de Sociedades is biased in terms of scale and legal type of company. The results might be explained also by the way in which foreign involvement is measured. Instead of using foreign ownership (expressed as a percentage of total assets), it might be necessary to measure directly foreign involvement in the management of the affiliate (flows of knowledge and experience), and the type and intensity of institutional arrangements and/or technological dependence between affiliates and headquarters. Finally, it might also be necessary to consider longer periods of time so that learning curves could become visible.

On the other hand, the coefficient capturing FDI at the sectoral level is positive and statistically significant, although very small. An increase of 10% in foreign participation in a sector would augment the production of local firms in 0.04%, *ceteris paribus*. These effects continue to be positive and small if we limit the estimation to local firms without FDI. The value of the coefficients is very similar although it is only statistically significant when the assets variable is used for the measurement of the sectoral FDI presence.

In a comparative perspective, whereas the studies performed with aggregate data and cross-section estimations found evidence that the presence of foreign companies is beneficial for the domestic firms, estimations with firm-level panel data revealed less optimistic conclusions. The study on Venezuela found a significant negative coefficient for the sectoral FDI variable, the one on Morocco a negative but not significant coefficient, whereas the study on Spain revealed a small but not significant effect, with changing signs according to the model specification. The results for Colombia seem thus to confirm the weak evidence of positive productivity spillovers from FDI.[21]

A number of authors have pointed to the fact that positive FDI spillovers are more likely when the local firms have the management and production capacity to absorb them, and/or when the technological knowledge gap is not too important (Kokko, 1994; Kokko *et al.*, 1996; Barrios, 2000). In order to confirm these results, separate estimations were performed for subsamples with high and low labor productivity levels. We found that the existence of significant positive spillovers is indeed limited to the case of sectors with higher productivity levels.

Finally, our results showing the small magnitude of the spillovers are consistent with the conclusions obtained by Steiner and Giedion (1995) in their qualitative assessment of FDI in Colombian manufacturing industries.[22] They found that the manufacturing firms with foreign participation make apparently little effort to transfer and diffuse technology, even internally, even though foreign affiliates consider that one of their principle advantages vis-à-vis local firms is the possession of technological resources.

Conclusions

The change in the FDI policy regime in the Andean region in the beginning of the 1990s has had a clear positive impact on the volume of incoming FDI flows in the region. Colombia also liberalized its FDI regime, in line with the new orientations of the economic chapters in the Constitution of 1991, the policy orientations of the governments in power, business interests in Colombia, and the priorities set in its relationship with the US, its principal economic and political partner.

Colombia was initially less successful in attracting FDI than its neighbors, in part because of the intensification of the conflict and the violence generated by the drug cartels in the early 1990s. But from the mid-1990s onwards, it systematically performed slightly above the regional average with respect to attracting FDI. UNCTAD's methodology shows that although Colombia has a potential that is below the average (because of factors including those that are related to the existence of the conflict), over the last years it has almost continuously performed "above potential".

The available estimates of the costs of the conflict do not allow firm conclusions to be drawn about the cost in terms of foregone FDI. Surveys among private businesses indicate, however, that the indirect costs (including foregone FDI) could be significantly higher than what comes out of the macro-economic estimates.

Finally, although there are good theoretical reasons to believe that FDI generates positive spillover effects for domestic firms, estimates with firm-level panel data do not always reveal their existence. The econometric results for Colombia show no or very weak (and not significant) spillover effects. If positive effects on the productivity of domestic firms are found at all, they appear to be completely absorbed by the most productive domestic firms. Positive productivity spillovers should thus not be taken for granted, or at least not be overestimated. This being said, it can be affirmed that foreign companies are on average more productive than the local ones, although scale effects obviously also play a role in this respect.

Notes

[1]   See also, De Lombaerde *et al.* (2009) on which the following paragraphs are based.

[2]   Considering indicators of state legitimacy, such as participation rates in national elections, legal opacity, corruption perceptions, or corruption, Colombia scores better than the lowest score available for the EU [see: http://www.election world.org; http://www.opacity-index.com; http://www.transparency.org]. The legal environment and the freedom of the press are comparable to Italy's (Deutsch 2004). It is also true, however, that Colombia scores significantly below the EU benchmark on the Gini coefficient, demonstrating the limited redistributive capacity of the Colombian state (*Human Development Report 2005*).

[3]   Foreign firms were defined as firms with foreign ownership of total capital of more than 49%. Mixed companies were defined as companies with a participation of foreign shareholders between 20 and 49%, and national companies as those with 20% or less foreign participation. For an early discussion of the common FDI regime incorporated in Decision 24, see Tironi (1978).

[4]   Applying to Bolivia and Ecuador.

5   Later, this percentage was raised to 20% by Decision 103.

6   In Colombia, this Decision was adopted through Resolution 49 of 1989.

7   The applicable legislation to FDI in Colombia includes: Law 45 of 1990, Decree Law 663 of 1993 (financial system), Decree 2080 of 2000, Law 680 of 2001, Decree 1844 of 2003, Decree 4210 of 2004, Resolution 8 of 2000 issued by the Banco de la República (as amended), Regulatory Circular Letter DCIN 83 issued on 15 December 2005 by the Banco de la República, Decree 4474 of 2005, Law 963 of 2005 (Investor's Legal Stability Law), Decree 1940 of 2006, Decree 1888 of 2008, and Decree 1999 of 2008.

8   Colombia also entered into BIT negotiations with the US, Germany, Canada, Argentina, the Netherlands, France (Ramírez, 1996; Lizarazo, 1997:122). Because of objections from the Constitutional Court with respect to the clauses on expropriation and compensation, the BITs negotiated in the 1990s could not immediately be ratified (Sentences C-358 of 1996 and C-379 of 1996) (Lizarazo, 1997:119-121). Article 58 of the Constitution was reformed by Legislative Act 01 of 1999.

9   On Colombia's participation in multilateral investment protection mechanisms, see for example, Restrepo (1997).

10   In addition, investors who invest a value greater than 7,500 legal monthly minimum wages can enter into a contract of legal stability with the government (Law 963 of 2005, declared constitutional by Sentence C-242 of 2006). This possibility does not apply to portfolio investments. Recently, these and other measures to protect foreign investment are being criticized by various analysts (Semana, 2008; Umaña, 2008).

11   See also, Agosín (1996).

12   Mesa and Parra (2006) add relatively high tax levels and relatively low productivity increases in Colombia as additional adverse factors for attracting FDI.

13   On the role of the private sector in the peace processes in Colombia, El Salvador and Guatemala, see, for example, Rettberg (2007). The study does not, however, discriminate between the domestic and the foreign private sector (multinational enterprises).

14   The indicators were calculated by manufacturing establishment, but because of the statistical secrecy obligation, we were not given access to the results at that level. It was necessary to aggregate the results by industrial sector at the 3-digit level ISIC Rev 2.

15   For examination of the comparisons according to firm size, see Pedraza (2003).

16   Foreign firms were defined here as companies with a positive (> 0%) ratio of foreign capital.

17   The Superintendencia de Sociedades sample has certain particularities. First, the companies included are mostly large, given the fact that the Superintendencia has a controlling function over large companies (Decree 3100 of 1997). Second, the companies included have mainly legal personality as "*sociedad limitada*" or "*sociedad anónima*", and exclude companies with financial activities. The firm-level data from the Annual Manufacturing Survey (DANE) are not available for the public, only on an aggregated level. This would however be an interesting alternative source of information on firms, and would also permit analysis of spillover effects via vertical linkages. Disclosure of the information by the authorities is a necessary prerequisite.

18   This definition of foreign firms was also used in Aitken and Harrison (1999) for Venezuela. However, other criteria for foreign ownership have also been used (> 5% or > 10% of total assets), without altering the conclusions. See, Pedraza (2002).

19   See also, Misas (1993) and Steiner and Giedion (1995).

20   Blömstrom and Sjöholm (1999), and Haddad and Harrison (1993) also failed to find significant positive coefficients for this variable.

21   These results were confirmed by separate estimations for subsamples of firms, classified according to size. These estimations never resulted in statistically significant coefficients for the firm-level FDI variable. They were positive for large and medium-sized firms, but negative for small firms. The coefficients showing the spillover effects continued to be significant in most cases, although they were not important in magnitude. Certain variation has been observed with varying measurements of foreign participation (assets *versus* sales) (Pedraza, 2002). "Better" results with the sales variable suggest that the effect of FDI on competition levels might be crucial for explaining positive spillovers. Further re-

search, involving direct measurements of the effect of FDI policies on the level and nature of competition, would be needed on this point. On the nexus between *apertura* and industrial concentration in Colombia, see, De Lombaerde (2004).

22 Steiner and Giedion (1995) report on the results of a questionnaire among foreign-owned firms based in Colombia; they analyzed the determinants of FDI and the contribution of foreign firms to development and the transfer of technology.

References

Agudelo, M.I. and J.M. Silva (1996), "Inversión Extranjera y Desempeño de la Industria Colombiana", Master thesis, Universidad Nacional de Colombia, Bogotá.

Agosín, M.R. (1996), "El retorno de la inversión extranjera a América Latina", in: M.R. Agosín (ed.) *Foreign Direct Investment in Latin America*, Inter-American Development Bank, Washington DC, pp. 1-45.

Aitken, B. and A. Harrison (1999), "Do Domestic Firms Benefit from Direct Foreign Investment? Evidence from Venezuela", *American Economic Review*, 89(3):605-618.

Anzola, M. (1997), "Las normas de inversión en el marco de la Comunidad Andina y G-3", in: P. De Lombaerde (ed.), *La Inversión Extranjera en Colombia. Régimen Jurídico y Análisis Económico*, Universidad Sergio Arboleda, Bogotá, pp. 47-91.

Barrios, S. (2000), "Foreign Direct Investment and Productivity Spillovers, Evidence from the Spanish Experience", *Documento de trabajo*, Fundación de Estudios de Economía Aplicada.

Blomström, M. and F. Sjöholm (1999), "Technology Transfer and Pullovers: Does Local participation in Multinationals Matter?", *European Economic Review*, 43(4/6):915-923.

Buzan, B. (1991), People, States and Fear: An Agenda for International Security Studies in the Post-Cold War Era, London: Harvester Wheatsheaf.

Collier, P. and A. Hoeffler (1998), "On Economic Causes of Civil War", *Oxford Economic Papers*, 50:563-73.

Collier, P. and A. Hoeffler (2004), "Greed and Grievance in Civil War", *Oxford Economic Papers*, 56:563-95.

Crisis Group (2003), "President Uribe's Democratic Security Policy", *Latin America Report*, (6).

Crisis Group (2005), "War and Drugs in Colombia", *Latin America Report*, (11).

CSIS (2007), "Back from the Brink: Evaluating Progress in Colombia, 1999–2007", *Americas Program Report*, Center for Strategic and International Studies.

Cubillos, M. and V. Navas (2000), *Inversión Extranjera Directa en Colombia: Características y Tendencias*, Departamento Nacional de Planeación, Bogotá.

De Lombaerde, P. (2004), "Liberación comercial, concentración industrial y política de competencia en Colombia", in: M. Anzola and C.L. Lizarazo (eds), *Regulación Económica: Tendencias y Desafíos*, Universidad del Rosario-Temis, Bogotá. pp. 103-113.

De Lombaerde, P. and Lizarazo, C. (2001), "Comercio Exterior e Inversión Extranjera", in: L.A. Restrepo Moreno (ed.), *Síntesis 2001. Anuario Social, Político y Económico de Colombia*, IEPRI, Tercer Mundo Editores, Bogotá.

De Lombaerde, P. and E.B. Pedraza (2005), "FDI Productivity Spillovers in the Andean Region: Econometric Evidence from Colombian Firm-level Panel Data", in: L. Cuyvers and F. De Beule (eds), *Transnational Corporations and Economic Development: From Internationalisation to Globalisation*, Palgrave Macmillan, London.

De Lombaerde, P., G. Haghebaert, S. Ramírez and A. Vranckx (2009), "EU Conflict Management in the Andean Region: The Case of Colombia", in: F. Söderbaum and P. Stålgren (eds), *European Union and the Global South*, Boulder: Lynne Rienner [forthcoming].

Deutsch, K. (ed.) (2004), Freedom of the Press 2004. A Global Survey of Media Independence, New York: Freedom House.

Echeverry, J.C., G. Piraquive and N. Salazar (1999), "El balance del sector público y la sostenibilidad fiscal en Colombia", *Archivos de Economía*, (115).

Echeverry, J.C., N. Salazar and V. Navas (2001), "¿Nos parecemos al resto del mundo? El conflicto colombiano en el contexto internacional", *Archivos de Economía*, (143).

Granada, C. and L. Rojas (1995), "Los costos del conflicto armado 1990-1994", *Planeación y Desarrollo*, XXVI(4).

Gurr, T.R. *et al.* (1998), "The State Failure Project: Early Warning Research for US Foreign Policy Planning", Paper presented at the Seminar *Failed States and International Security: Causes, Prospects, and Consequences*, Purdue University, 25-27 February.

Haddad, M. and Harrison. A.E. (1993), "Are There Positive Pullovers from Direct Foreign Investment? Evidence from Panel Data for Morocco", *Journal of Development Economics*, 42:51-74.

Hommes, R., A. Montenegro and P. Roda (eds) (1994), *Una apertura hacia el futuro: balance económico 1990-1994*, Minhacienda-DNP-Fonade, Bogotá.

Kokko, A. (1994), "Technology, Market Characteristics and Pullovers". *Journal of Development Economics*, 43(2):279-293.

Kokko, A., R. Tansini and M. Zejan. (1996), "Local Technological Capability and Spillovers from FDI in the Uruguayan Manufacturing Sector". *Journal of Development Studies*, 34(4):602-611.

Rodríguez, L. and C. Liliana. (1997), "Acuerdos bilaterales de promoción y protección a la inversión (APPI)", in: P. De Lombaerde (ed.), *La Inversión Extranjera en Colombia. Régimen Jurídico y Análisis Económico*, Universidad Sergio Arboleda, Bogotá, pp. 93-150.

Londoño, J.L. and R. Guerrero (1999), "Violencia en América Latina: epidemiología y costos", *IDB Working Papers*, (R-375).

McLean, P. (2002), "Colombia – Thinking Clearly about the Conflict", *Policy Papers on the Americas*, XIII(7).

Mesa Parra, F. and R.I. Parra Peña (2006),"Política tributaria como instrumento competitivo para captar la inversión extranjera directa: Caso de América Latina", *Archivos de Economía*, (313).

Misas, G. (1993), "El Papel de las Empresas Trasnacionales en la Reestructuración Industrial de Colombia: Una Síntesis", *Estudios e Informes de la CEPAL*, Santiago de Chile, (90).

OECD (1999), Política y promoción de la inversión extranjera directa en América Latina, OECD, Paris.

Pedraza, E.B. (2002), "Efectos indirectos de la inversión extranjera directa: evidencia para la economía colombiana," Master thesis, Faculty of Economics, Universidad Nacional de Colombia, Bogotá.

Pedraza, E.B. (2003), "Desempeño económico por tipo de firma: Empresas nacionales vs. grandes y pequeñas receptoras de inversión extranjera", *Archivos de Economía*, DNP, (225).

Perilla Jiménez, J.R. (2006), "Colombian Growth Determinants: What Do We Really Know?", *Archivos de Economía*, DNP, (326).

Pinto, Borrego, M.E., A. Vergara Ballen and Y. Lahuerta Percipiano (2005), "Costos generados por la violencia armada en Colombia: 1999-2003", *Archivos de Economía*, (277).

Pizarro Leongómez, E. (2002), "Colombia: ¿guerra civil, Guerra contra la sociedad, Guerra antiterrorista o Guerra ambigua?", *Análisis Político*, (46):164-80.

Posada Carbó, E. (2001), *¿Guerra civil? El lenguaje del conflicto en Colombia*, Bogotá: Libros de Cambio—Alfaomega.

Proexport (2008), *Legal Framework 2008*, Proexport Colombia, Bogotá.

Ramírez, J.C. (1996), "El Tratado de Inversión Bilateral Estados Unidos-Colombia. Perspectiva Colombiana", in: H. Osorio (ed.), *Tratado Bilateral de Protección a la Inversión: Perspectiva Colombiana y Norteamericana*, CLADEI, Bogotá, pp. 35-51.

Ramírez Tobón, W. (2002), "¿Guerra civil en Colombia?", *Análisis Político*, (46):151-63.

Reina, M. and S. Zuluaga (1998), *Colombia: siete años de apertura a la inversión extranjera 1991-1997*, Coinvertir-Fedesarrollo, Bogotá.

Restrepo, J., M. Spagat and J.F. Vargas (2003), "The Dynamics of the Colombian Civil Conflict: A New Data Set", *CEPR Discussion Paper*, (4108).

Restrepo Uribe, E. (1997), "Mecanismos multilaterales de protección a la inversión (MIGA, ICSID) y OPIC", in: P. De Lombaerde (ed.), *La Inversión Extranjera en Colombia. Régimen Jurídico y Análisis Económico*, Universidad Sergio Arboleda, Bogotá, pp. 3-29.

Rettberg, A. (2007), "The Private Sector and Peace in El Salvador, Guatemala, and Colombia", *Journal of Latin American Studies*, 39:463-494.

Rettberg, A. (2008), Explorando el dividendo de la paz: impactos del conflicto armado en el sector privado colombiano. Resultados de una encuesta nacional, Bogotá: Universidad de Los Andes.

Rogers, P. (2002), "Political Violence and Global Order" in K. Booth and T. Dunne (eds), *Worlds in Collision. Terror and the Future of Global Order*, Basingstoke: Palgrave Macmillan, pp. 215-25.

Rubio, M. (1995), *Violencia y conflicto en los noventa*, Bogotá: Universidad de Los Andes.

Semana (2008), "Fórmula peligrosa", www.semana.com [visited, 3 Mar. 2008].

Singer, D. and M. Small (1982), Resort to Arms: International and Civil Wars, 1816-1980, Beverly Hills: Sage.

Steiner, R., and U. Giedion (1995), "Characteristics, Determinants and Effects of Foreign Direct Investment in Colombia", in: M.R. Agosin (ed.) *Foreign Direct Investment in Latin America*, Washington D.C.: Inter-American Development Bank, pp.161-209.

Tironi, E. (1978), "Políticas frente al capital extranjero: la Decisión 24", in: E. Tironi (comp.), *Pacto Andino. Carácter y Perspectivas*, Instituto de Estudios Peruanos, Lima, pp. 71-110.

Trujillo, E. and M. Badel (1998), Los costos económicos de la criminalidad y la violencia en Colombia: 1991-1996", *Archivos de Economía*, (76).

Umaña, G. (2008), "La protección a la inversión", www.portafolio.com.co [visited, 27 Nov. 2008].

UNDP (Programa de Naciones Unidas para el Desarrollo (PNUD)) (2003), *El conflicto: callejón con salida*. Informe Nacional de Desarrollo Humano 2003, Bogotá.

Vial, J. (2002), "Foreign Investment in the Andean Countries", *CID Working Paper*, (085).

Wieland, C. (2008a), "¿El comienzo del fin de las FARC?", *KAS Länderbericht*, (June).

Wieland, C. (2008b), "Díez tesis sobre el cambio del conflicto en Colombia", *KAS Länderbericht*, (Nov.).

Annex 1: FDI inflows as a percentage of Gross Fixed Capital Formation, by host region and economy, 1985 - 2007

Region/economy	1985	1986	1987	1988	1989	1990	1991	1992	1993	1994	1995	1996	1997	1998	1999	2000	2001	2002	2003	2004	2005	2006	2007
South America	4,3	1,6	2,3	4,1	2,9	3,2	3,8	6,5	4,3	6,6	6,9	11,8	16,0	17,2	31,2	25,6	18,6	17,4	13,8	17,0	15,4	12,0	15,4
Argentina	5,9	3,1	-0,1	4,8	8,6	9,3	8,8	11,6	6,2	7,1	12,1	14,1	16,1	12,2	46,9	22,6	5,7	17,6	8,4	14,1	13,4	10,1	9,0
Bolivia	2,2	3,2	8,2	5,7	6,4	11,0	12,4	13,3	12,9	14,7	35,9	35,9	56,8	52,2	63,9	49,0	62,2	54,4	19,0	7,7	-23,2	17,2	9,6
Brazil	3,8	0,6	1,8	3,7	1,0	1,0	1,5	2,9	1,5	1,9	3,0	7,2	11,8	18,6	28,2	30,3	23,9	20,0	12,0	17,0	10,7	10,6	15,0
Chile	4,4	8,9	18,9	16,9	16,9	8,0	10,2	8,5	8,0	18,6	16,2	24,1	23,5	22,3	57,6	31,2	28,2	17,8	28,9	38,9	27,9	25,8	42,9
Colombia	11,4	7,4	3,4	1,8	5,5	5,1	5,2	7,3	6,9	7,8	4,7	14,8	25,6	15,1	13,1	23,0	22,6	17,9	13,0	16,6	41,8	21,5	22,9
Ecuador	2,4	3,8	5,1	7,2	7,8	6,4	6,9	7,2	16,6	16,4	11,9	13,0	17,1	18,8	22,9	22,1	29,3	13,5	14,3	11,9	6,0	3,0	1,8
Guyana	1,9	-6,6	3,8	2,4	-1,6	4,7	10,0	73,0	28,7	43,0	26,4	30,0	15,7	14,8	17,2	24,5	20,4	15,8	10,0	11,9	28,8	24,8	31,5
Paraguay	0,9	2,6	0,9	0,5	1,4	6,6	5,9	8,9	5,0	7,8	5,5	7,6	12,0	22,3	7,1	8,4	7,5	1,1	2,6	2,9	3,7	9,6	8,3
Peru	0,0	0,5	0,5	0,4	0,9	0,7	-0,1	-1,3	11,9	34,5	19,8	27,7	15,2	12,3	17,3	7,5	11,4	21,6	12,2	12,8	17,7	19,4	22,8
Uruguay	-1,7	6,4	6,0	5,2	4,2	4,6	2,7	0,6	4,6	6,1	6,0	4,8	4,0	4,8	7,8	7,5	12,8	15,6	39,4	22,3	40,8	49,9	27,4
Venezuela, Bolivarian Republic of	0,7	-1,4	3,5	3,9	6,7	9,9	1,9	11,4	2,8	6,7	5,9	15,2	28,4	19,1	12,4	19,1	12,5	3,8	15,8	7,2	8,8	-1,5	1,2

Source: UNCTAD World Investment Report

Annex 2: Inward FDI stock as a percentage of GDP, by host region and economy, 1985 - 2007

Region/ economy	1985	1986	1987	1988	1989	1990	1991	1992	1993	1994	1995	1996	1997	1998	1999	2000	2001	2002	2003	2004	2005	2006	2007
South America	10,1	9,5	9,9	9,4	9,4	9,6	9,8	11,3	11,8	11,7	9,6	10,9	13,9	17,0	22,4	23,6	27,4	28,6	31,6	29,7	27,6	26,4	27,7
Argentina	3,6	3,6	3,4	3,9	7,7	5,5	5,4	6,5	7,1	7,9	9,9	11,2	14,3	16,0	21,8	23,8	29,6	42,3	37,2	34,3	30,1	27,9	25,2
Bolivia	15,1	15,3	14,5	13,8	15,0	21,1	20,5	21,1	22,9	24,0	23,3	26,9	28,4	38,5	51,7	61,8	72,4	82,9	56,9	56,5	51,4	44,7	40,6
Brazil	11,5	10,4	10,7	9,7	7,7	8,5	9,5	12,1	12,5	11,3	6,8	7,1	8,6	12,6	17,4	19,0	22,1	19,9	24,0	24,3	22,2	22,0	25,0
Chile	65,8	62,8	57,7	53,1	50,7	48,1	44,2	38,6	38,5	38,2	33,9	38,6	41,7	47,4	59,6	60,8	63,4	62,9	73,1	63,3	62,7	55,0	64,4
Colombia	5,4	6,4	6,9	6,5	7,0	7,3	7,4	7,4	7,1	6,4	6,9	12,1	18,5	16,9	15,6	13,3	18,8	22,2	25,9	25,3	30,0	33,2	32,7
Ecuador	5,8	8,9	10,2	11,5	12,5	14,5	14,4	14,7	17,2	17,0	17,9	19,4	20,5	24,6	38,1	44,4	39,6	30,8	29,8	28,7	26,5	24,5	23,2
Guyana	9,0	6,3	10,7	9,4	9,7	11,3	16,4	54,5	58,6	69,7	73,1	77,6	80,0	89,7	99,2	106,1	114,1	117,9	118,7	115,7	119,8	121,2	119,7
Paraguay	6,8	6,3	7,8	6,0	8,6	8,5	8,5	10,2	10,9	11,6	8,0	9,5	11,0	15,1	16,7	18,7	17,6	17,7	19,6	16,5	17,2	19,2	16,7
Peru	7,7	5,3	3,3	4,0	3,7	4,5	4,0	4,2	4,7	9,9	10,3	12,0	13,1	14,6	19,0	20,7	21,9	22,1	21,0	19,1	20,0	20,8	22,7
Uruguay	9,7	8,4	7,4	7,8	8,1	8,0	7,0	5,6	5,4	5,6	5,8	6,2	6,4	7,0	8,6	10,4	13,0	11,4	16,1	16,0	17,1	21,7	22,0
Venezuela, Bolivarian Republic of	2,6	2,3	3,9	4,3	7,4	8,2	7,9	10,3	11,1	12,8	11,0	15,3	28,8	31,7	32,1	30,3	31,8	42,0	49,5	37,7	30,6	24,6	19,3

Source: UNCTAD World Investment Report.

Annex 3: Inward FDI stock as a percentage of GDP, by host region and economy, 1986 - 2007 (annual percentage point variations)

Region/economy	1986	1987	1988	1989	1990	1991	1992	1993	1994	1995	1996	1997	1998	1999	2000	2001	2002	2003	2004	2005	2006	2007
South America	-0,6	0,3	-0,5	0,0	0,2	0,2	1,5	0,5	-0,1	-2,1	1,3	3,1	3,1	5,4	1,2	3,8	1,1	3,0	-1,9	-2,2	-1,2	1,3
Argentina	-0,1	-0,1	0,4	3,9	-2,2	-0,1	1,1	0,6	0,9	1,9	1,4	3,1	1,6	5,9	1,9	5,8	12,7	-5,0	-3,0	-4,2	-2,2	-2,7
Bolivia	0,2	-0,8	-0,7	1,1	6,1	-0,6	0,6	1,8	1,1	-0,7	3,6	1,5	10,2	13,2	10,1	10,6	10,5	-26,0	-0,4	-5,1	-6,7	-4,1
Brazil	-1,1	0,3	-0,9	-2,1	0,8	1,0	2,6	0,4	-1,1	-4,5	0,3	1,6	4,0	4,8	1,5	3,1	-2,1	4,1	0,3	-2,1	-0,1	3,0
Chile	-3,0	-5,1	-4,6	-2,3	-2,7	-3,9	-5,6	-0,1	-0,3	-4,3	4,7	3,1	5,7	12,2	1,3	2,6	-0,5	10,2	-9,8	-0,5	-7,8	9,4
Colombia	1,1	0,5	-0,5	0,5	0,4	0,0	0,1	-0,4	-0,7	0,6	5,2	6,3	-1,6	-1,3	-2,2	5,4	3,4	3,7	-0,6	4,7	3,2	-0,5
Ecuador	3,0	1,3	1,3	1,0	2,0	0,0	0,3	2,5	-0,2	0,9	1,4	1,1	4,1	13,6	6,3	-4,9	-8,8	-1,0	-1,1	-2,2	-2,0	-1,3
Guyana	-2,7	4,5	-1,3	0,3	1,6	5,1	38,1	4,1	11,1	3,4	4,5	2,4	9,7	9,6	6,9	7,9	3,8	0,8	-3,0	4,1	1,4	-1,5
Paraguay	-0,5	1,4	-1,8	2,6	-0,1	0,0	1,7	0,7	0,7	-3,7	1,5	1,5	4,1	1,5	2,0	-1,1	0,1	1,9	-3,1	0,6	2,0	-2,5
Peru	-2,4	-2,0	0,8	-0,4	0,9	-0,6	0,2	0,5	5,2	0,4	1,8	1,1	1,5	4,4	1,7	1,2	0,2	-1,1	-1,9	0,9	0,8	1,9
Uruguay	-1,3	-1,0	0,4	0,3	-0,1	-1,0	-1,5	-0,1	0,1	0,3	0,3	0,2	0,5	1,6	1,8	2,6	-1,5	4,7	-0,1	1,1	4,6	0,3
Venezuela, Bolivarian Republic of	-0,3	1,6	0,5	3,1	0,8	-0,3	2,4	0,8	1,7	-1,8	4,3	13,5	2,9	0,5	-1,8	1,5	10,2	7,5	-11,9	-7,1	-6,0	-5,4

Source: Calculations of the authors on the basis of Annex 2.

Annex 4: Comparison of productivity indicators, 1995-1999

ISIC	Manufacturing sectors	PL[a]	UR[a]	K/L[a]	ULC[a]
311	Food	1.73*	1.22	1.46	0.77*
312	Other food	2.50*	1.39*	3.11*	0.84
313	Beverages	1.49	1.01	1.76*	0.62*
321	Textiles	1.72*	1.22*	1.29	0.71*
322	Garments	1.57*	1.24*	1.74	0.95
323	Leather products	0.68*	1.18	1.10	1.82*
324	Footwear	1.32*	1.41*	1.71*	1.07
331	Wooden products	1.21	1.24*	1.10	1.18
332	Furniture etc.	2.35*	1.49*	2.84*	0.62*
341	Wood pulp, paper and cardboard	1.40*	1.28*	1.60	0.94
342	Printing and editorials	1.51*	1.10	1.13	0.80*
351	Industrial chemical substances	2.66*	1.38*	2.98*	0.58*
352	Pharmaceuticals, soaps	2.27*	1.68*	2.80*	0.84
354	Derivatives of oil and coal	1.66	2.02*	2.36*	1.37
355	Rubber products	2.00*	1.54	3.23	0.74*
356	Plastic products	1.94*	1.31	2.65*	0.69*
361	Objects of clay, porcelain, etc.	1.23	1.08	1.77*	0.63
362	Glass	3.37*	1.85*	4.54*	0.55*
369	Non-metal mineral products	1.89*	1.30*	2.24*	0.59*
371	Basic iron and steel industry	2.65*	1.63*	3.69*	0.57*
372	Basic manufacturing of non-ferrous metals	1.07	1.27*	1.52	0.92
381	Metal products, except machines and equipment	2.01*	1.37*	1.91*	0.74*
382	Machines, except electrical	1.62*	1.31*	1.93*	0.87
383	Electrical machines and equipment	2.23*	1.87*	2.42*	0.93
384	Transportation material	2.76*	1.44*	1.66*	0.47*
385	Professional and scientific material	3.71*	1.49*	2.22*	0.51*
390	Other manufacturing industries	1.60*	1.47*	1.19	0.99

Source: Annual Manufacturing Survey (AMS) DANE 1995-1999; De Lombaerde and Pedraza (2005).

PL = productivity of labor, UR = unit remuneration, K/L = capital/labour ratio, ULC = unit labor cost.

[a] Ratio of average performance of foreign affiliates over average performance of local firms.

* = differences between averages statistically significant at 5% level.

Chapter 9

Post-Conflict Countries and Foreign Investment: Obstacles and Benefits

Nicholas Turner and Obijiofor Aginam

The preceding chapters have identified and critically evaluated a range of approaches to attracting, regulating and managing foreign direct investment (FDI) in post-conflict countries, with each case study providing deep insights into the respective country's successes and failures. This conclusion will draw out some of the unique and common practices emerging from the chapters, in order to highlight lessons for policymakers and areas that could potentially benefit from future research.

Before doing so, it would be instructive to outline the context within which these chapters are set, including the characteristics of post-conflict states that create such an urgent need for foreign investment, and yet at the same time make it so difficult to attract.

Countries recovering from violent conflict have been a subject of rising international attention, largely due to recently emerging trends in the nature and incidence of armed conflict, as well as the rise in UN peacemaking efforts following the end of the Cold War. The number of international wars has declined significantly since the late 1970s, while the 1990s brought the end of numerous civil wars – most of which first arose due to Cold War hostilities and conflicts over control of new states created by decolonisation.[1] The wars of today are largely between government forces and poorly-funded rebel groups, with civilians bearing the brunt of the impact and casualties. Ending hostilities remains a crucial goal, but sustaining peace in the following years has become a pressing concern owing to the high risk of renewed violence. Paul Collier and Anke Hoeffler's research on the 'conflict trap' finds that 40% of post-conflict countries fall back into war within the first five years,[2] a vulnerability affirmed across the UN, regional organizations and civil society in their increased focus on post-conflict peacebuilding.

The challenges of rebuilding in the aftermath of conflict are many and varied, calling for swift and robust policy responses. Clearly, the needs of post-conflict transition countries vary according to their particular circumstances. While the overriding priority in those countries emerging from complete collapse – such as Liberia and Somalia – is to restore stability and security, in other countries where institutions are still intact to some degree, efforts can concentrate more on improving economic and social conditions by establishing effective, accountable governance mechanisms. Nevertheless, the latest research and doctrine suggest the early post-conflict years provide unique opportunities to lay the foundations for sustainable economic development that will benefit the country in the following years.[3]

Economic Development to Escape the Conflict Trap

There is a strong negative relationship between the wealth of a country and the probability that it will suffer civil war. Macartan Humphreys and Ashutosh Varshney find that for a country with per capita GDP of US$250 there is a 15% probability of conflict over the next five years, while for a country with per capita GDP of US$600 this probability is halved.[4] If economic development and poverty reduction are so effective in reducing the incidence of conflict, this should be of particular significance for countries recovering from violent conflicts, considering they are often among the poorest – even compared with other developing countries. Most post-conflict countries fall into the category of least developed countries (LDCs).[5] Indeed, rapid economic growth in the aftermath of conflict is very effective in reducing the risk of future conflict, and significantly more so than in pre-conflict countries.[6]

Thus there is a strong case that alongside such imperatives as maintaining security and building public institutions, economic recovery plays a key role in sustaining the fragile peace. In the longer term, low income is an underlying issue that, unless solved, will maintain a high risk of conflict in future. These goals are complementary – improving economic conditions sets in motion a virtuous circle, as success in avoiding conflict then helps maintain economic growth. In addition, it should not be forgotten that economic development has intrinsic moral and practical value, improving conditions for citizens to live in freedom from fear and freedom from want.

FDI and Economic Development

In the post-conflict recovery process, reconstruction and development of physical and institutional infrastructure depend mainly upon foreign aid and FDI. It is revealing that LDCs are the most reliant upon aid among all developing countries, with official development assistance (ODA) an average of 8% of GDP in 2006. LDCs are also the most lacking in FDI, with only 0.7% of world FDI inflows, compared with 27% for developing countries as a whole.[7] Post-conflict countries, and even those that are categorized as developing countries rather than LDCs, desperately need increased foreign investment to supplement the flow of aid into the country, revitalize their industries and rebuild their infrastructures. While aid is crucial and effective, particularly if well-timed and structured, foreign investment can also provide intangible advantages for post-conflict countries that go above and beyond any economic contribution – which are outlined in more detail below.

As discussed in several of the chapters, the possible existence of a positive relationship between FDI and economic development is a subject of considerable disagreement among scholars and practitioners, with some suggesting that the relationship in fact runs in the opposite direction. Although the overall amount of investment does not have a significant effect on growth, the quality and form of FDI are seen as important determining factors. It is generally assumed that FDI can bring benefits when carefully managed as part of a comprehensive investment strategy. Investment from abroad brings a direct increase in capital stock and subsequent capital flows, while there is a potential indirect spill-over effect on the host economy, stimulating local spin-off industries, and transferring modern technology and new skills.

There exists a considerable body of academic research and lively policy debate regarding the general impact of FDI in developing countries. However, assessments of foreign investment laws and policies have not yet formed a significant part of peacebuilding research. This is particularly surprising considering the well-established links in the war economy literature between greed and conflict, which remain relatively unexplored in the context of peace. [8] As we know greed is a strong factor in conflict, there is a clear need for research to develop our understanding of its role in peacetime, particularly in the vulnerable early years after conflict.

Barriers to FDI in Post-Conflict Countries

The challenges of post-conflict economies are very different to those of developed, and even of other developing economies; therefore the means by which foreign investment can be facilitated and encouraged must be carefully tailored to these specific demands. As well as those conditions arising as direct effects of the conflict itself, there may be those that existed prior to the conflict, and may very well have been factors in causing it in the first place.

Many of these characteristics that make investment in recovering countries so risky and complicated are the same ones that make it so desperately needed. In addition to the omnipresent threat of relapse into violence, post-conflict countries are afflicted by a range of other serious risks and capacity deficits, including political instability, severe security problems, and a lack of institutional capacity. In developing countries generally, and even more so in post-conflict countries, weak institutions are known to hamper entre-preneurial investments, exacerbating underdevelopment. The lack of an adequate legal framework for foreign investment is among the most power-ful discouraging factors for potential investors, examined in more detail later in this chapter. After conflict, physical infrastructure is often damaged or unavailable, including electricity, water, transport and access to land. Corruption is often endemic, while transparency and rule of law are either absent or extremely weak. These are all strong limiting factors on economies shattered by conflict, and deprived of skilled labour as they struggle to cope with the effects of brain drain and capital flight.

Benefits of FDI in Post-Conflict Countries

Development aid alone cannot transform damaged economies into vibrant, self-sufficient systems – it is here that FDI has the ability to bring added advantages, and can eventually even eliminate the need for foreign aid. FDI creates the job opportunities which are so desperately needed for post-conflict countries to achieve long-term economic stability. It provides capital to increase the productive capacity of the host economy, and access to inter-national markets – helping countries to move from aid-dependent to in-vestment-driven reconstruction. By providing legitimate economic activities, FDI reintegrates former combatants and removes the incentives of the war economy.

There are also intangible benefits of foreign investment, such as the building of public confidence through employment generation and the return of those who previously fled the country. This kind of 'peace divi-dend' can instil the people with a stronger sense of hope and provide incentives to further consolidate peace.

Investment by transnational corporations (TNCs) in developing count-ries brings new technologies and working practices, along with increased competition. This competition may in the short term have negative effects in reducing the market share of local companies, but over time these local companies can gain as they are forced to use their existing technology and resources more efficiently in response to the greater competitive pressure. Local companies may copy the new technology introduced to the country by a TNC, while locals who have been trained in new technology or techniques by TNCs are able to subsequently set up their own companies or find jobs in other local companies. It is often in the interest of TNCs to provide support and training down the supply chain, improving the productivity of local companies. Much-needed improvements in product quality and labour standards may also result from the relatively high standards imposed by TNCs on local firms.

FDI can have both positive and negative impacts, which must be carefully considered when designing strategic policy to attract and regulate foreign investment. Any potential contribution by FDI to economic growth of the host country depends upon creating links with the local economy. Indeed, Kojo Yelpaala warns in his chapter that 'if FDI is left to its own devices, it is unlikely to generate growth, lead to meaningful technology transfer or create the internal links necessary for development.' Attracting unsuitable or inappropriate forms of FDI not only risks forfeiting potential benefits to the host economy, but can even actively hinder development and visit negative consequences on local communities and on the environment.

Natural Resources

This dilemma is prominent when seen in the context of post-conflict countries. The prevailing conditions largely render such countries attractive only to certain forms of FDI which have limited transformative possibilities. As Yelpaala notes, 'the poorest of poor countries are hardly ever attractive to TNCs in search of markets and profits unless those countries are endowed with abundant natural resources.' It is therefore unsurprising that investments in extractive industries such as oil, diamonds or minerals account for the majority of FDI flows to many developing countries, especially in Africa. Natural resource extraction is primarily export-oriented, with significant potential for income generation but with very limited opportunity for employment creation and linkages with the local economy. Such industrial activities also inevitably bring associated negative environmental and social impacts; this phenomenon is prevalent in most of Africa's resource-rich countries, including Angola, Congo-Brazzaville, the Democratic Republic of the Congo (DRC), Gabon, Nigeria, Cameroon, Sudan and Sierra Leone.

More importantly for post-conflict countries, a dependence on natural resource exports has been shown to significantly increase the risk of conflict and damage host-state governance.[9] The valuable contracts involved create powerful incentives for corruption among government and company employees. Price volatility can also have a destabilizing effect on the economy, especially for countries heavily dependent on exporting one resource – and indeed, natural resource extraction is inherently unsustainable, only lasting until the resource is exhausted.

Seeking to mitigate these negative impacts, efforts have been made to regulate resource extraction, particularly in low-income – and therefore conflict-prone – countries. A good example is the Kimberley Process, which has introduced certification to the diamond trade, distinguishing legitimate and illegitimate supply to reduce revenues for rebel groups. The Extractive Industries Transparency Initiative (EITI) provides a voluntary template for low-income natural resource exporting countries, improving governance through adoption of transparent accounting for revenues by companies and governments. Unfortunately, despite promotion by the World Bank, efforts to implement the EITI have been largely unsuccessful because most resource-rich developing countries lack the institutional capacity for such initiatives. Here research is needed to identify means for facilitating adoption of such measures, and potential alternatives.

Attracting Beneficial Foreign Investment

The chapters are in general agreement that to encourage a form of FDI that benefits post-conflict countries, the quality of investment must be prioritized, rather than focusing purely on the size of investment flows. FDI can only be justified if it is high value and makes a real contribution to the host economy, in terms of job-creation and spill-over of knowledge or technology. Above all, any investment regime must recognize that foreign investment is a tool to achieve the wider goal of economic development within a reconstruction and peacebuilding process, and not an end in itself.

Foreign investment policy must balance this need for caution with the recognition that developing countries are competing to attract investment. Potential investors will naturally consider the opportunities, the legal regime and incentives available at various destinations, and decide on that basis where to invest. The investment regime is important not only for attracting new investment – it can also encourage existing investors to re-invest or to increase levels of investment. In addition, it can offer protection and privileges for diasporas to return and assist in the reconstruction of their countries.

Clearly, there is no 'one-size-fits-all' policy solution for post-conflict investment promotion and regulation. As evident in the preceding case studies, there is a wide variety of complex difficulties that are unique to each country's particular situation. Meeting these challenges requires the adoption of a post-conflict private investment regime that is specifically tailored to the country's economic landscape, as well as being informed by its social, historical, and cultural character. Nevertheless, on the basis of the experiences detailed in this volume, some broad conclusions can be drawn which suggest policy measures that are generally successful in attracting and facilitating appropriate forms of FDI, and maximizing its benefits.

The Legal Framework for FDI

Violent conflict tends to leave states with a desperate shortage of judicial capacity – many judges and lawyers may have fled or been killed, and low-paid law enforcement officials may have joined militias. Courthouses, law libraries and other basic infrastructure necessary for a functioning legal system may have been destroyed. For post-conflict states lacking these basic elements of a legal system, it can be next to impossible to develop, review and enforce legislation.

This clearly presents a powerful deterrent to foreign investors who might otherwise consider making an investment in a post-conflict country. Those that do make investments may require much higher rates of return, given the increased risks of conducting business without effective legal recourse for unlawful actions. Post-conflict countries must therefore establish a legal framework that can overcome these difficulties and create a more attractive investment environment, by enacting legislation, rebuilding courthouses, and training judges and lawyers. Put simply, establishing a comprehensive legal framework for FDI is key to attracting foreign investment. But doing so can be all but impossible, when faced with tight constraints on financial and human resources and high competition for public spending priority, to say nothing of security challenges – particularly in the immediate aftermath of conflict

An alternative, explored in detail within this volume, is for the post-conflict government to utilize the laws, infrastructure and expertise of another legal system, including lawyers, judges and arbitrators, as well as courthouses and tribunals. This can be accomplished through investment contracts with individual foreign investors, and through international treaties.

Post-conflict governments can enter into individual contractual arrangements with foreign investors, in each case adopting the laws of a foreign state and providing for adjudication of disputes exclusively in its courts. Tai-Heng Cheng explores one solution in his chapter – designating the courts and laws of the investor's country as the adjudication forum and governing law of the investment agreement with the post-conflict country. Although this may satisfy investors' concerns when contracting directly with the government of the post-conflict country, there are legitimate concerns when an investor enters into a joint venture with a corporation of that country. In the event that the government takes regulatory actions which harm the investor, the investor may have no recourse against the government, which was not a party to the agreement, or against the corporation, which did not breach its agreement.

To address this gap and provide a more complete solution, a post-conflict country can consider additionally adopting the international legal framework for FDI, which unlike some regional or industry-specific frameworks is global in reach and applies to investments generally. A combination of the International Centre for the Settlement of Investment Disputes (through the ICSID Convention), the UN Convention on the Recognition and Enforcement of Arbitral Awards (New York Convention), and bilateral investment treaties (BITs) permits a post-conflict country and foreign investors to resolve disputes by using neutral arbitrators and to enforce the awards in the courts of any signatory state. ICSID provides a neutral arbitral forum for settling investor-state disputes, while the New York Convention enforces any international arbitral award between a foreign and a domestic corporation. BITs are designed to promote investment between signatory states, by prescribing that each state will accord substantive protections to the investments from the other state, including protection against direct and indirect expropriation.

Exploring ICSID in the context of Democratic Republic of Congo (DRC), Sierra Leone and Liberia, Virtus Igbokwe highlights a major concern for prospective investors in post-conflict countries: that governments may exercise their sovereign right to change laws, and even withdraw from guarantees of international arbitration at a later date. Investors have a legitimate expectation that the host state will act consistently, and not arbitrarily revoke guarantees – so Igbokwe asserts that 'further legislative assurance is imperative to preserve the guarantee of international arbitration in the event of adverse legislative changes.' Therefore, it is imperative for post-conflict countries to include a stability clause in their investment codes, specifically granting such protection to foreign investors for a certain period following their investment. He suggests that such a stability clause would reassure potential investors of the availability of dispute settlement by a neutral arbitral tribunal, and thereby encourage them to commit their capital resources in a post-conflict country.

Build, Operate and Transfer

The most beneficial arrangement for those post-conflict countries with abundant natural resources is to persuade TNCs to establish local processing facilities, which can bring the infusion of capital, technology and know-how necessary for sustainable economic growth. Kojo Yelpaala explores the possibilities for this to be achieved through a form of project financing known as Build, Operate and Transfer (BOT), whereby the government grants concessions to companies to finance and build a particular service or facility, operate it, and subsequently transfer it back to government ownership after the project has paid for itself. Yelpaala suggests that local processing facilities funded by BOT could allow countries such as Angola to refine their crude oil for export, while coffee bean producers such as Rwanda could establish flexible facilities with the capacity to roast beans to the specifications of any foreign buyer, and eventually even develop their own national brands for the global marketplace.

Incentives

Tax incentives are one area where it is particularly important to distinguish between investment flows and real contributions to socio-economic development. Here the overriding concern is that corporations may invest in a country solely to benefit from the incentives, without making any real contribution to the sustainability of the country's economy. Ibironke Odumosu's chapter notes the ability of some investors in Rwanda's 'free economic zones' to operate at zero percent income tax (with tax-free repatriation of profits), highlighting the risks of such counterproductive policies which sacrifice any beneficial effect in order to attract investment.

But incentives can even go further and have the unintended consequence of actively discouraging beneficial activity. Implementing extremely liberal tax policies in pursuit of foreign investment tends to attract a certain form of FDI, entirely motivated by the benefits conferred by a tax haven. This is evident in Liberia, where taxes are not levied on income earned outside the country's territorial borders, so that TNCs are only subject to taxation for income earned inside the country. In effect, this means foreign investors strive as far as possible to conduct income-generating activities outside the country, with a negative incentive to make beneficial contributions to the host country's economy. Several of the chapters suggest that incentives are not only a burden on the treasuries of the host countries, but in fact work as reverse subsidies to affluent countries and their investors by poor developing countries. In addition, incentives schemes which grant discretionary powers to administrators often induce corruption, increase costs and discourage serious investors. Such policies can result from institutional factors – where investment promotion agencies are created with the singular aim of increasing investment flows, they are likely to pursue this goal regardless of wider developmental objectives and the costs to society.

Long-term investments are more beneficial in development terms to the host country. For such investors, the stability and certainty of the tax regime are of equal or greater importance than the incentives offered. In this sense, a tax policy with long-term guarantees can effectively attract foreign investors by allaying their concerns, even if the incentives are not as immediately attractive as those offered by other countries.

Privatization

Privatization is a central element of the neo-liberal economic policies generally advocated for developing countries by international financial institutions (IFIs). Hence the economic policies of post-conflict countries have often
been overly concerned with the investment flows privatization can attract,
without adequately anticipating and mitigating the attendant negative
consequences such as downsizing of labor and price increases.

Indeed, privatization remains an extremely controversial and divisive
policy choice. When implemented poorly, under-regulated, or pursued in an
inappropriate situation, it can in effect bring the disadvantages of mo-
nopolization rather than the benefits of free market competition. Privatization should be seen as one available option within the wider economic
development and investment strategy of post-conflict countries – with the
choice of whether and how to privatize specific services guided by detailed
analysis of socio-economic costs and benefits, rather than an all-
encompassing philosophy. Unfortunately, pursuing such a measured approach may be impractical for many developing countries in the face of
politicized pressures applied by the IFIs.

Cautionary Notes

Desperation for investment to provide the capital to fuel a domestic economy can result in policies that focus on investment promotion without
adequate regard for the potential impacts of FDI, at the expense of vulnerable peoples and economies. Such policies may crowd out local investment,
through offering discriminatory incentives and by providing better legal
protections to regional (such as those within COMESA, the Common Market
for Eastern and Southern Africa) and international investors. In addition,
aggressive private sector-led development may have negative impacts on
the majority of the population, and result in wealth being concentrated in
the hands of the very wealthy. Many post-conflict countries have suffered
crises with roots in economic grievances, and must be wary of fuelling
tensions between different groups by allowing economic inequalities to go
unchecked. Indeed, economic policies may not substantially reduce the
incidence of conflicts if they do not alleviate the plights of citizens, or are not
tailored to address their concerns.

The narrow pursuit of neo-liberal economic policies of the form prescribed by many IFIs, including a minimal-statist, market-oriented approach
to development policy, has proved largely unsuccessful in many countries.
These prescriptions, advocating a state that is active in promoting and
protecting investment, but passive in regulating the activities of private

investors, might very well be successful in attracting FDI, but at the same time they often have very limited automatic benefits for the local economy. It is highly questionable whether adopting this prevailing wisdom in its entirety is appropriate and sustainable in post-conflict countries. Unfortunately their weak governments often have little option but to do so, particularly when geopolitics enters the equation, and pressure is brought to bear by powerful states offering the tantalizing prospect of increased development aid in return for improved and deregulated investment conditions.

These shortcomings are highlighted in Odumosu's chapter, where she observes that Rwanda is generally seen as an FDI 'success story', having adopted policies considered by IFIs to be ideal, by implementing a largely deregulated investment regime in order to attract FDI. But despite this perceived success in attracting FDI, the UNDP *Human Development Report 2007/2008* ranks Rwanda 161st out of 177 countries on the Human Development Index.[10] Nigeria has one of the highest levels of FDI flows in Africa, but was ranked 158th in the same report, demonstrating that FDI alone cannot make countries socially sustainable – even countries without the immediate challenges of post-conflict recovery.

Clearly, addressing the plight of poor developing countries, and particularly those emerging from years of conflict, cannot be entrusted solely to market forces. Post-conflict countries should be aiming to build a state with functioning institutions that drive confidence in the investment sector, without sacrificing the wellbeing of the population in the competition for foreign capital. Above all, policy decisions aimed at promoting FDI should be informed by detailed analysis of their potential side-effects on local people and the local economy.

While the editors hope that this volume will provide useful insights into successful and unsuccessful frameworks for FDI in post-conflict countries, it is clear that further research is desperately needed to better understand the dynamics of the issue, and in particular to develop approaches for assessing FDI's positive and negative impacts.

Notes

[1]   *Human Security Report 2005*, Human Security Centre, Oxford: Oxford University Press (2005).

[2]   Paul Collier and Anke Hoeffler, 'The Challenge of Reducing the Global Incidence of Civil War', *Copenhagen Consensus Challenge Paper*, March 2004, p.8, available at: www.copenhagenconsensus.com/Files/Filer/CC/Papers/Conflicts_230404.pdf (accessed 7 September 2009).

3   The 2009 Report of the UN Secretary General draws on the latest research and reflects on past experiences to emphasize the need for coherent responses and national ownership from the start. It highlights the early window of opportunity for implementing vital basic security measures and developing political processes, but also for 'laying the foundations for sustainable development.' *Report of the Secretary-General on Peacebuilding in the Immediate Aftermath of Conflict,* A/63/881, United Nations, 2009. Available at: http://www.un.org/ga/search/ view_doc.asp?symbol=A/63/881 (PDF).

     For a comprehensive overview of peacebuilding in the 1990s see *At War's End: Building Peace after Civil Conflicts,* Roland Paris, 2004, Cambridge: Cambridge University Press.

4   Macartan Humphreys and Ashutosh Varshney, 'Violent Conflict and the Millennium Development Goals: Diagnosis and Recommendations', CGSD Working Paper No. 19, August 2004, p.9, available at: http://www.earthinstitute. columbia.edu/cgsd/documents/humphreys_conflict_and_MDG.pdf (accessed 10 September 2009)

5   The UN Economic and Social Council (ECOSOC) defines LDCs using three criteria: low national income (per capita GDP under $750 for inclusion, above $900 for graduation), weak human assets (a composite index based on nutrition, health, education and adult literacy indicators), and high economic vulnerability (a composite index based on indicators of instability of agricultural production and exports, inadequate diversification, and economic size). See http://www.un. org/special-rep/ohrlls/ldc/ldc%20criteria.htm for the criteria for the identifycation of LDCs. ECOSOC reviews the list of LDCs on an annual basis; the list is available at: http://www.unohrlls.org/en/ldc/related/62/

6   Betty Bigombe, Paul Collier and Nicholas Sambanis, 'Policies for Building Post-Conflict Peace', *Journal of African Economies,* 2001.

7   LDCs received 26.7% of total ODA in 2006 (an average of 8% of GDP in each LDC). While developing countries received 27% of world FDI inflows, the share for LDCs was only 0.7%. All figures from 2006, in *The Least Developed Countries Report 2008: Growth, poverty and the terms of the development partnership,* United Nations Conference on Trade and Development (UNCTAD), available at http://www.UNCTAD.org/en/docs/ldc2008_en.pdf (PDF), accessed 1 September 2009.

8   See Mats R. Berdal and David M. Malone (eds),*Greed and Grievance: Economic Agendas in Civil Wars*. Boulder: Lynne Rienner, 2000; Paul Collier and Anke Hoeffler, *Greed and Grievance in Civil War*. Oxford: Oxford University Press, 2004.

9   *Ibid.* (*Greed and Grievance in Civil War*, Collier and Hoeffler, 2004)

10   *Human Development Report 2008/2009*, United Nations Development Programme. Available at: http://hdr.undp.org/en/media/HDR_20072008_EN_Complete.pdf

Index

www.ingramcontent.com/pod-product-compliance
Lightning Source LLC
Chambersburg PA
CBHW070558270326
41926CB00013B/2350